Mathematical Logic through Python

T0201403

Using a unique pedagogical approach, this text introduces mathematical logic by guiding students in implementing the underlying logical concepts and mathematical proofs via Python programming. This approach, tailored to the unique intuitions and strengths of the ever-growing population of programming-savvy students, brings mathematical logic into the comfort zone of these students and provides clarity that can only be achieved by a deep hands-on understanding and the satisfaction of having created working code. While the approach is unique, the text follows the same set of topics typically covered in a one-semester undergraduate course, including propositional logic and first-order predicate logic, culminating in a proof of Gödel's completeness theorem. A sneak peek to Gödel's incompleteness theorem is also provided. The textbook is accompanied by an extensive collection of programming tasks, code skeletons, and unit tests. Familiarity with proofs and basic proficiency in Python is assumed.

Yannai A. Gonczarowski is Assistant Professor of both Economics and Computer Science at Harvard University, and is the first faculty at Harvard to be appointed to both of these departments. He received his PhD in Mathematics and Computer Science from The Hebrew University of Jerusalem. Among his research awards are the ACM SIGecom Dissertation Award and INFORMS AMD Junior Researcher Paper Prize. He is also a professionally trained opera singer.

Noam Nisan is Professor of Computer Science and Engineering at The Hebrew University of Jerusalem, serving as Dean of the School of Computer Science and Engineering during 2018–2021. He received his PhD in Computer Science from the University of California, Berkeley. Among the awards for his research on computational complexity and algorithmic game theory are the Gödel Prize and Knuth Award. This is his fifth book.

Mathematical Logic through Python

YANNAI A. GONCZAROWSKI

Harvard University

NOAM NISAN

Hebrew University of Jerusalem

CAMBRIDGE
UNIVERSITY PRESS

University Printing House, Cambridge CB2 8BS, United Kingdom

One Liberty Plaza, 20th Floor, New York, NY 10006, USA

477 Williamstown Road, Port Melbourne, VIC 3207, Australia

314–321, 3rd Floor, Plot 3, Splendor Forum, Jasola District Centre, New Delhi – 110025, India

103 Penang Road, #05–06/07, Visioncrest Commercial, Singapore 238467

Cambridge University Press is part of the University of Cambridge.

It furthers the University's mission by disseminating knowledge in the pursuit of
education, learning, and research at the highest international levels of excellence.

www.cambridge.org
Information on this title: www.cambridge.org/9781108845076
DOI: 10.1017/9781108954464

First published 2022

Printed in the United Kingdom by TJ Books Limited, Padstow Cornwall

A catalogue record for this publication is available from the British Library.

Library of Congress Cataloging-in-Publication Data
Names: Gonczarowski, Yannai A., 1981- author. | Nisan, Noam, author.
Title: Mathematical logic through Python / Yannai A. Gonczarowski, Harvard
    University, Massachusetts, Noam Nisan, Hebrew University of Jerusalem.
Description: Cambridge, United Kingdom ; New York, NY : Cambridge
    University Press, [2022] | Includes index.
Identifiers: LCCN 2021057959 (print) | LCCN 2021057960 (ebook) |
    ISBN 9781108845076 (hardback) | ISBN 9781108949477 (paperback) |
    ISBN 9781108954464 (epub)
Subjects: LCSH: Logic, Symbolic and mathematical. | Python (Computer
    program language) | BISAC: COMPUTERS / Languages / General
Classification: LCC QA9 .G64 2022 (print) | LCC QA9 (ebook) |
    DDC 005.13/1–dc23/eng/20220125
LC record available at https://lccn.loc.gov/2021057959
LC ebook record available at https://lccn.loc.gov/2021057960

ISBN 978-1-108-84507-6 Hardback
ISBN 978-1-108-94947-7 Paperback

To Eshed, whose syntax and semantics logically evolved while this book did

Y.A.G.

To Michal, logically and illogically

N.N.

Contents

Preface   *page* xi

0   Introduction and Overview   1
    0.1   Our Final Destination: Gödel's Completeness Theorem   2
    0.2   Our Pedagogical Approach   4
    0.3   How We Travel: Programs That Handle Logic   5
    0.4   Our Roadmap   8

Part I   Propositional Logic

1   Propositional Logic Syntax   13
    1.1   Propositional Formulas   13
    1.2   Parsing   18
    1.3   Infinite Sets of Formulas   21
    1.A   Optional Reading: Polish Notations   22

2   Propositional Logic Semantics   24
    2.1   Detour: Semantics of Programming Languages   24
    2.2   Models and Truth Values   25
    2.3   Truth Tables   28
    2.4   Tautologies, Contradictions, and Satisfiability   30
    2.5   Synthesis of Formulas   31
    2.A   Optional Reading: Conjunctive Normal Form   33
    2.B   Optional Reading: Satisfiability and Search Problems   35

3   Logical Operators   41
    3.1   More Operators   41
    3.2   Substitutions   43
    3.3   Complete Sets of Operators   46
    3.4   Proving Incompleteness   49

4   Proof by Deduction   53
    4.1   Inference Rules   53
    4.2   Specializations of an Inference Rule   56
    4.3   Deductive Proofs   59

	4.4 Practice Proving	64
	4.5 The Soundness Theorem	66
5	**Working with Proofs**	69
	5.1 Using Lemmas	69
	5.2 Modus Ponens	73
	5.3 The Deduction Theorem	76
	5.4 Proofs by Way of Contradiction	79
6	**The Tautology Theorem and the Completeness of Propositional Logic**	84
	6.1 Our Axiomatic System	84
	6.2 The Tautology Theorem	86
	6.3 The Completeness Theorem for Finite Sets	92
	6.4 The Compactness Theorem and the Completeness Theorem for Infinite Sets	94
	6.A Optional Reading: Adding Additional Operators	97
	6.B Optional Reading: Other Axiomatic Systems	101
Part II	**Predicate Logic**	
7	**Predicate Logic Syntax and Semantics**	109
	7.1 Syntax	110
	7.2 Semantics	121
8	**Getting Rid of Functions and Equality**	129
	8.1 Getting Rid of Functions	129
	8.2 Getting Rid of Equality	138
9	**Deductive Proofs of Predicate Logic Formulas**	143
	9.1 Example of a Proof	144
	9.2 Schemas	145
	9.3 Proofs	160
	9.4 Getting Rid of Tautology Lines	171
10	**Working with Predicate Logic Proofs**	178
	10.1 Our Axiomatic System	178
	10.2 Syllogisms	184
	10.3 Some Mathematics	195
11	**The Deduction Theorem and Prenex Normal Form**	211
	11.1 The Deduction Theorem	211
	11.2 Prenex Normal Form	215
12	**The Completeness Theorem**	231
	12.1 Deriving a Model or a Contradiction for a Closed Set	236
	12.2 Closing a Set	240

12.3 The Completeness Theorem 252

12.4 The Compactness Theorem and the "Provability" Version of the
Completeness Theorem 253

13 Sneak Peek at Mathematical Logic II: Gödel's Incompleteness Theorem 256

13.1 Complete and Incomplete Theories 256

13.2 Gödel Numbering 258

13.3 Undecidability of the Halting Problem 260

13.4 The Incompleteness Theorem 262

Cheatsheet: Axioms and Axiomatic Inference Rules Used in This Book 266

Index 268

Preface

Mathematical Logic 101 is a beautiful course. Gödel's Theorems are arguably the most profound and deep truths taught throughout the entire undergrad theoretical curriculum. Nonetheless, it seems that among many computer science and engineering students this course suffers from the reputation of being an unintelligible course full of technical, uninsightful proofs. Students lose themselves in endless inductions and do not fully understand what it means, e.g., to "prove that anything that is true can be proven." Indeed, how can this not be confusing when the two occurrences of "prove" in that sentence have two distinct meanings – the latter referring to a precise very strict mathematical "proof" object that is defined during this course, while the former refers to the free-text proofs that we have been taught since our first year of undergrad? This book drastically reenvisions the Mathematical Logic 101 course, conveying the same material but tapping into the strengths of the ever-growing cohort of programming-oriented students to do so.

How does one help programming-oriented students to not lose themselves among endless little details in proofs, failing to see the overarching message of the course? We set out to make this course less abstract, more intuitive, and maybe even exciting, by tapping into the context where such students are used to comfortably dealing with endless little details on the way to a larger goal without ever missing the forest for the trees: computer programming. We redesigned the entirety of this very theoretical course from scratch to be based upon a series of programming exercises, each corresponding to either a theorem/lemma/corollary or a step toward such.

For example, the main result of the first half of a standard Mathematical Logic 101 course is the "Tautology Theorem" (a variant of the Completeness Theorem for propositional logic), which asserts that every tautology – every statement that holds in every possible model or setting – can be proven to hold using a small set of axioms. The corresponding programming exercise in this book is to write a function (based on functions from previous exercises, of course) whose input is a formula (an object of class `Formula`, which the students implement in a previous exercise) and whose output is either a model in which this formula does not hold (i.e., a counterexample to the formula being a tautology) or a proof (an object of class `Proof`, which the students implement in a previous exercise) of this formula. Obviously, whoever can write such a function, including all its recursively implemented helper functions, completely understands the reasoning in the proof of the Tautology Theorem, including all its inductively proven lemmas. (And this holds even more so for students who naturally grasp recursive code far better than they do inductive proofs.) In our experience, students with a background in programming for the most part even understand this proof better having actively coded its functionality themselves than had they only passively seen the proof being written on the blackboard by a teacher. In the process of moving from proving to programming, we have in fact also disambiguated the two meanings of "prove" in the earlier statement of "prove that whatever is true can be proven": we transformed the former "prove" into "program in code" and the latter "can be proven" into "is the conclusion of a valid `Proof` object." This disambiguation by way of defamiliarization of each of these occurrences of "prove" achieves great clarity and furthermore allows the students to more easily reexamine their intuitions and unconscious assumptions about proofs.

This book evolved from a course that we have been teaching at the Hebrew University of Jerusalem since 2017, first as an elective (we limited our class to 50 and then to 100 students as we fine-tuned the course, and there had been a waiting list) and later as an alternative for computer science and engineering students to the mandatory Mathematical Logic 101, to the clear satisfaction of the students, who continuously rank this course highly. In our experience, having the tasks of a single chapter due each week (if the schedule permits, then we try to allow an additional week for Chapter 10), with the tasks of Part I (Chapters 1 through 6) being solved by each student individually and the tasks of Part II (Chapters 7 through 12) being solved in pairs, has consistently proven to work well.

We are grateful to the Hebrew University students who took our course for their valuable questions and comments, and to our earlier students also for the faith they have put in us. We are indebted to our first TA and beta-solver, Alon Ziv, as well as to our subsequent TAs Noam Wies, Asaf Yehudai, Ofer Ravid, and Elazar Cohen, and beta-solvers Omri Cohen and Matan Harsat. A special thanks goes to Chagit Schiff-Blass, at the time a Law and Cognitive Science student, who showed us that our way of teaching Mathematical Logic really does appeal to an even more diverse student population than we had imagined, by first being an excellent beta-solver and then joining our teaching team. We thank Henry Cohn for valuable advice, and thank Aviv Keren and Shimon Schocken for their valuable detailed feedback on portions of earlier drafts of this book. We especially thank David Kashtan for careful and valuable scientific editing of this book on the logic side; any deviations from standard definitions or nomenclature are, of course, our own responsibility. Finally, we thank Kaitlin Leach, Rebecca Grainger, and the entire team at Cambridge University Press for their support and for their flexibility throughout the COVID pandemic. The cover picture by Vasily Kandinsky is titled "Serious-Fun," and we hope that this will describe your experience as you work through this book. We always appreciate feedback from readers.

0   Introduction and Overview

Assume that all Greeks are men. Assume also that all men are mortal. It follows logically that all Greeks are mortal.

This deduction is remarkable in the sense that we can make it even without understanding anything about Greeks, men, or mortality. The same deduction can take the assumptions that all Greeks are fish and that all fish fly and conclude that all Greeks fly. As long as the assumptions are correct, so is the conclusion. If one or more of the assumptions is incorrect, then all bets are off and the conclusion need not hold. How are such "content-free" deductions made? When is such a deduction valid? For example, assume that some Greeks are men and that some men are mortal; does it follow that some Greeks are mortal? No!

The field of logic deals exactly with these types of deductions – those that do not require any specific knowledge of the real world, but rather take statements about the world and deduce new statements from them, new statements that must be true if the original ones are. Such deductions are a principal way by which we can extend our knowledge beyond any facts that we directly observe. While in many fields of human endeavor logical deductions go hand in hand with other techniques of observing and understanding the actual facts of the world, in the field of mathematics logical deductions serve as the sole paradigmatic foundation.

A crucial property of logical deduction is that it is purely **syntactic** rather than **semantic**. That is, the validity of a logical deduction can be completely determined by its form, its syntax. Nothing about the actual meaning of the assumptions or conclusion, such as their truth or falsehood, is involved. The usefulness, however, of such deductions comes from the, perhaps surprising, fact that their conclusions do turn out to be true in the meaningful, semantic, sense. That is, whenever the assumptions are true, the conclusion also happens to be true – and this happens despite the fact that the deduction process itself was completely oblivious to said truth! Indeed, the clear separation between syntactic notions and semantic ones, as well as establishing the connections between them, are the core of the study of logic. There are several different possible motivations for such study, and these different motivations influence the type of issues emphasized.

Philosophers usually use logic as a tool of the trade, and mostly focus on the difficult process of translating between natural human language and logical **formulas**.[1] These are tricky questions mostly due to the human part of this mismatch: Human language is not completely precise, and to really understand the meaning of a sentence may require not only

---

[1] Another frequently used plural form of "formula," which you may encounter in many books, is "formulae." For simplicity, in this book we will stick with "formulas."

logical analysis but also linguistic analysis and even social understanding. For example, who exactly is included in the set of Greeks? When we assumed that they are all men, does that include or exclude women? Without coming to grips with these thorny questions, one cannot assess whether the assumptions are true and cannot benefit from the logical deduction that all Greeks are mortal.

Mathematicians also study logic as a tool of the trade. Mathematicians usually apply logic to precise mathematical statements, so they put less emphasis on the mismatch with the imprecise human language, but are rather focused on the exact rules of logic and on exactly understanding the formalization process and power of logic itself. Indeed, to understand the power of logic is to understand the limits of the basic paradigm of mathematics and mathematical proofs, and thus the field of mathematical logic is sometimes called **meta-mathematics**, mathematically studying *mathematics* itself.

Computer scientists use logic as a tool of the trade in a somewhat different sense, often relying on logical formalisms to represent various computational abstractions. Thus, for example, a language to access databases (e.g., SQL) may be based on some logical formalism (e.g., predicate logic), and abstract computational search problems (e.g., NP problems) may be treated as finding assignments to logical formulas (e.g., SAT).

The approach of this book is to proceed toward the goal of mathematicians who study logic, using the tools of computer scientists, and in fact not those computer scientists who study logic, but rather more applied computer scientists. Specifically, our main goal is to precisely formalize and understand the notions of a logical formula and a deductive logic proof, and to establish their relationship with mathematical truth. Our technique is to actually implement all these logical formulas and logical proofs as bona fide objects in a software implementation: You will actually be asked to implement, in the Python programming language, methods and functions that deal with Python objects such as Formula and Proof. For example, in Chapter 2 you will be asked to implement a function is_tautology(formula) that determines if the given logical formula is a tautology, i.e., logically always true; while in Chapter 6 you will be asked to implement a function proof_or_counterexample(formula) that returns either a formal logical proof of the given formula – if it happens to be a tautology – or else a counterexample that demonstrates that this formula is in fact *not* a tautology.

0.1   Our Final Destination: Gödel's Completeness Theorem

This book has a very clear end point to which everything leads: Gödel's completeness theorem, named after its discoverer, the Austrian (and later American) logician and mathematician Kurt Gödel. To understand it, let us first look at the two main syntactic objects that we will study and their semantics. Our first focus of attention is the **formula**, a formal representation of certain logical relations between basic simpler notions. For example a formalization of "All men are mortal" in the form, say, '∀x[Man(x)→Mortal(x)]' (we will, of course, specify exact syntactic rules for such formulas). Now comes the semantics, that is, the notion of truth of such a formula. A formula may be true or false in a particular setting, depending on the specifics of the setting. Specifically, a formula can be evaluated only relative to a particular **model**, where this model must specify all the particulars of the setting. In our example, such particulars would include which x in the "universe" are men and which are mortal. Once such a model is given, it is determined whether a given formula is true in this model or not.

Our second focus of attention is the notion of a **proof**. A proof again is a syntactic object: It consists of a set of formulas called **assumptions**, an additional formula called **conclusion**, and the core of the proof is a list of formulas that has to conform to certain specific rules ensuring that each formula in the list "follows" in some precise *syntactic* sense from previous ones or from assumptions, and that the last formula in the list is the conclusion. If such a formal proof exists, then we say that the conclusion is (syntactically) provable from the assumptions, which we denote by *assumptions* $\vdash$ *conclusion*. Now, again, enter the semantics, which deal with the following question: Is it the case that in *every* model in which all the assumptions are true, the conclusion is also true? (This question is only about the assumptions and the conclusion, and is agnostic of the core of any proof.) If that happens to be the case, then we say that the conclusion (semantically) follows from the assumptions, which we denote by *assumptions* $\models$ *conclusion*. Gödel's **completeness theorem** states the following under certain conditions.

THEOREM (Gödel's Completeness Theorem) *For any set of assumptions and any conclusion, it holds that "assumptions* $\vdash$ *conclusion" if and only if "assumptions* $\models$ *conclusion".*

This is a very remarkable theorem connecting two seemingly unrelated notions: The existence of a certain long list of formulas built according to some syntactic rules (this long list is the syntactic proof just defined), and the mathematical truth that whenever all assumptions are true, so invariably is the conclusion. On second thought, it does make sense that if something is syntactically provable then it is also semantically true: We will deliberately choose the syntactic rules of a proof to only allow true deductions. In fact, this is the whole point of mathematics: In order to know that whenever we add two even numbers we get an even number, we do not need to check all possible (infinitely many!) pairs of even numbers, but rather it suffices to "prove" the rule that if the two numbers that we add up are even then the result is even as well, and the whole point is that our proof system is **sound**: A "proved" statement must be true (otherwise the concept of a proof would not have been of any use). The other direction, the fact that any mathematical truth can be proven, is much more surprising: We could have expected that the more possibilities we build into our proof system, the more mathematical truths it can prove. It is far from clear, though, that any specific, finite, syntactic set of rules for forming proofs should suffice for proving, given any set of assumptions, *every* conclusion that follows from it. And yet, for the simple syntactic set of logical rules that we will present, this is exactly what Gödel's completeness theorem establishes.

One can view this as the final triumph of mathematical reasoning: Our logical notion of proof completely suffices to establish any consequence of any set of assumptions. Given a set of axioms of, e.g., a mathematical **field** (or any other mathematical structure), anything that holds for all fields can actually be logically proven from the field axioms!

Unfortunately, shortly after proving this completeness theorem, Gödel turned his attention to the question of finding the "correct" set of axioms to capture the properties of the natural numbers. What was desired at the time was to find for every branch of mathematics a simple set of axioms that suffices for proving or disproving any possible mathematical statement in that branch.[2] We say "unfortunately" since Gödel showed this to fail in a most spectacular way, showing that no such set of axioms exists even for the natural numbers: for every set of axioms there will remain mathematical statements about the natural numbers that can neither be proved nor disproved! This is called Gödel's **incompleteness theorem**. Despite its name, this theorem does not in fact contradict the completeness theorem: It is still true that anything that (semantically) follows from a set of axioms is syntactically provable from it, but unfortunately there will always remain statements such that neither they nor their negation follow from the set of axioms.

One can view Gödel's incompleteness theorem as the final defeat of mathematical reasoning: There will always remain questions beyond the reach of any specific formalization of mathematics. But this book – a first course in mathematical logic – focuses only on the triumph, i.e., on Gödel's completeness theorem, leaving the defeat, the incompleteness theorem, for a second course in mathematical logic.

0.2   Our Pedagogical Approach

The mathematical content covered by this book is quite standard for a first course in mathematical logic. Our pedagogical approach is, however, unique: We will "prove" everything by writing computer programs.

Let us motivate this unusual choice. We find that among academic courses in mathematics, the introductory mathematical logic course stands out as having an unusual gap between student perceptions and our own evaluation of its content: While we (and, we think, most mathematicians) view the mathematical content as rather easy, students seem to view it as very confusing relative to other mathematics courses. While we view the conceptual message of the course as unusually beautiful, students often fail to see this beauty – even those that easily see the beauty of, say, calculus or algebra. We believe that the reason for this mismatch is the very large gap that exists between the very abstract point of view – proving things about proofs – and the very low-level technical proofs themselves. It is easy to get confused between the proofs that we are writing and the proofs that are our subjects of discussion. Indeed, when we say that we are "writing proofs to prove things about proofs," the first "proofs" and the second "proofs" actually mean two very different things even though many introductory mathematical logic courses use the same word for both. This turns out to become even more confusing as the "mechanics" of both the proof we are writing and the proof that we are discussing are somewhat cumbersome while the actual point that we are making by writing these proofs is something that we usually take for granted, so it is almost impossible to see the forest for the trees.

Computer scientists are used to combining many "mechanical details" to get a high-level abstract goal (this is known as "programming"), and are also used to writing programs that handle objects that are as complex as the programs themselves (such as compilers). A large part of computer science exactly concerns the discussion of how to handle such challenges both in terms of tools (debuggers, assemblers, compilers) and it terms of paradigms

---

[2] This desire, formulated by the German mathematician David Hilbert, was called "Hilbert's Program."

(interfaces, object-orientation, testing). So this book utilizes the tools of a computer scientist to achieve the pedagogical goal of teaching the mathematical basis of logic.

We have been able to capture maybe 95% of the mathematical content of a standard first course in mathematical logic as programming tasks. These tasks capture the notions and procedures that are studied, and the solution to each of these programming tasks can be viewed as capturing the proof for some lemma or theorem. The reader who has actually implemented the associated function has in effect proved the lemma or theorem, a proof that has been verified for correctness (to some extent) once it has passed the extensive array of tests that we provide for the task. The pedagogical gain is that confusing notions and proofs become crystal clear once you have implemented them yourself. Indeed, in the earlier sentence "writing proofs to prove things about proofs," the first "proofs" becomes "code" and the second "proofs" becomes "Python objects of class `Proof`." Almost all the lemmas and theorems covered by a typical introductory course in mathematical logic are captured this way in this book. Essentially the only exceptions are theorems that consider "infinite objects" (e.g., an infinite set of formulas), which cannot be directly captured by a program that is constrained to dealing with finite objects. It turns out, however, that most of the mathematical content of even these infinitary proofs can be naturally captured by lemmas dealing with finite objects. What remains to be made in a purely non-programmatic mathematical way is just the core of the infinite argument, which is the remaining 5% or so that we indeed then lay out in the classical mathematical way.

0.3   How We Travel: Programs That Handle Logic

This book is centered around a sequence of programming projects in the Python programming language.[3] We provide a file directory that contains a small amount of code that we have already implemented, together with many skeletons of functions and methods that you will be asked to complete, and an extensive array of tests that will verify that your implementation is correct. Each chapter of this book is organized around a sequence of tasks, each of which calls for completing the implementation of a certain function or method for which we have supplied the skeleton (which also appears as a code snippet in the book). All of our code-base, including the already implemented parts of the code, the skeletons, and the tests, can be downloaded from the book website at `www.LogicThruPython.org`.

Let us take as an example Task 2 in Chapter 1. Chapter 1 deals with **propositional formulas**. You will handle such objects using code that appears in the Python file `propositions/syntax.py`, which already contains the constructor for a Python class `Formula` for holding a propositional formula as a tree-like data structure.[4]

---

[3] Specifically, the code snippets in this book have been tested with Python 3.7. Please refer to the book website at `www.LogicThruPython.org` for updated information regarding compatibility of newer Python versions with our code-base.

[4] The annotations following various colon signs, as well as following the -> symbol, are called Python **type annotations** and specify the types of the variables/parameters that they follow, and respectively of the return values of the functions that they follow.

```
┌──────────────────( propositions/syntax.py )──────────────────┐
│ class Formula:                                                │
│     """An immutable propositional formula in tree representation, composed from │
│     variable names, and operators applied to them.           │
│                                                               │
│     Attributes:                                               │
│         root: the constant, variable name, or operator at the root of the │
│             formula tree.                                     │
│         first: the first operand of the root, if the root is a unary or binary │
│             operator.                                         │
│         second: the second operand of the root, if the root is a binary │
│             operator.                                         │
│     """                                                       │
│     root: str                                                 │
│     first: Optional[Formula]                                  │
│     second: Optional[Formula]                                 │
│                                                               │
│     def __init__(self, root: str, first: Optional[Formula] = None, │
│                  second: Optional[Formula] = None):           │
│         """Initializes a `Formula` from its root and root operands. │
│                                                               │
│         Parameters:                                           │
│             root: the root for the formula tree.             │
│             first: the first operand for the root, if the root is a unary or │
│                 binary operator.                              │
│             second: the second operand for the root, if the root is a binary │
│                 operator.                                     │
│         """                                                   │
│         if is_variable(root) or is_constant(root):           │
│             assert first is None and second is None          │
│             self.root = root                                  │
│         elif is_unary(root):                                  │
│             assert first is not None and second is None      │
│             self.root, self.first = root, first              │
│         else:                                                 │
│             assert is_binary(root)                            │
│             assert first is not None and second is not None  │
│             self.root, self.first, self.second = root, first, second │
└───────────────────────────────────────────────────────────────┘
```

The main content of Chapter 1 is captured by asking you to implement various methods and functions related to objects of class Formula. Task 2 in Chapter 1, for example, asks you to implement the method variables() of this class, which returns a Python set of all variable names used in the formula. The file propositions/syntax.py thus already contains also the skeleton of this method.

```
┌──────────────────( propositions/syntax.py )──────────────────┐
│ class Formula:                                                │
│         ⋮                                                     │
│     def variables(self) -> Set[str]:                          │
│         """Finds all variable names in the current formula.  │
│                                                               │
│         Returns:                                              │
│             A set of all variable names used in the current formula. │
│         """                                                   │
│         # Task 1.2                                            │
└───────────────────────────────────────────────────────────────┘
```

To check that your implementation is correct, we also provide a corresponding test file, propositions/syntax_test.py, which contains the following test:

```
                          propositions/syntax_test.py
def test_variables(debug=False):
    for formula, expected_variables in [
            (Formula('T'), set()),
            (Formula('x1234'), {'x1234'}),
            (Formula('~', Formula('r')), {'r'}),
            (Formula('->', Formula('x'), Formula('y')), {'x','y'}),
                         ⋮
            (Formula(···), {···})]:
        if debug:
            print('Testing variables of', formula)
        assert formula.variables() == expected_variables
```

We encourage you to always browse through the examples within the test code before starting to implement the task, to make sure that you fully understand any possible nuances in the specifications of the task.

All the tests of all tasks in Chapter 1 can be invoked by simply executing the Python file test_chapter01.py, which we also provide. The code for testing the optional tasks of Chapter 1 is commented out in that file, so if you choose to implement any of these tasks (which is not required in order to be able to implement any of the non-optional tasks that follow them), simply uncomment the corresponding line(s) in that file. If you run this file and get no assertion errors, then you have successfully (as far as we can check) solved all of the tasks in Chapter 1.

This chapter – Chapter 0 – contains a single task, whose goal is to verify that you have successfully downloaded our code base from the book website at www.LogicThruPython.org, and that your Python environment is correctly set up.

TASK 1   Implement the missing code for the function half(x) in the file prelim/prelim.py, which halves an even integer. Here is the skeleton of this function as it already appears in the file:

```
                          prelim/prelim.py
def half(x: int) -> int:
    """Halves the given even integer.

    Parameters:
        x: even integer to halve.

    Returns:
        An integer `z` such that `z+z=x`.
    """
    assert x % 2 == 0
    # Task 0.1
```

The solution to Task 1 is very simple, of course (return x//2, or alternatively, return int(x/2)), but the point that we want you to verify is that you can execute the file test_chapter00.py without getting any assertion errors, but only getting the expected verbose listing of what was tested.

```
$ python test_chapter00.py
Testing half of 42
Testing half of 8
$
```

For comparison, executing the file test_chapter00.py with a faulty implementation of Task 1 would raise an assertion error. For example, implementing Task 1 with, say, return x//3, would yield the following output:

```
$ python test_chapter00.py
Testing half of 42
Traceback (most recent call last):
  File "test_chapter00.py", line 13, in <module>
    test_task1(True)
  File "test_chapter00.py", line 11, in test_task1
    test_half(debug)
  File "prelim/prelim_test.py", line 15, in test_half
    assert result + result == 42
AssertionError
$
```

and implementing Task 1 with, say, return x/2 (which returns a float rather than an int), would yield the following output:

```
$ python test_chapter00.py
Testing half of 42
Traceback (most recent call last):
  File "test_chapter00.py", line 13, in <module>
    test_task1(True)
  File "test_chapter00.py", line 11, in test_task1
    test_half(debug)
  File "prelim/prelim_test.py", line 14, in test_half
    assert isinstance(result, int)
AssertionError
$
```

0.4   Our Roadmap

We conclude this chapter by giving a quick overview of our journey in this book. We study two logical formalisms: Chapters 1–6 deal with the limited **propositional logic**, while Chapters 7–12 move on to the fuller (first-order) **predicate logic**. In each of these two parts of the book, we take a somewhat similar arc:

a. Define a syntax for logical formulas (Chapter 1/Chapter 7).
b. Define the semantics of said formulas (Chapter 2/Chapter 7).

c. Pause a bit in order to simplify things (Chapter 3/Chapter 8).

d. Define (syntactic) formal proofs (Chapter 4/Chapter 9).

e. Prove useful lemmas about said formal proofs (Chapter 5/Chapters 10 and 11).

f. Prove that any formula that is semantically true also has a syntactic formal proof (Chapter 6/Chapter 12).

Of course, the results that we prove for the simpler propositional logic in Part I of this book are then also used when dealing with predicate logic in Part II of the book. Here is a more specific chapter-by-chapter overview:

1. Chapter 1 defines a syntax for propositional logic and shows how to handle it.

2. Chapter 2 defines the notion of the semantics of a propositional formula, giving every formula a truth value in every given model.

3. Chapter 3 looks at the possible sets of logical operations allowed and discusses which such subsets suffice.

4. Chapter 4 introduces the notion of a formal deductive proof.

5. Chapter 5 starts analyzing the power of formal deductive proofs.

6. Chapter 6 brings us to the pinnacle of Part I of this book, obtaining the "tautology theorem," which is the mathematical heart of the completeness theorem for propositional logic (which we will indeed derive from it), and is also a key result that we will use in Part II of this book when proving the completeness theorem for predicate logic.

7. Chapter 7 starts our journey into predicate logic, introducing both its syntax and its semantics.

8. Chapter 8 is concerned with allowing some simplifications in our predicate logic, specifically getting rid of the notions of functions and of equality without weakening the expressive power of our formalism.

9. Chapter 9 introduces and formalizes the notion of a deductive proof of a formula in predicate logic.

10. Chapter 10 fixes a set of logical axioms and demonstrates their capabilities by applying them to several domains from syllogisms, through mathematical structures, to the foundations of mathematics, e.g., formalizing Russell's paradox about "the set of all sets that do not contains themselves."

11. Chapter 11 proves key results about the power of proofs in predicate logic.

12. Chapter 12 reaches the culmination of our journey by proving Gödel's completeness theorem. We also get, "for free," the "compactness theorem" of predicate logic.

13. Finally, Chapter 13 provides a "sneak peek" into a second course in mathematical logic, sketching a proof of Gödel's incompleteness theorem.

Part I

Propositional Logic

1 Propositional Logic Syntax

In this chapter we present a formal **syntax** for formalizing statements within logic. Consider the following example of a natural language sentence that has some logical structure: "If it rains on Monday then we will either hand out umbrellas or rent a bus." This sentence is composed of three basic **propositions**, each of which may potentially be either true or false: p1="it rains on Monday", p2="we will hand out umbrellas", and p3="we will rent a bus". We can interpret this English-language sentence as logically connecting these three propositions as follows: "p1 implies (p2 or p3)", which we will write as '(p1→(p2|p3))'.

Our goal in this chapter is to formally define a language for capturing these types of sentences. The motivation for defining this language is that it will allow us to precisely and formally analyze their *implications*. For example, we should be able to formally deduce from this sentence that if we neither handed out umbrellas nor rented a bus, then it did not rain on Monday. We purposefully postpone to Chapter 2 a discussion of **semantics**, of the meaning, that we assign to sentences in our language, and focus in this chapter only on the **syntax**, i.e., on the rules of grammar for forming sentences.

1.1 Propositional Formulas

Our language for Part I of this book is called **propositional logic**. While there are various variants of the exact rules of this language (allowing for various logical operators or for various rules about whether and when parentheses may be dropped), the exact variant used is not very important, but rather the whole point is to fix a single specific set of rules and stick with it. Essentially everything that we say about this specific variant will hold with only very minor modifications for other variants as well. Here is the formal definition with which we will stick.

DEFINITION 1.1 (Propositional Formula)   The following strings are (valid[1]) **propositional formulas**:

- A **variable name**: a letter in 'p'... 'z', optionally followed by a sequence of digits. For example, 'p', 'y12', or 'z035'.
- 'T'.
- 'F'.
- A **negation** '~ϕ', where ϕ is a (valid) propositional formula.

---

[1] What we call **valid** formulas are often called **well-formed** formulas in other textbooks.

- '$(\phi\&\psi)$' where each of ϕ and ψ is a propositional formula.
- '$(\phi|\psi)$' where each of ϕ and ψ is a propositional formula.
- '$(\phi\rightarrow\psi)$' where each of ϕ and ψ is a propositional formula.

These are the only (valid) propositional formulas. For example, '$\sim((\sim x\&(p007|x))\rightarrow F)$' is a propositional formula.

This definition is **syntactic**: it specifies which **strings**, that is, finite sequences of characters, are valid propositional formulas and which are not, by describing the rules through which such strings can be formed. (Again, we have deliberately not yet assigned any interpretation to such strings, but the reader will surely guess that the **constants** 'T' and 'F' stand for *True* and *False*, respectively, that the **unary** (operating on one **subformula**) **operator** '$\sim$' stands for *Not*, and that the **binary** (operating on two **subformulas**) **operators** '&', '|', and '$\rightarrow$' stand for *And*, *Or*, and *Implies*, respectively.) We remark that in many logic textbooks, the symbol '$\neg$' (**negation**) is used instead of '$\sim$', the symbol '$\wedge$' (**conjunction**) is used instead of '&', and the symbol '$\vee$' (**disjunction**) is used instead of '|'.

Our choice of symbols in this book was indeed influenced by which symbols are easy to type on a computer. For your convenience, the file `propositions/syntax.py` defines functions for identifying strings that contain the various **tokens**, or basic building blocks, allowed in propositional formulas.[2] The symbol '$\rightarrow$' is not a standard character, so in Python code we will represent it using the two-character sequence `'->'`.

```
                              ┤ propositions/syntax.py ├
def is_variable(string: str) -> bool:
    """Checks if the given string is a variable name.

    Parameters:
        string: string to check.

    Returns:
        ``True`` if the given string is a variable name, ``False`` otherwise.
    """
    return string[0] >= 'p' and string[0] <= 'z' and \
           (len(string) == 1 or string[1:].isdecimal())

def is_constant(string: str) -> bool:
    """Checks if the given string is a constant.

    Parameters:
        string: string to check.

    Returns:
        ``True`` if the given string is a constant, ``False`` otherwise.
```

---

[2] The decorator that precedes the definition of each of these functions in the code that you are given **memoizes** the function, so that if any of these functions is called more than once with the same argument, the previous return value for that argument is simply returned again instead of being recalculated. This has no effect on code correctness since running these functions has no side effects, and their return values depend only on their arguments and are immutable, but this does speed-up the execution of your code. It may seem silly to perform such optimizations with such short functions, but this will in fact dramatically speed-up your code in later chapters, when such functions will be called many many times from within various recursions. We use this decorator throughout the code that you are given in various places where there are speed improvements to be gained.

```
    """
    return string == 'T' or string == 'F'

def is_unary(string: str) -> bool:
    """Checks if the given string is a unary operator.

    Parameters:
        string: string to check.

    Returns:
        ``True`` if the given string is a unary operator, ``False`` otherwise.
    """
    return string == '~'

def is_binary(string: str) -> bool:
    """Checks if the given string is a binary operator.

    Parameters:
        string: string to check.

    Returns:
        ``True`` if the given string is a binary operator, ``False`` otherwise.
    """
    return string == '&' or string == '|' or string == '->'
```

Notice that Definition 1.1 is very specific about the use of parentheses: '$(\phi\&\psi)$' is a valid formula, but '$\phi\&\psi$' is not and neither is '$((\phi\&\psi))$'; likewise, '$\sim\phi$' is a valid formula but '$(\sim\phi)$' is not, etc. These restrictive choices are made to ensure that there is a unique and easy way to **parse** a formula: to take a string that is a formula and figure out the complete **derivation tree** of how it is decomposed into simpler and simpler formulas according to the derivation rules from Definition 1.1. Such a derivation tree is naturally expressed in a computer program as a tree data structure, and this book's pedagogical approach is to indeed implement it as such. So, the bulk of the tasks of this chapter are focused on translating formulas back and forth between representation as a string and as an expression-tree data structure.

The file propositions/syntax.py defines a Python class Formula for holding a propositional formula as a data structure.

```
                          ┌─────────────────────────┐
                          │ propositions/syntax.py  │
                          └─────────────────────────┘
@frozen
class Formula:
    """An immutable propositional formula in tree representation, composed from
    variable names, and operators applied to them.

    Attributes:
        root: the constant, variable name, or operator at the root of the
            formula tree.
        first: the first operand of the root, if the root is a unary or binary
            operator.
        second: the second operand of the root, if the root is a binary
            operator.
    """
    root: str
    first: Optional[Formula]
```

```
second: Optional[Formula]

def __init__(self, root: str, first: Optional[Formula] = None,
             second: Optional[Formula] = None):
    """Initializes a `Formula` from its root and root operands.

    Parameters:
        root: the root for the formula tree.
        first: the first operand for the root, if the root is a unary or
            binary operator.
        second: the second operand for the root, if the root is a binary
            operator.
    """
    if is_variable(root) or is_constant(root):
        assert first is None and second is None
        self.root = root
    elif is_unary(root):
        assert first is not None and second is None
        self.root, self.first = root, first
    else:
        assert is_binary(root)
        assert first is not None and second is not None
        self.root, self.first, self.second = root, first, second
```

The constructor of this class (which we have already implemented for you) takes as arguments the components (between one and three) of which the formula is composed, and constructs the composite formula. For instance, to represent the formula '$(\phi\&\psi)$', the constructor will be given the three "components": the operator '&' that will serve as the "root" of the tree and the two subformulas ϕ and ψ.

EXAMPLE 1.1   The data structure for representing the formula '~(p&q76)' is constructed using the following code:

```
my_formula = Formula('~', Formula('&', Formula('p'), Formula('q76')))
```

The various components of `my_formula` from Example 1.1 can then be accessed using the instance variables `my_formula.root` for the root, `my_formula.first` for the first subformula (if any), and `my_formula.second` for the second subformula (if any). To enable the safe reuse of existing formula objects as building blocks for other formula objects (and even as building blocks in more than one other formula object, or as building blocks that appear more than once in the same formula object), we have defined the Formula class to be **immutable**, i.e., we have defined it so that `my_formula.root`, `my_formula.first`, and `my_formula.second` cannot be assigned to after `my_formula` has been constructed. For example, you can verify that after `my_formula` is constructed as in Example 1.1, attempting to assign `my_formula.first = Formula('q4')` fails. This is achieved by the @frozen decorator that appears just before the class definition.[3] Most of the classes that you will implement as you work through this book will be made immutable in this way.

Your first task is to translate the expression-tree representation of a formula into its string representation. This can be done using recursion: suppose that you know how to

---

[3] The definition of this decorator is in the file `logic_utils.py` that we have provided to you, and which we imported for you into `propositions/syntax.py`.

convert two tree data structures `formula1` and `formula2` (that are both Python objects of type `Formula`) into strings; how can you convert, into such a string, a tree data structure of type `Formula` that has `'&'` at its root, and `formula1` and `formula2` as its two children/subformulas?

TASK 1 Implement the missing code for the method[4] `__repr__()` of class `Formula`, which returns a string that represents the formula (in the syntax defined in Definition 1.1). Note that in Python, the string returned by, e.g., `formula.__repr__()` is also returned by `str(formula)`, so by solving this task you will also be implementing the functionality of the latter.

```
                          propositions/syntax.py
class Formula:
        ⋮

    def __repr__(self) -> str:
        """Computes the string representation of the current formula.

        Returns:
            The standard string representation of the current formula.
        """
        # Task 1.1
```

Example: For the formula `my_formula` defined in Example 1.1, `my_formula.__repr__()` (and hence also `str(my_formula)`) should return the string `'~(p&q76)'`.

The next two tasks ask for getting a summary of the components of a given formula: the variable names used in it, and the operators used in it (where we treat 'T' and 'F' as operators too – we will discuss the rationale behind this definition in Chapter 3).

TASK 2 Implement the missing code for the method `variables()` of class `Formula`, which returns all of the variable names that appear in the formula. Recall that a variable name is a leaf of the tree whose label is a letter in 'p'...'z' optionally followed by a nonnegative integer.

```
                          propositions/syntax.py
class Formula:
        ⋮

    def variables(self) -> Set[str]:
        """Finds all variable names in the current formula.

        Returns:
            A set of all variable names used in the current formula.
        """
        # Task 1.2
```

---

[4] The decorator that precedes the definition of `__repr__()` in the code that you are given **memoizes** this method, so that any subsequent calls to this method (on the same `Formula` object) after the first call simply return the value returned by the first call instead of recalculating it. This has no effect on code correctness since the `Formula` class is immutable, running this method has no side effects, and the returned is immutable, but this will dramatically speed-up your code in later chapters, when you handle complex formulas. We use this decorator throughout the code that you are given in various places where there are speed improvements to be gained.

Example: For the formula `my_formula` defined in Example 1.1, `my_formula`
`.variables()` should return `{'p', 'q76'}`.

TASK 3   Implement the missing code for the method `operators()` of class `Formula`,
which returns all of the operators that appear in the formula. By operators we mean '~',
'&', '|', '→', 'T', and 'F'.

```
                      ┌─────────────────────┐
                      │ propositions/syntax.py │
                      └─────────────────────┘
class Formula:
    ⋮

    def operators(self) -> Set[str]:
        """Finds all operators in the current formula.

        Returns:
            A set of all operators (including 'T' and 'F') used in the current
            formula.
        """
        # Task 1.3
```

Example: For the formula `my_formula` defined in Example 1.1, `my_formula`
`.operators()` should return `{'~', '&'}`.

1.2   Parsing

Going in the opposite direction, i.e., taking a string representation of a formula and **parsing**
it into the corresponding derivation tree, is usually a bit more difficult since you need to
algorithmically figure out where to "break" the complex string representation of the formula into the different components of the formula. This type of parsing challenge is quite
common when dealing with many cases of formal "languages" that need to be "understood"
by a computer program, the prime example being when compilers need to understand
programs written in a programming language. There is a general theory that deals with
various classes of languages as well as algorithms for parsing them, with an emphasis
on the class of **context-free languages**, whose grammar can be defined by a recursive
definition. The language for formulas that we chose for this book is in this class, and is
simple enough so that a simple "recursive descent" algorithm, which we will now describe,
can handle its parsing.

The idea is to first read the first **token** in the string, where a token is a basic "word" of our
language: either one of the single-letter tokens `'T'`, `'F'`, `'('`, `')'`, `'~'`, `'&'`, `'|'`, or the
two-letter "implies" token `'->'`, or a variable name like `'p'` or `'q76'`. This first token will
tell you in a unique way how to continue reading the rest of the string, where this reading
can be done recursively. For example, if the first token is an open parenthesis, `'('`, then
we know that a formula ϕ must follow, which can be read by a recursive call. Once ϕ was
recursively read, we know that the following token must be one of `'&'`, `'|'`, or `'->'`, and
once this token is read then a formula ψ must follow, and then a closing parenthesis, `')'`.
This will become concrete as you implement the following task.

TASK 4   Implement the missing code for the static method _parse_prefix(string) of class Formula, which takes a string that has a prefix that represents a formula, and returns a formula tree created from the prefix, and a string containing the unparsed remainder of the string (which may be empty, if the parsed prefix is in fact the entire string).

```
                        ┌─────────────────────────┐
                        │ propositions/syntax.py  │
┌───────────────────────┴─────────────────────────┴───────────────────────┐
│ class Formula:                                                           │
│     ⋮                                                                    │
│     @staticmethod                                                        │
│     def _parse_prefix(string: str) -> Tuple[Optional[Formula], str]:     │
│         """Parses a prefix of the given string into a formula.          │
│                                                                          │
│         Parameters:                                                      │
│             string: string to parse.                                    │
│                                                                          │
│         Returns:                                                         │
│             A pair of the parsed formula and the unparsed suffix of the string. │
│             If the given string has as a prefix a variable name (e.g.,  │
│             'x12') or a unary operator followed by a variable name, then the │
│             parsed prefix will include that entire variable name (and not just a │
│             part of it, such as 'x1'). If no prefix of the given string is a │
│             valid standard string representation of a formula then returned pair │
│             should be of ``None`` and an error message, where the error message │
│             is a string with some human-readable content.               │
│         """                                                              │
│         # Task 1.4                                                       │
└──────────────────────────────────────────────────────────────────────────┘
```

Example: Formula._parse_prefix('(p&q)') should return a pair whose first element is a Formula object equivalent to Formula('&', Formula('p'), Formula('q')) and whose second element is '' (the empty string), while Formula._parse_prefix('p3&q') should return a pair whose first element is a Formula object equivalent to Formula('p3') and whose second element is the string '&q', and Formula._parse_prefix('((p&q))') should return the Python pair (None, 'Unexpected symbol)') (or some other error message in the second entry). See the test function test_parse_prefix in the file propositions/syntax_test.py for more examples (as we already remarked, it is always a good idea to consult the test function for a task before starting to solve the task).

The fact that given a string, the code that you wrote is able to clearly decide, without any ambiguity, on what exactly is the prefix of this string that constitutes a valid formula, relies on the fact that indeed our syntactic rules ensure that no prefix of a formula is also a formula itself (with the mentioned caveat that this holds as long as a variable name cannot be broken down so that only its prefix is taken, since, e.g., 'x1' *is* a prefix of 'x12'). Had our definitions been different, e.g., had we allowed '$\phi\&\psi$' as a formula as well, then this would have no longer been true. For example, under such definitions, the string 'x&y' would have been a valid formula, and so would have its prefix 'x'. The code behind your implementation and the reasoning of why it solves the task in the unique correct way thus essentially prove the following lemma.

LEMMA 1.1 (Prefix-Free Property of Formulas)   *No formula is a prefix of another formula, except for the case of a variable name as a prefix of another variable name.*

Since this is the first lemma in the book, let us take just a moment to consider how this lemma would be proven in a "standard mathematical way." The overall structure of the proof would be by induction on the length of the formula (which we need to show has no proper prefix that is also a formula). The proof would then proceed with a case-by-case analysis of the first token of the formula. The significant parts of the proof would be the ones that correspond to the inductive definitions, specifically to a formula starting with a '('. By definition, this formula must be parsed as '$(\phi*\psi)$' (where $*$ is one of the three allowed binary operators), and so must any supposed formula prefix of it (for perhaps some other '$(\phi'*'\psi')$'). We would then use the induction hypothesis claiming that neither ϕ nor ϕ' can be the prefix of the other if they are different, to show that $\phi = \phi'$, which then forces $* = *'$, and then we can apply the induction hypothesis again to show that neither ψ nor ψ' can be the prefix of the other if they are different, to conclude the proof (of this case).[5] The structure of this proof is in direct correspondence to your parsing algorithm and its justification: both the code and the proof have the same case-by-case analysis, only with mathematical induction in the proof replacing recursion in the algorithm. Furthermore, the reasoning for why you wrote your code the way you did – e.g., why your code can safely rely on the values returned by the induction calls and can safely expect to find certain tokens in certain places in the string – directly corresponds to the proof arguments. We thus feel that if you were able to solve this task, then you have a complete understanding of all the important mathematical elements of the proof – an understanding that possibly misses only the formalistic wrapping but has the advantage of being very concrete (and executable!). In this book we will thus not provide formal mathematical proofs that just repeat in a formal mathematical way conceptual steps taken in a programmatic solution of a task.

TASK 5   Implement the missing code for the static method `is_formula(string)` of class `Formula`, which checks whether a given string represents a valid formula (according to Definition 1.1).

```
                            ┤ propositions/syntax.py ├
class Formula:
     ⋮

    @staticmethod
    def is_formula(string: str) -> bool:
        """Checks if the given string is a valid representation of a formula.

        Parameters:
            string: string to check.

        Returns:
            ``True`` if the given string is a valid standard string
            representation of a formula, ``False`` otherwise.
        """
        # Task 1.5
```

---

[5] The "caveat case" of a variable name as a prefix of another variable name would come up when dealing with formulas whose first token is a variable name (rather than with a '(' as in the case just detailed). In this case, to get uniqueness we must indeed enforce that the entire variable-name token be part of the parsed prefix.

Hint: Use the `_parse_prefix()` method.

TASK 6 Implement the missing code for the static method `parse(string)` of class `Formula`, which parses a given string representation of a formula. (You may assume that the input string is valid, i.e., satisfies the precondition `Formula.is_formula(string)`, as indicated by the assertion that we already added for you.)

```
                        ┌─ propositions/syntax.py ─┐
class Formula:
        ⋮

    @staticmethod
    def parse(string: str) -> Formula:
        """Parses the given valid string representation into a formula.

        Parameters:
            string: string to parse.

        Returns:
            A formula whose standard string representation is the given string.
        """
        assert Formula.is_formula(string)
        # Task 1.6
```

Hint: Use the `_parse_prefix()` method.

The reasoning and code that allowed you to implement Task 6 (and the preceding Task 4) without any ambiguity essentially prove the following theorem.

THEOREM 1.1 (Unique Readability of Formulas) *There is a unique derivation tree for every valid propositional formula.*

1.3 Infinite Sets of Formulas

Our programs, like all computer programs, only handle finite data. This book however aims to teach mathematical logic and thus needs to also consider infinite objects. We shall aim to make a clear distinction between objects that are mathematically finite (like a single integer number[6]) and those that can mathematically be infinite (like a set of integers) but practical representations in a computer program may limit them to be finite. So, looking at the definition of formulas, we see that every formula has a *finite* length and thus formulas are finite objects in principle. Now, there is no uniform upper bound on the possible length of a formula (much like there is no uniform upper bound on the possible length of an integer), which means that there are infinitely many formulas. In particular, a set of formulas can in principle be an infinite object: It may contain a finite number of distinct formulas or an infinite number of distinct (longer and longer) formulas, but each of these formulas has only a finite length. Of course, when we actually represent sets of formulas in our programs, the represented sets will always be only of finite size.

---

[6] Indeed, while there is no upper bound on the length of an integer number, any given single integer number is of finite length.

As some readers may recall, in mathematics there can be different **cardinalities** of infinite sets, where the "smallest" infinite sets are called **countably infinite** (or **enumerable**). An infinite set S is called countably infinite, or **countable**, if there exists a way to list its items one after another without "forgetting" any of them: $S = \{s_1, s_2, s_3, \ldots\}$. (Formally if there exists a function f from the natural numbers *onto* S.)[7] The set of formulas is indeed countable in this sense: Each formula is a finite-length string whose letters come from a finite number of characters, and thus there is a finite number of formulas of any given fixed length. Thus one may first list all the formulas of length 1, then those of length 2, etc. We thus get the following simple fact.

THEOREM 1.2   *The set of formulas is countably infinite.*

While according to our definition of variable names and formulas there are only countably many variable names and therefore only countably many formulas, all of the results in this book extend naturally via analogous proofs to sets of variable names of arbitrary cardinality, which imply also formula sets of arbitrary cardinality. In the few places throughout this book where the generalization is not straightforward, we will explicitly discuss this.

1.A   Optional Reading: Polish Notations

The notation that we used to represent our formulas is only one possible format, and there are other notations by which a tree data structure can be represented as a string. The notation that we used is called **infix notation** since the operator at the root of the tree is given *in*-between the representations of the left and right subtrees. Another commonly used notation is **polish** notation.[8] In this notation, the operator is printed *before* the (two, in the case of a binary operator) subformulas that it operates on. Of course, these subformulas themselves are recursively printed in the same way. In another commonly used notation, **reverse polish notation**, the operator is printed *after* these subformulas.[9] One nice advantage of polish and reverse polish notations is that it turns out that parentheses are no longer needed. Thus, for example, the formula whose regular, infix notation is '~(p&q76)' would be represented in polish notation as '~&pq76' and in reverse polish notation as 'pq76&~'.

OPTIONAL TASK 7   Implement the missing code for the static method `polish()` of class `Formula`, which returns a string that represents the formula in polish notation.

---

[7] For the benefit of readers who are not familiar with cardinalities of infinite sets, we note that while when first encountering this definition it may be hard to think of any set that does *not* satisfy this property, in fact many sets that you have encountered do not satisfy it. A prime example is the infinite set of all real numbers between 0 and 1, which is not countable.

[8] So called after the Polish logician Jan Łukasiewicz who invented it.

[9] Polish notation and reverse polish notations are also called **prefix notation** and **postfix notation**, respectively, analogously to infix notation, describing where the operator comes with respect to the representations of the subtrees. We avoid these terms here in order not to confuse prefix as the name of the notation with prefix as the word describing the beginning of a string as in "prefix-free" or as in `_parse_prefix()`.

```
                          ( propositions/syntax.py )
class Formula:
        ⋮

    def polish(self) -> str:
        """Computes the polish notation representation of the current formula.

        Returns:
            The polish notation representation of the current formula.
        """
        # Optional Task 1.7
```

Example: For the formula `my_formula` defined in Example 1.1, `my_formula.polish()` should return the string `'~&pq76'`. (Remember that there are no parentheses in polish notation.) Once again, it is always a good idea to consult the test function for more examples.

Parsing polish notation is usually a bit easier than parsing infix notation, even though there are no parentheses.

OPTIONAL TASK 8   Implement the missing code for the static method `parse_polish(string)` of class `Formula`, which parses a given polish notation representation of a formula. As in Task 6, you may assume (without checking) that the input string is valid.

```
                          ( propositions/syntax.py )
class Formula:
        ⋮

    @staticmethod
    def parse_polish(string: str) -> Formula:
        """Parses the given polish notation representation into a formula.

        Parameters:
            string: string to parse.

        Returns:
            A formula whose polish notation representation is the given string.
        """
        # Optional Task 1.8
```

Hint: First implement an analogue of Task 4 for polish notation.

2 Propositional Logic Semantics

In Chapter 1 we defined the **syntax** of propositional formulas, that is, we defined which strings constitute valid propositional formulas. We were however careful not to assign any meaning, any **semantics**, to propositional formulas. The notion of the semantics of propositional formulas may be somewhat difficult to grasp, as the meaning of formulas may seem "obvious" but its formal definition may at first seem elusive. This chapter provides this formal definition.

Our intention for these semantics is as follows: Every variable name (e.g., 'p' or 'q76') will stand for a certain **primitive proposition** that may be *either true or false*, independently of other primitive propositions. A compound formula that contains more than one variable name will describe a more complex proposition, whose truth or lack thereof depends on *which primitive propositions are true and which are not*. For example, we may have 'p' represent "It is raining," 'q' represent "My umbrella is open," 'r' represent "I am singing," and 's' represent "I am dancing." A compound formula such as '((p&~q)&(r|s))' evaluates to *true* if it is raining and my umbrella is *not* open, and furthermore either I am singing or I am dancing.

Before moving forward with the formal definition of the semantics of propositional formulas, it may perhaps be instructive to take a short detour to another domain where we have a distinction between syntax and semantics, a domain where we expect many of our readers to have a good feel for semantics: programming languages.

2.1 Detour: Semantics of Programming Languages

Consider the following valid program:

```
#include <stdio.h> /*
print("wonderland")
""" */
int main() { printf("looking-glass\n"); }
// """
```

What would this program output? Well, since in Python comments start with the symbol # and continue until the end of the line, and multiline strings (which are ignored on their own) are enclosed between triple quotations, then graying out Python comments and ignored strings, the program would be interpreted as follows:

```
                          ( mystery_program.py )
#include <stdio.h> /*
print("wonderland")
""" */
int main() { printf("looking-glass\n"); }
// """
```

and when executed would simply print `wonderland`. This answer, as we will now explain, while partially correct, does make some assumptions. As it turns out, the proper answer to the question of what would the program print is "it depends on which language you consider this program to be written in." Indeed, this program is not only a valid program in Python, but also in the C programming language![1] While the *syntax* of this program is valid both in Python and in C, its *semantics* in each of these programming languages turn out however to be completely different. In C, comments are either enclosed between /* and */, or start with // and continue until the end of the line. Therefore, as a C program, graying out C comments, the above program would be interpreted as follows:

```
                          ( mystery_program.c )
#include <stdio.h> /*
print("wonderland")
""" */
int main() { printf("looking-glass\n"); }
// """
```

and when compiled and executed, would simply print `looking-glass`.

So what is our point with this example? First, that the semantics are very important: In the case of programming languages they determine what the program *does*. Second, that even if usually a short glance suffices for you to "more-or-less understand" a piece of code (or a formula), carefully defining the "right" semantics is still very important, and may be tricky and not at all obvious. With this appreciation, let us return to propositional formulas and proceed to assign *semantics* to them.

2.2 Models and Truth Values

Formally, the **semantics** we will give to a formula are the respective truth values that it gets in every possible setting of its variable names. We view a possible setting of these variable names as a "possible world," and the semantics of a formula are whether it is true or not in each of these possible worlds. We will call such a possible world a **model**.

DEFINITION 2.1 (Model)   Let S be the set of variable names. A **model** M over S is a function that assigns a truth value to every variable name in S. That is, $M: S \to \{True, False\}$.

The file `propositions/semantics.py`, which contains all of the functions that you are asked to implement in the next few sections, deals with the semantics of propositional formulas. A formula is represented as an instance of the class `Formula` that was defined

---

[1] Fear not if you have no familiarity with the C programming language. We will explain the little that is needed to know about C in order to drive the point of this discussion home.

in Chapter 1. We will represent a model as a Python `dict` (dictionary) that maps every variable name to a Boolean value:

```
                          propositions/semantics.py
#: A model for propositional-logic formulas, a mapping from variable names to
#: truth values.
Model = Mapping[str, bool]

def is_model(model: Model) -> bool:
    """Checks if the given dictionary is a model over some set of variable
    names.

    Parameters:
        model: dictionary to check.

    Returns:
        ``True`` if the given dictionary is a model over some set of variable
        names, ``False`` otherwise.
    """
    for key in model:
        if not is_variable(key):
            return False
    return True

def variables(model: Model) -> AbstractSet[str]:
    """Finds all variable names over which the given model is defined.

    Parameters:
        model: model to check.

    Returns:
        A set of all variable names over which the given model is defined.
    """
    assert is_model(model)
    return model.keys()
```

Having defined a model, we can now give each formula its semantics – the truth value that it gets in every possible model.

DEFINITION 2.2 (Truth Value of Formula in Model)   Given a formula ϕ and a model M over a set of variable names that contains (at least) all those used in ϕ, we define the **(truth) value** of the formula ϕ in the model M recursively in the natural way:

- If ϕ is the constant 'T', its value is *True*; if ϕ is the constant 'F', its value is *False*.
- If ϕ is a variable name p, then its value is as specified by the model: $M(p)$.
- If ϕ is of the form '$\sim\psi$', then its value is *True* if the (recursively defined) value of ψ in M is *False* (and is *False* otherwise).
- If ϕ is of the form '$(\psi\&\xi)$', then its value is *True* if the (recursively defined) values of both ψ and ξ in M are *True* (and is *False* otherwise); if ϕ is of the form '$(\psi|\xi)$', then its value is *True* if the (recursively defined) value of either ψ or ξ (or both) in M is *True* (and is *False* otherwise); if ϕ is of the form '$(\psi\rightarrow\xi)$', then its value is *True* if either the (recursively defined) value of ψ in M is *False* or the (recursively defined) value of ξ in M is *True* (and is *False* otherwise).

Returning to the example we started with, one possible model M is $M('p') = $ *True* (it is raining), $M('q') = $ *False* (my umbrella is NOT open), $M('r') = $ *True* (I am singing), and $M('s') = $ *False* (I am NOT dancing), and in this model the formula '$((p\&\sim q)\&(r|s))$' evaluates to the value *True* as defined recursively: '$\sim q$' evaluates to *True* (since 'q' evaluates to *False*), and so '$(p\&\sim q)$' evaluates to *True* (since both 'p' and '$\sim q$' evaluate to *True*); furthermore, '$(r|s)$' evaluates to *True* (since 'r' evaluates to *True*); and finally '$((p\&\sim q)\&(r|s))$' evaluates to *True* (since both '$(p\&\sim q)$' and '$(r|s)$' evaluate to *True*). Of course there are more possible models, and for some of them the formula evaluates to *True* while for the others it evaluates to *False*.

While the semantics of the *not* ('$\sim$'), *or* ('$|$'), and *and* ('$\&$') operators are quite natural and self-explanatory, the *implies* ('$\rightarrow$') operator may seem a bit more cryptic. The way to think about '$(\psi \rightarrow \xi)$' is as stating that if ψ is *True*, then ξ is *True* as well. This statement would be *False* only if both ψ were *True* and ξ were *False*, so this statement is *True* whenever either ψ is *False* or ξ is *True*, which coincides with Definition 2.2. Yet, it may still intuitively seem unnatural that the statement "if ψ is *True*, then ξ is *True* as well" is considered to be *True* if ψ is *False* (indeed, how should one interpret this conditional if ψ is false?). The reason for this definition is that we would generally be interested in whether a given formula is *True* in each of a *set* of models. In this context, the formula '$(\psi \rightarrow \xi)$' can be naturally interpreted as "whenever ψ is *True*, so is ξ," that is, in any model in this set in which ψ is *True*, so is ξ. (This of course still does not tell us anything about models in this set in which ψ is *False*, but replacing "if" with "whenever" may somewhat further motivate this definition, and help make this operator a bit less cryptic.)

TASK 1   Implement the missing code for the function `evaluate(formula, model)`, which returns the truth value of the given formula in the given model.

```
                    ┌─ propositions/semantics.py ─┐
def evaluate(formula: Formula, model: Model) -> bool:
    """Calculates the truth value of the given formula in the given model.

    Parameters:
        formula: formula to calculate the truth value of.
        model: model over (possibly a superset of) the variable names of the
            given formula, to calculate the truth value in.

    Returns:
        The truth value of the given formula in the given model.

    Examples:
        >>> evaluate(Formula.parse('~(p&q76)'), {'p': True, 'q76': False})
        True

        >>> evaluate(Formula.parse('~(p&q76)'), {'p': True, 'q76': True})
        False
    """
    assert is_model(model)
    assert formula.variables().issubset(variables(model))
    # Task 2.1
```

2.3   Truth Tables

Once we have defined the value that a formula gets in a given model, we now turn to handling sets of possible models. If we have a set of n variable names, then there are exactly 2^n possible models over this set: All possible combinations where each of the variable names is mapped to either *True* or *False*. In the next task we ask you to list all these possible models.

Before jumping to the task, we should explicitly note the exponential jump in the size of the objects that we are dealing with. While all the code that you have written so far would have no problem dealing with formulas with millions of variable names, once we want to list *all* the possible models over a given set of variable names, we will not be able to handle more than a few dozen variable names at most: already with 40 variable names we have more than a trillion models ($2^{40} \approx 10^{12}$).

TASK 2   Implement the missing code for the function `all_models(variables)`, which returns a list[2] of all possible models over the given variable names.

```
                          ╭─ propositions/semantics.py ─╮
def all_models(variables: Sequence[str]) -> Iterable[Model]:
    """Calculates all possible models over the given variable names.

    Parameters:
        variables: variable names over which to calculate the models.

    Returns:
        An iterable over all possible models over the given variable names. The
        order of the models is lexicographic according to the order of the given
        variable names, where False precedes True.

    Examples:
        >>> list(all_models(['p', 'q']))
        [{'p': False, 'q': False}, {'p': False, 'q': True},
         {'p': True, 'q': False}, {'p': True, 'q': True}]

        >>> list(all_models(['q', 'p']))
        [{'q': False, 'p': False}, {'q': False, 'p': True},
         {'q': True, 'p': False}, {'q': True, 'p': True}]
    """
    for v in variables:
        assert is_variable(v)
    # Task 2.2
```

---

[2] While in this book we will not pay much attention to complexities and running times, we do pay here just a bit of attention to this first exponential blowup. Even though for simplicity the task asks to return a `list`, we recommend that readers familiar with Python *iterables* return an iterable that *iterates* over all possible models (which does not require keeping them all together in memory) rather than actually return a `list` of all possible models (which would require them to all be together in memory). The test that we provide allows for any iterable, and not merely a `list`, to be returned by this function. We do not, however, intend to run any of this code on more than a few variable names, so we do not impose any efficiency requirements on your code, and we do allow solving this task by returning a `list` of all models.

Guidelines: The standard term "lexicographic order" that specifies the order of the models refers to considering each model as a "word" in the alphabet consisting of the two "letters" *False* and *True*, considering the "letter" *False* to precede the "letter" *True*, and listing all the "words" (models) "alphabetically" in the sense that every word that starts with *False* precedes every word that starts with *True*, and more generally for any prefix of a "word," words that start with that prefix and then *False* (regardless of which "letters" follow) precede words that start with that prefix and then *True* (regardless of which "letters" follow).

Hint: The product method (with its `repeat` argument) from the standard Python `itertools` module may be useful here.

TASK 3   Implement the missing code for the function `truth_values(formula, models)`, which returns a list of the respective truth values of the given formula in the given models.[3]

```
                    propositions/semantics.py

def truth_values(formula: Formula, models: Iterable[Model]) -> Iterable[bool]:
    """Calculates the truth value of the given formula in each of the given
    models.

    Parameters:
        formula: formula to calculate the truth value of.
        models: iterable over models to calculate the truth value in.

    Returns:
        An iterable over the respective truth values of the given formula in
        each of the given models, in the order of the given models.

    Examples:
        >>> list(truth_values(Formula.parse('~(p&q76)'),
        ...                    all_models(['p', 'q76'])))
        [True, True, True, False]
    """
    # Task 2.3
```

We are now able to print the full semantics of a formula: its truth value for every possible model over its variable names. There is a standard way to print this information, called a **truth table**: A table with a line for each possible model, where this line lists each of the truth values of the variable names in the model, and then the truth value of the formula in the model.

TASK 4   Implement the missing code for the function `print_truth_table(formula)`, which prints the truth table of the given formula (according to the format demonstrated in the *docstring* of this function).

---

[3] Readers who implemented Task 2 to return a memory-efficient iterable rather than a `list` are encouraged to implement this method to accept `models` also as an arbitrary iterable, and to also return a memory-efficient iterable rather than a `list` from this function. The test that we provide allows for any iterable to be returned by this function, but only requires the function to support taking a `list` of models.

```
                        ┌─ propositions/semantics.py ─┐
def print_truth_table(formula: Formula) -> None:
    """Prints the truth table of the given formula, with variable-name columns
    sorted alphabetically.

    Parameters:
        formula: formula to print the truth table of.

    Examples:
        >>> print_truth_table(Formula.parse('~(p&q76)'))
        | p | q76 | ~(p&q76) |
        |---|-----|----------|
        | F | F   | T        |
        | F | T   | T        |
        | T | F   | T        |
        | T | T   | F        |
    """
    # Task 2.4
```

2.4   Tautologies, Contradictions, and Satisfiability

We are going to pay special attention to two types of formulas – those that get the value *True* in *some* model and those that get the value *True* in *all* models.

DEFINITION 2.3 (Satisfiable Formula; Contradiction; Tautology)

- A formula is said to be **satisfiable** if it gets the value *True* in some (at least one) model. A formula that is not satisfiable is said to be a **contradiction**.
- A formula is said to be a **tautology** if it gets the value *True* in all models over its variable names.

For example, the formula '(p&~p)' is a contradiction (why?) and thus is not satisfiable and is certainly not a tautology, while '(p|~p)' is a tautology (why?) and in particular is also satisfiable. The formula '(p&q)' is neither a contradiction nor a tautology, but is satisfiable (why?). Note that a formula ϕ is a contradiction if and only if '~ϕ' is a tautology, and thus a formula ϕ is satisfiable if and only if its negation '~ϕ' is not a tautology. One may figure out whether a given formula satisfies each of these conditions by going over all possible models.

TASK 5   Implement the missing code for the three functions is_tautology(formula), is_contradiction(formula), and is_satisfiable(formula), which respectively return whether the given formula is a tautology, is a contradiction, and is satisfiable.

```
                        ┌─ propositions/semantics.py ─┐
def is_tautology(formula: Formula) -> bool:
    """Checks if the given formula is a tautology.

    Parameters:
        formula: formula to check.
```

```
    Returns:
        ``True`` if the given formula is a tautology, ``False`` otherwise.
    """
    # Task 2.5a

def is_contradiction(formula: Formula) -> bool:
    """Checks if the given formula is a contradiction.

    Parameters:
        formula: formula to check.

    Returns:
        ``True`` if the given formula is a contradiction, ``False`` otherwise.
    """
    # Task 2.5b

def is_satisfiable(formula: Formula) -> bool:
    """Checks if the given formula is satisfiable.

    Parameters:
        formula: formula to check.

    Returns:
        ``True`` if the given formula is satisfiable, ``False`` otherwise.
    """
    # Task 2.5c
```

Examples: If f is the formula that represents '~(p&q76)', then is_tautology(f) should return False, is_contradiction(f) should return False, and is_satisfiable(f) should return True. If g is the formula that represents '(x|~x)', then is_tautology(g) should return True, is_contradiction(g) should return False, and is_satisfiable(g) should return True.

Hint: Once you implement one of these functions by going over all possible models, it should be easy to use it to implement the other two.

2.5 Synthesis of Formulas

All of the tasks so far accepted a formula as their input, and answered questions about its truth value in a given model or in some set of models. In the next two tasks you are asked to implement the "reversed" functionality: to take as input desired semantics, and output – synthesize – a formula that conforms to it. Remarkably, this can be done for any desired semantics.

Our first step will be to create a formula whose truth table has a single row with value *True*, with all other rows having value *False*. This can be done in the form of a **conjunctive clause**: a conjunction (i.e., a concatenation using '&' operators) of (one or more) variable names or negation-of-variable-names.

TASK 6 Implement the missing code for the function _synthesize_for_model(model), which returns a propositional formula in the form of a conjunctive clause that is *True* for the given model and *False* for every other model over the same variable names.

```
┌─────────────────( propositions/semantics.py )─────────────────┐
def _synthesize_for_model(model: Model) -> Formula:
    """Synthesizes a propositional formula in the form of a single conjunctive
    clause that evaluates to ``True`` in the given model, and to ``False`` in
    any other model over the same variable names.

    Parameters:
        model: model over a nonempty set of variable names, in which the
            synthesized formula is to hold.

    Returns:
        The synthesized formula.
    """
    assert is_model(model)
    assert len(model.keys()) > 0
    # Task 2.6
```

Your solution to Task 6 (programmatically) proves the following lemma.

LEMMA 2.1   *Let* $M : S \to \{True, False\}$ *be a model over some nonempty finite set of variable names S. There exists a formula in the form of a conjunctive clause that evaluates to True in M and to False in all other models over S.*

If we want to create a formula that has some arbitrary given truth table, that is, that has value *True* for all models in some arbitrary set of models and *False* for any other model, then we can easily just take a disjunction (i.e., a concatenation using '|' operators) of the conjunctive clauses that Lemma 2.1 guarantees for each of the models in the set. This would give us a formula in the form called **disjunctive normal form (DNF)**: a disjunction of (one or more) conjunctive clauses.

TASK 7 (Programmatic Proof of the DNF Theorem (2.1))   Implement the missing code for the function `synthesize(variables, values)`, which constructs a propositional formula in DNF from the given description of its truth table.[4]

```
┌─────────────────( propositions/semantics.py )─────────────────┐
def synthesize(variables: Sequence[str], values: Iterable[bool]) -> Formula:
    """Synthesizes a propositional formula in DNF over the given variable names,
    that has the specified truth table.

    Parameters:
        variables: nonempty set of variable names for the synthesized formula.
        values: iterable over truth values for the synthesized formula in every
            possible model over the given variable names, in the order returned
            by `all_models(variables)`.

    Returns:
        The synthesized formula.

    Examples:
        >>> formula = synthesize(['p', 'q'], [True, True, True, False])
        >>> for model in all_models(['p', 'q']):
```

_____
[4] Once again, readers who implemented Task 3 to return a memory-efficient iterable rather than a `list` are encouraged to implement this method to also accept `values` as an arbitrary iterable.

```
        ...       evaluate(formula, model)
      True
      True
      True
      False
    """
    assert len(variables) > 0
    # Task 2.7
```

Hints: Use the function `_synthesize_for_model` that you implemented in Task 6. Note that the case in which the set of models with value *True* is empty is a special case since we are not allowing to simply return the formula 'F', so you will need to return an equivalent DNF of your choice (over the given variable names).

The fact that you were able to complete Task 7 proves the following rather remarkable theorem.

THEOREM 2.1 (The DNF Theorem) *Let S be a nonempty finite set of variable names. For every Boolean function f over the variable names in S (i.e., f arbitrarily assigns a truth value to every tuple of truth values for the variable names in S) there exists a formula in disjunctive normal form whose truth table is exactly the Boolean function f.*

2.A   Optional Reading: Conjunctive Normal Form

In this section we will consider an alternative approach to synthesizing formulas. While this approach is a precise dual to the one used in Section 2.5, it may be slightly more challenging conceptually. Our first step will be to create a formula whose truth table has all rows except one having value *True*, with the remaining row having value *False*. This can be done in the form of a **disjunctive clause**: a disjunction of (one or more) variable names or negation-of-variable-names.

OPTIONAL TASK 8   Implement the missing code for the function `_synthesize_for_all_except_model(model)`, which returns a propositional formula in the form of a disjunctive clause that is *False* for the given model and *True* for every other model over the same variable names.

```
                    propositions/semantics.py

def _synthesize_for_all_except_model(model: Model) -> Formula:
    """Synthesizes a propositional formula in the form of a single disjunctive
    clause that evaluates to ``False`` in the given model, and to ``True`` in
    any other model over the same variable names.

    Parameters:
        model: model over a nonempty set of variable names, in which the
            synthesized formula is to not hold.

    Returns:
        The synthesized formula.
    """
    assert is_model(model)
```

```
    assert len(model.keys()) > 0
    # Optional Task 2.8
```

Analogously to the way Lemma 2.1 is proven by your solution to Task 6, your solution to Optional Task 8 proves the following lemma.

LEMMA 2.2   *Let $M : S \to \{True, False\}$ be a model over some nonempty finite set of variable names S. There exists a formula in the form of a disjunctive clause that evaluates to False in M and to True in all other models over S.*

If we want to create a formula that has some arbitrary given truth table, that is, that has value *True* for all models in some arbitrary set of models and *False* for any other model, then we can just take a conjunction of the disjunctive clauses that Lemma 2.2 guarantees for each of the models *not* (!) in the set. This would give us a formula in the form called **conjunctive normal form (CNF)**: a conjunction of (one or more) disjunctive clauses.

OPTIONAL TASK 9 (Programmatic Proof of the CNF Theorem (2.2))   Implement the missing code for the function synthesize_cnf(variables, values), which constructs a propositional formula in CNF from the given description of its truth table.[5]

```
                        ┌─ propositions/semantics.py ─┐
def synthesize_cnf(variables: Sequence[str], values: Iterable[bool]) -> Formula:
    """Synthesizes a propositional formula in CNF over the given variable names,
    that has the specified truth table.

    Parameters:
        variables: nonempty set of variable names for the synthesized formula.
        values: iterable over truth values for the synthesized formula in every
            possible model over the given variable names, in the order returned
            by `all_models(variables)`.

    Returns:
        The synthesized formula.

    Examples:
        >>> formula = synthesize_cnf(['p', 'q'], [True, True, True, False])
        >>> for model in all_models(['p', 'q']):
        ...     evaluate(formula, model)
        True
        True
        True
        False
    """
    assert len(variables) > 0
    # Optional Task 2.9
```

Hints: Use the function _synthesize_for_all_except_model that you implemented in Optional Task 8. Note that the case in which the set of models with value *False* is empty is a special case since we are not allowing to simply return the formula 'T', so you will need to return an equivalent CNF of your choice (over the given variable names).

---

[5] Once again, readers who implemented Task 3 to return a memory-efficient iterable rather than a list are encouraged to implement this method to also accept values as an arbitrary iterable.

The fact that you were able to complete Optional Task 9 proves the following theorem, which is as remarkable as the DNF theorem (2.1).

THEOREM 2.2 (The CNF Theorem)   *Let S be a nonempty finite set of variable names. For every Boolean function f over the variable names in S (i.e., f arbitrarily assigns a truth value to every tuple of truth values for the variable names in S) there exists a formula in Conjunctive Normal Form whose truth table is exactly the Boolean function f.*

Attentive readers would notice the **duality** between constructing a DNF formula and a CNF formula. Given a model, `_synthesize_for_model_all_except_model()` returns a disjunctive clause with the exact same structure – only with each variable name replaced by its negation and vice versa (and with *and* operators replaced by *or* operators) – as the conjunctive clause returned by `_syntehsize_for_model()` for the same model. More generally, given a truth table, `_synthesize_cnf()` returns a CNF formula with the exact same structure – only with each variable name replaced by its negation and vice versa (and with *and* operators replaced with *or* operators and vice versa) – as the DNF formula returned by `_syntehsize()` for *the negation of* that truth table. The reason for this is in fact quite simple: These invocations create formulas that are negations of one another, and by De Morgan's laws, the negation of a DNF or CNF formula is a formula with the exact same structure, only with *and* operators replaced with *or* operators and vice versa, and with each variable name replaced by its negation and vice versa.

2.B   Optional Reading: Satisfiability and Search Problems

As already noted, in this book we will mostly ignore questions of computational complexity, i.e., of the running time of the algorithms that we use, and usually focus only on correctness, which is what guarantees the validity of the corresponding proofs. However, since handling truth values of propositional formulas turns out to be a central issue of study in computational complexity theory, we will now shortly discuss these computational complexity aspects.

Looking at the various tasks of this chapter, one may observe that there are two very different levels of running times involved. Tasks that deal with a single model, such as `evaluate(formula, model)` or `_synthesize_for_model(model)` (or `_synthesize_for_all_except_model(model)`), can easily be solved very efficiently and your solution should easily work for formulas with thousands or even millions of variable names. On the other hand, as we have noted, tasks that deal with *all* models of a given formula, such as `print_truth_table(formula)` or `synthesize(models, values)` (or `synthesize_cnf(models, values)`), have inputs or outputs whose size is exponential in the number of variable names used in the formula. Thus, it is certain that there is no hope that *any* solution of any of these latter tasks could operate on formulas that have more than a few dozen variable names, as otherwise the input and/or output would not be able to fit into your computer's memory.

The most interesting tasks to study from the point of view of their computational complexity, though, are rather tasks such as implementing `is_tautology(formula)` or `is_satisfiable(formula)`, whose inputs and outputs don't explicitly involve the set of all models and yet the natural algorithm for solving them is precisely to go over all possible models (as your solution does). In these cases the natural algorithm that goes over all models will take an exponential amount of time and thus this algorithm would not be able to handle formulas with more than a few dozen variable names. Are there other algorithms for determining whether a given formula is satisfiable (or equivalently, whether a given formula is tautology[6]) that are more efficient than simply trying each and every possible model? It is true that for some special classes of formulas, there exists such an algorithm. For example, efficiently checking whether a DNF formula is satisfiable turns out to be possible and even quite easy[7] (and dually, so does checking whether a CNF formula is a tautology[8]). Furthermore, much effort was spent on the problem of efficiently finding a satisfying assignment to a formula, mostly using clever backtracking techniques, and there are programs that, *heuristically*, work rather well on formulas encountered when translating some real-world challenges into satisfiability of propositional formulas. But does there exist an algorithm that is *guaranteed* to efficiently find a satisfying solution if such exists? While this may seem to be a rather specific algorithmic question that may interest few people who are not logicians, it turns out that quite the opposite is true. In fact, the far-reaching implications of this problem cannot be overstated, since an immense variety of computational problems can be converted into a question of whether some propositional formula is satisfiable or not.

A paradigmatic example of such a "conversion" is that of **computational search problems**. A typical such computational problem asks to find some kind of entity x that satisfies a certain set of given properties. To solve such a task, an algorithm may encode the required x as a sequence of bits $x_1, \ldots, x_n$ and encode the required properties as a propositional formula over these variable names such that a satisfying assignment encodes the desired solution. To make this concrete, let's take as an example the **graph coloring problem**: given a graph, find a **graph coloring** of the vertices of the graph, using at most k colors, such that no two vertices connected by an edge are colored by the same. The file `propositions/reductions.py`, which contains all of the functions that you are asked to implement in this section, already contains the definition of how we will represent graphs in Python in this section:

```
propositions/reductions.py
#: A graph on a vertex set of the form (1,...,`n_vertices`), represented by the
#: number of vertices `n_vertices` and a set of edges over the vertices.
Graph = Tuple[int, AbstractSet[Tuple[int, int]]]
```

---

[6] We write "equivalently" since a formula is satisfiable if and only if its negation is not a tautology. This immediately tells us that the existence of an efficient algorithm for checking whether a formula is a tautology would be equivalent (and as hard to find, if one exists) to the existence of an efficient algorithm for satisfiability, since an algorithm for any one of these problems could easily be converted to an algorithm for the other problem by checking the negation of the input formula.

[7] Indeed, it is not hard to verify that a DNF formula is NOT satisfiable if and only if every one of its clauses is NOT satisfiable, which in turn occurs if and only if every one of its clauses contains both a variable name and its own negation.

[8] Indeed, dually to checking the satisfiability of a DNF formula, it is not hard to verify that a CNF formula is a tautology if and only if every one of its clauses is a tautology, which in turn occurs if and only if every one of its clauses contains both a variable name and its own negation.

```
def is_graph(graph: Graph) -> bool:
    """Checks if the given data structure is a valid representation of a graph.

    Parameters:
        graph: data structure to check.

    Returns:
        ``True`` if the given data structure is a valid representation of a
        graph, ``False`` otherwise.
    """
    (n_vertices, edges) = graph
    for edge in edges:
        for vertex in edge:
            if not 1 <= vertex <= n_vertices:
                return False
        if edge[0] == edge[1]:
            return False
    return True
```

This file also contains the function `is_valid_3coloring(graph, coloring)`, which we have already implemented for you and which verifies that the given coloring is a valid coloring of the given graph:

```
                    ┤ propositions/reductions.py ├
def is_valid_3coloring(graph: Graph, coloring: Mapping[int, int]) -> bool:
    """Checks whether the given coloring is a valid coloring of the given graph
    by the colors 1, 2, and 3.

    Parameters:
        graph: graph to check.
        coloring: mapping from the vertices of the given graph to colors, to
            check.

    Returns:
        ``True`` if the given coloring is a valid coloring of the given graph by
        the colors 1, 2, and 3; ``False`` otherwise.
    """
    assert is_graph(graph)
    (n_vertices, edges) = graph
    for vertex in range(1, n_vertices + 1):
        if vertex not in coloring.keys() or coloring[vertex] not in {1, 2, 3}:
            return False
    for edge in edges:
        if coloring[edge[0]] == coloring[edge[1]]:
            return False
    return True
```

A coloring of the graph can be encoded by having, for every vertex v and possible color c, a Boolean variable x_{vc} that represents that vertex v is colored by color c, and then the constraints that state that an assignment of values to the variables names – a model – represents a valid coloring of the graph can be expressed as whether a certain propositional formula over these variable names is satisfied by this model.

OPTIONAL TASK 10   Implement the missing code for the two functions `graph3coloring_to_formula(graph)` and `assignment_to_3coloring(graph,` assignment). The former function returns a propositional formula that "encodes" the 3-coloring problem of the given graph in the sense that it is satisfiable if and only if that graph is colorable by at most three colors. Moreover, we require that any satisfying assignment to the generated formula can actually be converted into a 3-coloring of the graph, which the latter function accomplishes. Your implementation should be computationally efficient in the sense that each of these functions should be able to easily handle graphs with hundreds or even thousands of vertices.

```
                        propositions/reductions.py

def graph3coloring_to_formula(graph: Graph) -> Formula:
    """Efficiently reduces the 3-coloring problem of the given graph into a
    satisfiability problem.

    Parameters:
        graph: graph whose 3-coloring problem to reduce.

    Returns:
        A propositional formula that is satisfiable if and only if the given
        graph is 3-colorable.
    """
    assert is_graph(graph)
    # Optional Task 2.10a

def assignment_to_3coloring(graph: Graph, assignment: Model) -> \
        Mapping[int, int]:
    """Efficiently transforms an assignment to the formula corresponding to the
    3-coloring problem of the given graph, to a 3-coloring of the given graph so
    that the 3-coloring is valid if and only if the given assignment is
    satisfying.

    Parameters:
        graph: graph to produce a 3-coloring for.
        assignment: assignment to the variable names of the formula returned by
            `graph3coloring_to_formula(graph)`.

    Returns:
        A 3-coloring of the given graph by the colors 1, 2, and 3 that is valid
        if and only if the given assignment satisfies the formula
        `graph3coloring_to_formula(graph)`.
    """
    assert is_graph(graph)
    formula = graph3coloring_to_formula(graph)
    assert evaluate(formula, assignment)
    # Optional Task 2.10b
```

Once you have implemented the two functions from Optional Task 10, we get an algorithm for 3-coloring a graph.

```
                        propositions/reductions.py

def tricolor_graph(graph: Graph) -> Union[Mapping[int, int], None]:
    """Computes a 3-coloring of the given graph.

    Parameters:
        graph: graph to 3-color.
```

```
Returns:
    An arbitrary 3-coloring of the given graph if it is 3-colorable,
    ``None`` otherwise.
"""
assert is_graph(graph)
formula = graph3coloring_to_formula(graph)
for assignment in all_models(list(formula.variables())):
    if evaluate(formula, assignment):
        return assignment_to_3coloring(graph, assignment)
return None
```

Your solution to Optional Task 10 was required to be computationally efficient;[9] it is probably able to easily handle graphs with thousands of vertices and formulas with thousands of variable names. The only efficiency bottleneck in the function `tricolor_graph(graph)` is in its main loop:

```
for assignment in all_models(list(formula.variables())): ...
```

There are exponentially many possible models and this directly means that once the number of variable names is more than a few dozen, this algorithm becomes impractical. But, an efficient algorithm for finding a satisfying assignment (if such exists) to a formula could immediately be used to replace this loop and yield an efficient algorithm for graph coloring. As it turns out, not only can the coloring problem be efficiently converted – **reduced** – to the formula satisfiability problem, but so can also an immense gamut of other diverse and seemingly unrelated problems. In fact, Cook's theorem, a central result in the field of **computational complexity**, states that *any* computational search problem can be efficiently reduced to finding a satisfying assignment to a propositional formula. This class of problems includes most computational tasks of interest including, e.g., the traveling salesmen problem, breaking any cryptographic code, solving arbitrary sets of equations, automatically proving theorems, finding bugs in programs, and much more. An enormous amount of effort has gone into trying to find efficient algorithms for many of these problems, all in vain. Since an efficient algorithm for satisfiability would, in one fell swoop, provide efficient algorithms for all of these, the existence of one seems rather unlikely.

In the notation of computational complexity, the class of efficiently solvable problems (formally, those that have a polynomial-time algorithm) is called *P*, and the class of computational search problems is called *NP*. The fact that any problem in *NP* can be reduced to a satisfiability problem is stated as satisfiability being ***NP*-complete**. So, an efficient algorithm for determining whether a given formula is satisfiable exists if and only if *every* problem in *NP* also has an efficient algorithm, i.e., if and only if "*P* = *NP*." The question of whether "*P* = *NP* ?" is arguably considered to be the main open problem in computer science, and as already mentioned the general belief is that the answer is negative, i.e., that satisfiability does not have an efficient algorithm.

Recall that we said earlier that efficiently checking whether a DNF formula is satisfiable (or dually, whether a CNF formula is a tautology) is in fact easy. Supposedly, one could

---

[9] Our test for this task takes a while to run, though, since the test – not the task – enumerates over all possible models to check the solution.

have then proposed the following algorithm for satisfiability of an arbitrary formula: First convert the formula to an equivalent formula (i.e., with the same truth table) in DNF, and then efficiently check whether that formula is satisfiable. The problem here is that we know of no efficient way of converting a formula into DNF (or into CNF). We do know, however, given an arbitrary formula ϕ, to efficiently construct a formula ϕ' in CNF such that while these two formulas may not be equivalent, it does hold that ϕ' is satisfiable if and only if ϕ is, and furthermore, given a satisfying assignment for ϕ', it is easy to efficiently find a satisfying assignment for ϕ. This of course immediately implies that satisfiability continues to be as difficult even when we restrict the input formula to be in CNF.[10]

In fact, for a similar reason, satisfiability continues to be as difficult even when restricting to **3-CNF**: The special case of CNF where each clause is a disjunction of *at most three* variable names or negation-of-variable-names, e.g., '(((((p|q)|~r)&(~p|~s))&((q|s)|~r))&t)'.[11] The significance of this fact is that it gives us a general way for proving that other computational search problems are *NP*-complete: 3-CNF formulas intuitively are easier to reason about than general formulas, and this helped computer scientists to show over the years that the question of whether a 3-CNF formula is satisfiable can be reduced into a variety of computational search problems (i.e., to show that an efficient algorithm for any of a variety of computation search problems could be used to construct an efficient algorithm for satisfiability). Exhibiting such a reduction for some computational search problem Q implies that the problem Q itself is *NP*-complete, and thus cannot be solved efficiently unless $P = NP$. Thousands of problems have been proven to be *NP*-complete this way, including many optimization problems, for example the traveling salesman problem, the knapsack problem, and many other problems including even the 3-coloring problem that was discussed in this section.[12] So, finding an efficient algorithm for the seemingly innocent task of 3-coloring a graph would immediately give an efficient algorithm for any NP-complete problem, including breaking any cryptographic code!

---

[10] Recall however that for formulas in CNF it is easy to tell whether they are tautologies: The only way that a CNF formula may be a tautology is if each of its clauses contains some of variable name and its own negation. The special form that retains the hardness of the tautology problem is the dual DNF. This duality is an implication (why?) of the previously discussed connection between the problems of satisfiability and checking whether a given formula is a tautology.

[11] And dually, of course, for the above previously discussed reasons (why?), tautology continues to be as difficult even when restricting to 3-DNF: The special case of DNF where each clause is a conjunction of at most three variable names or negation-of-variable-names.

[12] We emphasize that this reduction is in the opposite direction to the reduction shown in Optional Task 10, which is from the 3-coloring problem to satisfiability: There we used an algorithm for satisfiability to construct an algorithm for 3-coloring a graph.

3 Logical Operators

Our formulas so far have used a fixed set of logical operators: three binary operators, '|', '&', and '→', a single unary operator, '~', and two constants, 'T' and 'F', which can be viewed as **nullary** operators (operators that take zero operands – see the beginning of Section 3.1), and to which we will indeed refer as operators in this chapter. In this chapter we take a wider point of view of the allowed set of operators. This wider view has two aspects: On the one hand we may want to gain richness by adding more operators, and on the other hand, for the sake of minimalism and succinctness we may want to remove operators. We will explore both options, but the bottom line of this chapter will be that this does not matter much and any "reasonable" set of operators will basically give rise to the "same kind" of logic. We will thus be confident that there is no loss of generality in continuing to stick with the set of operators that we have originally chosen.

3.1 More Operators

Abstractly speaking, an n-**ary** operator, i.e., an operator that takes n operands – where n is called the **arity** of the operator – is simply a function from n-tuples of Boolean values to a Boolean value. Since there are 2^n different n-tuples of Boolean values and since each of them can get mapped to one of the two possible Boolean values, the total number of n-ary operators is 2^{2^n}.

Let us start by considering $n = 0$: nullary operators. There are two of these: one that maps the 0-length-tuple to *True* and the other that maps it to *False*. These two nullary operators are already in our language: 'T' and 'F'. Let us move to considering $n = 1$: unary operators. There are four of these. Two of them completely disregard their input and always output the same value: one of them always outputs *True* and the other always outputs *False*. In this sense they are equivalent to the nullary operators 'T' and 'F'. A third operator is the identity operator that maps *True* to *True* and *False* to *False*, so we require no notation for it. Only the fourth unary operator is interesting: it maps *True* to *False* and *False* to *True*, i.e., it is none other than our beloved negation operator '~'.

We finally get some interesting new operators when considering $n = 2$: binary operators. Indeed, there are 16 possible binary operators, including the binary operators that we already met: | (or), & (and), and → (implies).[1] We will now give names and assign symbols to four of the new ones among these:

---

[1] Similarly to what we observed with unary operators, eight of these 16 possible binary operators are no more than unary (or nullary) operators in disguise: two such operators disregard their input and always output the

- '⊕' (**xor**, short for *exclusive or*): *True* whenever exactly one of its two operands is *True* and the other is *False*.
- '↔' (**iff**, short for *if and only if*): *True* whenever either both operands are *True* or both are *False*. (This operator is sometimes also called **double implication**.)
- '$\overline{\&}$', (**nand**, short for *not and*): negation of the conjunction ("and") of its two operands. (This operator is sometimes also called the **Sheffer stroke** and denoted by '↑' or, confusingly enough, by '|'.)
- '$\overline{|}$' (**nor**, short for *not or*): negation of the disjunction ("or") of its two operands. (This operator is sometimes also called the **Quine arrow** and denoted by '↓'.)

The following table lists these new binary operators, the way we denote each of them in our Python code (note that most are denoted by a sequence of two or even three characters), and the truth table by which their semantics are defined.

Operator:	⊕	↔	$\overline{\&}$	$\overline{|}$
name:	xor	iff	nand	nor
Python representation:	+	<->	-&	-|
Value of '*False* operator *False*':	*False*	*True*	*True*	*True*
Value of '*False* operator *True*':	*True*	*False*	*True*	*False*
Value of '*True* operator *False*':	*True*	*False*	*True*	*False*
Value of '*True* operator *True*':	*False*	*True*	*False*	*False*

TASK 1   Extend the `Formula` class from Chapter 1 to also support the four new binary operators just defined. Start by changing the function `is_binary()` in the file `propositions/syntax.py` from:

```
                    propositions/syntax.py (old)
def is_binary(string: str) -> bool:
    """Checks if the given string is a binary operator.

    Parameters:
        string: string to check.

    Returns:
        ``True`` if the given string is a binary operator, ``False`` otherwise.
    """
    return string == '&' or string == '|' or string == '->'
```

to:

```
                    propositions/syntax.py (new)
def is_binary(string: str) -> bool:
    """Checks if the given string is a binary operator.

    Parameters:
        string: string to check.
```

same value and correspond to the nullary operators; another two simply output one of the inputs (one always outputs its first input, the other always outputs its second input), disregarding the other input – these correspond to the identity operator; and another two simply output the negation of one of the inputs, disregarding the other – these correspond to the negation operator.

```
Returns:
    ``True`` if the given string is a binary operator, ``False`` otherwise.
"""
return string in {'&', '|', '->', '+', '<->', '-&', '-|'}
```

Next, make the necessary changes to the method `_parse_prefix()` of class `Formula`. Finally, verify that all the methods (both instance methods and static methods) that you have implemented in this class in Chapter 1 now function properly for all of the seven (old and new) binary operators; with some luck (and good software engineering) you will require no further changes in your code beyond the above changes to `is_binary()` and `_parse_prefix()`. (As with every task, we provide tests also for the above, to help you check your implementation of this extended functionality.)

TASK 2 Extend the `evaluate()` function from Chapter 2 to also support the four new operators just defined. Verify that the functions `truth_values()`, `print_truth_table()`, `is_tautology()`, `is_contradiction()`, and `is_satisfiable()` from that chapter "inherit" the support for these operators from your changes to the `evaluate()` function.

We may, of course, decide to add operators with even higher **arity**. For example the **ternary** (taking three operands) operator **mux** (short for *multiplexer*) takes three Boolean values a, x, and y, and evaluates to x if a is *True* and to y if a is *False*. There is no semantic difficulty with adding such higher-arity operators, and the only issue to consider is which syntax to choose to represent them. A simple choice is to use a functional notation like '$mux(a,x,y)$', a solution that can apply to any operator of any arity and only requires that we fix a name for the operator. Another option is to use some specific notation for ternary operators. For example, in some programming languages the notation `a?x:y` is used for the ternary mux operator. Everything that we discuss in the rest of this chapter also applies to any additional operators of any arity. As you have shown in Chapter 2, though, that any operator of any higher arity can be expressed (i.e., its truth table can be synthesized) using operators of arity two or less, in order to avoid the technical details of fixing a syntax for higher-arity operators, our discussion will safely avoid operators of higher arity.

3.2 Substitutions

So, adding operators to our logic turned out to be quite easy. We now start looking at doing the opposite: removing operators. The idea is very simple: If you can "express" one operator using others, then you can take any formula that uses the former operator and convert it to one that does not use it by substituting each instance of this operator with the appropriate combination of other operators. In this section we will focus on the mechanics of this type of substitution, which as we will see can be done in a completely syntactic manner.

Before we consider the task of substituting for an operator, we handle a simpler task of substituting for variable names, which is essentially a way of *composing* formulas. Suppose that we have a formula ϕ that uses some variable names $v_1, \ldots, v_n$ and a sequence of formulas $\psi_1, \ldots, \psi_n$ (over some set of other variable names), then we can compose ϕ with the ψ_is by (simultaneously) replacing in ϕ each occurrence of any v_i with the (sub)formula ψ_i, obtaining a single formula of which we can think as $\phi(\psi_1, \ldots, \psi_n)$, over the set of the variable names of the ψ_is (without the original v_is). For example, taking the formula '$((x \rightarrow x)|y)$' and replacing the variable name 'x' with the formula '$(q\&r)$' and the variable name 'y' with the formula 'p', we obtain the single formula '$(((q\&r) \rightarrow (q\&r))|p)$'.

TASK 3   Implement the missing code for the method `substitute_variables(substitution_map)` of class `Formula`, which takes a dictionary that maps some variable names to formulas, and returns the composition of the current formula with these formulas.

```
┌─────────────── propositions/syntax.py ───────────────┐
class Formula:
    ⋮

    def substitute_variables(self, substitution_map: Mapping[str, Formula]) -> \
            Formula:
        """Substitutes in the current formula, each variable name `v` that is a
        key in `substitution_map` with the formula `substitution_map[v]`.

        Parameters:
            substitution_map: mapping defining the substitutions to be
                performed.

        Returns:
            The formula resulting from performing all substitutions. Only
            variable name occurrences originating in the current formula are
            substituted (i.e., variable name occurrences originating in one of
            the specified substitutions are not subjected to additional
            substitutions).

        Examples:
            >>> Formula.parse('((p->p)|r)').substitute_variables(
            ...     {'p': Formula.parse('(q&r)'), 'r': Formula.parse('p')})
            (((q&r)->(q&r))|p)
        """
        for variable in substitution_map:
            assert is_variable(variable)
        # Task 3.3
```

Guidelines: When replacing occurrences of a variable name v with the formula ψ to which v is mapped by the given dictionary, you should not duplicate the formula ψ for each substitution of an occurrence of v, but rather have the *same* Formula object for ψ (the object from the given dictionary) be pointed to from all locations in the new formula tree that correspond to places where v appears in the original formula. For example, say that the current formula is '$((p\&q)|(\sim p\&\sim q))$', and you are asked to replace 'p' in this formula with the formula '$(x \rightarrow y)$', to obtain '$(((x \rightarrow y)\&q)|(\sim(x \rightarrow y)\&\sim q))$'. While in the textual representation of the formula, each occurrence of '$(x \rightarrow y)$' is fully spelled out, when building the Formula data structure for the composition, we ask you to use a single Formula object (the one from the given substitution map) for both occurrences of '$(x \rightarrow y)$', by pointing to this object from both places in the returned formula where '$(x \rightarrow y)$' appears. While this means that the returned formula data structure is no longer a tree, but a **directed acyclic graph (DAG)**, this is completely fine and causes no problems in our implementation since Formula objects are immutable. (So, for example, we would never find ourselves modifying one occurrence of '$(x{\rightarrow}y)$' in the formula and by doing so unintentionally modify the other as well.) Moreover, this sharing of sub-data-structures clearly leads to a data structure that is more memory-efficient than straightforward parsing of the composed textual formula.[2]

We are now ready to substitute formulas for operators. Suppose that we have a general substitution rule that allows us to replace '$(p{*}q)$', where '$*$' is some given operator, by some formula ϕ whose variable names are 'p' and 'q'; for example this rule may be to replace '$(p\&q)$' with '$\sim(\sim p|\sim q)$'. Now we can take any formula of the form '$(\psi_1{*}\psi_2)$' where ψ_1 and ψ_2 are arbitrary subformulas, and replace it with $\phi(\psi_1, \psi_2)$ (as defined in the beginning of this section); for example, if ψ_1 is '$(x|y)$' and ψ_2 is '$\sim x$', then '$(\psi_1\&\psi_2)$' is '$((x|y)\&\sim x)$', and we can replace it with '$\sim(\sim(x|y)|\sim\sim x)$'. Despite the fact that this substitution is completely syntactic ("copy–paste," if you wish), it should be clear that if '$(p{*}q)$' and ϕ both have the same truth table, then it is also true that '$(\psi_1{*}\psi_2)$' and $\phi(\psi_1, \psi_2)$ both have the same truth table, but this semantic discussion will be left for Section 3.3. In this section we only ask you to perform this syntactic substitution, but in a general way, that is, finding all matching subformulas and (simultaneously) replacing them, and also handling substitution rules for several different operators at the same time.

TASK 4   Implement the missing code for the method `substitute_operators(substitution_map)` of class `Formula`. This method takes as input a dictionary that maps some operators to formulas, where each of these formulas is over the variable names 'p' and 'q', where 'p' is agreed to serve as a placeholder for the first operand of the operator mapped to the formula (if the operator is unary or binary), and 'q' is agreed to serve as a placeholder for the second operand of the operator (if the operator is binary). The method returns a formula obtained from the current formula by replacing, for each operator that is a key in the given dictionary, each occurrence of this operator with the formula to which the dictionary maps this operator, where in that formula every occurrence of 'p' is replaced with the first operand of the operator in the original formula and every occurrence of 'q' is replaced with the second operand of the operator in the original formula. (In particular, if the operator is 'T' or 'F', then it is simply replaced with the formula to which the dictionary maps it, without making any substitutions in that formula.)

---

[2] Conceptually, either of these data structure representations are just representations of the composed formula, and in this book we continue to just think about the formula and ignore any such "internal sharing" in the code. For the benefit of interested readers, we do note, though, that the field of **computational complexity** that studies the *size* of formulas, does however care much about the distinction of whether sharing sub-data-structures is or is not allowed: In the language of that field, the term **formula size** refers to the size of a tree representation that does *not* allow sharing, while the term **circuit size** is used for a DAG representation that is allowed to share intermediate results. Naturally, the latter may be smaller than the former, and in fact it turns out that sometimes even significantly so. It is still a central open problem of computational complexity theory whether the gap between the formula size and the circuit size can be *super-polynomial* (grow faster than any polynomial). This is called the "$NC^1 = P$?" question (an equality here would mean that the gap cannot be super-polynomial), and it turns out to precisely capture the question of whether every computation can be significantly parallelized. This is already the second example that we see (the first was the question of efficient satisfiability, discussed in Chapter 2) of a question that may seem at first glance to be a purely theoretical question of interest mainly to logic aficionados, but in fact turns out to have far-reaching applied implications to virtually any computationally heavy task that you could imagine.

```
                    ┌──────────────────────────┐
                    │ propositions/syntax.py   │
                    └──────────────────────────┘
class Formula:
    ⋮

    def substitute_operators(self, substitution_map: Mapping[str, Formula]) -> \
            Formula:
        """Substitutes in the current formula, each constant or operator `op`
        that is a key in `substitution_map` with the formula
        `substitution_map[op]` applied to its (zero or one or two) operands,
        where the first operand is used for every occurrence of 'p' in the
        formula and the second for every occurrence of 'q'.

        Parameters:
            substitution_map: mapping defining the substitutions to be
                performed.

        Returns:
            The formula resulting from performing all substitutions. Only
            operator occurrences originating in the current formula are
            substituted (i.e., operator occurrences originating in one of the
            specified substitutions are not subjected to additional
            substitutions).

        Examples:
            >>> Formula.parse('((x&y)&~z)').substitute_operators(
            ...     {'&': Formula.parse('~(~p|~q)')})
            ~(~~(~x|~y)|~~z)
        """
        for operator in substitution_map:
            assert is_constant(operator) or is_unary(operator) or \
                   is_binary(operator)
            assert substitution_map[operator].variables().issubset({'p', 'q'})
        # Task 3.4
```

Guidelines: You should once again be frugal in your duplications of subformulas. That is, whichever subformulas (subtrees) of the original formula that you can use in their entirety in the returned formula, you should point to instead of duplicating.

3.3 Complete Sets of Operators

Now that we have the mechanics of substituting for operators in place, we can proceed to the heart of the issue of "getting rid" of unnecessary logical operators. The following is a key definition that will guide us to make sure that we don't "get rid" of too many operators:

DEFINITION 3.1 (Complete Set of Operators) A set of logical operators is called **complete** if every Boolean function (of any arity) can be expressed using only the operators in the set.

The notion of "expressed" here is a semantic one: there exists a formula that uses only these operators, whose truth table is the one of the given Boolean function. In this language, the main result proved in Chapter 2 was that the set of operators $\{`\sim`,`\&`,`|`\}$ is complete (since the DNF theorem (2.1) states that every Boolean function can be represented in disjunctive normal form, a form that only uses these three operators).

In this chapter we will demonstrate other sets of operators that are complete, a task that will turn out to be easier using the fact that we already have one such set in our toolbox. The basic idea is simple: Once we know that we can represent a Boolean function using one set of operators, if we can in turn represent each of the operators in this set using a second set of operators, then using substitution we can get a representation of the original Boolean function using (only) the latter set of operators.

To get used to this type of substitution, your next task is to take an arbitrary formula that uses any of the extended family of operators introduced so far and convert it to a formula that uses only the set of operators {'~','&','|'}. Of course, from Chapter 2 we already know that this is possible as there exists a DNF formula that has the same truth table as the original formula. Indeed, one semantic way to achieve this would be to calculate the truth table of the given formula, and then synthesize a formula in DNF that has the same truth table:

```
synthesize(formula.variables(),
           truth_values(formula(), all_models(formula.variables()))))
```

The problem with this approach is that it takes exponential time. Therefore, in the next task, you are asked to implement the same functionality in a syntactic rather than semantic way that, beyond being a good exercise, has the additional advantage of being far more efficient.

The file `propositions/operators.py` contains a list of functions that you are asked to implement in the remainder of this chapter.

TASK 5   Implement the missing code for the function `to_not_and_or(formula)`, which returns a formula that is equivalent to the given formula (i.e., a formula having the same truth table) but may only use the operators *not*, *and*, and *or* in it.

```
propositions/operators.py

def to_not_and_or(formula: Formula) -> Formula:
    """Syntactically converts the given formula to an equivalent formula that
    contains no constants or operators beyond '~', '&', and '|'.

    Parameters:
        formula: formula to convert.

    Returns:
        A formula that has the same truth table as the given formula, but
        contains no constants or operators beyond '~', '&', and '|'.
    """
    # Task 3.5
```

Hint: Substitute (using your solution for Task 4) each other operator with an equivalent formula that uses only the allowed operators.

We are now ready for the crux of this chapter: showing that a few other sets of operators are complete. As we know that the set {'~','&','|'} is complete, to show that another set of operators is complete, it suffices to represent only each of the three operators '~', '&', and '|' using operators from that latter set.

TASK 6   Implement the missing code for the four functions `to_not_and(formula)`, `to_nand(formula)`, `to_implies_not(formula)`, and `to_implies_false(formula)`, each of which returns a formula that is equivalent to the given formula, but may only use the operators listed in the name of that function.

```
propositions/operators.py

def to_not_and(formula: Formula) -> Formula:
    """Syntactically converts the given formula to an equivalent formula that
    contains no constants or operators beyond '~' and '&'.

    Parameters:
        formula: formula to convert.

    Returns:
        A formula that has the same truth table as the given formula, but
        contains no constants or operators beyond '~' and '&'.
    """
    # Task 3.6a

def to_nand(formula: Formula) -> Formula:
    """Syntactically converts the given formula to an equivalent formula that
    contains no constants or operators beyond '-&'.

    Parameters:
        formula: formula to convert.

    Returns:
        A formula that has the same truth table as the given formula, but
        contains no constants or operators beyond '-&'.
    """
    # Task 3.6b

def to_implies_not(formula: Formula) -> Formula:
    """Syntactically converts the given formula to an equivalent formula that
    contains no constants or operators beyond '->' and '~'.

    Parameters:
        formula: formula to convert.

    Returns:
        A formula that has the same truth table as the given formula, but
        contains no constants or operators beyond '->' and '~'.
    """
    # Task 3.6c

def to_implies_false(formula: Formula) -> Formula:
    """Syntactically converts the given formula to an equivalent formula that
    contains no constants or operators beyond '->' and 'F'.

    Parameters:
        formula: formula to convert.

    Returns:
        A formula that has the same truth table as the given formula, but
```

```
              contains no constants or operators beyond '->' and 'F'.
    """
    # Task 3.6d
```

Your solution to Task 6 proves the following theorem.

THEOREM 3.1   *The following four sets of operators are each (separately) a complete set of operators:*

a. *The set containing only '~' (not) and '&' (and).*
b. *The singleton set containing only '$\overline{\&}$' (nand).*
c. *The set containing only '→' (implies) and '~' (not).*
d. *The set containing only '→' (implies) and 'F' (False).*

   This is not an exhaustive list of complete sets of operators, of course: Any superset of a complete set of operators is itself complete. There are also a few other minimal complete sets of operators; in particular the singleton set of '$\overline{|}$' (nor) by itself is also a complete set. There are also minimal complete sets of operators that contain operators of arity higher than 2, such as the set containing only *mux* and '~' (not). Nevertheless, the above are arguably the most interesting complete sets of operators.

   Once we know that a set of operators is complete, we can limit ourselves to using only this set, knowing that nothing of the essence is lost in the sense that still every truth table can be expressed using some formula in our logic. This will be our approach in the rest of our discussion of propositional logic, where we will restrict ourselves to the complete set that only contains '→' (implies) and '~' (not), shunning not only the new operators introduced in this chapter but also the familiar disjunction and conjunction binary operators '&' and '|', as well as the constants 'T' and 'F'. This will naturally simplify all technicalities without affecting anything substantial.

3.4   Proving Incompleteness

It is natural to wonder which other sets of operators are complete. For example, as we have seen that the set containing only '→' and 'F' is complete, it is natural to ask whether the set containing only '→' and 'T' is also complete, or maybe even the singleton set containing only '→'. Similarly, as we have seen that the set containing only '&' and '~' is complete, it is natural to ask whether the set containing only '&' and '|' is also complete, etc. In this section we will prove negative answers to these and other questions. As expected, since these are negative results, they will not be proven by programming, but rather by classical mathematical arguments.

   How can one go about proving that there is *no way* to represent some function using a given set of operators? Well, one very useful proof technique is actually quite simple: identify a property of Boolean functions that must hold for all Boolean functions that can be represented using only this given set of operators, and then exhibit some Boolean function that does not have this property. As we will see, though, pinpointing the right property to use is somewhat of an art. The following theorem, which answers (among others) the two specific questions raised in the previous paragraph, has an especially simple proof of this form:

THEOREM 3.2   *The set of operators containing '&', '|', '→', 'T', '↔', and 'mux'[3] is not complete. In particular it cannot represent the constant function with value False, or the negation function.*

Proof   The property that all functions composed only of the operators '&', '|', '→', 'T', '↔', and 'mux' share is the following:

DEFINITION 3.2 (T-Preservation)   A Boolean function f is called **T-preserving** if whenever the values of all its input values are *True*, the function also outputs *True*.

To see that every function composed of these operators is T-preserving, we need to note two things: First that all six operators in the list have this property (this can be seen directly by simply plugging in all-*True* values into each of these and evaluating) and second that composing functions with this property also maintains the property. The second point is true since if you take T-preserving functions f and g and look at their composition $f(g(\cdot), \cdot)$ (where $\cdot$ denotes an arbitrary set of values), then if all input values are *True* then so is $g(\cdot)$ and then all input values to f are *True* so thus is also $f(\cdot)$. Formally, this is then proved by induction on the length of the formula.[4]

We next need to identify a function that does not have this property, and conclude that it cannot be composed of the operators listed in the statement of Theorem 3.2 (so they do not form a complete set). As this function we can choose, e.g., the constant function that always has value *False*, or the negation function, both of which are not T-preserving.   □

Theorem 3.2 provides a rather satisfactory answer to the question of why '→' and 'T' do not comprise a complete set of operators, and while it also shows that '&' and '|' (and 'T') do not comprise a complete set, the really interesting question is whether the set containing '&' and '|' in addition to both constants 'T' and 'F' is complete. As we will now prove, it turns out that it is not the case:

THEOREM 3.3   *The set of operators containing '&', '|', 'T', and 'F' is not complete. In particular it cannot represent the negation function.*

Proof   The key property here will be that of **monotonicity**:

DEFINITION 3.3 (Monotonicity)   A Boolean function f is called **monotone** if whenever for some input (that is, for some tuple of input values) f evaluates to *True*, it also continues

---

[3] Recall that 'mux' is the ternary operator such that 'mux(x, y, z)' evaluates to the same value as '$((x \& y)|(\tilde{\ }x \& z))$'.

[4]   Here is the formalistic argument: We are given a formula composed only of these operators and need to show that when the input values are all *True* the formula also evaluates to *True*. The base case is if the formula is either a variable name or the nullary operator 'T', and in these two cases clearly the value of the function is *True*. Otherwise, we apply the induction hypothesis to each of the two (or three in the case of 'mux') operands of the root operator to obtain that they evaluate to *True*, which then implies that the value of the whole formula is *True*.

to evaluate to *True* even if we modify the input by changing some of the input values from *False* to *True*.[5]

For a monotone function, changing some of the input values from *False* to *True* can only lead to the function's value changing from *False* to *True* (or not changing at all) and never to the value changing in the opposite direction, from *True* to *False*. It is clear that '&', '|', 'T', and 'F' are all monotone, and that composition maintains monotonicity: if f and g are monotone, then looking at the effect of changing the value of some input from *False* to *True* on the value of $f(g(\cdot), \cdot)$, we observe that since $g(\cdot)$ can only change from *False* to *True* then this is true for all of the input values to f and thus also for its output.

In contrast, the negation function is not monotone, since when its input changes from *False* to *True* its output changes form *True* to *False*. We conclude that the negation function cannot be composed of the above operators, and so they do not form a complete set. □

All of the sets that we have so far proven to be incomplete do not contain the negation operator (and moreover, negation cannot be composed of any of these sets, and in fact adding the negation operator to any of these sets yields a complete set of operators). We will now show that a different set, which contains also the negation operator, is incomplete. The property that we will use to achieve this is more subtle, and to pinpoint it will require somewhat more thought.

THEOREM 3.4 *The set of operators containing 'T', 'F', '~', '$\oplus$', and '$\leftrightarrow$' is not complete. In particular it cannot represent the conjunction ("and") function or the disjunction ("or") function.*

Proof The key property here, **affineness**, may seem at first glance to have been hard to come up with, but as we will discuss, it in fact can be seen to be quite natural from an algebraic point of view that views {*False*, *True*} as a field with two elements.

DEFINITION 3.4 (Affineness)   A Boolean function f is called **affine** if it is equivalent (in the sense of having the same truth table) either to the *xor* of a subset[6] of its inputs[7] or to the negation of the *xor* of a subset of its inputs.[8]

It is easy to see that each of the operators 'T', 'F', '~', and '$\oplus$' is affine since it can be written as a *xor* of a subset of its inputs, or as the negation of such a *xor*.

Affine functions are precisely those functions that have the property that each of their inputs either never affects their output (this is the case when this input is *not* one of the

---

[5] The name "monotonicity" comes from viewing these functions as functions from vectors of zeros and ones to zeros and ones, with *False* corresponding to zero and *True* corresponding to one. A function is monotone in the above sense if and only if when viewed this way it is monotone in each of its coordinates in the standard numeric sense.

[6] Like the operators '&' and '|' (but unlike the operator '$\rightarrow$', for example), the *xor* operator is **commutative** and **associative**: if we *xor* several values, the order in which we *xor* them does not alter the output, so for any given set of values, their *xor* is well-defined with no need to specify any ordering, placement of parentheses, etc.

[7] By convention, we consider the *xor* of an empty set of inputs to be *False*.

[8] The name "affineness" comes from viewing these functions (somewhat similarly to the explanation of monotonicity in Footnote 5) as mappings from the vector space over the two-element field (note that *xor* is simply the addition operation of this field), to that field. A function is affine in the sense Definition 3.4 if and only if when viewed this way it is an affine transformation in the standard linear-algebraic sense, i.e., a linear transformation plus a constant (since over the two-element field, adding the constant one is equivalent to negating the value).

*xor*ed inputs) or always affects their output in the sense that regardless of the other inputs, changing this input changes the output (this is the case when this input is one of the *xor*ed inputs). We can therefore immediately conclude that the conjunction and disjunction functions are not affine: for example, for the conjunction function we note that if the first input is *False* then the second input does *not* affect the output but if the first input is *True* then the second input *does* affect the output, so it is not true that the second input either never affects the output regardless of the other inputs or always affects the output regardless of the other inputs. It therefore remains to check that any composition of affine functions is affine.

There are two ways to complete the proof. One of them is via the algebraic point of view that led us to consider affineness to begin with: It is a well-known fact from linear algebra that the composition of affine transformations is itself an affine transformation. For those who are unfamiliar with this property of affine transformations, the second way to complete this proof is that it is easy to reprove this property in our special case of Boolean functions: If we replace one of the inputs of an affine function by an affine function, then any input that is *xor*ed with itself simply "cancels out," as do two negations, leaving us with an affine function. □

We have seen that the set containing *not* and *and* is complete, and so is the singleton set containing only *nand*. We have seen that the set containing *not* and *or* is complete, and so is the singleton set containing only *nor*. We have seen that the set containing *not* and *implies* is complete. It is natural to therefore ask whether the singleton set containing only what one may be tempted to analogously call "*nimplies*," **non-implication**, is complete. That is, whether the singleton set containing only the binary operator '$\Rightarrow$', whose semantics we define by defining its output to be the negation of the output of the *implies* operator on the same inputs,[9] is complete. This turns out not to be true, and you are invited to try and prove this yourself, using the same technique of finding a property that every Boolean function that can be built from instances of this operator satisfies, and then exhibiting a Boolean function that does not satisfy this property. **Hint:** Search for a property, inspired by one of the properties above, that is common to '$\Rightarrow$', 'F', '&', '|', '$\oplus$', and 'mux', and to every function constructed using only them, that would enable you to show that the set of operators containing all of these is not complete (and hence, every subset of this set, including the singleton set containing only the operator '$\Rightarrow$', is not complete).

---

[9] Attentive readers may notice that this is the last binary operator that we have not discussed so far. Recall that there are 16 possible binary operators, eight of which are unary (or nullary) operators in disguise and eight "really are" binary operators (in the sense that none of them always disregards one or more of its inputs). Of the latter, we already defined three in Chapter 2 and four more in the beginning of this chapter, and the last remaining one is this so-called "nimplies" operator.

4 Proof by Deduction

In this chapter, we will define the syntax of a **deductive proof**, i.e., a formal proof that starts from a set of assumptions and proceeds step by step by inferring additional intermediate results, until the intended conclusion is inferred. Specifically, a significant portion of this chapter will be focused on verifying the syntactic validity of a given proof.

4.1 Inference Rules

Before getting into proofs, we will define the notion of an **inference rule** that allows us to proceed in a proof by **deducing** a "conclusion line" from previous "assumption lines." Moreover, what a proof proves is a "lemma" or a "theorem," which, as we will see, may itself be viewed as an inference rule that states that the conclusion of the lemma or theorem follows from its assumptions.

DEFINITION 4.1 (Inference Rule)   An **inference rule** is composed of a list of zero or more propositional formulas called the **assumptions** of the rule and one additional propositional formula called the **conclusion** of the rule.

An example of an inference rule is as follows: Assumptions: '(p|q)', '(~p|r)'; Conclusion: '(q|r)'. An inference rule need not necessarily have any assumptions. An example of an assumptionless (i.e., with zero assumptions) inference rule is as follows: (Assumptions: none;) Conclusion: '(~p|p)'.

The file propositions/proofs.py defines (among other classes) a Python class InferenceRule for holding an inference rule as a list of assumptions and a conclusion, all of type Formula.

```
                            ┌─ propositions/proofs.py ─┐
@frozen
class InferenceRule:
    """An immutable inference rule in Propositional Logic, comprised of zero
    or more assumed propositional formulas, and a conclusion propositional
    formula.

    Attributes:
        assumptions: the assumptions of the rule.
        conclusion: the conclusion of the rule.
    """
    assumptions: Tuple[Formula, ...]
    conclusion: Formula
```

```
def __init__(self, assumptions: Sequence[Formula], conclusion: Formula):
    """Initializes an `InferenceRule` from its assumptions and conclusion.

    Parameters:
        assumptions: the assumptions for the rule.
        conclusion: the conclusion for the rule.
    """
    self.assumptions = tuple(assumptions)
    self.conclusion = conclusion
```

TASK 1   Implement the missing code for the method `variables()` of class `InferenceRule`, which returns all of the variable names that appear in any of the assumptions and/or in the conclusion of the rule.

```
                              ┌─ propositions/proofs.py ─┐
class InferenceRule:
    ⋮

    def variables(self) -> Set[str]:
        """Finds all variable names in the current inference rule.

        Returns:
            A set of all variable names used in the assumptions and in the
            conclusion of the current inference rule.
        """
        # Task 4.1
```

Examples: If `rule` is the first inference rule (the one with two assumptions) given as an example earlier, then `rule.variables()` should return `{'p', 'q', 'r'}`, and if `rule` is the second inference rule (the assumptionless one) given as an example earlier, then this call should return `{'p'}`.

In most of this chapter we will allow for arbitrary inference rules (arbitrary assumptions and arbitrary conclusion) and focus solely on the syntax of using them in deductive proofs. This syntax in particular will not depend much on whether any of these inference rules is semantically "correct" or not. We will later however be more specific about our inference rules, and the first requirement that we will want is for all of them to indeed be semantically **sound**.

DEFINITION 4.2 (Entailment; Soundness)   We say that a set of assumption formulas A **entails** a conclusion formula ϕ if every model that satisfies all the assumptions in A also satisfies ϕ. We denote this by $A \models \phi$.[1] We say that the inference rule whose assumptions are the elements of the set A and whose conclusion is ϕ is **sound**[2] if $A \models \phi$.

For example, it is easy to verify that {'p','(p→q)'} $\models$ 'q', and thus the inference rule having assumptions 'p' and '(p→q)' and conclusion 'q' is sound.[3] Similarly, the two

---

[1] The symbol $\models$ is sometimes used also in a slightly different way: for a model M and a formula ϕ one may write $M \models \phi$ (i.e., M **is a model of** ϕ) to mean that ϕ evaluates to *True* in the model M. For example, {'p' : *True*, 'q' : *False*} $\models$ '(p&~q)'.

[2] What we call **sound** inference rules are often called **truth-preserving** inference rules in other textbooks.

[3] This inference rule is called **modus ponens**, and it will be of major interest starting in Chapter 5.

inference rules given as examples earlier are also sound. On the other hand, the inference rule with the single assumption '(p→q)' and the conclusion '(q→p)' is not sound since the model that assigns *False* to 'p' and *True* to 'q' satisfies the assumption but not the conclusion. If A is a singleton set, then we sometimes remove the set notation and write, for example, '~~p' $\models$ 'p' (the inference rule having these assumption and conclusion is called **Double-Negation Elimination**). If A is the empty set then we simply write $\models \phi$, which is equivalent to saying that ϕ is a tautology. Thus, for example, $\models$ '(p|~p)' (the assumptionless inference rule having this conclusion is called the **Law of Excluded Middle**).

The next two tasks explore the semantics of inference rules. Accordingly, the functions that you are asked to implement in these tasks are contained in the file propositions/ semantics.py.

TASK 2   Implement the missing code for the function evaluate_inference(rule, model), which returns whether the given inference rule holds in the given model, that is, whether it is *not* the case that all assumptions hold in this model but the conclusion does not.

```
                    ┌─ propositions/semantics.py ─┐

def evaluate_inference(rule: InferenceRule, model: Model) -> bool:
    """Checks if the given inference rule holds in the given model.

    Parameters:
        rule: inference rule to check.
        model: model to check in.

    Returns:
        ``True`` if the given inference rule holds in the given model, ``False``
        otherwise.

    Examples:
        >>> evaluate_inference(InferenceRule([Formula('p')], Formula('q')),
        ...                     {'p': True, 'q': False})
        False

        >>> evaluate_inference(InferenceRule([Formula('p')], Formula('q')),
        ...                     {'p': False, 'q': False})
        True
    """
    assert is_model(model)
    # Task 4.2
```

TASK 3   Implement the missing code for the function is_sound_inference(rule), which returns whether the given inference rule is sound, i.e., whether it holds in every model.

```
                    ┌─ propositions/semantics.py ─┐

def is_sound_inference(rule: InferenceRule) -> bool:
    """Checks if the given inference rule is sound, i.e., whether its
    conclusion is a semantically correct implication of its assumptions.
```

```
        Parameters:
            rule: inference rule to check.

        Returns:
            ``True`` if the given inference rule is sound, ``False`` otherwise.
        """
        # Task 4.3
```

4.2   Specializations of an Inference Rule

We will usually think of an inference rule as a template where the variable names serve as placeholders for formulas. For example if we look at the Double-Negation Elimination rule, the inference rule having assumption '~~p' and conclusion 'p', we may plug any formula into the variable name 'p' and get a "special case," or a **specialization**, of the rule. For example, we may substitute '(q→r)' for 'p' and get the inference rule having assumption '~~(q→r)' and conclusion '(q→r)'. Or, we may substitute 'x' for 'p' and get the inference rule having assumption '~~x' and conclusion 'x'. Both of these inference rules are specializations of the original inference rule.[4]

DEFINITION 4.3 (Specialization)   An inference rule β is a **specialization** of an inference rule α if there exist a number of formulas $\phi_1, \ldots, \phi_n$ and a matching number of variable names $v_1, \ldots, v_n$, such that β is obtained from α by (simultaneously) substituting the formula ϕ_i for each occurrence of the variable name v_i in all of the assumptions of α (while maintaining the order of the assumptions) as well as in its conclusion.

Given an inference rule and a desired substitution/specialization map, it is quite easy to obtain the specialized inference rule.

TASK 4   Implement the missing code for the method `specialize(specialization_map)` of class `InferenceRule`, which returns the specialization of the inference rule according to the given specialization map.

```
                                    propositions/proofs.py
#: A mapping from variable names to formulas.
SpecializationMap = Mapping[str, Formula]
    .
    .
    .
class InferenceRule:
        .
        .
        .
    def specialize(self, specialization_map: SpecializationMap) -> \
            InferenceRule:
        """Specializes the current inference rule by simultaneously substituting
        each variable name `v` that is a key in `specialization_map` with the
        formula `specialization_map[v]`.
```

---

[4] We do not primarily think of the variable names in specializations, such as the specialization having assumption '~~(q→r)' and conclusion '(q→r)' or the specialization having assumption '~~x' and conclusion 'x' in this example, as placeholders for further substitutions. Nonetheless, we still call these specializations **inference rules**, just like we do the "general" rule having assumption '~~p' and conclusion 'p' (in which we *do* think of the variable name as a placeholder), as it will be very convenient to use the same Python object for both "general" rules and specializations.

```
            Parameters:
                specialization_map: mapping defining the specialization to be
                    performed.

            Returns:
                The resulting inference rule.
            """
            for variable in specialization_map:
                assert is_variable(variable)
            # Task 4.4
```

Hint: Use the `substitute_variables()` method of class `Formula`, which you implemented in Chapter 3 and which performs a similar substitution for a single formula.

Given two inference rules, it is only slightly more difficult to tell whether one is a specialization of the other. First, the number of assumptions should match. Then, for every formula in the assumptions or the conclusion there should be a match between the formula in the "general" rule and the corresponding formula in the alleged specialization: if the "general" formula is a variable name then the specialized formula may be any formula; otherwise, the root of the specialized formula must be identical to the root of the general formula, and the subtrees should match recursively in the same way. Moreover, there is an important additional consistency condition: all occurrences of each variable name in the general rule must correspond to the same subformula throughout the specialization. In the following task you are asked to implement this procedure.

TASK 5   In this task you will not only determine whether a given inference rule is a specialization of another, but you will also, if this is the case, find the appropriate specialization map. We will continue to represent a specialization map as a Python dictionary (mapping variable names of the general rule to subformulas of the specialized rule) and use Python's `None` value to represent that no specialization map exists since the alleged specialization is in fact not a specialization of a given general rule.

a. Start with the basic check that ensures all occurrences of each variable name are consistently mapped to the same subformula. Implement the missing code for the static method `_merge_specialization_maps(specialization_map1, specialization_map2)` of class `InferenceRule`, which takes two specialization maps, checks whether they are consistent with each other in the sense that no variable name appears in both but is mapped to a different formula in each, and if so, returns the merger of the maps, and otherwise returns `None`.

```
                          ┤ propositions/proofs.py ├
class InferenceRule:
        ⋮
        ⋮
    @staticmethod
    def _merge_specialization_maps(
            specialization_map1: Union[SpecializationMap, None],
            specialization_map2: Union[SpecializationMap, None]) -> \
            Union[SpecializationMap, None]:
        """Merges the given specialization maps while checking their
        consistency.
```

```
        Parameters:
            specialization_map1: first mapping to merge, or ``None``.
            specialization_map2: second mapping to merge, or ``None``.

        Returns:
            A single mapping containing all (key, value) pairs that appear in
            either of the given maps, or ``None`` if one of the given maps is
            ``None`` or if some key appears in both given maps but with
            different values.
        """
        if specialization_map1 is not None:
            for variable in specialization_map1:
                assert is_variable(variable)
        if specialization_map2 is not None:
            for variable in specialization_map2:
                assert is_variable(variable)
        # Task 4.5a
```

b. Proceed to figuring out which specialization map (if any) makes a given for-mula a specialization of another. Implement the missing code for the static method _formula_specialization_map(general, specialization) of class InferenceRule, which takes two formulas and returns such a specialization map if the second given formula is indeed a specialization of the first, and None otherwise.

propositions/proofs.py

```
class InferenceRule:
        :
        :

    @staticmethod
    def _formula_specialization_map(general: Formula, specialization: Formula) \
            -> Union[SpecializationMap, None]:
        """Computes the minimal specialization map by which the given formula
        specializes to the given specialization.

        Parameters:
            general: non-specialized formula for which to compute the map.
            specialization: specialization for which to compute the map.

        Returns:
            The computed specialization map, or ``None`` if `specialization` is
            in fact not a specialization of `general`.
        """
        # Task 4.5b
```

Hint: Use the _merge_specialization_maps() method that you have just imple-mented.

c. Finally, put everything together to tell if and how one inference rule is a specialization of another. Implement the missing code for the method specialization_map(specialization) of class InferenceRule, which takes an alleged specialization of the current rule, and returns the corresponding specialization map, or None if the alleged specialization is in fact not a specialization of the current rule. Remember that the definition of a specialization requires that the order of the assumptions be preserved.

```
                           ┤ propositions/proofs.py ├
class InferenceRule:
        .
        .
        .

    def specialization_map(self, specialization: InferenceRule) -> \
            Union[SpecializationMap, None]:
        """Computes the minimal specialization map by which the current
        inference rule specializes to the given specialization.

        Parameters:
            specialization: specialization for which to compute the map.

        Returns:
            The computed specialization map, or ``None`` if `specialization` is
            in fact not a specialization of the current rule.
        """
        # Task 4.5c
```

Note that if we just want to tell whether one rule is or is not a specialization of another, all we need to check is whether `specialization_map()` returns a specialization map rather than None, which we have already implemented for you as a method of class InferenceRule.

```
                           ┤ propositions/proofs.py ├
class InferenceRule:
        .
        .
        .

    def is_specialization_of(self, general: InferenceRule) -> bool:
        """Checks if the current inference rule is a specialization of the given
        inference rule.

        Parameters:
            general: non-specialized inference rule to check.

        Returns:
            ``True`` if the current inference rule is a specialization of
            `general`, ``False`` otherwise.
        """
        return general.specialization_map(self) is not None
```

4.3 Deductive Proofs

We are now ready to introduce the main concept of this chapter, the (deductive) proof. Such a proof is a syntactic derivation of a conclusion formula (the conclusion of the "lemma" or "theorem" being proven) from a set of assumption formulas (the assumptions of the "lemma" or "theorem" being proven) via a set of inference rules (which we already take as given). We will use the very standard form of a proof that proceeds line by line. Each line in the proof may either be a direct quote of one of the assumptions of the lemma (or theorem) that we are proving or be derived from previous lines in the proof using a specialization of one of the inference rules that the proof may use. The last line of the proof should exactly be the conclusion of the lemma that we are proving. As noted in Section 4.1, in this chapter we will allow for arbitrary inference rules to be specified for use by a proof, and so we will explicitly specify the set of inference rules that may be used in each proof.[5] Here is an example of a proof.

Lemma to be proven: Assumption: '(x|y)'; Conclusion: '(y|x)'

Inference rules allowed:

1. Assumptions: '(p|q)', '(~p|r)'; Conclusion: '(q|r)'
2. (Assumptions: none;) Conclusion: '(~p|p)'

Proof:

1. '(x|y)'. Justification: assumption of the lemma to be proven.
2. '(~x|x)'. Justification: (conclusion of a) specialization of (the assumptionless) Allowed Inference Rule 2.
3. '(y|x)'. Justification: conclusion of a specialization of Allowed Inference Rule 1; Assumption 1 of the specialization: Line 1, Assumption 2 of the specialization: Line 2.

When we quote an assumption of the lemma to be proven, we must quote it verbatim, with no substitutions whatsoever. Thus, for example, Line 1 of the proof just given precisely quotes the assumption '(x|y)' and could *not* have quoted instead, say, '(w|z)', which indeed does *not* follow from the assumption '(x|y)'. On the other hand, when we use an inference rule to derive a line from previous lines, our derivation can use any specialization of that rule. Thus, for example, Line 2 of the proof uses the assumptionless inference rule whose conclusion is '(~p|p)' to derive '(~x|x)' from an empty set of assumptions, as this is a specialization obtained from that inference rule by substituting the formula 'x' for the variable name 'p'. Similarly, Line 3 of the proof uses an inference rule having assumptions '(x|y)' and '(~x|x)' and conclusion '(y|x)', which is a specialization of the first allowed inference rule, obtained by substituting 'x' for 'p' and for 'r', and 'y' for 'q'. When we formally define a proof, as already noted, we think of the "lemma" or "theorem" to be proven as an inference rule that states that the conclusion of the lemma follows from its assumptions. As we will see in Chapter 5, this will turn out to be very convenient as it will easily allow us to use the proved "lemma" as an inference rule in a subsequent proof.

DEFINITION 4.4 (Proof; Provability)   Given a formula ϕ, a set of formulas A, and a set of inference rules $\mathcal{R}$, a **proof** via $\mathcal{R}$ of the inference rule having conclusion ϕ and assumptions A, or simply a **proof** via $\mathcal{R}$ of the conclusion ϕ from the assumptions A,[6] is a list of formulas whose last formula is ϕ, such that each of the formulas in the list is either in A or the conclusion of a specialization of a rule in $\mathcal{R}$ such that the assumptions of this specialization are preceding formulas in the list. We say that the inference rule having assumptions A and conclusion ϕ is **provable** via $\mathcal{R}$, or simply that ϕ is **provable** from A via $\mathcal{R}$, if there exists a proof of that rule via $\mathcal{R}$. We denote this by $A \vdash_{\mathcal{R}} \phi$.

---

[5] As we progress in the following chapters, we will converge to a single specific set of rules that will be used from then onward.
[6] While a proof of an inference rule having assumptions A and conclusion c could be seen as mathematically distinct from a proof of the conclusion c from the assumption A, we will not require such a distinction in this book.

We emphasize that the notion of a proof is completely **syntactic**, and therefore so is the definition of $A \vdash_{\mathcal{R}} \phi$. However, when we think about a "proof" we intuitively desire also some semantic property: that a "proof" indeed "proves" what it claims. That is, that if we have a "proof" of some rule whose assumptions are correct, then indeed the conclusion of the "proof" is also correct; in other words, that the rule that was proven is sound. As we will see in Section 4.5, the notion of proof that we just described indeed has this semantic property, as long as it is *only allowed to use sound inference rules*. But for now, let us proceed to handle the syntax.

The file `propositions/proofs.py` also defines a class `Proof` for holding a deductive proof. Each line of the proof, including its full justification, is held by the inner class `Proof.Line` defined in the same file. (Note that unlike in the proof example just given, in the code all line numbers are 0-based.)

```
                        propositions/proofs.py

@frozen
class Proof:
    """An immutable deductive proof in Propositional Logic, comprised of a
    statement in the form of an inference rule, a set of inference rules that
    may be used in the proof, and a list of lines that prove the statement via
    these inference rules.

    Attributes:
        statement: the statement proven by the proof.
        rules: the allowed rules of the proof.
        lines: the lines of the proof.
    """
    statement: InferenceRule
    rules: FrozenSet[InferenceRule]
    lines: Tuple[Proof.Line, ...]

    def __init__(self, statement: InferenceRule,
                 rules: AbstractSet[InferenceRule],
                 lines: Sequence[Proof.Line]):
        """Initializes a `Proof` from its statement, allowed inference rules,
        and lines.

        Parameters:
            statement: the statement to be proven by the proof.
            rules: the allowed rules for the proof.
            lines: the lines for the proof.
        """
        self.statement = statement
        self.rules = frozenset(rules)
        self.lines = tuple(lines)

    @frozen
    class Line:
        """An immutable line in a deductive proof, comprised of a formula that
        is justified either as an assumption of the proof, or as the conclusion
        of a specialization of an allowed inference rule of the proof, the
        assumptions of which are justified by previous lines in the proof.

        Attributes:
            formula: the formula justified by the line.
```

```
            rule: the inference rule, out of those allowed in the proof, that
                has a specialization that concludes the formula; or ``None`` if
                the formula is justified as an assumption of the proof.
            assumptions: tuple of zero or more numbers of previous lines in the
                proof whose formulas are the respective assumptions of the
                specialization of the rule that concludes the formula, if the
                formula is not justified as an assumption of the proof.
        """

    formula: Formula
    rule: Optional[InferenceRule]
    assumptions: Optional[Tuple[int, ...]]

    def __init__(self, formula: Formula,
                 rule: Optional[InferenceRule] = None,
                 assumptions: Optional[Sequence[int]] = None):
        """Initializes a `Proof.Line` from its formula, and optionally its
        rule and numbers of justifying previous lines.

        Parameters:
            formula: the formula to be justified by the line.
            rule: the inference rule, out of those allowed in the proof,
                that has a specialization that concludes the formula; or
                ``None`` if the formula is to be justified as an assumption
                of the proof.
            assumptions: numbers of previous lines in the proof whose
                formulas are the respective assumptions of the
                specialization of the rule that concludes the formula, or
                ``None`` if the formula is to be justified as an assumption
                of the proof.
        """
        assert (rule is None and assumptions is None) or \
               (rule is not None and assumptions is not None)
        self.formula = formula
        self.rule = rule
        if assumptions is not None:
            self.assumptions = tuple(assumptions)

    def is_assumption(self) -> bool:
        """Checks if the current proof line is justified as an assumption of
        the proof.

        Returns:
            ``True`` if the current proof line is justified as an assumption
            of the proof, ``False`` otherwise.
        """
        return self.rule is None
```

TASK 6   The goal of this task is to check whether a given (alleged) proof is indeed a **valid** one, i.e., whether the lines of the proof in fact derive the conclusion of the statement from its assumptions via the allowed inference rules as in the definition of a proof.

a. Start by implementing the missing code for the method `rule_for_line(line_number)` of class `Proof`, which returns an inference rule comprised of the formulas in the specified line and in all the lines by which it is justified.

```
                         ╭─────────────────────────╮
                         │ propositions/proofs.py  │
                     ╭───┴─────────────────────────┴───╮
class Proof:
    ⋮

    def rule_for_line(self, line_number: int) -> Union[InferenceRule, None]:
        """Computes the inference rule whose conclusion is the formula justified
        by the specified line, and whose assumptions are the formulas justified
        by the lines specified as the assumptions of that line.

        Parameters:
            line_number: number of the line according to which to compute the
                inference rule.

        Returns:
            The computed inference rule, with assumptions ordered in the order
            of their numbers in the specified line, or ``None`` if the specified
            line is justified as an assumption.
        """
        assert line_number < len(self.lines)
        # Task 4.6a
```

b. Continue by implementing the missing code for the method is_line_valid(
   line_number) of class Proof, which returns whether the specified line is either
   an assumption and justified as such or the result of applying a specialization of the
   inference rule by which the line is justified to the previous lines by which the line is
   justified.

```
                         ╭─────────────────────────╮
                         │ propositions/proofs.py  │
                     ╭───┴─────────────────────────┴───╮
class Proof:
    ⋮

    def is_line_valid(self, line_number: int) -> bool:
        """Checks if the specified line validly follows from its justifications.

        Parameters:
            line_number: number of the line to check.

        Returns:
            If the specified line is justified as an assumption, then ``True``
            if the formula justified by this line is an assumption of the
            current proof, ``False`` otherwise. Otherwise (i.e., if the
            specified line is justified as a conclusion of an inference rule),
            ``True`` if the rule specified for that line is one of the allowed
            inference rules in the current proof, and it has a specialization
            that satisfies all of the following:

            1. The conclusion of that specialization is the formula justified by
               that line.
            2. The assumptions of this specialization are the formulas justified
               by the lines that are specified as the assumptions of that line
               (in the order of their numbers in that line), all of which must
               be previous lines.
        """
        assert line_number < len(self.lines)
        # Task 4.6b
```

Hint: Use the `rule_for_line()` method that you have just implemented.

c. Finally, implement the missing code for the method `'is_valid()'` of class `Proof`, which returns whether the proof is a valid proof of the statement it claims to prove, using the allowed inference rules.

```
                          propositions/proofs.py
class Proof:
    ⋮

    def is_valid(self) -> bool:
        """Checks if the current proof is a valid proof of its claimed statement
        via its inference rules.

        Returns:
            ``True`` if the current proof is a valid proof of its claimed
            statement via its inference rules, ``False`` otherwise.
        """
        # Task 4.6c
```

4.4   Practice Proving

Before continuing with our agenda of reasoning about the formal deductive proofs that we have just defined, it is worthwhile to first get comfortable in simply using them. Here are two basic exercises in writing formal proofs using the `Proof` class. The functions that you are asked to implement in these tasks are contained in the file `propositions/some_proofs.py`. We warmly recommend to first try and figure out the proof strategy with a pen and a piece of paper, and only then write the code that returns the appropriate `Proof` object.

TASK 7   Prove the following inference rule: Assumption: '(p&q)'; Conclusion: '(q&p)'; via the following three inference rules:

- Assumptions: 'x', 'y'; Conclusion: '(x&y)'
- Assumption: '(x&y)'; Conclusion: 'y'
- Assumption: '(x&y)'; Conclusion: 'x'

The proof should be returned by the function `prove_and_commutativity()`, whose missing code you should implement.

```
                          propositions/some_proofs.py
# Some inference rules that only use conjunction.

#: Conjunction introduction inference rule
A_RULE = InferenceRule([Formula.parse('x'), Formula.parse('y')],
                       Formula.parse('(x&y)'))
#: Conjunction elimination (right) inference rule
AE1_RULE = InferenceRule([Formula.parse('(x&y)')],Formula.parse('y'))
#: Conjunction elimination (left) inference rule
AE2_RULE = InferenceRule([Formula.parse('(x&y)')],Formula.parse('x'))
```

```
def prove_and_commutativity() -> Proof:
    """Proves '(q&p)' from '(p&q)' via `A_RULE`, `AE1_RULE`, and `AE2_RULE`.

    Returns:
        A valid proof of '(q&p)' from the single assumption '(p&q)' via the
        inference rules `A_RULE`, `AE1_RULE`, and `AE2_RULE`.
    """
    # Task 4.7
```

The next and final task requires some more ingenuity. It focuses on inference rules that only involve the *implies* operator and uses the following three inference rules, which in the following chapters will end up being part of our "chosen" set of inference rules (which, as we will see in Chapter 6, suffice for proving all sound inference rules):

MP: Assumptions: 'p', '(p→q)'; Conclusion: 'q'

 I1: (Assumptions: none;) Conclusion: '(q→(p→q))'

 D: (Assumptions: none;) Conclusion: '((p→(q→r))→((p→q)→(p→r)))'

These inference rules, alongside the rule that you are asked to prove in the next task, are defined in the file propositions/axiomatic_systems.py.[7]

```
                    propositions/axiomatic_systems.py

# Axiomatic inference rules that only contain implies

#: Modus ponens / implication elimination
MP = InferenceRule([Formula.parse('p'), Formula.parse('(p->q)')],
                   Formula.parse('q'))
#: Self implication
I0 = InferenceRule([], Formula.parse('(p->p)'))
#: Implication introduction (right)
I1 = InferenceRule([], Formula.parse('(q->(p->q))'))
#: Self-distribution of implication
D = InferenceRule([], Formula.parse('((p->(q->r))->((p->q)->(p->r)))'))
```

TASK 8 Prove the following inference rule via the inference rules MP, I1, and D.

I0: (Assumptions: none;) Conclusion: '(p→p)'

The proof should be returned by the function prove_I0(), whose missing code you should implement.

```
                    propositions/some_proofs.py

def prove_I0() -> Proof:
    """Proves `I0` via `MP`, `I1`, and `D`.

    Returns:
        A valid proof of `I0` via the inference rules `MP`, `I1`, and `D`.
    """
    # Task 4.8
```

---

[7] You will not be asked to implement anything in this file throughout this book.

Hint: Start by using the rule D with '(p→p)' substituted for 'q' and with 'p' substituted for 'r'. Notice that this would give you something that looks like '(ϕ→(ψ→(p→p)))'. Now try to extract the required '(p→p)' using the rules MP and I1.

4.5   The Soundness Theorem

Let us emphasize again what should be clear up to this point: The validity of a proof is a purely **syntactic** matter. However at this point we are ready for the first relation between the syntactic world of proofs and the semantic world of truths: Any inference rule that is provable via sound inference rules must be sound, or equivalently, any conclusion that is provable, via sound inference rules, from true assumptions must be true.

THEOREM 4.1 (The Soundness Theorem for Propositional Logic)   *Any inference rule that is provable via (only) sound inference rules is itself sound as well. That is, if $\mathcal{R}$ contains only sound inference rules, and if $A \vdash_\mathcal{R} \phi$, then $A \models \phi$.*

In fact, this trivial-yet-magical theorem provides the basic justification for the whole concept of mathematics: proving something to be convinced that it is true. Otherwise, there would have been no point in proving anything! This theorem also makes it clear why we will always only allow using sound inference rules in our proofs, as otherwise we might prove claims that are wrong.

The following two tasks prove the soundness theorem (4.1). The functions that you are asked to implement in these tasks are contained in the file `propositions/soundness.py`. Our first order of business is to tackle the use of specializations in a proof: Recall that a proof that uses a set $\mathcal{R}$ of inference rules is allowed to use, in every line, any specialization of any rule in $\mathcal{R}$ rather than just these rules verbatim. This turns out not to be an issue, since if we start with any sound inference rule like the one having assumption 'x' and conclusion '~~x', and then "plug into x" any formula, for example '(p&q)', then we get a *sound* specialization: the inference rule having assumption '(p&q)' and conclusion '~~(p&q)'. The reason for this is that had there been a counterexample to the specialized inference rule, then it would directly yield a counterexample to the original inference rule as well. The following task makes this explicit.

TASK 9 (Programmatic Proof of the Specialization Soundness Lemma (4.1))   Implement the missing code for the function `rule_nonsoundness_from_specialization_nonsoundness(general, specialization, model)`, which takes an inference rule, a specialization of this rule, and a model that is a counterexample to the soundness of this specialization, and returns a model that is a counterexample to the soundness of the general inference rule.

```
                    ( propositions/soundness.py )
def rule_nonsoundness_from_specialization_nonsoundness(
        general: InferenceRule, specialization: InferenceRule, model: Model) \
        -> Model:
    """Demonstrates the non-soundness of the given general inference rule given
    an example of the non-soundness of the given specialization of this rule.
```

```
    Parameters:
        general: inference rule to the soundness of which to find a
            counterexample.
        specialization: non-sound specialization of `general`.
        model: model in which `specialization` does not hold.

    Returns:
        A model in which `general` does not hold.
    """
    assert specialization.is_specialization_of(general)
    assert not evaluate_inference(specialization, model)
    # Task 4.9
```

Guidelines: This function will be tested on inference rules with many variable names, so iterating over all models to find a model to return (similarly to your implementation of `is_sound_inference()`) is not an adequate solution strategy (and more importantly, does not programmatically prove what we have set out to prove). Instead, try to understand how to use the given model to find a suitable model to return.

Your solution to Task 9 proves the following lemma.

LEMMA 4.1 (Specialization Soundness) *Every specialization of a sound inference rule is itself sound as well.*

Once we have this lemma under our belt we can proceed to prove the soundness theorem (4.1). Assume by way of contradiction that we have a (valid) proof that starts with a set of assumptions and proves a conclusion that is not (semantically) entailed by them. If we look at any model that purports to be a counterexample to this proved inference rule then we can obtain from it a counterexample to one of the inference rules that are used in the proof. Which one? Look at the sequence of lines of the proof. In the beginning of the proof we have assumptions that evaluate to *True* in the model and at the end of the proof we have a conclusion that evaluates to *False* in this model (this is exactly what it means for the model to be a counterexample to the proved inference rule). If we look at the first line in the proof that evaluates to *False* in the model, it must have used an inference rule that is not sound, since if it were sound, then by the specialization soundness lemma (4.1) so would have been its specialization that justifies the line, and therefore a model that satisfies all of the specialization's assumptions (like our counterexample model) would have also satisfied the specialization's conclusion. The following task makes this explicit.

TASK 10 (Programmatic Proof of the Soundness Theorem (4.1) for Propositional Logic) Implement the missing code for the function `nonsound_rule_of_nonsound_proof(proof, model)`, which takes a valid proof and a model that is a counterexample to the statement of the given proof, and returns a non-sound inference rule that is used in the given proof, along with a model that is a counterexample to the soundness of the returned inference rule.

propositions/soundness.py

```
def nonsound_rule_of_nonsound_proof(proof: Proof, model: Model) -> \
        Tuple[InferenceRule, Model]:
    """Finds a non-sound inference rule used by the given valid proof of a
    non-sound inference rule, and demonstrates the non-soundness of the former
    rule.
```

```
Parameters:
    proof: valid proof of a non-sound inference rule.
    model: model in which the inference rule proved by the given proof does
        not hold.

Returns:
    A pair of a non-sound inference rule used in the given proof and a model
    in which this rule does not hold.
"""
assert proof.is_valid()
assert not evaluate_inference(proof.statement, model)
# Task 4.10
```

Guidelines: This function will be tested on proofs with inference rules with many variable names, so running `is_sound_inference()` on each inference rule used in the given proof is not an adequate solution strategy (and more importantly, does not programmatically prove the soundness theorem (4.1)). Instead, try to understand how to use the given model to find a suitable rule (and model) to return.

The soundness theorem (4.1) gives us a clear one-sided connection between the syntactic notion of $A \vdash_{\mathcal{R}} \phi$ and the semantic notion of $A \models \phi$, i.e., that for some interesting sets of inference rules (i.e., if $\mathcal{R}$ is a set of sound inference rules), the former implies the latter. Our goal in the next two chapters will be to prove a converse called the **completeness theorem**: that for some interesting sets of sound inference rules, the latter implies the former as well.

5 Working with Proofs

In Chapter 4 we introduced the syntactic notion of a formal deductive proof in propositional logic and you wrote code that checked whether a given alleged proof is indeed a syntactically valid proof. In this chapter we proceed to mathematically analyze such syntactic formal proofs and prove theorems about formal proofs. Notice the two very different uses of "proof" in the last sentence: In "proving theorems...," the meaning is the usual mathematical notion of presenting a mathematically convincing, but not syntactically formal, argument of correctness; in "...about formal proofs" we mean syntactically formal propositional-logic proofs. The former is usually done in mathematical language but in this book will be achieved – as we have done so far – by writing Python programs with the claimed functionality, while the latter are usually viewed as mathematical objects (formally, strings of symbols), and we will use Python objects of the class `Proof` (which you implemented in Chapter 4), handled by said programs, to represent them. Disambiguating these two very different notions of "proof" by defamiliarizing them from what we intuitively grasp as a proof, turning one of them into "programming" and the other into "object of class `Proof`," is at the heart of the pedagogical approach of this book, and we hope that it will help avoid the confusion that is sometimes stirred by this ambiguity and by our intuition of what a proof is.

While one of our long-term goals in this book is to be able to completely formalize mathematically convincing proofs of the former kind as syntactically formal proofs of the latter kind, and thus to explain why there is in fact no ambiguity here and that both are called "proof" for a good reason, this will have to wait for the stronger **predicate logic** studied in Part II of this book. For now, we are happy with using "regular" mathematics (or programming) to prove claims regarding our formal syntactic propositional-logic proofs (or equivalently, the corresponding `Proof` objects).

5.1 Using Lemmas

Recall that each of our formal proofs has a well-defined set of inference rules that it can use, and each step (line) in the proof is confined to applying one of these rules. In "regular" mathematics we often abstract away a subargument as a **lemma**, prove the lemma once, and from that point allow ourselves to continue using the lemma as an additional inference rule without needing to reprove it every time that we use it in some other proof. In fact, the way that mathematics progresses is exactly by proving a richer and richer set of lemmas and theorems, all of them to be used "as inference rules" later on at will. This seems to be such a basic element of mathematical reasoning, that one may well expect such a capability of proving lemmas and then using them to be an integral part of our definition of formal proofs (just as high-level programming languages have, as an integral part of the definition of the language, the ability to implement and then use functions and methods). As we will now see, we do not need to define this capability, and in fact having the capability of defining lemmas is only for the *human* convenience of writing proofs, while our formal proofs can mimic this ability without having it be part of the definition. (To some extent, this is similar to machine languages often not having any notion of a procedure or function call, and yet being able to implement that functionality when higher-level languages are compiled into such machine languages.)

The functions that you are asked to implement in this section are contained in the file propositions/proofs.py. The first thing that we have to verify is that if some lemma is proven, then specializations of that lemma can also be proven. In "regular" mathematics we take this as a triviality of course: Every first-year mathematics or computer science student has at some point applied a lemma whose statement begins with "for any function f" to a specific function g, treating both the assumptions and the conclusion of the lemma as if they were originally phrased for this specific g rather than for f. But, once we have limited ourselves to formal proofs of the very specific form defined in Chapter 4, we need to show that this property still holds for this specific form of formal proofs.

TASK 1 (Programmatic Proof of the Specialization Provability Lemma (5.1))   Implement the missing code for the function prove_specialization(proof, specialization), which takes a (valid) deductive proof of some inference rule, and returns a deductive proof of the given specialization of that rule, via the same inference rules.

```
┌─────────────────── propositions/proofs.py ───────────────────┐

def prove_specialization(proof: Proof, specialization: InferenceRule) -> Proof:
    """Converts the given proof of an inference rule to a proof of the given
    specialization of that inference rule.

    Parameters:
        proof: valid proof to convert.
        specialization: specialization of the rule proven by the given proof.

    Returns:
        A valid proof of the given specialization via the same inference rules
        as the given proof.
    """
    assert proof.is_valid()
    assert specialization.is_specialization_of(proof.statement)
    # Task 5.1
```

Example: If proof is a proof of the inference rule having assumptions '(p|q)', '(~p|r)' and conclusion '(q|r)', then specialization could be, e.g., the inference rule with assumptions '(x|p)', '(~x|(y&z))' and conclusion '(p|(y&z))'.

Hint: Start by using the specialization_map() method of class InferenceRule to get the map that specializes the rule that proof proves into specialization.

Your solution to Task 1 proves the following lemma.

LEMMA 5.1 (Specialization Provability)   *Let $\mathcal{R}$ be a set of inference rules. Every specialization of every lemma that is provable via $\mathcal{R}$ is itself provable via $\mathcal{R}$ as well.*

With the specialization provability lemma (5.1) in hand, we are now ready to show that the formal proof system that we defined in Chapter 4 does indeed have the power to allow for gradual building of lemmas and their usage – a result that we will formally state subsequently and call the **lemma theorem**.

TASK 2 (Programmatic Proof of the Lemma Theorem (5.1))   In this task you will implement the missing code for the function `inline_proof(main_proof, lemma_proof)`, which takes a deductive proof `main_proof` of some inference rule via a set of inference rules $\mathcal{R}$, takes a deductive proof `lemma_proof` of one of the inference rules $\lambda \in \mathcal{R}$ (short for lemma) via a set of inference rules $\mathcal{R}'$ (where $\lambda \notin \mathcal{R}'$ of course), and returns a deductive proof of the inference rule proved by `main_proof`, however via the inference rules $(\mathcal{R} \setminus \{\lambda\}) \cup \mathcal{R}'$.

a. First implement the missing code for the function `_inline_proof_once(main_proof, line_number, lemma_proof)`, which replaces only a single instance of the use of the given lemma, and thus the returned proof is allowed to use all of the inference rules in $\mathcal{R} \cup \mathcal{R}'$, including λ, but must use λ one time less than in the given proof.

```
                        ┌─ propositions/proofs.py ─┐
def _inline_proof_once(main_proof: Proof, line_number: int,
                       lemma_proof: Proof) -> Proof:
    """Inlines the given proof of a "lemma" inference rule into the given proof
    that uses that "lemma" rule, eliminating the usage of (a specialization of)
    that "lemma" rule in the specified line in the latter proof.

    Parameters:
        main_proof: valid proof to inline into.
        line_number: number of the line in `main_proof` that should be replaced.
        lemma_proof: valid proof of the inference rule of the specified line (an
            allowed inference rule of `main_proof`).

    Returns:
        A valid proof obtained by replacing the specified line in `main_proof`
        with a full (specialized) list of lines proving the formula of the
        specified line from the lines specified as the assumptions of that line,
        and updating justification line numbers specified throughout the proof
        to maintain the validity of the proof. The set of allowed inference
        rules in the returned proof is the union of the rules allowed in the two
        given proofs, but the "lemma" rule that is used in the specified line in
        `main_proof` is no longer used in the corresponding lines in the
        returned proof (and thus, this "lemma" rule is used one less time in the
        returned proof than in `main_proof`).
    """
    assert main_proof.is_valid()
    assert line_number < len(main_proof.lines)
    assert main_proof.lines[line_number].rule == lemma_proof.statement
    assert lemma_proof.is_valid()
    # Task 5.2a
```

Guidelines: Implement the easiest implementation, which does not generate a proof with a minimal number of lines but does avoid a lot of clutter, by returning a proof that contains three batches of lines:

1. All the lines of `proof` up to line `line_number-1`, unmodified.
2. All the lines of a proof of the specialization (of the lemma) that is used in line `line_number` of `proof`, only with the following two modifications:
   - All line numbers justifying assumptions of specializations that are used in this batch of lines should be shifted by `line_number`.
   - Each line that corresponds to any assumption of the proof of the specialization that is not also an assumption of `proof` should be modified by adding an appropriate rule and an appropriate assumption list to that line (these can simply be copied from the line whose number is used in line `line_number` of `proof` to justify the corresponding assumption).
3. All the lines of `proof` from line `line_number+1` onward, modified so that all line numbers greater than or equal to `line_number` that justify assumptions of specializations are shifted by the same appropriate number.

b. Now you can implement the function `inline_proof(main_proof, lemma_proof)` by using `_inline_proof_once()` repeatedly, until all uses of the given lemma in the original proof are eliminated.

```
                          ┌─────────────────────────┐
                          │ propositions/proofs.py  │
─────────────────────────┴─────────────────────────┴──────────────────
def inline_proof(main_proof: Proof, lemma_proof: Proof) -> Proof:
    """Inlines the given proof of a "lemma" inference rule into the given proof
    that uses that "lemma" rule, eliminating all usages of (any specializations
    of) that "lemma" rule in the latter proof.

    Parameters:
        main_proof: valid proof to inline into.
        lemma_proof: valid proof of one of the allowed inference rules of
            `main_proof`.

    Returns:
        A valid proof obtained from `main_proof` by inlining (an appropriate
        specialization of) `lemma_proof` in lieu of each line that specifies the
        "lemma" inference rule proved by `lemma_proof` as its justification. The
        set of allowed inference rules in the returned proof is the union of the
        rules allowed in the two given proofs but without the "lemma" rule
        proved by `lemma_proof`.
    """
    assert main_proof.is_valid()
    assert lemma_proof.is_valid()
    # Task 5.2b
```

Your solution to Task 2 proves the following theorem, which formalizes the fact that while we have not explicitly allowed the usage of lemmas in our definition of a deductive proof, this is in fact not required for us to be able to use them (for our great convenience!).

THEOREM 5.1 (The Lemma Theorem)   *If an inference rule ρ is provable via a set of inference rules $\mathcal{R} \cup \{\lambda\}$, and if λ is provable via $\mathcal{R}$, then ρ is provable via only the set $\mathcal{R}$.*

5.2   Modus Ponens

Suppose that you have a mathematical proof – in "regular mathematics" – of some conclusion ψ from some assumption ϕ. Outside the logic classroom we may say that this proves that "ϕ implies ψ" – which in the logic classroom we formalize as '$(\phi \to \psi)$'. However, notice that in our logical formalization, a proof of ψ from the assumption ϕ, i.e., of $\{\phi\} \vdash \psi$, is formally different than a proof of the implication, i.e., of $\vdash$ '$(\phi \to \psi)$'. Once we fix the set $\mathcal{R}$ of allowed inference rules, $\{\phi\} \vdash \psi$ means that there is a valid proof of the formula ψ from the single assumption ϕ (via $\mathcal{R}$) while $\vdash$ '$(\phi \to \psi)$' means that there is a valid proof of the single formula '$(\phi \to \psi)$' from no assumptions (again, via $\mathcal{R}$).

Our next order of business on our "working with proofs" agenda is understanding and formalizing the connection between these two notions, and indeed reaching a state of affairs where we can syntactically move freely between the two notions, as our mathematical intuition dictates we should be able to, and as will be very convenient for us to do when we prove the completeness theorem for propositional logic in Chapter 6. Before proceeding with the syntactic issues of proofs, let us underscore this intuition using an analogous semantic question: What is the relation between $\{\phi\} \models \psi$ and $\models$ '$(\phi \to \psi)$'? Here the answer is that these two are equivalent: $\{\phi\} \models \psi$ (i.e., ϕ entails ψ, or equivalently, the rule having assumption ϕ and conclusion ψ is sound) means that in every model in which ϕ holds, so does ψ. But this exactly means that the formula '$(\phi \to \psi)$' is a tautology, i.e., that $\models$ '$(\phi \to \psi)$'.

So we now return to the syntactic question of $\{\phi\} \vdash \psi$ versus $\vdash$ '$(\phi \to \psi)$'. This section will discuss the "easy" direction of the desired equivalence: that if $\vdash$ '$(\phi \to \psi)$' then $\{\phi\} \vdash \psi$. Section 5.3 will discuss the "harder" converse direction: that if $\{\phi\} \vdash \psi$ then $\vdash$ '$(\phi \to \psi)$', which is called the **deduction theorem**. In each of these two directions we will find sufficient conditions on the set of allowed inference rules, $\mathcal{R}$, that ensures the desired implication. Our final fixed set of allowed inference rules – our **axiomatic system** – which will be presented in Chapter 6, will naturally satisfy both sets of conditions, and so for that set of inference rules we will indeed have the desired equivalence.

The only condition on our set of inference rules $\mathcal{R}$ that we require for the "easy direction" is that it contains the simple inference rule called **modus ponens**, or **MP** for short, which is one of the most natural and basic inference rules, already known in Ancient Greece. You were already briefly introduced to this inference rule in Task 8 of Chapter 4.

Modus Ponens (MP): Assumptions: 'p', '(p→q)'; Conclusion: 'q'

```
┌─────────────────────────────────┐
│ propositions/axiomatic_systems.py │
# Axiomatic inference rules that only contain implies

#: Modus ponens / implication elimination
MP = InferenceRule([Formula.parse('p'), Formula.parse('(p->q)')],
                   Formula.parse('q'))
                          ⋮
```

It is straightforward to verify that MP is indeed sound, and your implementation of `is_sound_inference()` has in fact already done so: one of the ways in which we have tested it is by making sure that it successfully verifies the soundness of MP.

Using MP, we can immediately see the easy direction of the desired equivalence, that if $\vdash$ '$(\phi{\rightarrow}\psi)$' then $\{\phi\} \vdash \psi$: To create a proof of ψ from $\{\phi\}$, given proof for '$(\phi{\rightarrow}\psi)$', take the given proof, append an assumption line ϕ (which is now is indeed an assumption), and directly apply MP to the last two lines (i.e., to ϕ and to '$(\phi{\rightarrow}\psi)$') to deduce ψ. This simple technique continues to hold even regardless of any other assumptions that the original proof of '$(\phi{\rightarrow}\psi)$' uses. (These assumptions are simply used by the new proof as well.) This proves the following lemma, which states the "easy direction" of the equivalence that we are after.

LEMMA 5.2 *Let $\mathcal{R}$ be a set of inference rules that includes MP, let A be an arbitrary set of formulas, and let ϕ and ψ be two additional formulas. If $A \vdash_{\mathcal{R}}$ '$(\phi{\rightarrow}\psi)$', then $A \cup \{\phi\} \vdash_{\mathcal{R}} \psi$.*

Once we have MP at our disposal, we can "replace" a desired inference rule that has an assumption ϕ (called the **antecedent**) and conclusion ψ (called the **consequent**) by the assumption-less inference rule conclusion '$(\phi{\rightarrow}\psi)$'. Thus, for example, if we want our axiomatic system to be able to (validly) deduce '$(\phi{\rightarrow}\psi)$' from 'ψ', then we will just introduce the assumptionless inference rule '$(q{\rightarrow}(p{\rightarrow}q))$' that will allow us to make this deduction using MP. We can also similarly "encode" an inference rule with more than one assumption. For example, we can "encode" an inference rule with two assumptions ϕ_1, ϕ_2 and conclusion ψ by the assumptionless inference rule with conclusion '$(\phi_1{\rightarrow}(\phi_2{\rightarrow}\psi))$' that will allow us to perform the deduction of the encoded inference rule using two invocations[1] of MP. Thus, for example, if we want to be able to deduce 'ψ' from the two assumptions '$(\phi{\rightarrow}\psi)$' and '$(\~\phi{\rightarrow}\psi)$', then the assumptionless inference rule '$((q{\rightarrow}p){\rightarrow}((\~q{\rightarrow}p){\rightarrow}p))$' will do the trick. More generally, we could encode any inference rule with any number of assumptions $\phi_1, \ldots, \phi_n$ and conclusion ξ by the assumptionless inference rule with conclusion '$(\phi_1{\rightarrow}(\phi_2{\rightarrow}\cdots(\phi_n{\rightarrow}\xi)\cdots))$' (similarly to the discussion on semantics in the beginning of this section, the latter rule is sound if and only if the former one is) without losing any "proving power" as long as we have MP at our disposal. As you will see in Chapter 6, in our axiomatic system, MP will be the only inference rule that has a nonempty set of assumptions, and all other inference rules will be assumptionless ones (this will be important for technical reasons, as you will see in Section 5.3) that in fact "encode" various inference rules that have one or two assumptions.

The following task mechanizes the process of making deductions using such encoded rules and MP. The functions that you are asked to implement in the remainder of this chapter are contained in the file `propositions/deduction.py` unless otherwise noted.

TASK 3

a. Start by implementing the missing code for the function `prove_corollary(`
`antecedent_proof, consequent, conditional)`, which takes a proof of some "antecedent" formula ϕ from some assumptions, a desired consequent ψ, and an assumptionless inference rule `conditional` of which '$(\phi{\rightarrow}\psi)$' is a specialization, and returns a proof of ψ from the same assumptions, via the same inference rules as well as MP and `conditional`.

---

[1] Similarly to the last part of your proof of I0 in Chapter 4.

```
                        ┌─ propositions/deduction.py ─┐
def prove_corollary(antecedent_proof: Proof, consequent: Formula,
                    conditional: InferenceRule) -> Proof:
    """Converts the given proof of a formula `antecedent` to a proof of the
    given formula `consequent` by using the given assumptionless inference rule
    of which '(`antecedent`->`consequent`)' is a specialization.

    Parameters:
        antecedent_proof: valid proof of `antecedent`.
        consequent: formula to prove.
        conditional: assumptionless inference rule of which the assumptionless
            inference rule with conclusion '(`antecedent`->`consequent`)' is a
            specialization.

    Returns:
        A valid proof of `consequent` from the same assumptions as the given
        proof, via the same inference rules as the given proof and in addition
        `MP` and `conditional`.
    """
    assert antecedent_proof.is_valid()
    assert InferenceRule([],
                    Formula('->', antecedent_proof.statement.conclusion,
                            consequent)).is_specialization_of(conditional)
    # Task 5.3a
```

b. Now, implement the missing code for the slightly more complex variant function combine _ proofs(antecedent1 _ proof, antecedent2_proof, consequent, double_conditional), which takes *two* proofs of two "antecedent" formulas ϕ_1 and ϕ_2, both from the same[2] assumptions and via the same inference rules, a desired consequent ψ, and an assumptionless inference rule double_conditional of which '$(\phi_1 \to (\phi_2 \to \psi))$' is a specialization, and, as in the previous part of this task, returns a proof of ψ from the same assumptions, via the same inference rules as well as MP and conditional.

```
                        ┌─ propositions/deduction.py ─┐
def combine_proofs(antecedent1_proof: Proof, antecedent2_proof: Proof,
                   consequent: Formula, double_conditional: InferenceRule) -> \
        Proof:
    """Combines the given proofs of two formulas `antecedent1` and `antecedent2`
    into a proof of the given formula `consequent` by using the given
    assumptionless inference rule of which
    '(`antecedent1`->`antecedent2`->`consequent`)' is a specialization.

    Parameters:
        antecedent1_proof: valid proof of `antecedent1`.
        antecedent2_proof: valid proof of `antecedent2` from the same
            assumptions and inference rules as `antecedent1_proof`.
        consequent: formula to prove.
        double_conditional: assumptionless inference rule of which the
            assumptionless inference rule with conclusion
            '(`antecedent1`->`antecedent2`->`consequent`)' is a specialization.
```

[2] We require that the assumptions of the two given proofs are exactly the same and in the same order for simplicity and since this is what we will use, even though the same solution would also work with no requirements on the assumptions, and only returning a proof from all the assumptions that are used in any of the given proofs.

```
    Returns:
        A valid proof of `consequent` from the same assumptions as the given
        proofs, via the same inference rules as the given proofs and in addition
        `MP` and `double_conditional`.
    """
    assert antecedent1_proof.is_valid()
    assert antecedent2_proof.is_valid()
    assert antecedent1_proof.statement.assumptions == \
           antecedent2_proof.statement.assumptions
    assert antecedent1_proof.rules == antecedent2_proof.rules
    assert InferenceRule(
        [], Formula('->', antecedent1_proof.statement.conclusion,
        Formula('->', antecedent2_proof.statement.conclusion, consequent))
        ).is_specialization_of(double_conditional)
    # Task 5.3b
```

5.3   The Deduction Theorem

We now move to the hard part of the equivalence: showing that if $\{\phi\} \vdash \psi$ then $\vdash$ '$(\phi{\rightarrow}\psi)$', and even more generally, that for any set of additional assumptions A, if $A \cup \{\phi\} \vdash \psi$ then $A \vdash$ '$(\phi{\rightarrow}\psi)$'. This result is called the **deduction theorem**, it will help us in many proofs, and its proof is a significant milestone toward the goal of Part I of this book. We will prove this theorem for any set $\mathcal{R}$ of inference rules that also contains, in addition to MP, the following three **axioms** (we will use the term **axioms** to refer to the assumptionless inference rules that will be part of our axiomatic system – our set of allowed inference rules), to which you were also already introduced in Chapter 4:

I0: '(p→p)'
I1: '(q→(p→q))'
D: '((p→(q→r))→((p→q)→(p→r)))'

propositions/axiomatic_systems.py

```
# Axiomatic inference rules that only contain implies
    ⋮

#: Self implication
I0 = InferenceRule([], Formula.parse('(p->p)'))
#: Implication introduction (right)
I1 = InferenceRule([], Formula.parse('(q->(p->q))'))
#: Self-distribution of implication
D = InferenceRule([], Formula.parse('((p->(q->r))->((p->q)->(p->r)))'))
```

It is straightforward to verify that these three axioms (and the additional axioms that will be presented in the remainder of this chapter and in Chapter 6) are sound, and once again, your implementation of `is_sound_inference()` has in fact already done this: One of the ways in which we have tested it is by making sure that it successfully verifies the soundness of all of these axioms.

Recall that in Chapter 4 you have already proved I0 via {MP, I1, D}, so by the lemma theorem (5.1), anything that is provable via {MP, I0, I1, D} is in fact provable without I0, via only {MP, I1, D}. So, we allow ourselves to also use I0 just for convenience, even though this is in fact not really needed.

We will place one additional restriction on our set $\mathcal{R}$ of inference rules: that all of these inference rules, except MP, have no assumptions. In the strictest technical sense, this will be sufficient for our purposes since from this point on, our sets of inference rules will always have this property. On a more conceptual level, since we have MP at our disposal, as discussed above we can always, instead of adding some inference rule to our axiomatic system, add instead an assumptionless inference rule that "encodes" it without losing any "proving power."

Let us think about what we have to do to show that if $A \cup \{\phi\} \vdash \psi$ then $A \vdash \text{'}(\phi \rightarrow \psi)\text{'}$. We are given a proof of ψ from an assumption ϕ, as well as some other assumptions A, and need to create a new proof of the conclusion '$(\phi \rightarrow \psi)$' from only the assumptions in A. How can we do this? The idea is to go over the original proof line by line, and if the ith line of the original proof contains a formula ξ_i, then to add to our new proof a line containing '$(\phi \rightarrow \xi_i)$' instead. In terms of the conclusion, this is exactly what we want since the last line of the original proof is ψ and therefore the last line of the new proof will be '$(\phi \rightarrow \psi)$', as needed. The problem is that the new list of lines need not really constitute a valid proof: it's quite possible that none of these lines is an assumption or follows from previous ones using one of the allowed inference rules. The point is that, assuming that we have the required inference rules at our disposal, we will be able to add some "intermediate lines" in between each pair of line of the new proof, to turn it into a valid proof. Let us consider which kinds of lines we can have in the original proof, and see how we can deal with each of them:

- It may be that the line ξ_i is one of the assumptions that also remains an assumption in the new proof (i.e., $\xi_i \in A$). The problem is that our strategy requires us to deduce a line with '$(\phi \rightarrow \xi_i)$' while only ξ_i is an allowed assumption. Conveniently, it is possible to deduce '$(\phi \rightarrow \xi_i)$' from ξ_i via I1 along with MP (hint: take inspiration from the implementation of `prove_corollary()`).

- It may be that ξ_i is exactly the assumption ϕ that we are no longer allowed to use in the new proof. Our strategy calls for deducing a line with '$(\phi \rightarrow \xi_i)$', which in this case is '$(\phi \rightarrow \phi)$'. Conveniently, I0 allows to deduce this *without* using ϕ as an assumption.

- It may be that ξ_i is deduced by MP from two previous lines containing some formulas ξ_j and ξ_k. We need to deduce '$(\phi \rightarrow \xi_i)$', but can rely on the fact that we have already deduced '$(\phi \rightarrow \xi_j)$' and '$(\phi \rightarrow \xi_k)$' in the new proof (in the lines corresponding to the lines containing ξ_j and ξ_k in the original proof). Conveniently, a clever usage of D along with MP allows us to deduce this (hint: take inspiration from the implementation of `combine_proofs()`).

- The last option is that ξ_i is deduced by some inference rule that is not MP. As we assume that all inference rules except MP have no assumptions, ξ_i is therefore (the conclusion of) a specialization of an allowed assumptionless inference rule. So, we can deduce ξ_i in the new proof as well, and we conveniently already know how to deduce '$(\phi \rightarrow \xi_i)$' from it via I1 along with MP.

You are now asked to implement this proof strategy.

TASK 4 (Programmatic Proof of the Deduction Theorem (5.2) for Propositional Logic)
Implement the missing code for the function `remove_assumption(proof)`. This function
takes as input a deductive proof of a conclusion ψ from a nonempty list of assumptions via
inference rules that, except for MP, have no assumptions. The function returns a deductive
proof of '$(\phi \rightarrow \psi)$', where ϕ is the last assumption of the given proof, from the same
assumptions except for ϕ, via the same inference rules as well as MP, I0, I1, and D.

```
propositions/deduction.py

def remove_assumption(proof: Proof) -> Proof:
    """Converts the given proof of some `conclusion` formula, the last
    assumption of which is an assumption `assumption`, to a proof of
    '(`assumption`->`conclusion`)' from the same assumptions except
    `assumption`.

    Parameters:
        proof: valid proof to convert, with at least one assumption, via some
            set of inference rules all of which have no assumptions except
            perhaps `MP`.

    Returns:
        A valid proof of '(`assumption`->`conclusion`)' from the same
        assumptions as the given proof except the last one, via the same
        inference rules as the given proof and in addition `MP`, `I0`, `I1`,
        and `D`.
    """
    assert proof.is_valid()
    assert len(proof.statement.assumptions) > 0
    for rule in proof.rules:
        assert rule == MP or len(rule.assumptions) == 0
    # Task 5.4
```

Your solution to Task 4 proves the final, hard direction, of the deduction theorem.

THEOREM 5.2 (The Deduction Theorem for Propositional Logic)   *Let $\mathcal{R}$ be a set of*
inference rules that includes MP, I1, and D, and may additionally include only inference
rules with no assumptions. Let A be an arbitrary set of formulas, and let ϕ and ψ be two
additional formulas. Then $A \cup \{\phi\} \vdash_{\mathcal{R}} \psi$ if and only if $A \vdash_{\mathcal{R}}$ '$(\phi \rightarrow \psi)$'.

Recall that while we allowed using also I0 in Task 4, since you have already shown
in Chapter 4 that I0 is provable via $\{MP, I1, D\}$, then by the lemma theorem (5.1), the
statement of the deduction theorem (5.2) need not assume (and indeed, does not assume)
that using I0 is allowed. The deduction theorem (5.2) is an extremely useful tool for writing
proofs. Many results that are quite tedious to prove directly from the above (and other)
inference rules are easily proven using the deduction theorem (5.2). The final task of this
section demonstrates such a result.

TASK 5   Prove the following inference rule: Assumptions: '$(p \rightarrow q)$', '$(q \rightarrow r)$';
Conclusion: '$(p \rightarrow r)$'; via the inference rules MP, I0, I1, and D. The proof should
be returned by the function `prove_hypothetical_syllogism()` in the file
`propositions/some_proofs.py`, whose missing code you should implement.

```
                    ┌─ propositions/some_proofs.py ─┐
#: Hypothetical syllogism
HS = InferenceRule([Formula.parse('(p->q)'), Formula.parse('(q->r)')],
                   Formula.parse('(p->r)'))

def prove_hypothetical_syllogism() -> Proof:
    """Proves `HS` via `MP`, `I0`, `I1`, and `D`.

    Returns:
        A valid proof of `HS` via the inference rules `MP`, `I0`, `I1`, and `D`.
    """
    # Task 5.5
```

Hint: Use the deduction theorem (5.2).

Indeed, while it is not very intricate to prove that 'r' holds given that 'p', '(p→q)', and '(q→r)' hold, proving the hypothetical syllogism above without using the deduction theorem (5.2) would have been more intricate and considerably less straightforward (even for this simple example) – just examine the resulting proof that your solution returns!

5.4   Proofs by Way of Contradiction

A ubiquitous proof strategy throughout mathematics is that of proof by way of contradiction: to prove a formula ϕ, we assume that its negation '~ϕ' holds. Based on this contrived assumption we attempt to prove an "obvious contradiction," for example that ψ holds even though we know that '~ψ' holds. If we succeed in proving such an "obvious contradiction," then we deduce from this that our contrived assumption '~ϕ' was flawed to begin with, that is, that ϕ in fact holds. As it turns out, while this proof strategy seems at first glance to be quite far from the "step-by-step" notion of deductive proofs that we have defined in Chapter 4, the ability to prove by way of contradiction in fact, as we will see in this section, follows from, and is one of the most profound consequences of, the deduction theorem (5.2).

To formalize the notion of proof by way of contradiction, we have to start with a **syntactic** definition of (proving) an "obvious contradiction." We emphasize that we may not resort to the semantic notion of a **contradiction**, which we have defined in Chapter 2 to be a formula that has no model, i.e., a formula whose negation is a tautology. (Indeed, in Section 2.B, we discussed that the question of whether a given formula is not a semantic contradiction is NP-complete – e.g., as hard as breaking any cryptographic code (!) – so identifying any semantic contradiction as such is not in any way an "obvious" thing to do.) The intuitive syntactic notion of an "obvious contradiction" is the formula 'F', and intuitively we aim to show that if one can prove the formula 'F' from some set of assumptions, then this uncovers an inconsistency in the set of assumptions. In particular, if one manages to prove 'F' from '~ϕ' as well as some other assumptions (i.e., assume the negation of ϕ and reach an "obvious contradiction"), then one can prove ϕ directly from these assumptions (without '~ϕ'). For technical reasons, though, we will wish to be able to work without the constant 'F' necessarily being part of our allowed operators throughout the bulk of Chapter 6 (more on this in that chapter), so instead of taking 'F' to be our "obvious contradiction," it will be more convenient to take the negation of our axioms as our "obvious contradiction." We will indeed do so, and we encourage you to disambiguate the syntactic notion of proofs by way of contradiction from the semantic notion of a contradiction by thinking about such proofs as **proofs by way of contradicting an axiom**. This way of thinking about such proofs will continue to be useful for us also in Part II of this book. (We will nonetheless continue to use the term "proof by way of contradiction" as it is standard.) For concreteness, we will take '~(p→p)' (the negation of the axiom I0) as our "obvious contradiction." While this may seem a bit arbitrary, we will in fact momentarily show that the details of the negation of which axiom is chosen do not really matter and all turn out to be equivalent. In fact, we will give five definitions that are equivalent as long as our axiomatic system contains the inference rules MP and I0, as well as the following (sound) inference rule:

I2: '(~p→(p→q))'

```
                    ┌─ propositions/axiomatic_systems.py ─┐
  # Axiomatic inference rules for not (and implies)

  #: Implication introduction (left)
  I2 = InferenceRule([], Formula.parse('(~p->(p->q))'))
                     ⋮
```

DEFINITION 5.1 (Consistency)   Let $\mathcal{R}$ be a set of inference rules that includes MP, I0, and I2, and may additionally include only inference rules with no assumptions. A set of formulas A is said to be (syntactically) **inconsistent** (with respect to $\mathcal{R}$) if one of the following five equivalent conditions holds:

1. The formula '~(p→p)' is provable (via $\mathcal{R}$) from the assumptions A.
2. The negation of *some* axiom (assumptionless inference rule from $\mathcal{R}$)[3] is provable from the assumptions A.
3. There exists some formula ϕ such that both ϕ and '~ϕ' are provable from the assumptions A.
4. Every formula ψ is provable from the assumptions A.
5. The negation of *every* axiom (assumptionless inference rule from $\mathcal{R}$) is provable from the assumptions A.

A set of formulas that is not inconsistent is called **consistent**.

   Definition 5.1 gives five equivalent syntactic definitions to the **syntactic** notion of an inconsistency. The equivalence of the first definition to the third and fourth definitions indeed shows that being able to prove '~(p→p)' is a natural (and not arbitrary) definition for an inconsistency of a set of assumptions. The equivalence of the first, second, and last definitions indeed shows that there is nothing special about '~(p→p)', in the sense that everything from this point onward would hold just the same if we replaced '~(p→p)' with the negation of any other axiom. (Indeed, by the above, if we can prove the negation of

---

[3] To avoid clutter, when we refer to an axiom as a formula, such as when talking about its negation, we more precisely mean the formula that is the axiom's conclusion (so "the negation of some axiom" more precisely means "the negation of the conclusion of some axiom").

any single axiom then we can prove '~(p→p)', and if we can prove '~(p→p)' then we can prove the negation of every other axiom.)

Let us see why these five definitions are equivalent: The fourth definition trivially implies the fifth one, the fifth one trivially implies the first one, and the first one trivially implies the second one. The second definition implies the third one since every axiom can be trivially proven, and thus if we take ϕ to be the axiom whose negation we can prove, then can prove both ϕ and '~ϕ'. It remains to show that the third definition implies the fourth one, which you will do in the next task using I2.

TASK 6   Implement the missing code for the function `proof_from_opposites(` `proof_of_affirmation, proof_of_negation, conclusion)`. This function takes as input a proof of some formula ϕ and a proof of its negation '~ϕ', both via the same inference rules and from the same assumptions (implying that these assumptions are inconsistent with respect to the used inference rules), and also takes as input some arbitrary `conclusion`. The function returns a proof of `conclusion` from the same assumptions via the same inference rules as well as MP and I2.

```
                      propositions/deduction.py

def prove_from_opposites(proof_of_affirmation: Proof,
                         proof_of_negation: Proof, conclusion: Formula) -> \
        Proof:
    """Combines the given proofs of a formula `affirmation` and its negation
    '~`affirmation`' into a proof of the given formula.

    Parameters:
        proof_of_affirmation: valid proof of `affirmation`.
        proof_of_negation: valid proof of '~`affirmation`' from the same
            assumptions and inference rules of `proof_of_affirmation`.
        conclusion: formula to prove.

    Returns:
        A valid proof of `conclusion` from the same assumptions as the given
        proofs, via the same inference rules as the given proofs and in addition
        `MP` and `I2`.
    """
    assert proof_of_affirmation.is_valid()
    assert proof_of_negation.is_valid()
    assert proof_of_affirmation.statement.assumptions == \
           proof_of_negation.statement.assumptions
    assert Formula('~', proof_of_affirmation.statement.conclusion) == \
           proof_of_negation.statement.conclusion
    assert proof_of_affirmation.rules == proof_of_negation.rules
    # Task 5.6
```

Hint: The function `combine_proofs()` that you implemented in Task 3 can ease the usage of the axiom I2.

Your solution to Task 6 concludes the proof of the following.

LEMMA 5.3   *The five definitions of inconsistency given above are indeed equivalent.*

We are now ready to formally justify the validity of the notion of a proof by way of contradiction. To do so, we will allow ourselves to use also the following additional (sound) axiom:

N: '$((\tilde{\ }q\rightarrow\tilde{\ }p)\rightarrow(p\rightarrow q))$'

```
                    propositions/axiomatic_systems.py
# Axiomatic inference rules for not (and implies)
                          ⋮
#: Converse contraposition
N = InferenceRule([], Formula.parse('((~q->~p)->(p->q))'))
```

TASK 7 (Programmatic Proof of the Theorem (5.3) on Soundness of Proofs by Way of Contradiction)   Implement the missing code for the function `prove_by_way_of_contradiction(proof)`, which takes a proof of '$\tilde{\ }(p\rightarrow p)$' from some assumptions as well as from the negation '$\tilde{\ }\phi$' of some formula, and returns a proof of the formula ϕ from these assumptions (without '$\tilde{\ }\phi$') via the same inference rules as well as MP, I0, I1, D, and N.

```
                       propositions/deduction.py
def prove_by_way_of_contradiction(proof: Proof) -> Proof:
    """Converts the given proof of '~(p->p)', the last assumption of which is an
    assumption '~`formula`', to a proof of `formula` from the same assumptions
    except '~`formula`'.

    Parameters:
        proof: valid proof of '~(p->p)' to convert, the last assumption of which
            is of the form '~`formula`', via some set of inference rules all of
            of which have no assumptions except perhaps `MP`.

    Returns:
        A valid proof of `formula` from the same assumptions as the given proof
        except the last one, via the same inference rules as the given proof and
        in addition `MP`, `I0`, `I1`, `D`, and `N`.
    """
    assert proof.is_valid()
    assert proof.statement.conclusion == Formula.parse('~(p->p)')
    assert len(proof.statement.assumptions) > 0
    assert proof.statement.assumptions[-1].root == '~'
    for rule in proof.rules:
        assert rule == MP or len(rule.assumptions) == 0
    # Task 5.7
```

Hint: Use the deduction theorem (5.2) (`remove_assumption(proof)`) and then the axiom N.

By your solution to Task 7, proving by way of contradiction (which would have indeed been more aptly named **proving by way of contradicting an axiom**) is a sound proof technique. Indeed, this is one of the most profound corollaries of the deduction theorem (5.2). What about the other direction? If we can prove ϕ from A, does this imply that $A\cup\{'\tilde{\ }\phi'\}$ is inconsistent? This turns out to trivially hold since if $A\vdash\phi$, then certainly $A\cup\{'\tilde{\ }\phi'\}\vdash\phi$, but also certainly $A \cup \{\text{`}\sim\phi\text{'}\} \vdash \text{`}\sim\phi\text{'}$. So we have proven not only that proving by way of contradiction is a sound proof technique, but in fact that anything that is provable can be proven by way of contradiction.

THEOREM 5.3 (Soundness of Proofs by Way of Contradiction)   *Let $\mathcal{R}$ be a set of inference rules that includes MP, I1, D, and N,[4] and may additionally include only inference rules with no assumptions. Let A be an arbitrary set of formulas, and let ϕ be an additional formula. Then $A \cup \{\text{`}\sim\phi\text{'}\}$ is inconsistent with respect to $\mathcal{R}$ if and only if $A \vdash_{\mathcal{R}} \phi$.*

---

[4] While we have actually proven this only for a set of inference rules that additionally includes also I0 and I2, you have already shown that I0 is provable via MP, I1, and D, and we will see in Chapter 6 that also I2 is provable via MP, I1, and D, so by the lemma theorem (5.1) we already phrase the theorem accordingly.

6 The Tautology Theorem and the Completeness of Propositional Logic

Recall from Chapter 4 the **soundness theorem** (4.1) for propositional logic: Any inference rule that is provable (using any set of sound inference rules) is sound. In this chapter, in which our analysis of propositional logic culminates, we will prove a converse of sorts: We will show that our proof system, with a specific small axiomatic set of sound inference rules – our **axiomatic system**, which specifically contains **modus ponens** as well as few **axioms** (assumptionless inference rules) – is **complete**, that is, can prove every sound inference rule. Our first and main step is to state and prove the **tautology theorem** (6.1): that every tautology is provable via our axiomatic system. Once we have that under our belt, it will not be difficult to extend this and show that also every sound inference rule is provable, i.e., that if some finite set of assumptions A entails a formula ϕ (i.e., if $A \models \phi$) then ϕ is indeed provable from A using our axiomatic system (i.e., $A \vdash \phi$). Finally, we will further extend this to infinite sets of assumptions, an extension which, due to its infinite nature, we will obviously not prove in a programmatic way but rather using "regular" mathematical reasoning. As we will see in Part II of this book, the tautology theorem (6.1) will also serve as a major building block of our proof of the pinnacle result of this entire book: the completeness theorem (6.5/6.6) for the richer predicate logic.

6.1 Our Axiomatic System

In the bulk of this chapter we will restrict ourselves to only allowing the logical operators '$\rightarrow$' and '$\sim$', disallowing '&', '|', 'T', and 'F'. As we have seen in Chapter 3, these two operators suffice for representing any Boolean function (i.e., synthesizing any truth table), and indeed many mathematical logic courses restrict their definitions to only these operators by either disallowing other operators completely or treating other operators as shorthands for expressions involving only these two operators (along the lines of the substitutions that you implemented in Chapter 3). In Section 6.A you will optionally see how the same results apply also to formulas that may use the other operators ('|', '&', 'T', 'F', and even others), provided that we add a few appropriate additional axioms to our axiomatic system.

Our axiomatic system – the set of inference rules that we will show to suffice for proving any inference rule – contains all the inference rules that were required for the various tasks of Chapter 5 (MP, I0, I1, D, I2, and N), as well as a few additional axioms:

MP: Assumptions: 'p', '(p→q)'; Conclusion: 'q'
  I0: '(p→p)'
  I1: '(q→(p→q))'
  D: '((p→(q→r))→((p→q)→(p→r)))'
  I2: '(~p→(p→q))'
  N: '((~q→~p)→(p→q))'
 NI: '(p→(~q→~(p→q)))'
NN: '(p→~~p)'
  R: '((q→p)→((~q→p)→p))'

```
                    propositions/axiomatic_systems.py
# Axiomatic inference rules that only contain implies

#: Modus ponens / implication elimination
MP = InferenceRule([Formula.parse('p'), Formula.parse('(p->q)')],
                   Formula.parse('q'))
#: Self implication
I0 = InferenceRule([], Formula.parse('(p->p)'))
#: Implication introduction (right)
I1 = InferenceRule([], Formula.parse('(q->(p->q))'))
#: Self-distribution of implication
D = InferenceRule([], Formula.parse('((p->(q->r))->((p->q)->(p->r)))'))

# Axiomatic inference rules for not (and implies)

#: Implication introduction (left)
I2 = InferenceRule([], Formula.parse('(~p->(p->q))'))
#: Converse contraposition
N = InferenceRule([], Formula.parse('((~q->~p)->(p->q))'))
#: Negative-implication introduction
NI = InferenceRule([], Formula.parse('(p->(~q->~(p->q)))'))
#: Double-negation introduction
NN = InferenceRule([], Formula.parse('(p->~~p)'))
#: Resolution
R = InferenceRule([], Formula.parse('((q->p)->((~q->p)->p))'))

#: Large axiomatic system for implication and negation, consisting of `MP`,
#: `I0`, `I1`, `D`, `I2`, `N`, `NI`, `NN`, and `R`.
AXIOMATIC_SYSTEM = frozenset({MP, I0, I1, D, I2, N, NI, NN, R})
```

It is straightforward to verify the soundness of each inference rule in this axiomatic system, and as already hinted in Chapter 5, your implementation of `is_sound_inference()` has in fact already done so: One of the ways in which we have tested it is by making sure that it successfully verifies the soundness of all of these inference rules.

Whenever we use the notation ⊢ in this chapter without explicitly specifying the allowed set $\mathcal{R}$ of inference rules (i.e., whenever we use ⊢ rather than ⊢$_\mathcal{R}$ for some $\mathcal{R}$), we will mean with respect to this axiomatic system as the allowed set of inference rules. This set was chosen for ease of use in the tasks of this chapter. Other, smaller, axiomatic systems that still give rise to complete proof systems are also possible. For example, notice that you have in fact already proven I0 via I1, D, and MP, so certainly by the lemma theorem (5.1) we can remove I0 from this axiomatic system without weakening its "proving power."

In fact, it turns out (you will optionally show this in Task 6.B) that the subset $\mathcal{H} = \{MP, I1, D, N\}$ of only four inference rules suggested by the nineteenth–twentieth-century German mathematician David Hilbert suffices for proving all the others in this axiomatic system. Thus, once we show that this axiomatic system can prove something, it follows by the lemma theorem (5.1) that also Hilbert's axiomatic system $\mathcal{H}$ can do so.[1] Thus, even though the tasks ahead allow using the full axiomatic system just defined, we will state our theorems for $\mathcal{H}$.

The full axiomatic system just defined was chosen as to directly match natural steps in the proofs to come. Specifically, if there is a proof step where we will need to soundly deduce some formula ψ from some other formula ϕ, then we have added to our axiomatic system an axiom of which '$(\phi \rightarrow \psi)$' is a specialization, which will allow us to directly derive ψ from ϕ as required, using an application of MP. If there is a proof step where we will need to soundly deduce some formula ψ from two other formulas ϕ_1 and ϕ_2, then we have added an axiom on which '$(\phi_1 \rightarrow (\phi_2 \rightarrow \psi))$' is a specialization to our axiomatic system. The functions `prove_corollary()` and `combine_proofs()` that you have implemented in Chapter 5 will therefore be very useful in applying these axioms – these encoded inference rules – in the corresponding proof steps.

The functions that you are asked to implement in this chapter are contained in the file `propositions/tautology.py` unless otherwise noted.

6.2   The Tautology Theorem

We now start our journey toward proving a tautology. The first step takes a single model (i.e., a single assignment of truth values to the variable names) and a formula ϕ that evaluates to *True* in this model (a central example being a formula ϕ that is a tautology, i.e., evaluates to *True* in *any* model) and proves the formula ϕ *in this model*. More formally, for each variable name x with value *True* in the given model we take the assumption 'x' and for each variable name x with value *False* in this model we take the assumption '~x'; from these assumptions (one for each variable name used in the formula), we wish to prove the formula ϕ (using the full axiomatic system defined above).

DEFINITION 6.1 (Formula(s) Capturing Assignment)   Given an assignment of a Boolean value b to a variable name x, the formula that **captures** this assignment is the formula 'x' if b is *True* and is the formula '~x' if b is *False*. Given a model $\{x_1 : b_1, x_2 : b_2, \ldots, x_n : b_n\}$, where each x_i is a variable name and each b_i is a Boolean value, the set of formulas that **captures** this model is the set of the n formulas that capture the n assignments in the model.

For example, the model $\{\text{'p'} : \textit{True}, \text{'q'} : \textit{False}, \text{'r'} : \textit{True}\}$ is captured by the set of formulas $\{\text{'p'}, \text{'~q'}, \text{'r'}\}$. Notice that this definition, while technically trivial, does achieve a transformation from the semantic world of models to the syntactic world of formulas, and as such is an important conceptual step in our proof of the tautology theorem (6.1). Now suppose that we have a formula ϕ that evaluates to *True* in this model, such as '$(p \rightarrow r)$', then our claim is that ϕ is provable, using our axiomatic system, from this set of formulas as assumptions. If, on the other hand, ϕ evaluates to *False* in this model then our claim is

---

[1] In fact, it is actually possible to derive all of our axioms from the following single axiom, in addition to MP: '$(((((p \rightarrow q) \rightarrow (\text{~}r \rightarrow \text{~}s)) \rightarrow r) \rightarrow t) \rightarrow ((t \rightarrow p) \rightarrow (s \rightarrow p)))$'.

that we can prove its negation '~ϕ', using our axiomatic system, from these assumptions. Given such a model and formula ϕ, such a proof (of ϕ or of '~ϕ') can with some care be constructed recursively:

- The base case is very simple since for a variable name x we already have the correct formula ('x' if x evaluates to *True*, and '~x' if x evaluates to *False*) in our set of assumptions.
- If ϕ is of the form '$(\phi_1 \to \phi_2)$' for some formulas ϕ_1 and ϕ_2, then:
  - If ϕ has value *True* in the given model, then either ϕ_1 has value *False* in this model or ϕ_2 has value *True* in it. In the former case we can recursively prove '~ϕ_1', while in the latter we can recursively prove ϕ_2. In the former case, the axiom I2 allows us to use '~ϕ_1' to prove ϕ, and in the latter case the axiom I1 allows us use ϕ_2 to prove ϕ.
  - Otherwise, ϕ has value *False* in the model, so both ϕ_1 is *True* and ϕ_2 is *False* in the model, and so we can recursively prove both ϕ_1 and '~ϕ_2'. Now, the axiom NI allows us to prove '~ϕ' from these two.
- Finally, if ϕ is of the form '~ψ' for some formula ψ, then:
  - If ϕ evaluates to *True*, then ψ evaluates to *False*, so we can recursively prove '~ψ' which is exactly ϕ, as needed.
  - Otherwise, ϕ evaluates to *False* so ψ evaluates to *True*, so we can recursively prove ψ, but our goal is to prove '~ϕ', that is, '~~ψ', which the axiom NN allows us to prove from ψ.

The fact that the axioms I2, NI, and NN (and I1), which this recursively constructed proof needs in order to work, are in our axiomatic system is of course no coincidence: We have added these axioms to our axiomatic system precisely to allow us to perform the various steps of the proof.

TASK 1

a. First, implement the missing code for the function `formulas_capturing_model(model)`, which returns the formulas that capture the given model.

```
propositions/tautology.py
```

```python
def formulas_capturing_model(model: Model) -> List[Formula]:
    """Computes the formulas that capture the given model: '`x`' for each
    variable name `x` that is assigned the value ``True`` in the given model,
    and '~`x`' for each variable name `x` that is assigned the value ``False``.

    Parameters:
        model: model to construct the formulas for.

    Returns:
        A list of the constructed formulas, ordered alphabetically by variable
        name.

    Examples:
        >>> formulas_capturing_model({'p2': False, 'p1': True, 'q': True})
        [p1, ~p2, q]
    """
    assert is_model(model)
    # Task 6.1a
```

b. Now, implement the missing code for the function `prove_in_model(formula, model)`, which takes a propositional formula (which may only contain '→' and '~' as operators) and a model, and returns a proof of either the formula (if it evaluates to *True* in the given model) or its negation (if the given formula evaluates to *False* in the given model) from the formulas that capture the given model as assumptions, via our axiomatic system.

propositions/tautology.py

```
def prove_in_model(formula: Formula, model:Model) -> Proof:
    """Either proves the given formula or proves its negation, from the formulas
    that capture the given model.

    Parameters:
        formula: formula that contains no constants or operators beyond '->' and
            '~', whose affirmation or negation is to prove.
        model: model from whose formulas to prove.

    Returns:
        If the `formula` evaluates to ``True`` in the given model, then a valid
        proof of `formula`; otherwise a valid proof of '~`formula`'. The
        returned proof is from the formulas that capture the given model, in the
        order returned by `formulas_capturing_model(model)`, via
        `AXIOMATIC_SYSTEM`.

    Examples:
        >>> proof = prove_in_model(Formula.parse('(p->q7)'),
        ...                        {'q7': False, 'p': False})
        >>> proof.is_valid()
        True
        >>> proof.statement.conclusion
        (p->q7)
        >>> proof.statement.assumptions
        (~p, ~q7)
        >>> proof.rules == AXIOMATIC_SYSTEM
        True

        >>> proof = prove_in_model(Formula.parse('(p->q7)'),
        ...                        {'q7': False, 'p': True})
        >>> proof.is_valid()
        True
        >>> proof.statement.conclusion
        ~(p->q7)
        >>> proof.statement.assumptions
        (p, ~q7)
        >>> proof.rules == AXIOMATIC_SYSTEM
        True
    """
    assert formula.operators().issubset({'->', '~'})
    assert is_model(model)
    # Task 6.1b
```

Your solution to Task 1 essentially[2] proves the following lemma.

---

[2] That is, up to using our full axiomatic system rather than $\mathcal{H}$. See Section 6.B for why $\mathcal{H}$ indeed suffices.

LEMMA 6.1   *Let ϕ be a formula that only uses the operators '$\rightarrow$' and '$\sim$'. If ϕ evaluates to True in a given model M, then ϕ is provable via $\mathcal{H}$ from the set of formulas that captures M. If ϕ evaluates to False in M, then '$\sim\phi$' is provable via $\mathcal{H}$ from the set of formulas that captures M.*

Lemma 6.1 implies, in particular, that if ϕ is a tautology, then we can prove it from any set of assumptions that correspond to any model over all of the variable names of ϕ. Our goal, though, is to show that a tautology is provable from no assumptions. We now take an additional step towards this goal by showing how to reduce the number of assumptions by one: How to combine proofs for two models that differ from each other by the value of a single variable name, to eliminate any assumptions regarding that variable name.

TASK 2   Implement the missing code for the function `reduce_assumption(proof_from_affirmation, proof_from_negation)`. This function takes as input two proofs, both proving the *same* conclusion via the same inference rules, from *almost* the same list of assumptions, with the only difference between the assumptions of the two proofs being that the last assumption of `proof_from_negation` is the negation of the last assumption of `proof_from_affirmation`. The function returns a proof of the same conclusion as both proofs, from the assumptions that are common to both proofs (i.e, all assumptions except the last one of each proof), via the same inference rules as well as MP, I0, I1, D, and R.

```
                    ( propositions/tautology.py )

def reduce_assumption(proof_from_affirmation: Proof,
                      proof_from_negation: Proof) -> Proof:
    """Combines the two given proofs, both of the same formula `conclusion` and
    from the same assumptions except that the last assumption of the latter is
    the negation of that of the former, into a single proof of `conclusion` from
    only the common assumptions.

    Parameters:
        proof_from_affirmation: valid proof of `conclusion` from one or more
            assumptions, the last of which is an assumption `assumption`.
        proof_from_negation: valid proof of `conclusion` from the same
            assumptions and inference rules of `proof_from_affirmation`, but
            with the last assumption being '~`assumption`' instead of
            `assumption`.

    Returns:
        A valid proof of `conclusion` from only the assumptions common to the
        given proofs (i.e., without the last assumption of each), via the same
        inference rules of the given proofs and in addition `MP`, `I0`, `I1`,
        `D`, and `R`.

    Examples:
        If `proof_from_affirmation` is of ``['p', '~q', 'r'] ==> '(p&(r|~r))'``,
        then `proof_from_negation` must be of
        ``['p', '~q', '~r'] ==> '(p&(r|~r))'`` and the returned proof is of
        ``['p', '~q'] ==> '(p&(r|~r))'``.
    """
    assert proof_from_affirmation.is_valid()
    assert proof_from_negation.is_valid()
    assert proof_from_affirmation.statement.conclusion == \
```

```
            proof_from_negation.statement.conclusion
    assert len(proof_from_affirmation.statement.assumptions) > 0
    assert len(proof_from_negation.statement.assumptions) > 0
    assert proof_from_affirmation.statement.assumptions[:-1] == \
           proof_from_negation.statement.assumptions[:-1]
    assert Formula('~', proof_from_affirmation.statement.assumptions[-1]) == \
           proof_from_negation.statement.assumptions[-1]
    assert proof_from_affirmation.rules == proof_from_negation.rules
    # Task 6.2
```

Hint: Use the deduction theorem (5.2) (`remove_assumption()` from Chapter 5) and the axiom R.

Once again, the fact that the axiom R, on which your solution to Task 2 relies, is in our axiomatic system is of course no coincidence: We have added this axioms to our axiomatic system precisely because of this. We also note that your solution to Task 2 is the crucial place where the deduction theorem (5.2) is used on the way to proving the tautology theorem (6.1), as well as the completeness theorem (6.5/6.6) for propositional logic.

Since Task 1 allows us to prove a tautology ϕ from the set of assumptions that correspond to *any* model, we can keep combining the "combined proofs" resulting from Task 2, each time reducing the number of variable names in the assumptions by one, until we remain with no assumptions. This is precisely how you will now prove the tautology theorem (6.1).

TASK 3 (Programmatic Proof of the Tautology Theorem (6.1))

a. Implement the missing code for the function `prove_tautology(tautology, model)`, which returns a proof of the given tautology, via our axiomatic system, from the assumptions that capture the given model, which is a model over a (possibly empty) prefix of the variable names of the given tautology. In particular, if the given model is over the empty set of variable names (the default) then the returned proof is of the given tautology from no assumptions.

propositions/tautology.py

```
def prove_tautology(tautology: Formula, model: Model = frozendict()) -> Proof:
    """Proves the given tautology from the formulas that capture the given
    model.

    Parameters:
        tautology: tautology that contains no constants or operators beyond '->'
            and '~', to prove.
        model: model over a (possibly empty) prefix (with respect to the
            alphabetical order) of the variable names of `tautology`, from whose
            formulas to prove.

    Returns:
        A valid proof of the given tautology from the formulas that capture the
        given model, in the order returned by `formulas_capturing_model(model)`,
        via `AXIOMATIC_SYSTEM`.

    Examples:
        >>> proof = prove_tautology(Formula.parse('(~(p->p)->q)'),
```

```
...                          {'p': True, 'q': False})
>>> proof.is_valid()
True
>>> proof.statement.conclusion
(~(p->p)->q)
>>> proof.statement.assumptions
(p, ~q)
>>> proof.rules == AXIOMATIC_SYSTEM
True

>>> proof = prove_tautology(Formula.parse('(~(p->p)->q)'))
>>> proof.is_valid()
True
>>> proof.statement.conclusion
(~(p->p)->q)
>>> proof.statement.assumptions
()
>>> proof.rules == AXIOMATIC_SYSTEM
True
"""
assert is_tautology(tautology)
assert tautology.operators().issubset({'->', '~'})
assert is_model(model)
assert sorted(tautology.variables())[:len(model)] == sorted(model.keys())
# Task 6.3a
```

Guidelines: If the given model is over all the variable names of the given tautology, simply construct the proof using `prove_in_model(tautology, model)`. Otherwise, recursively call `prove_tautology()` with models that also have assignments to the next variable name that is unassigned in the given model, and then use the `reduce_assumption()` function that you have just implemented.

b. Implement the missing code for the function `proof_or_counterexample( formula)`, which either returns a proof of the given formula from no assumptions via our axiomatic system (if this formula is a tautology) or returns a model in which the given formula does not hold (if this formula is not a tautology).

```
                    ┌─────────────────────────────┐
                    │ propositions/tautology.py   │
                    └─────────────────────────────┘
def proof_or_counterexample(formula: Formula) -> Union[Proof, Model]:
    """Either proves the given formula or finds a model in which it does not
    hold.

    Parameters:
        formula: formula that contains no constants or operators beyond '->' and
            '~', to either prove or find a counterexample for.

    Returns:
        If the given formula is a tautology, then an assumptionless proof of the
        formula via `AXIOMATIC_SYSTEM`, otherwise a model in which the given
        formula does not hold.
    """
    assert formula.operators().issubset({'->', '~'})
    # Task 6.3b
```

You have now shown that every tautology is provable via our (sound) axiomatic system, and since the soundness theorem (4.1) asserts (in particular) that any formula that is provable via any sound set of inference rules is a tautology, you have essentially proven the following theorem, giving a remarkable connection between the semantic and syntactic realms, by stating that any universal truth is provable.

THEOREM 6.1 (The Tautology Theorem)   *Every tautology is provable from no assumptions via* $\mathcal{H}$. *Thus, for any formula ϕ it is the case that $\models \phi$ if and only if $\vdash_{\mathcal{H}} \phi$.*

6.3   The Completeness Theorem for Finite Sets

The tautology theorem (6.1) directly implies also more general variants of basically the same idea. The first generalization shows that our axiomatic system can be used not only to prove any tautology – that is, any sound inference rule *that has no assumptions* – but in fact to prove any sound inference rule *whatsoever*. Despite its strength, this is in fact a relatively easy corollary as we have already seen in Chapter 5 that one may easily "encode" any inference rule as one without assumptions, such that if the rule is sound then its encoding is a tautology, and such that it is rather easy to get a proof of the rule from a proof of its encoding. In the next task, you will prove this generalization.

TASK 4 (Programmatic Proof of the "Provability" Version of the Completeness Theorem (6.2) for Finite Sets)

a. Start by implementing the missing code for the function `encode_as_formula(rule)`, which returns a single formula that "encodes" the given inference rule.

```
                    ┌──────────────────────────────┐
                    │ propositions/tautology.py    │
┌───────────────────┴──────────────────────────────┴───────────────────┐
│ def encode_as_formula(rule):                                          │
│     """Encodes the given inference rule as a formula consisting of a chain of │
│     implications.                                                     │
│                                                                       │
│     Parameters:                                                       │
│         rule: inference rule to encode.                               │
│                                                                       │
│     Returns:                                                          │
│         The formula encoding the given rule.                          │
│                                                                       │
│     Examples:                                                         │
│         >>> encode_as_formula(InferenceRule([Formula('p1'), Formula('p2'), │
│         ...                                   Formula('p3'), Formula('p4')], │
│         ...                                   Formula('q')))          │
│         (p1->(p2->(p3->(p4->q))))                                     │
│                                                                       │
│         >>> encode_as_formula(InferenceRule([], Formula('q')))        │
│         q                                                             │
│     """                                                               │
│     # Task 6.4a                                                       │
└───────────────────────────────────────────────────────────────────────┘
```

b. Implement the missing code for the function `prove_sound_rule(rule)`, which takes a sound inference rule, and returns a proof for it via our axiomatic system.

```
                       ┌─ propositions/tautology.py ─┐
def prove_sound_inference(rule: InferenceRule) -> Proof:
    """Proves the given sound inference rule.

    Parameters:
        rule: sound inference rule whose assumptions and conclusion contain no
            constants or operators beyond '->' and '~', to prove.

    Returns:
        A valid proof of the given sound inference rule via `AXIOMATIC_SYSTEM`.
    """
    assert is_sound_inference(rule)
    for formula in {rule.conclusion}.union(rule.assumptions):
        assert formula.operators().issubset({'->', '~'})
    # Task 6.4b
```

Your solution to Task 4 proves that if a set of assumptions entails a conclusion, then it is indeed possible to prove this conclusion from these assumptions via our (sound) axiomatic system. Thus (similarly to the proof of the tautology theorem (6.1)), together with the soundness theorem (4.1) that gives the converse (for any sound axiomatic system), you have essentially proven the following theorem, expanding our understanding of the connection between the semantic and syntactic realms that we unearthed with the tautology theorem (6.1).

THEOREM 6.2 (The Completeness Theorem for Finite Sets: "Provability" Version)   *For any finite set of formulas A and any formula ϕ, it is the case that $A \models \phi$ if and only if $A \vdash_{\mathcal{H}} \phi$.*

A somewhat more minimalistic and symmetric way to look at the completeness theorem (6.2) is to "move" the conclusion ϕ into the set of assumptions. More specifically, note that by definition, $A \models \phi$ is equivalent to $A \cup \{`\sim\phi`\}$ not having a model, and by the theorem (5.3) on soundness of proofs by way of contradiction, $A \vdash \phi$ is equivalent to $A \cup \{`\sim\phi`\}$ being inconsistent. This allows us to rephrase the completeness theorem (6.2) as an equivalence between the semantic notion of a set of formulas (analogous to $A \cup \{`\sim\phi`\}$, but note that '$\sim\phi$' no longer plays a different role here than any of the formulas in A!) not having a model, and the syntactic notion of the same set of formulas being inconsistent.

TASK 5 (Programmatic Proof of the "Consistency" Version of the Completeness Theorem (6.3) for Finite Sets)   Implement the missing code for the function `model_or_inconsistency(formulas)`, which returns either a model of the given formulas (if such a model exists) or a proof of '$\sim(p\rightarrow p)$' via our axiomatic system from the given formulas as assumptions (if such a model does not exist).

```
                       ┌─ propositions/tautology.py ─┐
def model_or_inconsistency(formulas: Sequence[Formula]) -> Union[Model, Proof]:
    """Either finds a model in which all the given formulas hold, or proves
    '~(p->p)' from these formulas.

    Parameters:
        formulas: formulas that use only the operators '->' and '~', to either
            find a model of, or prove '~(p->p)' from.
```

```
Returns:
    A model in which all of the given formulas hold if such exists,
    otherwise a valid proof of '~(p->p)' from the given formulas via
    `AXIOMATIC_SYSTEM`.
"""
for formula in formulas:
    assert formula.operators().issubset({'->', '~'})
# Task 6.5
```

Hint: If a model of the given formulas does not exist, what can you say about the inference rule with the given formulas as assumptions, and with conclusion '~(p→p)'? Is it sound? Why? Now how can you use your solution to Task 4 to complete your solution? Make sure that you completely understand why your solution works, and do not just be content with it passing our tests.

Your solution for Task 5 indeed proves a version of the completeness theorem (6.2) that is phrased in a more symmetric manner using the semantic notion of having a model and the syntactic notion of consistency.

THEOREM 6.3 (The Completeness Theorem for Finite Sets: "Consistency" Version) *A finite set of formulas has a model if and only if it is consistent with respect to $\mathcal{H}$.*

6.4   The Compactness Theorem and the Completeness Theorem for Infinite Sets

The theorems we have proven so far in this chapter only proved equivalences between syntactic and semantic notions for *finite* sets of formulas. For example, our last version of the completeness theorem (6.3) stated that a *finite* consistent set of formulas has a model. Does an infinite consistent set of formulas necessarily also have a model? Before providing an answer to this question, let us examine the syntactic definitions of proofs and consistency, and the semantic notions of truth and having a model, for infinite sets of formulas/assumptions.

The definition of a formula ϕ being provable from a set A of assumptions is that a proof exists, and by definition a proof has a *finite* number of lines in it (much like in our discussion of the length of a formula toward the end of Chapter 1, the number of lines of a proof is finite yet unbounded).[3] If the set A is infinite, then any of its infinitely many formulas can be used as an assumption in the proof, but since the proof has finite length, only some finite subset of the assumptions will actually be used in any given proof. Therefore, since inconsistency is defined as having a proof of both a formula and its negation, we have that if an infinite set A is inconsistent, then some finite subset of A (the formulas that appear in the finite proof of the formula and/or in the finite proof of its negation) is already inconsistent. This shows the following trivial lemma.

---

[3] Indeed, trying to define any alternative notion of "proofs of infinite length" would completely circumvent the most fundamental goal of mathematical logic: understanding what is possible for humans to prove.

LEMMA 6.2 *A set of propositional formulas is consistent if and only if every finite subset of it is consistent.*

Thus there is really "nothing new" when dealing with infinite sets in terms of the syntactic notions of proofs and consistency – everything can be reduced to finite sets.

Let us now consider the semantic notion of an infinite set A of formulas having a model. The definition requires that the model satisfy every formula in the infinite set. While every formula is, by definition, finite, and thus uses only finitely many variable names, since there are infinitely many formulas in the set, there may be infinitely many variable names that are used altogether in all formulas in the set, so our model will have to be an infinite object: an assignment of a truth value to every variable name that appears in any formula in the set. Determining whether the model satisfies any given formula is still a finite question since any single formula uses only finitely many of the variable names in the model, but the whole notion of an infinite model is new. In particular, so far we have not developed any method of constructing infinite models, so it is not clear how we can construct a model that satisfies an infinite set of formulas.

Surprisingly, it turns out that the question of whether an infinite set of formulas has a model can also be reduced to whether all of its finite subsets have models. For reasons that we will touch on soon, this result is called the **compactness theorem** for propositional logic.

THEOREM 6.4 (The Compactness Theorem for Propositional Logic) *A set of propositional formulas has a model if and only if every finite subset of it has a model.*

The "only if" direction of this theorem is trivial: if the set A has a model, then this model is a model of every subset of A (finite or otherwise). The "if" direction of this theorem is actually quite surprising. Let us look at an analogous statement with "formulas" over real numbers. Consider the set of inequalities $\{x \geq 1, x \geq 2, x \geq 3, \ldots\}$. Clearly every finite subset of these inequalities has a model, i.e., a real number x that satisfies every inequality in this finite subset (say, take the maximum of all of the numbers that are "mentioned" in this finite subset). However, no model, i.e., no value of x, satisfies *all* of these infinitely many inequalities (the set of natural numbers contains no maximum element!). In mathematics, and specifically in the branch of mathematics called **topology**, the property that an infinite set of constraints is guaranteed to have a "solution" (a.k.a. a model, a.k.a. nonempty intersection) if every finite subset of it has one is called **compactness**. Thus, the compactness theorem (6.4) for propositional logic is so named since it asserts that for any family of variable names, the space of models over these variable names is **compact** with respect to the constraints of satisfying formulas, and this theorem is in fact a special case one of the cornerstone theorems of topology, **Tychonoff's theorem**, which asserts that all of the spaces in a very large family of spaces (including, for any family of variable names, the space of all models over these variable names, and also including many other spaces) have this property.[4] We will now give a direct proof of the

---

[4] A remark for readers with a background in topology: viewing the set of all models as the set of Boolean assignments to countably many variable names, $\{True, False\}^{\mathbb{N}}$, it turns out that the set of models satisfying a

compactness theorem (6.4) for propositional logic that does not require any background in topology.

Proof of the Compactness Theorem for Propositional Logic   We prove the "if" direction, that is, we assume that every finite subset of a set F of formulas has a model, and we will construct a model of F. Let us enumerate the variable names used anywhere in the set of formulas as $x_1, x_2, \ldots$, and let us enumerate the formulas in the set as $\phi_1, \phi_2, \ldots$. (By Theorem 1.2 there are only countably many of each, so we can indeed enumerate them.[5]) A model is an assignment of a truth value to each of the (possibly infinitely many) variable names. We will build the desired model step by step, at each step i deciding which truth value to assign to x_i. Our goal is to pick the truth value to assign to x_i at the ith step to maintain the following property: For every finite subset of the formulas in F, there exists a model that satisfies all of them and has the already-fixed truth values for $x_1, \ldots, x_i$.

Clearly, at the beginning before the first step, the required property holds as we have not fixed any truth values yet, so the assumption of the theorem is exactly this property for $i = 0$. Now let us assume that we already fixed truth values for $x_1, \ldots, x_{i-1}$ with the required property for $i-1$, and see that we can also fix a truth value for x_i in a way that maintains the required property for i. For each j let us examine the finite set of formulas $F_j = \{\phi_1, \phi_2, \ldots, \phi_j\}$. Given the required property for $i-1$, for every j there exists a model of F_j with the already-fixed truth values of $x_1, \ldots, x_{i-1}$, so let us consider such a model for each j. Each of these models (that correspond to different values of j) assigns some truth value to x_i, and since there are only two possible truth values, one (at least) of these two values is assigned to x_i by infinitely many of these models. We will pick such a value as our fixed value for x_i. To see that we have the required property for i, consider any finite set $G \subseteq F$. Since G is finite, it is contained in some F_k, and since the value that we fixed for x_i is assigned to it by models corresponding to infinitely many values of j, there exists some $j \geq k$ such that the model that satisfies all of F_j assigns this truth value to x_i (and also has the already-fixed truth values for $x_1, \ldots, x_{i-1}$ since we only looked at models with

---

given formula is **closed** with respect to the **product topology** over $\{True, False\}^{\mathbb{N}}$, since belonging to this set depends only on finitely many variable name assignments. So, since Tychonoff's theorem asserts that the product of any collection of compact topological spaces is compact with respect to the product topology, we have as a special case that $\{True, False\}^{\mathbb{N}}$ is compact with respect to the product topology, and so its closed sets satisfy the **finite intersection property**: Any collection of closed sets with an empty intersection has a finite subcollection with an empty intersection, which proves the compactness theorem (6.4) for propositional logic. Unsurprisingly, the direct proof that we will give for the compactness theorem (6.4) for propositional logic is in fact quite similar to a popular proof of the special case of Tychonoff's theorem for countable products of general metric spaces (the latter proof proves that the product space is sequentially compact, which suffices since the product of countably many metric spaces is metrizable, and for metrizable spaces sequential compactness is equivalent to compactness).

[5] As discussed in Chapter 1, according to our definitions the set of variable names is countably infinite and therefore so is the set of formulas, so we can enumerate each of them. If we allowed using variable names from a set of greater infinite cardinality (e.g., constant names like c_α where α is a real number, which are impossible to enumerate), then the set of all possible formulas would also no longer be countable, and therefore we would not be able to enumerate either of these sets. The compactness theorem (6.4) would still hold, though, and could be proven via analogous core arguments but with some additional supporting arguments that would require some background in set theory. Alternatively, even for variable name sets of arbitrary cardinality, the compactness theorem (6.4) for propositional logic is still a special case of, and therefore implied by, Tychonoff's theorem.

these fixed values). Since $G \subseteq F_k \subseteq F_j$, this model satisfies G as required and therefore the required property holds also for i.

We have finished describing the construction of the model – a construction that assigned a truth value to every variable name x_i. To complete the proof, we need to show that this model indeed satisfies all of F. Take any formula $\phi \in F$, and let n be the largest index of a variable name that appears in it. The truth value of ϕ depends only on the truth values of the variable names $x_1, \ldots, x_n$, and since we picked the n fixed truth values of these variable names in a way that guarantees that there exists a model with these truth values that satisfies any finite subset of F, and in particular satisfies the singleton set $\{\phi\}$, we conclude that all models that have these fixed values for $x_1, \ldots, x_n$ satisfy ϕ, including the model that we constructed. □

We are now in an enviable state where both the syntactic question of being consistent and the semantic question of having a model can be reduced to finite sets, for which we have already proven the equivalence between the two, so we can now get the same equivalence for infinite sets as well:

THEOREM 6.5 (The Completeness Theorem for Propositional Logic: "Consistency" Version) *A set of formulas has a model if and only if it is consistent with respect to $\mathcal{H}$.*

Proof By the compactness theorem (6.4), a set of formulas has a model if and only if every finite subset of it has a model, which by the "consistency" version of the completeness theorem (6.3) for finite sets holds if and only if every finite subset of it is consistent, which by Lemma 6.2 holds if and only if the entire set is consistent. An illustration of this argument is given in Figure 6.1. □

Again, the formalism of the **completeness theorem** that we have just proven is directly equivalent to the other formalism, completing our understanding of the equivalence within propositional logic of the semantic notion of entailment and the syntactic notion of provability.

THEOREM 6.6 (The Completeness Theorem for Propositional Logic: "Provability" Version) *For any set of formulas A and any formula ϕ, it is the case that $A \models \phi$ if and only if $A \vdash_{\mathcal{H}} \phi$.*

Proof $A \models \phi$ is by definition equivalent to $A \cup \{\sim\phi\}$ not having a model, and by the theorem (5.3) on soundness of proofs by way of contradiction, $A \vdash \phi$ is equivalent to $A \cup \{\sim\phi\}$ being inconsistent (nothing in the proof of that theorem depended on the finiteness of A). Therefore, this version of the completeness theorem follows immediately from its "consistency" version (Theorem 6.5). □

6.A Optional Reading: Adding Additional Operators

Throughout this chapter we limited ourselves to formulas that only used negation ('$\sim$') and implication ('$\rightarrow$'). As we have seen in Chapter 3 that these two operators form a complete set of operators, we have not lost any proving power by limiting ourselves this way. But what if we want to consider general formulas that may also contain the additional operators '&', '|', 'T', and 'F'? One way to treat this question is to view these operators as simply

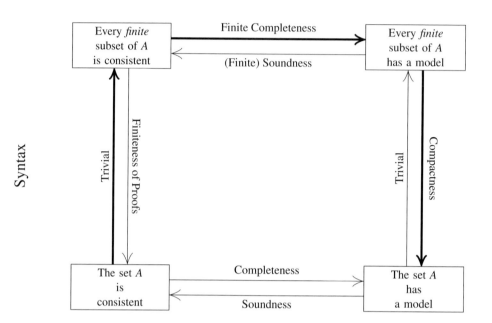

Figure 6.1 Diagram relating the completeness and compactness theorems. The **thick** arrows trace our proof of the "hard direction" of the completeness theorem (6.5) for propositional logic using finite completeness (Theorem 6.3) and compactness (Theorem 6.4).

shorthand notation for a full expression that is always only written using negation and implication (along the lines of the substitutions that you implemented in Chapter 3). Under this point of view, it is clear that everything that we proved in this chapter continues to hold, since the new operators are only "syntactic sugar" while the "real" formulas continue to be of the form discussed.

A more direct approach would nonetheless want to actually consider general formulas that may contain '&', '|', 'T', and 'F' as primitive operators, as we have done up to this chapter.[6] It is clear that without further axioms we will not be able to prove anything about a formula like '(p|~p)'. We will thus have to add to our axiomatic systems additional (sound) axioms that essentially capture the properties of these additional operators:

A: '(p→(q→(p&q)))'
NA1: '(~q→~(p&q))'
NA2: '(~p→~(p&q))'

---

[6] One may similarly want to handle as primitives even more operators as introduced in Chapter 3. While this can be similarly done, we will stick to these four operators for the purposes of this section.

O1: '(q→(p|q))'
O2: '(p→(p|q))'
NO: '(~p→(~q→~(p|q)))'
T: 'T'
NF: '~F'

```
                    propositions/axiomatic_systems.py

# Axiomatic inference rules for conjunction (and implication and negation)

#: Conjunction introduction
A = InferenceRule([], Formula.parse('(p->(q->(p&q)))'))
#: Negative-conjunction introduction (right)
NA1 = InferenceRule([], Formula.parse('(~q->~(p&q))'))
#: Negative-conjunction introduction (left)
NA2 = InferenceRule([], Formula.parse('(~p->~(p&q))'))

# Axiomatic inference rules for disjunction (and implication and negation)

# Disjunction introduction (right)
O1 = InferenceRule([], Formula.parse('(q->(p|q))'))
# Disjunction introduction (left)
O2 = InferenceRule([], Formula.parse('(p->(p|q))'))
# Negative-disjunction introduction
NO = InferenceRule([], Formula.parse('(~p->(~q->~(p|q)))'))

# Axiomatic inference rules for constants (and implication and negation)

#: Truth introduction
T =  InferenceRule([], Formula.parse('T'))
#: Negative-falsity introduction
NF = InferenceRule([], Formula.parse('~F'))

#: Large axiomatic system for all operators, consisting of the rules in
#: `AXIOMATIC_SYSTEM`, as well as `A`, `NA1`, `NA2`, `O1`, `O2`, `NO`, `T`, and
#: `NF`.
AXIOMATIC_SYSTEM_FULL = \
    frozenset(AXIOMATIC_SYSTEM.union({A, NA1, NA2, O1, O2, NO, T, NF}))
```

So our augmented axiomatic system contains all together seventeen rules: the original nine rules, as well as these additional eight rules. As in the beginning of this chapter, these additional axioms were chosen not for frugality in the number of axioms or for aesthetic reasons, but rather for ease of use. Indeed, once again it turns out (you will optionally show this in Section 6.B) that a smaller and in a sense also more aesthetic subset $\hat{\mathcal{H}}$ of only twelve inference rules suffices for proving all the others in the above augmented axiomatic system, so once again even though the subsequent Optional Task 6 allows using the full augmented axiomatic system just defined, the lemma theorem (5.1) allows us to state the corresponding theorem for $\hat{\mathcal{H}}$.

Essentially the only place where something has to be augmented in our analysis so far (and in your already-coded solution to the previous tasks of this chapter) to support these additional operators is Lemma 6.1 (corresponding to the function `prove_in_model()` that you have implemented in your solution to Task 1). That proof of that lemma proceeded by induction (recursion) on the formula structure and was tailored closely to the two operators that we allowed to appear there. The same induction/recursion however can be very similarly extended to also handle the additional operators using the new axioms that we have introduced in this section.

OPTIONAL TASK 6   Implement the missing code[7] for the function `prove_in_model_full(formula, model)`, which has the same functionality as `prove_in_model(formula, model)` except that the given formula may contain also the operators '&', '|', 'T', and 'F', and the returned proof is via the seventeen inference rules in `AXIOMATIC_SYSTEM_FULL`.

propositions/tautology.py

```
def prove_in_model_full(formula: Formula, model: Model) -> Proof:
    """Either proves the given formula or proves its negation, from the formulas
    that capture the given model.

    Parameters:
        formula: formula that contains no operators beyond '->', '~', '&', and
            '|' (and may contain constants), whose affirmation or negation is to
            prove.
        model: model from whose formulas to prove.

    Returns:
        If `formula` evaluates to ``True`` in the given model, then a valid
        proof of `formula`; otherwise a valid proof of '~`formula`'. The
        returned proof is from the formulas that capture the given model, in the
        order returned by `formulas_capturing_model(model)`, via
        `AXIOMATIC_SYSTEM_FULL`.

    Examples:
        >>> proof = prove_in_model_full(Formula.parse('(p&q7)'),
        ...                             {'q7': True, 'p': True})
        >>> proof.is_valid()
        True
        >>> proof.statement.conclusion
        (p&q7)
        >>> proof.statement.assumptions
        (p, q7)
        >>> proof.rules == AXIOMATIC_SYSTEM_FULL
        True

        >>> proof = prove_in_model_full(Formula.parse('(p&q7)'),
        ...                             {'q7': False, 'p': True})
        >>> proof.is_valid()
        True
        >>> proof.statement.conclusion
        ~(p&q7)
        >>> proof.statement.assumptions
        (p, ~q7)
        >>> proof.rules == AXIOMATIC_SYSTEM_FULL
        True
    """
    assert formula.operators().issubset({'T', 'F', '->', '~', '&', '|'})
```

---

[7] Start by copying the code of your implementation of `prove_in_model()`, and then extend it.

```
    assert is_model(model)
    # Optional Task 6.6
```

Your solution to Optional Task 6 gives us a general version of the lemma (6.1) that corresponds to Task 1, this time for formulas that may also use the operators *and*, *or*, *T*, and *F*, in addition to *not* and *implies*.

LEMMA 6.3   *Let ϕ be a formula (that may use any of the operators '~', '$\rightarrow$', '|', '&', 'T', and 'F'). If ϕ evaluates to True in a given model M, then ϕ is provable via $\hat{\mathcal{H}}$ from the set of formulas that captures M. If ϕ evaluates to False in M, then '~ϕ' is provable via $\hat{\mathcal{H}}$ from the set of formulas that captures M.*

Once you have solved Optional Task 6 and have thus proved the generalized Lemma 6.3, you could now replace every call to `prove_in_model()` in your code with a call to `prove_in_model_full()` (and replace every reference to Lemma 6.1 in our analysis with a reference to the generalized Lemma 6.3) and all your code should then run[8] (and all proofs should then hold) for general formulas, with our augmented axiomatic system in lieu of the old one.

6.B   Optional Reading: Other Axiomatic Systems

As noted throughout this chapter, we have chosen the axiomatic systems so far to allow for our proofs and code to be as simple as possible. In this section, we will explore other axiomatic systems that still give rise to a complete proof system that are popular due to their small size or due to other aesthetic reasons. Our first order of business is of course to show that the axiomatic system $\mathcal{H} = \{MP, I1, D, N\}$ still gives rise to a complete proof system (if our formulas may contain only *implies* and *not*).

```
                    propositions/axiomatic_systems.py
#: Hilbert axiomatic system for implication and negation, consisting of `MP`,
#: `I1`, `D`, and `N`.
HILBERT_AXIOMATIC_SYSTEM = frozenset({MP, I1, D, N})
```

To prove that $\mathcal{H}$ gives rise to a complete proof system, by the lemma theorem (5.1) it suffices to prove via only $\mathcal{H}$ all of the other axioms of the axiomatic system that we have already proven to give rise to a complete proof system, i.e., I0, I2, NI, NN, and R. As you have already proven I0 via (a subset of) $\mathcal{H}$ in Chapter 4, it in fact suffices to prove I2, NI, NN, and R, via MP, I0, I1, D, and N. The deduction theorem (5.2), both directly (by its explicit use) and indirectly (by using hypothetical syllogisms, via your implementation of `prove_hypothetical_syllogism()` from Chapter 5), will be instrumental in proving these. The functions that you are asked to implement in this section are contained in the file `propositions/some_proofs.py`.

---

[8] Some assertions would also have to be changed for this to actually run.

OPTIONAL TASK 7   Prove the rules I2, NI, NN, and R, each via (a subset of your choosing of) MP, I0, I1, D, and N. The proofs should be, respectively, returned by the functions `prove_I2()`, `prove_NI()`, `prove_NN()`, and `prove_R()`, whose missing code you should implement.

```
                                propositions/some_proofs.py

def prove_I2() -> Proof:
    """Proves `I2` via `MP`, `I0`, `I1`, `D`, `N`.

    Returns:
        A valid proof of `I2` via the inference rules `MP`, `I0`, `I1`, `D`, and
        `N`.
    """
    # Optional Task 6.7a
      ⋮

def prove_NN() -> Proof:
    """Proves `NN` via `MP`, `I0`, `I1`, `D`, `N`.

    Returns:
        A valid proof of `NN` via the inference rules `MP`, `I0`, `I1`, `D`, and
        `N`.
    """
    # Optional Task 6.7c
      ⋮

def prove_NI() -> Proof:
    """Proves `NI` via `MP`, `I0`, `I1`, `D`, `N`.

    Returns:
        A valid proof of `NI` via the inference rules `MP`, `I0`, `I1`, `D`, and
        `N`.
    """
    # Optional Task 6.7e
      ⋮

def prove_R() -> Proof:
    """Proves `R` via `MP`, `I0`, `I1`, `D`, `N`.

    Returns:
        A valid proof of `R` via the inference rules `MP`, `I0`, `I1`, `D`, and
        `N`.
    """
    # Optional Task 6.7g
```

Guidelines: Use the following strategy.

a. Prove I2 (implement the missing code for `prove_I2()`).

   Hint: Use a hypothetical syllogism (see Task 5 in Chapter 5) whose assumptions are specializations of I1 and N.

b. Prove that '($\sim\sim$p$\rightarrow$p)' (implement the missing code for the function `_prove_NNE()` in the same file).

   Hint: Use the deduction theorem (5.2), i.e., assume '$\sim\sim$p' and deduce 'p'. To do so, first prove that '($\sim\sim$p$\rightarrow$($\sim\sim$p$\rightarrow$p))' by "chaining" two hypothetical syllogisms (so the conclusion of the first hypothetical syllogism serves as the first assumption of the second hypothetical syllogism). As the first assumption for the first hypothetical syllogism, use '($\sim\sim$p→($\sim\sim\sim\sim$p→$\sim\sim$p))' (what is this a specialization of?), and as all other assumptions use specializations of N.

c. Prove NN (implement the missing code for `prove_NN()`).
   Hint: Apply MP to an appropriate specialization of N.

d. Prove that '((p→q)→($\sim$q→$\sim$p))' (implement the missing code for the function `_prove_CP()` in the same file).
   Hint: First use the deduction theorem (5.2) (twice) to prove '((p→q)→($\sim\sim$p→$\sim\sim$q))'.

e. Prove NI (implement the missing code for `prove_NI()`).
   Hint: Use a specialization of the assumptionless rule that you have proved in the previous step of this task to prove '($\sim$q→$\sim$(p→q))' from 'p'.

f. Prove the inference rule with assumption '($\sim$p→p)' and conclusion 'p' (implement the missing code for the function `_prove_CM()` in the same file).
   Hint: Start your proof with a single line whose conclusion is the formula '(($\sim$p→(p→$\sim$($\sim$p→p)))→(($\sim$p→p)→($\sim$p→$\sim$($\sim$p→p))))'.

g. Prove R (implement the missing code for `prove_R()`).
   Hint: Use the deduction theorem (5.2) twice, i.e., prove the inference rule with assumptions '(q→p)', '($\sim$q→p)' and conclusion 'p'. To do so, use a hypothetical syllogism whose assumptions are '($\sim$p→$\sim$q)' and '($\sim$q→p)'.

While $\mathcal{H}$ is a very popular axiomatic system due to its relative small size, it is by far not the only axiomatic system of its size that gives rise to a complete proof system. Just to give one example, another popular choice for such an axiomatic system is $\mathcal{H}' = \{MP, I1, D, N'\}$, the variant of $\mathcal{H}$ obtained by replacing N with the following (sound) axiom as the axiom that captures the properties of the operator '$\sim$':

N': '(($\sim$q→$\sim$p)→(($\sim$q→p)→q))'.

```
                    propositions/axiomatic_systems.py

# Alternative for N

#: Reductio ad absurdum
N_ALTERNATIVE = InferenceRule([], Formula.parse('((~q->~p)->((~q->p)->q))'))

#: Hilbert axiomatic system for implication and negation, with `N` replaced by
#: `N_ALTERNATIVE`.
HILBERT_AXIOMATIC_SYSTEM_ALTERNATIVE = frozenset({MP, I1, D, N_ALTERNATIVE})
```

Once again, to prove that $\mathcal{H}'$ gives rise to a complete proof system, by the lemma theorem (5.1) it suffices to prove that N via (only) MP, I0, I1, D, and N'.

OPTIONAL TASK 8 Prove the rule N via MP, I0, I1, D, and N'. The proof should be returned by the function `prove_N()`, whose missing code you should implement.

```
                    propositions/some_proofs.py

def prove_N() -> Proof:
    """Proves `N` via `MP`, `I0`, `I1`, `D`, and `N_ALTERNATIVE`.
```

```
    Returns:
        A valid proof of `N` via the inference rules `MP`, `I0`, `I1`, `D`, and
        `N_ALTERNATIVE`.
    """
    # Optional Task 6.8
```

Hint: Use the deduction theorem (5.2), i.e., assume '(~q→~p)' and prove '(p→q)'. To do so, apply MP to N' to obtain a formula that will serve as the second assumption of a hypothetical syllogism whose conclusion is '(p→q)'.

Axiomatic systems are sometimes chosen due to not only their size or practical reasons, but also aesthetic reasons. While we have chosen the axioms A, NA1, and NA2 to capture the properties of the operator '&', and the axioms O1, O2, and NO to capture the properties of the operator '|', because these axioms naturally fit into our proof strategy, a popular choice in mathematical logic courses is to replace NA1, NA2, and NO with the following respective three alternative (sound) axioms, which could be argued to be a more aesthetic choice as each of these alternative axioms contains only implication, and not also negation, in addition to the relevant operator ('&' or '|') whose properties are captured:

AE1: '((p&q)→q)'
AE2: '((p&q)→p)'
 OE: '((p→r)→((q→r)→((p|q)→r)))'

```
                              propositions/axiomatic_systems.py
# Alternatives for NA1, NA2, NO without negation

#: Conjunction elimination (right)
AE1 = InferenceRule([], Formula.parse('((p&q)->q)'))
#: Conjunction elimination (left)
AE2 = InferenceRule([], Formula.parse('((p&q)->p)'))
#: Disjunction elimination
OE = InferenceRule([], Formula.parse('((p->r)->((q->r)->((p|q)->r)))'))

#: Hilbert axiomatic system for all operators, consisting of the rules in
#: `HILBERT_AXIOMATIC_SYSTEM`, as well as `A`, `AE1`, `AE2`, `O1`, `O2`, `OE`,
#: `T`, and `NF`.
HILBERT_AXIOMATIC_SYSTEM_FULL = \
    frozenset(HILBERT_AXIOMATIC_SYSTEM.union({A, AE1, AE2, O1, O2, OE, T, NF}))
```

Your final optional task in this chapter is to show that the axiomatic system resulting from this replacement, $\hat{\mathcal{H}} = \{MP, I1, D, N, A, AE1, AE2, O1, O2, OE, T, NF\}$, indeed still gives rise to a complete proof system (even if our formulas may contain also '&', '|', 'T', and 'F'). You will once again rely on the power of the lemma theorem (5.1), by which it suffices to only show that NA1, NA2, and NO are provable via $\hat{\mathcal{H}}$.

OPTIONAL TASK 9   Prove each of the following inference rules via the respective specified axioms. Each of these proofs should be returned by the respective specified function, whose missing code you should implement.

a. Prove NA1 via MP, I0, I1, D, N, and AE1. The proof should be returned by `prove_NA1()`.
   Hint: Use AE1.

b. Prove NA2 via MP, I0, I1, D, N, and AE2. The proof should be returned by `prove_NA2()`.
   Hint: Use AE2.

c. Prove NO via MP, I0, I1, D, N, and OE. The proof should be returned by `prove_NO()`.
   Hint: Use OE; make use of I2 (more than once) and of the inference rule that you have proved in part f of Optional Task 7.

```
                         ( propositions/some_proofs.py )

def prove_NA1() -> Proof:
    """Proves `NA1` via `MP`, `I0`, `I1`, `D`, `N`, and `AE1`.

    Returns:
        A valid proof of `NA1` via the inference rules `MP`, `I0`, `I1`, `D`,
        and `AE1`.
    """
    # Optional Task 6.9a

def prove_NA2() -> Proof:
    """Proves `NA2` via `MP`, `I0`, `I1`, `D`, `N`, and `AE2`.

    Returns:
        A valid proof of `NA2` via the inference rules `MP`, `I0`, `I1`, `D`,
        and `AE2`.
    """
    # Optional Task 6.9b

def prove_NO() -> Proof:
    """Proves `NO` via `MP`, `I0`, `I1`, `D`, `N`, and `OE`.

    Returns:
        A valid proof of `NO` via the inference rules `MP`, `I0`, `I1`, `D`, and
        `OE`.
    """
    # Optional Task 6.9c
```

Part II

Predicate Logic

7 Predicate Logic Syntax and Semantics

Propositional logic, which we studied in Part I of this book up to this point, is not rich enough by itself to represent many common logical statements. Consider for example the simple **syllogism**: All men are mortal, some men exist; thus, some mortals exist. Propositional logic cannot even express the notions of "all" or "exists," let alone this type of logical deduction. We will therefore now switch to a different, richer logic, called **first-order predicate logic**, or for short, **predicate logic** (or **first-order logic**). This logic, which will be our language for part II of this book, will be strong enough to express and formalize such notions.

For example the above statement can be written in predicate logic as:[1]

> **Assumptions:** '$\forall x[(\text{Man}(x) \rightarrow \text{Mortal}(x))]$', '$\exists x[\text{Man}(x)]$'
>
> **Conclusion:** '$\exists x[\text{Mortal}(x)]$'

In fact, this logic is strong enough to represent every statement (and proof) that you have ever seen in mathematics! For example, the commutative law of addition can be represented as '$\forall x[\forall y[x+y=y+x]]$', which we will actually write in the slightly more cumbersome notation '$\forall x[\forall y[\text{plus}(x,y)=\text{plus}(y,x)]]$'. An integral part of allowing quantifications ("for all"/"exists") is that the reasoning is about variables that are no longer only placeholders for Boolean values, but rather placeholders for much richer "values." For example, wherever it appears in the syllogism example, the variable 'x' can be defined as a placeholder for any living thing, while in the commutative law example, the variables 'x' and 'y' can be placeholders for any number, or more generally for any group element or field element.

This new logic will enable a transformation in our thinking: until this point the formal logic that we were analyzing, propositional logic, was different – weaker – than the mathematical language (or programming) with which we were analyzing it. Now, since predicate logic is in fact a proper formalization of *all* of mathematics, the mathematical language that we will use to talk about logic can in fact itself be formalized as predicate logic. We will nonetheless keep allowing ourselves to talk "like in normal math courses" (as you have done since the beginning of your studies) rather than being 100% formal, but it is important to keep in mind that in principle we could convert all of the definitions and proofs in this whole book – or in any other mathematics book – to a completely formal form written entirely in predicate logic. This chapter, which parallels Chapters 1 and 2 only for predicate logic, defines the syntax and semantics of predicate logic.

---

[1] Notice that it takes some ingenuity to formalize "All men are mortal" as '$\forall x[(\text{Man}(x) \rightarrow \text{Mortal}(x))]$'. Indeed, formalizing human-language sentences as formulas may at times be far from a trivial task, but that is not the focus of this book.

7.1   Syntax

Propositional logic was created to reason about Boolean objects; therefore, every formula represents (that is, when we endow it with semantics) a Boolean statement. In predicate logic we will have **formulas** that represent Boolean statements, such as 'plus(x,y)=z', but we will also have more basic "formula-like" expressions called **terms**, such as 'plus(x,y)', which evaluate to not-necessarily-Boolean values such as numbers, other mathematical objects, or even people or more general living beings as in the case of the term 'x' in the example at the top of this chapter. As with propositional logic, we start by syntactically defining terms and formulas in predicate logic, and will only later give them semantic meaning. Nonetheless, remembering that formulas will eventually represent Boolean statements, while terms will eventually evaluate to arbitrary not-necessarily-Boolean values, will add an intuitive layer of understanding to our syntactic definitions and will help us understand where we are headed. We start by defining terms in predicate logic.

DEFINITION 7.1 (Term)   The following strings are (valid[2]) **terms** in predicate logic:

- A **variable name**: A sequence of alphanumeric characters that begins with a letter in 'u'...'z'. For example, 'x', 'y12', or 'zLast'.
- A **constant name**: A sequence of alphanumeric characters that begins with a digit or with a letter in 'a'...'e'; or an underscore (with nothing before or after it). For example, '0', 'c1', '7x', or '_'.
- An n-ary **function invocation** of the form '$f(t_1,\ldots,t_n)$', where f is a **function name** denoted by a sequence of alphanumeric characters that begins with a letter in 'f'...'t', where[3] $n \geq 1$, and where each t_i is itself a (valid) term. For example, 'plus(x,y)', 's(s(0))', or 'f(g(x),h(7,y),c)'.

These are the only (valid) terms in predicate logic.

The file `predicates/syntax.py` defines (among other classes) the Python class `Term` for holding a term as a data structure.

```
predicates/syntax.py

def is_constant(string: str) -> bool:
    """Checks if the given string is a constant name.

    Parameters:
        string: string to check.

    Returns:
        ``True`` if the given string is a constant name, ``False`` otherwise.
    """
    return  (((string[0] >= '0' and string[0] <= '9') or \
             (string[0] >= 'a' and string[0] <= 'e')) and \
            string.isalnum()) or string == '_'
```

---

[2] Similarly to the case of propositional formulas, what we call **valid** terms are often called **well-formed** terms in other textbooks.

[3] Another choice that we could have made would have been to not allow any constants, but to instead allow nullary functions, which would have "acted as" constants. The reason that we specifically allow constants (and therefore disallow nullary functions as they are not needed when constants are allowed), beyond avoiding the clutter of many empty pairs of brackets, will become clear in Chapter 12.

```
def is_variable(string: str) -> bool:
    """Checks if the given string is a variable name.

    Parameters:
        string: string to check.

    Returns:
        ``True`` if the given string is a variable name, ``False`` otherwise.
    """
    return string[0] >= 'u' and string[0] <= 'z' and string.isalnum()

def is_function(string: str) -> bool:
    """Checks if the given string is a function name.

    Parameters:
        string: string to check.

    Returns:
        ``True`` if the given string is a function name, ``False`` otherwise.
    """
    return string[0] >= 'f' and string[0] <= 't' and string.isalnum()

@frozen
class Term:
    """An immutable predicate-logic term in tree representation, composed from
    variable names and constant names, and function names applied to them.

    Attributes:
        root: the constant name, variable name, or function name at the root of
            the term tree.
        arguments: the arguments of the root, if the root is a function name.
    """
    root: str
    arguments: Optional[Tuple[Term, ...]]

    def __init__(self, root: str, arguments: Optional[Sequence[Term]] = None):
        """Initializes a `Term` from its root and root arguments.

        Parameters:
            root: the root for the formula tree.
            arguments: the arguments for the root, if the root is a function
                name.
        """
        if is_constant(root) or is_variable(root):
            assert arguments is None
            self.root = root
        else:
            assert is_function(root)
            assert arguments is not None and len(arguments) > 0
            self.root = root
            self.arguments = tuple(arguments)
```

The constructor of this class creates an expression-tree representations for a term. For example, the data structure for representing the term 'plus(s(x),3)' is constructed using the following code:

```
my_term = Term('plus', [Term('s', [Term('x')]), Term('3')])
```

Note that the terms that serve as arguments of function invocations are passed to the constructor together as a Python `list` rather than each argument separately (as was the case for, e.g., passing operands to operators in our code for propositional logic). We now move on to use terms to define formulas in predicate logic.

DEFINITION 7.2 (Formula)   The following strings are (valid[4]) **formulas** in predicate logic:

- An **equality** of the form '$t_1=t_2$', where each of t_1 and t_2 is a (valid) term. For example, '0=0', 's(0)=1', or 'plus(x,y)=plus(y,x)'.
- An n-ary **relation invocation**[5] of the form '$R(t_1,\ldots,t_n)$', where R is a **relation name** denoted by a string of alphanumeric characters that begins with a letter in 'F'... 'T', where $n \geq 0$ (note that we specifically allow nullary relations), and where each t_i is a term. For example, 'R(x,y)', 'Plus(s(0),x,s(x))', or 'Q()'.
- A (unary) **negation** of the form '$\sim\phi$', where ϕ is a (valid) formula.
- A **binary operation** of the form '$(\phi*\psi)$', where $*$ is one of the binary operators '|', '&', or '$\rightarrow$',[6] and each of ϕ and ψ is a formula.
- A **quantification** of the form '$Qx[\phi]$', where Q is either the **universal quantifier** '$\forall$', which we represent in Python as `'A'`, or the **existential quantifier** '$\exists$', which we represent in Python as `'E'`, where x is a variable name (denoted by a sequence of alphanumeric characters that begins a letter in 'u'... 'z', as defined in Definition 7.1), and where ϕ is a formula. The subformula ϕ that is within the square brackets in the quantification '$Qx[\phi]$' is called the **scope** of the quantification. For example, '$\forall x[x=x]$', '$\exists x[R(7,y)]$', '$\forall x[\exists y[R(x,y)]]$', or '$\forall x[(R(x)|\exists x[Q(x)])]$'.

These are the only (valid) formulas in predicate logic.

The file `predicates/syntax.py` also defines the Python class `Formula` for holding a predicate-logic formula as a data structure.

---
predicates/syntax.py

```
def is_equality(string: str) -> bool:
    """Checks if the given string is the equality relation.

    Parameters:
```

---

[4] As in propositional logic, what we call **valid** formulas are often called **well-formed** formulas in other textbooks.

[5] A relation invocation is sometimes called a **predication** in other textbooks. We use the term relation invocation to stress its technical similarity to a function invocation: Both function names and relation names can be invoked on an n-tuple of terms, with the difference being that a function invocation is a term while a relation invocation is a formula. (When we endow them with semantics later, a relation will correspond to a mapping that returns a Boolean value – a truth value – while a function will correspond to a mapping that returns a not-necessarily-Boolean object of the same type, in some sense, as its inputs.)

[6] We could have again used any other (larger or smaller) set of complete Boolean operators, including operators of various arities, as discussed in Chapter 3 for propositional logic. As the discussion for predicate logic would have been completely equivalent, we omit it here and stick with the unary negation operator and with these three binary operators for convenience as we did in Part I of this book. (We allow ourselves not to bother with nullary operators, though, to avoid terminologically confusing them with the similarly named predicate-logic constants.)

```
            string: string to check.

        Returns:
            ``True`` if the given string is the equality relation, ``False``
            otherwise.
        """
        return string == '='

def is_relation(string: str) -> bool:
    """Checks if the given string is a relation name.

    Parameters:
        string: string to check.

    Returns:
        ``True`` if the given string is a relation name, ``False`` otherwise.
    """
    return string[0] >= 'F' and string[0] <= 'T' and string.isalnum()

def is_unary(string: str) -> bool:
    """Checks if the given string is a unary operator.

    Parameters:
        string: string to check.

    Returns:
        ``True`` if the given string is a unary operator, ``False`` otherwise.
    """
    return string == '~'

def is_binary(string: str) -> bool:
    """Checks if the given string is a binary operator.

    Parameters:
        string: string to check.

    Returns:
        ``True`` if the given string is a binary operator, ``False`` otherwise.
    """
    return string == '&' or string == '|' or string == '->'

def is_quantifier(string: str) -> bool:
    """Checks if the given string is a quantifier.

    Parameters:
        string: string to check.

    Returns:
        ``True`` if the given string is a quantifier, ``False`` otherwise.
    """
    return string == 'A' or string == 'E'

@frozen
class Formula:
    """An immutable predicate-logic formula in tree representation, composed
    from relation names applied to predicate-logic terms, and operators and
    quantifications applied to them.
```

```
    Attributes:
        root: the relation name, equality relation, operator, or quantifier at
            the root of the formula tree.
        arguments: the arguments of the root, if the root is a relation name or
            the equality relation.
        first: the first operand of the root, if the root is a unary or binary
            operator.
        second: the second operand of the root, if the root is a binary
            operator.
        variable: the variable name quantified by the root, if the root is a
            quantification.
        statement: the statement quantified by the root, if the root is a
            quantification.
    """
    root: str
    arguments: Optional[Tuple[Term, ...]]
    first: Optional[Formula]
    second: Optional[Formula]
    variable: Optional[str]
    statement: Optional[Formula]

    def __init__(self, root: str,
                 arguments_or_first_or_variable: Union[Sequence[Term],
                                                       Formula, str],
                 second_or_statement: Optional[Formula] = None):
        """Initializes a `Formula` from its root and root arguments, root
        operands, or root quantified variable name and statement.

        Parameters:
            root: the root for the formula tree.
            arguments_or_first_or_variable: the arguments for the root, if the
                root is a relation name or the equality relation; the first
                operand for the root, if the root is a unary or binary operator;
                the variable name to be quantified by the root, if the root is a
                quantification.
            second_or_statement: the second operand for the root, if the root is
                a binary operator; the statement to be quantified by the root,
                if the root is a quantification.
        """
        if is_equality(root) or is_relation(root):
            # Populate self.root and self.arguments
            assert isinstance(arguments_or_first_or_variable, Sequence) and \
                   not isinstance(arguments_or_first_or_variable, str)
            if is_equality(root):
                assert len(arguments_or_first_or_variable) == 2
            assert second_or_statement is None
            self.root, self.arguments = \
                root, tuple(arguments_or_first_or_variable)
        elif is_unary(root):
            # Populate self.first
            assert isinstance(arguments_or_first_or_variable, Formula)
            assert second_or_statement is None
            self.root, self.first = root, arguments_or_first_or_variable
        elif is_binary(root):
            # Populate self.first and self.second
            assert isinstance(arguments_or_first_or_variable, Formula)
            assert second_or_statement is not None
            self.root, self.first, self.second = \
```

```
                root, arguments_or_first_or_variable, second_or_statement
        else:
            assert is_quantifier(root)
            # Populate self.variable and self.statement
            assert isinstance(arguments_or_first_or_variable, str) and \
                   is_variable(arguments_or_first_or_variable)
            assert second_or_statement is not None
            self.root, self.variable, self.statement = \
                root, arguments_or_first_or_variable, second_or_statement
```

The constructor of this class similarly creates an expression-tree representation for a (predicate-logic) formula. For example, given the term `my_term` defined in the example that followed Definition 7.1, the data structure for representing the formula '$(\exists x[plus(s(x), 3)=y] \to GT(y,4))$' is constructed using the following code:

```
my_formula = Formula('->',
                     Formula('E', 'x',
                             Formula('=', [my_term, Term('y')])),
                     Formula('GT', [Term('y'), Term('4')]))
```

Once again, note that the terms that serve as arguments of relation invocations (including arguments of the **equality relation**) are passed to the constructor together as a Python `list` rather than each argument separately (as is the case for, e.g., the operands of Boolean operators). Also note that for nullary relation invocations, this list will be of length zero. As with propositional formulas, to enable the safe reuse of existing formula and term objects as building blocks for (possibly even multiple) other formula and term objects, we have defined both of these classes to be **immutable** using the `@frozen` decorator.

As with propositional formulas, it is possible to represent predicate-logic terms and formulas as strings in a variety of notations, including infix, polish, and reverse polish notations. We will use the representation defined in Definitions 7.1 and 7.2, which for terms is a functional notation that is similar to polish notation (only with added parentheses and commas since we have not defined the arity of each function name in advance), and for formulas is infix notation for Boolean operations and for equality, once again is a functional notation that is similar to polish notation (in the same sense, for the same reasons) for relation invocations, and is also similar to polish notation (with the addition of square brackets for readability) for quantifications.

TASK 1 Implement the missing code for the method `__repr__()` of class Term, which returns a string that represents the term (in the usual functional notation defined in Definition 7.1).

predicates/syntax.py

```
class Term:
    :
    :

    def __repr__(self) -> str:
        """Computes the string representation of the current term.

        Returns:
            The standard string representation of the current term.
        """
        # Task 7.1
```

Example: For the term `my_term` defined in the example above, `my_term.__repr__()` (and hence also `str(my_term)`) should return the string `'plus(s(x),3)'`.

TASK 2   Implement the missing code for the method `__repr__()` of class `Formula`, which returns a string that represents the term (in the usual notation defined in Definition 7.2 – infix for Boolean operations and equality, functional for relation invocations, similar to polish for quantifications).

```
                          ( predicates/syntax.py )
class Formula:

    ⋮

    def __repr__(self) -> str:
        """Computes the string representation of the current formula.

        Returns:
            The standard string representation of the current formula.
        """
        # Task 7.2
```

Example: For the formula `my_formula` defined in the example above, `my_formula.__repr__()` (and hence also `str(my_formula)`) should return the string `'(Ex[plus(s(x),3)=y]->GT(y,4))'`.

We observe that similarly to the string representations (both infix and prefix) of propositional formulas, the string representations of predicate-logic terms and formulas are also **prefix-free**, meaning that there are no two valid distinct predicate-logic terms such that the string representation of one is a prefix of the string representation of the other (with a small caveat, analogous to that of propositional formulas, that a variable name or constant name cannot be broken down so that only its prefix is taken), and similarly for predicate-logic formulas:

LEMMA 7.1 (Prefix-Free Property of Terms)   *No term is a prefix of another term, except for the case of a variable name as a prefix of another variable name, or a constant name as a prefix of another constant name.*

LEMMA 7.2 (Prefix-Free Property of Formulas)   *No formula is a prefix of another formula, except for the case of an equality with a variable name or constant name on the right-hand side, as a prefix of another equality with the same left-hand-side term as the former equality, but with another variable name or constant name (respectively) on the right-hand side (e.g., 'f(x)=a1' as a prefix of 'f(x)=a123').*

The proofs of the lemma (7.1) on the prefix-free property of terms and of the lemma (7.2) on the prefix-property of (predicate-logic) formulas are completely analogous to the proof of the lemma (1.1) on the prefix-free property of propositional formulas from Chapter 1, since despite the richness of the language of predicate logic, we have taken care to define the various tokens in it – constant names, function names, variable names, relation names, quantifiers, etc. – so that they can be differentiated from one another based on their first character without the need to look beyond it (just like in propositional logic). Therefore, we omit these proofs (make sure that you can reconstruct their reasoning, though!). The prefix-free property allows for convenient parsing of predicate-logic expressions, using the same strategy that you followed for parsing propositional formulas in Chapter 1.

TASK 3

a. Implement the missing code for the static method _parse_prefix(string) of class Term, which takes a string that has a prefix that represents a term, and returns a term tree created from that prefix, and a string containing the unparsed remainder of the string (which may be empty, if the parsed prefix is in fact the entire string).

```
                        ┌─ predicates/syntax.py ─┐
class Term:
    :
    :

    @staticmethod
    def _parse_prefix(string: str) -> Tuple[Term, str]:
        """Parses a prefix of the given string into a term.

        Parameters:
            string: string to parse, which has a prefix that is a valid
                representation of a term.

        Returns:
            A pair of the parsed term and the unparsed suffix of the string. If
            the given string has as a prefix a constant name (e.g., 'c12') or a
            variable name (e.g., 'x12'), then the parsed prefix will be that
            entire name (and not just a part of it, such as 'x1').
        """
        # Task 7.3a
```

Example: Term._parse_prefix('s(x),3))' should return a pair whose first element is a Term object equivalent to Term('s', [Term('x')]), and whose second element is the string ',3))'.

Hint: Use recursion.

b. Implement the missing code for the static method parse(string) of class Term, which parses a given string representation of a term. You may assume that the input string represents a valid term.

```
                        ┌─ predicates/syntax.py ─┐
class Term:
    :
    :

    @staticmethod
    def parse(string: str) -> Term:
        """Parses the given valid string representation into a term.

        Parameters:
            string: string to parse.

        Returns:
            A term whose standard string representation is the given string.
        """
        # Task 7.3b
```

Example: `Term.parse('plus(s(x),3)')` should return a `Term` object equivalent to `my_term` from the example that followed Definition 7.1.
Hint: Use the `_parse_prefix()` method.

Similarly to the case of propositional formulas in Chapter 1, the reasoning and code that allowed you to implement the second (and the first) part of Task 3 without any ambiguity essentially prove the following theorem.

THEOREM 7.1 (Unique Readability of Terms)   *There is a unique derivation tree for every valid term in predicate logic.*

TASK 4

a. Implement the missing code for the static method `_parse_prefix(string)` of class `Formula`, which takes a string that has a prefix that represents a formula, and returns a formula tree created from that prefix, and a string containing the unparsed remainder of the string (which may be empty, if the parsed prefix is in fact the entire string).

```
                              predicates/syntax.py

class Formula:
        ⋮

    @staticmethod
    def _parse_prefix(string: str) -> Tuple[Formula, str]:
        """Parses a prefix of the given string into a formula.

        Parameters:
            string: string to parse, which has a prefix that is a valid
                representation of a formula.

        Returns:
            A pair of the parsed formula and the unparsed suffix of the string.
            If the given string has as a prefix a term followed by an equality
            followed by a constant name (e.g., 'f(y)=c12') or by a variable name
            (e.g., 'f(y)=x12'), then the parsed prefix will include that entire
            name (and not just a part of it, such as 'f(y)=x1').
        """
        # Task 7.4a
```

Example: `Formula._parse_prefix('Ex[plus(s(x),3)=y]->GT(y,4))')` should return a pair whose first element is a `Formula` equivalent to `Formula('E', 'x', Formula('=', [my_term, Term('y')]))` (for `my_term` from the example that followed Definition 7.2), and whose second element is the string `'->GT(y,4))'`.
Hint: Use recursion, and use the `_parse_prefix()` method of class `Term` when needed.

b. Implement the missing code for the static method `parse(string)` of class `Formula`, which parses a given string representation of a formula. You may assume that the input string represents a valid formula.

```
                              predicates/syntax.py

class Formula:
        ⋮
```

```
@staticmethod
def parse(string: str) -> Formula:
    """Parses the given valid string representation into a formula.

    Parameters:
        string: string to parse.

    Returns:
        A formula whose standard string representation is the given string.
    """
    # Task 7.4b
```

Example: `Formula.parse('(Ex[plus(s(x),3)=y]->GT(y,4))')` should return a Formula object equivalent to `my_formula` from the example that followed Definition 7.2.

Hint: Use the `_parse_prefix()` method.

Similarly to the case of terms, the reasoning and code that allowed you to implement the second (and the first) part of Task 4 without any ambiguity essentially prove the following theorem.

THEOREM 7.2 (Unique Readability of Formulas)   *There is a unique derivation tree for every valid formula in predicate logic.*

Completing the syntactic section of this chapter, you are now asked to implement a few methods that will turn out to be useful later on – methods that return all the constructs of a specific type (constant names, variable names, function names, or relation names) that are used in a term or a formula.

TASK 5   Implement the missing code for the methods `constants()`, `variables()`, and `functions()` of class `Term`, which respectively return all of the constant names that appear in the term, all of the variable names that appear in the term, and all of the function names that appear in the term – each function name in a pair with the arity of its invocations. For the latter, you may assume that any function name that appears multiple times in the term is always invoked with the same arity.

```
                        ┌─────────────────────┐
                        │ predicates/syntax.py │
                        └─────────────────────┘
class Term:
    :
    :

    def constants(self) -> Set[str]:
        """Finds all constant names in the current term.

        Returns:
            A set of all constant names used in the current term.
        """
        # Task 7.5a

    def variables(self) -> Set[str]:
        """Finds all variable names in the current term.

        Returns:
            A set of all variable names used in the current term.
        """
        # Task 7.5b
```

```
def functions(self) -> Set[Tuple[str, int]]:
    """Finds all function names in the current term, along with their
    arities.

    Returns:
        A set of pairs of function name and arity (number of arguments) for
        all function names used in the current term.
    """
    # Task 7.5c
```

For formulas, it turns out that we will sometimes be interested in the set of **free** variable names in a formula rather than all variable names in it. A **free occurrence** of a variable name in a formula is one that is not immediately next to a quantifier, nor **bound** by – that is, within the scope of – a quantification over this variable name. For example, in the formula '∀x[R(x,y)]', the occurrence of the variable name 'y' is free, but the occurrence of the variable name 'x' within 'R(x,y)' is not free since it is bound by the universal quantification '∀x'. To take a more delicate example, in the formula '(∃x[Q(x,y)]&x=0)', while the first occurrence of 'x' (not counting the one immediately next to the quantifier in '∃x') is bound (and therefore not free), the second one is free, and so the **free variable names** – the variable names that have free occurrences – in this formula are nonetheless 'x' and 'y'.

TASK 6   Implement the missing code for the methods constants(), variables(), free_variables(), functions(), and relations() of class Formula, which, respectively, return all of the constants names that appear in the formula, all of the variable names that appear in the formula, all of the variable names that have free occurrences in the formula, all of the function names that appear in the formula (each function name in a pair with the arity of its invocations), and all of the relation names that appear in the formula – each relation name in a pair with the arity of its invocations. For the latter two, you may assume that any function name or relation name that appears multiple times in the formula is always invoked with the same arity.

predicates/syntax.py

```
class Formula:
    ⋮

    def constants(self) -> Set[str]:
        """Finds all constant names in the current formula.

        Returns:
            A set of all constant names used in the current formula.
        """
        # Task 7.6a

    def variables(self) -> Set[str]:
        """Finds all variable names in the current formula.

        Returns:
            A set of all variable names used in the current formula.
        """
        # Task 7.6b
```

```
    def free_variables(self) -> Set[str]:
        """Finds all variable names that are free in the current formula.

        Returns:
            A set of every variable name that is used in the current formula not
            only within a scope of a quantification on that variable name.
        """
        # Task 7.6c

    def functions(self) -> Set[Tuple[str, int]]:
        """Finds all function names in the current formula, along with their
        arities.

        Returns:
            A set of pairs of function name and arity (number of arguments) for
            all function names used in the current formula.
        """
        # Task 7.6d

    def relations(self) -> Set[Tuple[str, int]]:
        """Finds all relation names in the current formula, along with their
        arities.

        Returns:
            A set of pairs of relation name and arity (number of arguments) for
            all relation names used in the current formula.
        """
        # Task 7.6e
```

Finally, before moving on to the semantics of predicate logic, we note as we did for propositional logic that each **expression** (term or formula) is a finite-length string whose letters come from a finite number of characters, and thus there is a finite number of expressions of any given fixed length. We thus once again get the following simple fact.[7]

THEOREM 7.3   *The set of terms and the set of formulas in predicate logic are both countably infinite.*

7.2   Semantics

We now move to the semantics of predicate-logic expressions (terms and formulas). Recall that in propositional logic both variables and formulas represent Boolean values, and a model directly specifies an **interpretation**, which is a Boolean value (a truth value), to each of the variable names, and the value of a formula is computed from the interpretations of its variable names according to the truth tables of the operators in the formula. As discussed in the beginning of Section 7.1, in predicate logic our variables do not represent Boolean values, but rather values from some **universe** of elements – this is the grand set of values over which the quantifiers '∀' and '∃' quantify. In this logic, not only is the mapping

---

[7] As in propositional logic, all of our results will extend naturally via analogous proofs to allow for sets of constant/variable/function/relation names of arbitrary cardinality, which would imply also term and formula sets of arbitrary cardinality. As in Part I of this book, in the few places where the generalization will not be straightforward, we will explicitly discuss this.

from variable/constant names to values (from the universe) defined by the model, but in fact the universe that these values belong to is itself also defined by the model and can differ between models. Accordingly, the interpretations of all predicate-logic expression constructs that can be applied to terms – i.e., the mappings by which relation names and function names are interpreted – are also defined by the model.

The universe of a model could be any set (though we will restrict ourselves to finite sets in our code), for example the set of all elements of some field. Models in predicate logic define this universe and additionally provide interpretations of the constant names (as elements of the universe[8]), function names (as maps from tuples of elements of the universe to an element of the universe), and relation names (as maps from tuples of elements of the universe to Boolean values) used in the formulas. Thus, as already hinted to in the beginning of this chapter, the semantic interpretation (value) that a model induces on a term will be an element from the universe, while the value induced by a model on a formula will be Boolean (a truth value). Variables are not assigned a specific interpretation by a model, and as we will see soon, will only get a value once it is assigned to them by an additional assignment – corresponding to a quantification – that complements the model (as a variable name is syntactically a term, the value assigned to a variable name will also be an element of the universe of the model).

DEFINITION 7.3 (Model)   A **model** in predicate logic consists of a set of elements Ω called the **universe** of the model, as well as an **interpretation** for a set of constant names, function names, and relation names. An **interpretation** of a constant name is an element in the universe Ω, an **interpretation** of an n-ary function name is a function $f : \Omega^n \to \Omega$, and an **interpretation** of an n-ary relation name is a subset of Ω^n (for which the relation holds[9]).

For example, the following describes the five-element field F_5 (sometimes also denoted as $\mathbb{Z}_5$ or $GF(5)$) as a model for a field:

- Universe $\Omega = \{0, 1, 2, 3, 4\}$.
- The interpretation of the constant name '0' is $0 \in \Omega$. The interpretation of the constant name '1' is $1 \in \Omega$.
- The interpretation of the binary function name 'plus' is addition modulo 5: $\text{plus}(0,0) = 0$, $\text{plus}(0,1) = 1$, ..., $\text{plus}(0,4) = 4$, $\text{plus}(1,0) = 1$, ..., $\text{plus}(1,3) = 4$, $\text{plus}(1,4) = 0, \ldots, \text{plus}(4,4) = 3$. The interpretation of the binary function name 'times' is multiplication modulo 5, for example, $\text{times}(3,3) = 4$.
- The interpretation of the unary relation name[10] 'IsPrimitive' is $\{(2), (3)\}$.

---

[8] In this sense, somewhat confusingly, constants in predicate logic are analogous to variables in propositional logic, while as we will see soon variables in predicate logic play a different role that has to do with quantifications and has no analogue in propositional logic.

[9] While this standard representation of a relation as the set of all n-tuples of universe elements for which the relation holds (i.e., is true) will be slightly more convenient for us in our code, and is also more aesthetic, we will at times continue to think of relations also as functions from n-tuples of universe elements to Boolean values when the analogy to functions (from n-tuples of universe elements to universe elements) is intuitively useful.

[10] A field element is called primitive if it *generates* the *multiplicative group* of the field, that is, if every nonzero element of the field can be written as an integer power of that element.

- Depending on the expressions that we wish to evaluate, we could also add corresponding interpretations for additional function names and relation names, such as the unary function names 'inverse' and 'multiplicativeInverse'.

The file `predicates/semantics.py` defines a class `Model` that holds a semantic model for predicate-logic expressions.

```
                          ┌─────────────────────────────┐
                          │ predicates/semantics.py     │
─────────────────────────────────────────────────────────────────
#: A generic type for a universe element in a model.
T = TypeVar('T')


@frozen
class Model(Generic[T]):
    """An immutable model for predicate-logic constructs.

    Attributes:
        universe: the set of elements to which terms can be evaluated and over
            which quantifications are defined.
        constant_interpretations: mapping from each constant name to the
            universe element to which it evaluates.
        relation_arities: mapping from each relation name to its arity, or to
            ``-1`` if the relation is the empty relation.
        relation_interpretations: mapping from each n-ary relation name to
            argument n-tuples (of universe elements) for which the relation is
            true.
        function_arities: mapping from each function name to its arity.
        function_interpretations: mapping from each n-ary function name to the
            mapping from each argument n-tuple (of universe elements) to the
            universe element that the function outputs given these arguments.
    """
    universe: FrozenSet[T]
    constant_interpretations: Mapping[str, T]
    relation_arities: Mapping[str, int]
    relation_interpretations: Mapping[str, AbstractSet[Tuple[T, ...]]]
    function_arities: Mapping[str, int]
    function_interpretations: Mapping[str, Mapping[Tuple[T, ...], T]]

    def __init__(self, universe: AbstractSet[T],
                 constant_interpretations: Mapping[str, T],
                 relation_interpretations:
                 Mapping[str, AbstractSet[Tuple[T, ...]]],
                 function_interpretations:
                 Mapping[str, Mapping[Tuple[T, ...], T]] = frozendict()):
        """Initializes a `Model` from its universe and constant, relation, and
        function name interpretations.

        Parameters:
            universe: the set of elements to which terms are to be evaluated
                and over which quantifications are to be defined.
            constant_interpretations: mapping from each constant name to a
                universe element to which it is to be evaluated.
            relation_interpretations: mapping from each relation name that is to
                be the name of an n-ary relation, to the argument n-tuples (of
                universe elements) for which the relation is to be true.
            function_interpretations: mapping from each function name that is to
                be the name of an n-ary function, to a mapping from each
                argument n-tuple (of universe elements) to a universe element
```

```
                   that the function is to output given these arguments.
     """
     for constant in constant_interpretations:
         assert is_constant(constant)
         assert constant_interpretations[constant] in universe
     relation_arities = {}
     for relation in relation_interpretations:
         assert is_relation(relation)
         relation_interpretation = relation_interpretations[relation]
         if len(relation_interpretation) == 0:
             arity = -1 # any
         else:
             some_arguments = next(iter(relation_interpretation))
             arity = len(some_arguments)
             for arguments in relation_interpretation:
                 assert len(arguments) == arity
                 for argument in arguments:
                     assert argument in universe
         relation_arities[relation] = arity
     function_arities = {}
     for function in function_interpretations:
         assert is_function(function)
         function_interpretation = function_interpretations[function]
         assert len(function_interpretation) > 0
         some_argument = next(iter(function_interpretation))
         arity = len(some_argument)
         assert arity > 0
         assert len(function_interpretation) == len(universe)**arity
         for arguments in function_interpretation:
             assert len(arguments) == arity
             for argument in arguments:
                 assert argument in universe
             assert function_interpretation[arguments] in universe
         function_arities[function] = arity

     self.universe = frozenset(universe)
     self.constant_interpretations = frozendict(constant_interpretations)
     self.relation_arities = frozendict(relation_arities)
     self.relation_interpretations = \
         frozendict({relation: frozenset(relation_interpretations[relation])
                     for relation in relation_interpretations})
     self.function_arities = frozendict(function_arities)
     self.function_interpretations = \
         frozendict({function: frozendict(function_interpretations[function])
                     for function in function_interpretations})
```

You have probably guessed by now how we would evaluate, in a model, terms that are simply constant names, and how we would recursively evaluate terms that are function invocations. What about variable names, though? A model specifies no interpretation for variable names. We evaluate variable names in the following way, which may seem a bit cryptic right now, but will become clearer once we talk about evaluating quantified formulas: A term that contains variable names has a defined value in a given model M for this term only once we additionally define an **assignment** A that assigns an element in the universe of M to each variable name in the term.

DEFINITION 7.4 (Value of Term in Model)   Given a term τ, a model M with interpretations for (at least) the constant and function names of τ, and an assignment A for (at least) the variable names of τ, the **value** of the term τ in the model M under the assignment A is an element in the universe Ω of M that we define recursively:

- If τ is a constant name c, then its value is given directly by the model M as the interpretation of this constant name.
- If τ is a variable name x, then its value is given directly by the assignment A.
- If τ is an n-ary function invocation $f(t_1,\ldots,t_n)$, then its value is the result of applying the interpretation of the function name f (which is a function from Ω^n to Ω that is given directly by the model) to the (recursively defined) values of its arguments $t_1,\ldots,t_n$ in M under A.

For example, the value of the term 'times(x,plus(1,1))' in the field model example under the assignment that assigns the value $4 \in \Omega$ to the variable name 'x' is $3 \in \Omega$. If a term has no variable names, then an assignment is not required in order to fully evaluate it in a model using Definition 7.4 (i.e., it has the same value in this model under any assignment). For example, the value of the term 'plus(plus(plus(plus(1,1),1),1),1)' in the field model example (under any assignment) is $0 \in \Omega$.

TASK 7   Implement the missing code for the method `evaluate_term(term, assignment)` of class `Model`, which returns the value (in the universe of the model) of the given term under the given assignment of values to its variable names.

```
                    ┌─────────────────────────────────┐
                    │  predicates/semantics.py        │
┌───────────────────┴─────────────────────────────────┴───────────────────┐
 class Model:
         ⋮

     def evaluate_term(self, term: Term,
                     assignment: Mapping[str, T] = frozendict()) -> T:
         """Calculates the value of the given term in the current model under the
         given assignment of values to variable names.

         Parameters:
             term: term to calculate the value of, for the constant and function
                 names of which the current model has interpretations.
             assignment: mapping from each variable name in the given term to a
                 universe element to which it is to be evaluated.

         Returns:
             The value (in the universe of the current model) of the given
             term in the current model under the given assignment of values to
             variable names.
         """
         assert term.constants().issubset(self.constant_interpretations.keys())
         assert term.variables().issubset(assignment.keys())
         for function,arity in term.functions():
             assert function in self.function_interpretations and \
                 self.function_arities[function] == arity
         # Task 7.7
```

Similarly, given a model, a predicate-logic formula, and an assignment for the free variable names of the formula, we can recursively associate a Boolean truth value with the formula:

DEFINITION 7.5 (Truth Value of Formula in Model)   Given a formula ϕ, a model M with interpretations for (at least) the constant, function, and relation names of ϕ, and an assignment for (at least) the free variable names of ϕ, we define the **(truth) value** of the formula ϕ in the model M under the assignment A recursively:

- If ϕ is an equality '$t_1{=}t_2$', then its value is *True* if and only if in M under A the value of the term t_1 is the same element of the universe Ω of M as the value of the term t_2 (where these values, each an element of Ω, are as recursively defined in Definition 7.4).

- If ϕ is an n-ary relation invocation '$R(t_1,\ldots,t_n)$', then its value is *True* if and only if the tuple of the values of these terms (ordered from 1 to n) in M under A is contained in the interpretation of the relation name R in M.

- Unary and binary Boolean operations are evaluated as in propositional formulas (see Chapter 2), with the subformulas evaluated also in M under A.

- If ϕ is a universally quantified formula '$\forall x[\psi]$', then its value is *True* if and only if ψ evaluates to *True* in M under *every* assignment created from A by assigning some element in Ω to the variable name x (this determines the values of the free occurrences of x in ψ) while leaving the values assigned to other variable names as in A; if ϕ is an existentially quantified formula '$\exists x[\psi]$', then its value is *True* if and only if ψ evaluates to *True* in M under *some* (i.e., one or more) assignment created from A by assigning some element in Ω to the variable name x (this determines the values of the free occurrences of x in ψ) while leaving the values assigned to other variable names as in A.

Note that analogously to the case of terms, a formula only has a defined value in a given model once we additionally define an assignment that gives a value to each of its *free* variable names (such an assignment is needed when evaluating any term in this formula that contains occurrences of variable names that are free occurrences with respect to the full formula). For example, since in the formula '$\forall x[times(x,y){=}x]$' the variable name 'y' is free, this formula only has a defined truth value if an additional assignment assigns a value to 'y', while the variable name 'x' need not be explicitly assigned a value by the assignment because by definition, since it is bound by a universal quantification, we go over all possible values for it when evaluating the formula. The truth value of this formula in the field model example is *True* under an assignment that assigns the value $1 \in \Omega$ to the variable name 'y', and *False* under any assignment that assigns any other value (in $\{0,2,3,4\}$) to 'y'.

Analogously to terms, if a formula has no free variable names, then an assignment is not required in order to fully evaluate it in a model using Definition 7.5 (i.e., it has the same value in the model under any assignment). For example, the truth value of the formula '$\forall x[\exists y[times(x,y){=}1]]$' in the field model example (under any assignment) is *False*, while that of the formula '$\forall x[(x{=}0|\exists y[times(x,y){=}1])]$' is *True*, and so is that of the formula '$\forall x[plus(plus(plus(plus(x,x),x),x),x){=}0]$'. Similarly, in that model the truth value of the formula '$\forall x[(x{=}0|IsPrimitive(x))]$' is *False*, and that of the formula '∀x[(IsPrimitive(x)→∀y[(y=0|(y=x|(y=times(x,x)|(y=times(times(x,x),x)| y=times(times(times(x,x),x),x)))))])]' is *True*.

Note that Definitions 7.4 and 7.5 imply that we interpret an occurrence of a variable name in any specific context by the innermost **scope** containing it that defines an assignment for it: The innermost quantification if such exists, or the given assignment (which in this sense defines an assignment for the "global scope" of the entire formula that is evaluated) if there exists no such quantification (i.e., if that occurrence of the variable name is free). Thus, in the (algebraically nonsensical) formula '(x=0|(∃x[IsPrimitive(x)→∀x[times(x,x)=1]]))', both occurrences of 'x' in 'times(x,x)' are **bound by** (i.e., when evaluated, will get their value from the assignment corresponding to) the universal quantifier, while the occurrence of 'x' in 'IsPrimitive(x)' is bound by the existential quantifier and the occurrence of 'x' in 'x=0' is free and its value must be given by an assignment in order to evaluate this formula. Note that the subformula '(∃x[IsPrimitive(x)→∀x[times(x,x)=1]])' can be evaluated in a model without requiring any value to be given to 'x' by an assignment, since there are no free occurrences of 'x' in it.

TASK 8 Implement the missing code for the method `evaluate_formula(formula, assignment)` of class `Model`, which returns the truth value of the given formula under the given assignment of values to its free variable names.

```
                          predicates/semantics.py
class Model:
    ⋮

    def evaluate_formula(self, formula: Formula,
                         assignment: Mapping[str, T] = frozendict()) -> bool:
        """Calculates the truth value of the given formula in the current model
        under the given assignment of values to free occurrences of variable
        names.

        Parameters:
            formula: formula to calculate the truth value of, for the constant,
                function, and relation names of which the current model has
                interpretations.
            assignment: mapping from each variable name that has a free
                occurrence in the given formula to a universe element to which
                it is to be evaluated.

        Returns:
            The truth value of the given formula in the current model under the
            given assignment of values to free occurrences of variable names.
        """
        assert formula.constants().issubset(
            self.constant_interpretations.keys())
        assert formula.free_variables().issubset(assignment.keys())
        for function,arity in formula.functions():
            assert function in self.function_interpretations and \
                   self.function_arities[function] == arity
        for relation,arity in formula.relations():
            assert relation in self.relation_interpretations and \
                   self.relation_arities[relation] in {-1, arity}
        # Task 7.8
```

Finally, as we will see we will many times be interested in checking whether a formula evaluates to *True* in a given model under *all* possible assignments to its free variable names. In this case, as in propositional logic, we will say that this model **is a model of** this formula. We will furthermore be interested in evaluating like this not merely a single formula but a whole set of formulas. The last task of this chapter is to implement a helper method that performs this.

TASK 9   Implement the missing code for the method is_model_of(formulas) of class Model, which returns whether the model is a model of each of the given formulas, regardless of which values from the universe of the model are assigned to its free variable names.

```
                         predicates/semantics.py
class Model:
    :
    :

    def is_model_of(self, formulas: AbstractSet[Formula]) -> bool:
        """Checks if the current model is a model of the given formulas.

        Parameters:
            formulas: formulas to check, for the constant, function, and
                relation names of which the current model has interpretations.

        Returns:
            ``True`` if each of the given formulas evaluates to true in the
            current model under any assignment of elements from the universe of
            the current model to the free occurrences of variable names in that
            formula, ``False`` otherwise.
        """
        for formula in formulas:
            assert formula.constants().issubset(
                self.constant_interpretations.keys())
            for function,arity in formula.functions():
                assert function in self.function_interpretations and \
                        self.function_arities[function] == arity
            for relation,arity in formula.relations():
                assert relation in self.relation_interpretations and \
                        self.relation_arities[relation] in {-1, arity}
        # Task 7.9
```

8   Getting Rid of Functions and Equality

Taking a bird's-eye view of Chapter 3, we have shown, within the context of propositional logic, that there exists a simple syntactic procedure to modify sets of "rich formulas" (in that chapter: formulas that use arbitrary operators) to sets of "less-rich formulas" (say, those using only the operators '$\rightarrow$' and '$\sim$') without losing any expressiveness, in the sense that a set of rich formulas has a model if and only if the corresponding set of less-rich formulas has a model (in that chapter, it in fact turned out to be the exact same model). In this chapter, we will follow a conceptually similar (yet technically quite different) path, and see that we can essentially eliminate two ingredients from our predicate-logic expressions with essentially no loss of any expressiveness. Specifically, you will show that we can syntactically replace all function invocations with invocations of appropriate relations, and that we can syntactically replace any equality with the invocation of an essentially equivalent relation. The point with all these replacements will be the same: that we do not lose expressive power in the same sense that if we take a set of formulas that may contain function invocations and equalities ("rich formulas"), and take the corresponding set of formulas that results from syntactically replacing all these with corresponding relation invocations ("less-rich formulas"), then while they do not share the same models (as was the case in Chapter 3), models can still be translated back and forth between these sets of formulas, and in particular, the former set of formulas has a model if and only if the latter does, so the question of "does a given set of formulas have a model" can encode the same set of problems whether or not we allow the usage of functions and equalities. This will allow us to use functions and equalities whenever we find it convenient to do so (e.g., in Chapter 10) and to ignore them when we find it inconvenient to use them (as will be the case in Chapter 12).

8.1   Getting Rid of Functions

In this section, we will show that we can eliminate all function invocations from predicate-logic formulas without losing expressive power. The idea is that a function $f : \Omega^n \rightarrow \Omega$ can be "encoded" as a relation $F \subset \Omega^{n+1}$ where for every $\alpha_1, \ldots, \alpha_n \in \Omega$ and $\beta \in \Omega$, we have that β is $f(\alpha_1, \ldots, \alpha_n)$ if and only if $F(\beta, \alpha_1, \ldots, \alpha_n)$ holds.[1] Of course, such an "encoding" relation F is not arbitrary but has the special property that for every $\alpha_1, \ldots, \alpha_n \in \Omega$

---

[1]   In fact, this is how functions are formally defined in the mathematical field known as **set theory**, where all mathematical objects, including functions, are defined as sets.

there exists a single (no more and no less) $\beta \in \Omega$ such that $F(\beta, \alpha_1, \ldots, \alpha_n)$. So, we will transform any formula ϕ that contains any invocations of function names $f_1, \ldots, f_k$ to an essentially equivalent formula that instead contains invocations of corresponding relation names $F_1, \ldots, F_k$. Specifically, each function invocation will be replaced by an invocation of a corresponding relation that has the same name as the function, except that the first letter is capitalized. For example, an invocation of the function named 'f' will be replaced by an invocation of the corresponding relation named 'F', an invocation of the function named 'f7' by an invocation of the corresponding relation named 'F7', and an invocation of the function named 'plus' by an invocation of the corresponding relation named 'Plus'. In the file `predicates/functions.py`, which contains all of the Python functions that you are asked to implement in this chapter, we have already implemented for you two functions that perform this translation from function names to relation names and back.

predicates/functions.py

```
def function_name_to_relation_name(function: str) -> str:
    """Converts the given function name to a canonically corresponding relation
    name.

    Parameters:
        function: function name to convert.

    Returns:
        A relation name that is the same as the given function name, except that
        its first letter is capitalized.
    """
    assert is_function(function)
    return function[0].upper() + function[1:]

def relation_name_to_function_name(relation: str) -> str:
    """Converts the given relation name to a canonically corresponding function
    name.

    Parameters:
        relation: relation name to convert.

    Returns:
        A function name `function` such that
        `function_name_to_relation_name(function)` is the given relation name.
    """
    assert is_relation(relation)
    return relation[0].lower() + relation[1:]
```

DEFINITION 8.1 (Relation Corresponding to Function; Function-Free Analog of Model)

- Given an n-ary function f defined over a universe Ω, we say that a given $n+1$-ary relation F defined over the same universe Ω is the relation that **corresponds to** the function f if for all $\beta, \alpha_1, \ldots, \alpha_n \in \Omega$ we have that $F(\beta, \alpha_1, \ldots, \alpha_n)$ holds if and only if $f(\alpha_1, \ldots, \alpha_n)$ is β.

- Given a model M that contains functions, we say that a model M' is the **function-free analog** of the model M if M' is identical to M except that each function interpretation in M is replaced in M' with the relation interpretation that corresponds to it (as just defined), where the latter interpretation is assigned to the relation name that is the same as the function name to which the former interpretation is assigned, except that the first letter of the relation name is capitalized.

For example, consider the following model with a single unary function and a single unary relation:

- Universe $\Omega = \{0, 1, 2\}$.
- The interpretation of the constant name '0' is $0 \in \Omega$.
- The interpretation of the unary function name 'inverse' is $\mathrm{inverse}(1) = 0$, $\mathrm{inverse}(2) = 1$, and $\mathrm{inverse}(0) = 2$.
- The interpretation of the unary relation name 'IsPrimitive' is $\{(2)\}$.

This model is encoded by its following function-free analog model with a single binary relation that corresponds to the above unary function, and the same single unary relation:

- Universe, as in the original model, $\Omega = \{0, 1, 2\}$.
- The interpretation of the constant name '0' is $0 \in \Omega$ as in the original model.
- The interpretation of the binary relation name 'Inverse' is $\{(0, 1), (1, 2), (2, 0)\}$.
- The interpretation of the unary relation name 'IsPrimitive' is $\{(2)\}$ as in the original model.

In the next two task, you will transform a given model to its function-free analog model and back.

TASK 1   Implement the missing code for the function `replace_functions_with_relations_in_model(model)`, which returns the function-free analog model of the given model that may contain function invocations.

```
                          predicates/functions.py

def replace_functions_with_relations_in_model(model: Model[T]) -> Model[T]:
    """Converts the given model to a canonically corresponding model without any
    function interpretations, replacing each function interpretation with a
    canonically corresponding relation interpretation.

    Parameters:
        model: model to convert, such that there exist no canonically
            corresponding function name and relation name that both have
            interpretations in this model.

    Returns:
        A model obtained from the given model by replacing every function
        interpretation of a function name with a relation interpretation of the
        canonically corresponding relation name, such that the relation
        interpretation contains any tuple (`x1`,...,`xn`) if and only if `x1`
        is the output of the function interpretation for the arguments
        (`x2`,...,`xn`).
    """
    for function in model.function_interpretations:
        assert function_name_to_relation_name(function) not in \
                model.relation_interpretations
    # Task 8.1
```

TASK 2   Implement the missing code for the function `replace_relations_with_functions_in_model(model, original_functions)`, which returns the model that has interpretations for the given function names (and not for any other function names), and whose function-free analog is the given model.

```
                        predicates/functions.py
def replace_relations_with_functions_in_model(model: Model[T],
                                    original_functions:
                                    AbstractSet[str]) -> \
        Union[Model[T], None]:
    """Converts the given model with no function interpretations to a
    canonically corresponding model with interpretations for the given function
    names, having each new function interpretation replace a canonically
    corresponding relation interpretation.

    Parameters:
        model: model to convert, that contains no function interpretations.
        original_functions: function names for the model to convert to,
            such that no relation name that canonically corresponds to any of
            these function names has an interpretation in the given model.

    Returns:
        A model `model` with the given function names such that
        `replace_functions_with_relations_in_mode(model)` is the given model, or
        ``None`` if no such model exists.
    """
    assert len(model.function_interpretations) == 0
    for function in original_functions:
        assert is_function(function)
        assert function not in model.function_interpretations
        assert function_name_to_relation_name(function) in \
            model.relation_interpretations
    # Task 8.2
```

Hint: You should return None unless for every one of the given function names there is a correspondingly named relation interpretation in the given model that corresponds to a function, i.e., if this relation interpretation is $n+1$-ary, then for every $\alpha_1, \ldots, \alpha_n$ in the universe of the given model, there exists a single (no more and no less) β in the universe of the given model such that $(\beta, \alpha_1 \ldots, \alpha_n)$ is in this relation interpretation.

We now move on to the task of converting a formula that may contain function invocations to a function-free analog formula that instead contains invocation of the corresponding relation names. Our goal is that the truth value of the former in any model M be the same as that of the latter in the function-free analog model of the same model M.

DEFINITION 8.2 (Function-Free Analog of Formula)   Given a formula ϕ that may contain function invocations, we say that a formula ϕ' that contains no function invocations is a **function-free analog**[2] of the formula ϕ if all of the following hold.

---

[2] While in Definition 8.1 we have defined *the* function-free analog of a model, we define here *a* function-free analog of a formula. While a formula may indeed have more than one function-free analog, we will for simplicity subsequently focus on a specific function-free analog for any given formula.

1. ϕ' uses the same relation names as ϕ, and in addition, for each function name in ϕ, the formula ϕ' also uses a relation with the same name except that the first letter of the relation name is capitalized.
2. ϕ' has the same set of free variable names as ϕ.
3. For every model M and for every assignment of elements from the universe of M to the free variable names of ϕ, the truth value of ϕ in the model M under the given assignment is the same as the truth value of ϕ' in the model M' that is the function-free analog of M under the same assignment.

The basic idea is to introduce a new variable name, say z, to hold the value of every function invocation '$f(x)$' in the original formula. We will then replace the usage of the value of the function invocation by the new variable name (i.e., replace '$f(x)$' with 'z') and add an assumption that indeed '$z=f(x)$', however this assumption will be specified using the corresponding relation name, i.e., it will be specified as '$F(z,x)$'. For example, a function-free analog of the formula 'IsPrimitive(inverse(x))' (which uses the function and relation names as in the first model in the example that followed Definition 8.1) is '$\exists z[(\text{Inverse}(z,x)\,\&\,\text{IsPrimitive}(z))]$' (which uses the two relation names as in the second model in that example).

With some more care, we can also handle formulas that contain function invocations whose arguments are themselves function invocations, such as '$R(f(g(x)))$'. In such a case, we will also introduce new variable names for all "intermediate" function invocations. To understand how to handle such formulas, let us first formalize the task of taking a term that contains multiple (hierarchical) function invocations and breaking it into steps while introducing explicit variable names for intermediate values. (This is exactly what a compiler for any programming language does when parsing such a term!)

TASK 3   Implement the missing code for the function `_compile_term(term)`, which takes a term whose root is a function invocation (possibly with nested function invocations further down the term tree) and returns "steps" that "break down" the given term, each of which is a formula of the form '$y=f(x_1,\dots,x_n)$', where y is a new variable name, f is a function name, and each x_i is either a constant name or a variable name, such that the left-hand-side variable name of the last step (the "y of the last step") evaluates to the value of the whole given term.

```
                        predicates/functions.py
def _compile_term(term: Term) -> List[Formula]:
    """Syntactically compiles the given term into a list of single-function
    invocation steps.

    Parameters:
        term: term to compile, whose root is a function invocation, and which
            contains no variable names that are ``z`` followed by a number.

    Returns:
        A list of steps, each of which is a formula of the form
        ''`y`=`f`(`x1`,...,`xn`)'', where `y` is a new variable name obtained by
        calling `next(fresh_variable_name_generator)`, `f` is a function name,
        and each of the `x`i is either a constant name or a variable name. If
        `x`i is a new variable name, then it is also the left-hand side of a
```

```
        previous step, where all of the steps "leading up to" `x1` precede those
        "leading up" to `x2`, etc. If all the returned steps hold in any model,
        then the left-hand-side variable name of the last returned step
        evaluates in that model to the value of the given term.
    """
    assert is_function(term.root)
    for variable in term.variables():
        assert not is_z_and_number(variable)
    # Task 8.3
```

Example: Given the term '$f(g(g(0)),h(x))$', the function should return the formulas '$z1=g(0)$', '$z2=g(z1)$', '$z3=h(x)$', and '$z4=f(z2,z3)$', in this order, coinciding with the following breakdown of the term:

$$\text{`}f(g(\underbrace{g(\underbrace{0}_{z1})}_{z2}),\underbrace{h(x)}_{z3})\text{'}$$
$$\underbrace{}_{z4}$$

Guidelines: The new variable names used in the returned steps, in the order of the steps, should be generated by calling next(fresh_variable_name_generator) (this generator, which makes sure that numbering continues to increase between successive calls to your function, is imported for you from logic_utils.py[3]), and you may assume that variable names generated this way do not occur anywhere in the given term.

We can now see how the "compiler" that you implemented in Task 3 can be used to find a function-free analog of a formula whose root is a relation invocation whose arguments contain multiple nested function invocations, such as '$R(f(g(x)),h(2,y),3)$'. Using this formula as an example, note that for the term '$f(g(x))$', your "compiler" returns the two steps '$z1=g(x)$' and '$z2=f(z1)$', and for the term '$h(2,y)$', your "compiler" subsequently returns the single step '$z3=h(2,y)$'. The function-free analog formula will go over all the new variable names (where it will go over the relation invocation arguments in left-to-right order, and for each argument it will go over the list of new variable names created for it in the order of the steps returned by your "compiler"). For each new variable name over which it goes, the function-free analog formula will existentially ($\exists$) quantify over it, stating that relation invocation that corresponds to the function invocation in the step for this variable name should be satisfied, and that all of these, as well as the root relation invocation being satisfied, should hold simultaneously. For example, in our example the equivalent resulting formula is

$$\text{`}\exists z1[(G(z1,x)\&\exists z2[(F(z2,z1)\&\exists z3[(H(z3,2,y)\&R(z2, z3, 3))])])]\text{'}$$

Finding a function-free analog of a formula whose root is an equality is very similar (in this context, an equality is no different than any other relation invocation), and finally finding function-free analogs of composite formulas (i.e., formulas whose root is a Boolean operator or a quantification) can be done recursively, by respectively compositing the function-free analogs of their subformulas.

---

[3] So a second call to _compile_term() with the same term '$f(g(g(0)),h(x))$' from the example just given will return the formulas '$z5=g(0)$', '$z6=g(z5)$', '$z7=h(x)$', and '$z8=f(z6,z7)$' if implemented using this generator, which is the behavior that we seek.

TASK 4 Implement the missing code for the function `replace_functions_with_relations_in_formula`(formula), which returns the function-free analog formula (constructed as just described) of the given formula that may contain function invocations.

```
                    predicates/functions.py
def replace_functions_with_relations_in_formula(formula: Formula) -> Formula:
    """Syntactically converts the given formula to a formula that does not
    contain any function invocations, and is "one-way equivalent" in the sense
    that the former holds in a model if and only if the latter holds in the
    canonically corresponding model with no function interpretations.

    Parameters:
        formula: formula to convert, which contains no variable names that are
            ``z`` followed by a number, and such that there exist no canonically
            corresponding function name and relation name that are both invoked
            in this formula.

    Returns:
        A formula such that the given formula holds in any model `model` if and
        only if the returned formula holds in
        `replace_function_with_relations_in_model(model)`.
    """
    assert len({function_name_to_relation_name(function) for
                function,arity in formula.functions()}.intersection(
                    {relation for relation,arity in formula.relations()})) == 0
    for variable in formula.variables():
        assert not is_z_and_number(variable)
    # Task 8.4
```

Hints: As with many (but not all) other tasks in this part of the book, here too it is possible to have the exact same code that handles relation names also handle equality, and you should do precisely this. Use recursion for formulas that have quantifiers or Boolean operators at their root.

Your solution to Task 4 guarantees the following: For every model `model`, if we take `new_formula=replace_functions_with_relations_in_formula(formula)` and `new_model=replace_functions_with_relations_in_model(model)`, then `new_model` is a model of `new_formula` (recall that we mean by this that `new_formula` holds in `new_model`) if and only if `model` is a model of `formula`. Note that this only gives us a guarantee regarding the truth values of the function-free `new_formula` in a model that is a function-free analog of some model (as opposed to in a model that is not the function-free analog of any model), that is, in a model where the interpretations of the new relation names correspond to functions. In particular, it is possible that `formula` has no model whereas `new_formula` has a model (in which some new relations names have interpretations that do not correspond to functions). We will now add a verification of this property of relations, thereby ensuring that the interpretation of each new relation name, in *any* model of the function-free `new_formula` (and not only in those returned by `replace_functions_with_relations_in_model()`), indeed corresponds to *some* function.

Note that, e.g., for the interpretation of a binary relation name F to indeed correspond to some unary function, we need both that (1) for every $\alpha \in \Omega$ there exists $\beta \in \Omega$

such that the function maps α to β: '$\forall x[\exists z[F(z,x)]]$' and (2) there exists only one such β: '$(\forall x[(\forall z1[(\forall z2[((F(z1,x)\&F(z2,x))\rightarrow z1=z2)])])])$'. So, we will construct a set of formulas by starting with the function-free equivalent of some original formula. For each relation name that corresponds to a function name in the original formula, we will then add to this set a formula – the conjunction of these two formulas, modified as appropriate according to the arity of the relation name[4] – that ensures that the interpretation of this relation name indeed corresponds to some function. This will guarantee that the obtained set of formulas has the property that any model of this *set* can be decoded into a model of the original formula (i.e., is returned by `replace_functions_with_relations_in_model()` given some model). We will now implement this procedure, not only for a single original formula, but more generally for a set of original formulas.

TASK 5 Implement in the missing code for the function `replace_functions_with_relations_in_formulas(formulas)`, which returns formulas containing (1) a function-free analog of each of the given formulas, obtained via Task 4, and (2) for every function name that appears in the given formulas, a formula that verifies that the interpretation of the corresponding relation name that replaced it indeed corresponds to a function.

---

predicates/functions.py

```
def replace_functions_with_relations_in_formulas(formulas:
                                        AbstractSet[Formula]) -> \
        Set[Formula]:
    """Syntactically converts the given set of formulas to a set of formulas
    that do not contain any function invocations, and is "two-way
    equivalent" in the sense that:

    1. The former holds in a model if and only if the latter holds in the
       canonically corresponding model with no function interpretations.
    2. The latter holds in a model if and only if that model has a
       canonically corresponding model with interpretations for the function
       names of the former, and the former holds in that model.

    Parameters:
        formulas: formulas to convert, which contain no variable names that are
            ``z`` followed by a number, and such that there exist no canonically
            corresponding function name and relation name that are both invoked
            in these formulas.

    Returns:
        A set of formulas, one for each given formula as well as one additional
        formula for each relation name that replaces a function name from the
        given formulas, such that:

        1. The given formulas hold in a model `model` if and only if the
           returned formulas hold in
           `replace_functions_with_relations_in_model(model)`.
        2. The returned formulas hold in a model `model` if and only if
           `replace_relations_with_functions_in_model(model,original_functions)`,
           where `original_functions` are all the function names in the given
```

---

[4] Throughout this book, whenever you are given a set of formulas, you may always assume that any function name or relation name that appears multiple times in these formulas is always invoked with the same arity.

```
                    formulas, is a model and the given formulas hold in it.
        """
        assert len(set.union(*[{function_name_to_relation_name(function) for
                                function,arity in formula.functions()}
                            for formula in formulas]).intersection(
                                set.union(*[{relation for relation,arity in
                                            formula.relations()} for
                                            formula in formulas]))) == 0
        for formula in formulas:
            for variable in formula.variables():
                assert not is_z_and_number(variable)
        # Task 8.5
```

For every formula set `formulas` and its corresponding function-free formula set `new_formulas=replace_functions_with_relations_in_formulas(formulas)`, we now have a two-way assurance. First, as before, we have for every model `model` of `formulas` that `replace_functions_with_relations_in_model(model)` is a model of `new_formulas`. Second, we now also have the other direction: If `functions` is the set of function names used in `formulas`, then we also have for every model `model` of `new_formulas` that `replace_relations_with_functions_in_model(model, functions)` is a model of `formulas`. Therefore, there exists a model of the set `formulas` (that may contain function invocations) if and only if there exists a model of the function-free set `new_formulas`. Your solutions in this chapter so far therefore prove the following theorem.

THEOREM 8.1 (Redundancy of Functions)   *For every set F of formulas (which may contain function invocations), there exists a set F' of function-free formulas obtainable from F via an efficient syntactic procedure, such that F has a model if and only if F' has a model. Moreover, given a model of F' there is a simple natural way to convert it into a model of F and vice versa.*

Admittedly, the theorem (8.1) on the redundancy of functions is stated in a somewhat informal manner. While as computer scientists we have a reasonable understanding of the word "efficient" in "efficient syntactic procedure," the phrase "simple natural way" justifiably seems less grounded and precise. We intentionally do not want to dive too deeply into the precise meaning of this phrase in this book but will note that the idea is that there is a one-to-one correspondence between models of F, and models of F' (so in a strong sense the sets of the models that F and F' can represent are "as rich") that has many additional desirable properties beyond the ability to convert models back and forth. For example, this correspondence is *local* in the sense that given a model of F', to find the interpretation of a single function name (or other construct name) in the corresponding model of F we need only look at a single interpretation in F' and do not need any "global" information about F'. Interested readers are advised to seek out a text on **model theory**, and specifically read about **homomorphisms** between models, for a deeper look into the beautiful world that here we merely peek into.

8.2   Getting Rid of Equality

We now move to the second simplification of this chapter, eliminating equalities in formulas. Since you have already shown how to eliminate function invocations from formulas without losing any expressive power, we will assume henceforth that our formulas and models are function-free. Unlike in Section 8.1, we will start with transforming formulas as in Task 5, and only then move to converting models back and forth as in Tasks 1 and 2. Our strategy here for transforming individual formulas into equality-free ones is very simple: replace any equality '$\tau=\sigma$' (where τ and σ are terms) with a matching invocation of the relation name 'SAME', i.e., 'SAME(τ,σ)'. Once again, we must also add some formulas that force 'SAME' to have the intended interpretation, but the catch is that we cannot use the equality symbol in these formulas (otherwise, we will have gained nothing). So, which conditions that can be expressed without using equalities capture the meaning of the equality relation? First, it is clear that 'SAME' should have the basic properties of reflexivity (SAME(x,x)), symmetry (SAME(x,y) iff SAME(y,x)), and transitivity (SAME(x,y) and SAME(y,z) imply SAME(x,z)). These do not suffice, however. Indeed, the main requirement that will connect this new relation name to its intended interpretation is that 'SAME(τ,σ)' implies that in *every* formula where we have τ we can replace it by σ. For any unary relation name R, this would mean requiring that '$\forall x[\forall y[(\text{SAME}(x,y)\to(R(x)\to R(y)))]]$', for any binary relation name 'R' it would mean requiring that '$\forall x1[\forall x2[\forall y1[\forall y2[((\text{SAME}(x1,y1)\&\text{SAME}(x2,y2))\to(R(x1,x2)\to R(y1,y2)))]]]]$', etc. If we introduce such a formula for each relation name that our formulas contain, then we are assured that in every formula we can replace any term by any "SAME term," without changing the truth value of the formula.

TASK 6   Implement the missing code for the function `replace_equality_with_SAME_in_formulas(formulas)`, which returns equality-free formulas containing (1) the equality-free analog of each of the given formulas (obtained by replacing every equality with a matching invocation of the relation name 'SAME') and (2) additional formulas that ensure that 'SAME' has the required semantics (reflexivity, symmetry, transitivity, and being respected by all relations).

predicates/functions.py

```
def replace_equality_with_SAME_in_formulas(formulas: AbstractSet[Formula]) -> \
        Set[Formula]:
    """Syntactically converts the given set of formulas to a canonically
    corresponding set of formulas that do not contain any equalities, consisting
    of the following formulas:

    1. A formula for each of the given formulas, where each equality is
       replaced with a matching invocation of the relation name 'SAME'.
    2. Formula(s) that ensure that in any model of the returned formulas, the
       interpretation of the relation name 'SAME' is reflexive, symmetric,
       and transitive.
    3. For each relation name from the given formulas, formula(s) that ensure
       that in any model of the returned formulas, the interpretation of this
       relation name respects the interpretation of the relation name 'SAME'.
```

```
    Parameters:
        formulas: formulas to convert, that contain no function names and do not
            contain the relation name 'SAME'.

    Returns:
        The converted set of formulas.
    """
    for formula in formulas:
        assert len(formula.functions()) == 0
        assert 'SAME' not in \
            {relation for relation,arity in formula.relations()}
    # Task 8.6
```

Having defined the transformation for formulas, similarly to Section 8.1 we now wish to convert a model of the original formulas to a model of the equality-free formulas, in a way that preserves the truth value.

TASK 7   Implement the missing code for the function add_SAME_as_equality_ in_model(model), which returns a model that is identical to the given model, with the addition of an interpretation of the relation name 'SAME' that behaves like equality.

```
                            ┤ predicates/functions.py ├
def add_SAME_as_equality_in_model(model: Model[T]) -> Model[T]:
    """Adds an interpretation of the relation name 'SAME' in the given model,
    that canonically corresponds to equality in the given model.

    Parameters:
        model: model that has no interpretation of the relation name 'SAME', to
            add the interpretation to.

    Returns:
        A model obtained from the given model by adding an interpretation of the
        relation name 'SAME', that contains precisely all pairs (`x`,`x`) for
        every element `x` of the universe of the given model.
    """
    assert 'SAME' not in model.relation_interpretations
    # Task 8.7
```

Your solutions to Tasks 6 and 7 guarantee that for every formula set formulas and its corresponding equality-free formula set new_formulas=replace_equality_ with_SAME_in_formulas(formulas), for every model model it is the case that model is a model of formulas if and only if add_SAME_as_equality_in_model(model) is a model of new_formulas. Once again, though, similarly to Section 8.1, we need to make sure that we have not introduced any additional models when removing equality. As in Task 2, we will do so by showing that every model of the new set of equality-free formulas can be converted into a model of the original set of formulas. When going in this "opposite direction," a conceptual difficulty arises: The semantics of equality is that for any two terms τ and σ, the truth value of the formula '$\tau=\sigma$' is *True* if and only if the *values* of these two terms are both the exact same element of Ω. There is no way to force such semantics without the equality symbol! This means that in some sense, the new set of formulas supports richer models not supported by the original set of formulas. For example, consider the formula '∀x[∀y[x=y]]'. It is easy to see that every model that satisfies it must have only a single element in its universe. There is no way to force a model to have only a single element without using equality: The formula '∀x[∀y[SAME(x,y)]]' can be satisfied by a model with two elements (and, in fact, can be satisfied by a model with any number of elements!), even if we demand that the interpretation of 'SAME' be reflexive, symmetric, and transitive. Nevertheless, the different elements in such a model really are *the same* as each other as we have put formulas in place requiring that they act in exactly the same way in every possible formula.

In general, whenever a model contains different elements that are "the SAME" as each other, if we keep only a single representative in our model for each such set of items that are "the SAME" as each other, then we force equality to behave like 'SAME'. Formally, the interpretation of 'SAME' partitions the elements of the universe into **equivalence classes**, and our new model will have a single representative for each equivalence class. As an example, consider the following model:

- Universe $\Omega = \{0, \ldots, 10\}$.
- The interpretation of the constant name '0' is $0 \in \Omega$.
- The interpretation of the constant name '4' is $4 \in \Omega$.
- The interpretation of the ternary relation name 'Plus' is such that for every $\alpha, \beta, \gamma \in \Omega$, we have that (γ, α, β) is in the interpretation of 'Plus' if and only if $\gamma = \alpha + \beta$ modulo 4.
- The interpretation of the ternary relation name 'Times' is such that for every $\alpha, \beta, \gamma \in \Omega$, we have that (γ, α, β) is in the interpretation of 'Times' if and only if $\gamma = \alpha \cdot \beta$ modulo 4.
- The interpretation of the (binary) relation name 'SAME' is such that for every $\alpha, \beta \in \Omega$, we have that (α, β) is in the interpretation of 'SAME' if and only if $\alpha = \beta$ modulo 4.

It is straightforward to verify that the interpretation of 'SAME' in this model is reflexive, symmetric, transitive, and respected by both other relations. For the latter property, note that indeed if $\alpha, \alpha' \in \Omega$ are "the SAME," $\beta, \beta' \in \Omega$ are "the SAME," and $\gamma, \gamma' \in \Omega$ are "the SAME," then (γ, α, β) is in the interpretation of one of these relation names if and only if $(\gamma', \alpha', \beta')$ is in the interpretation of that relation name. It is straightforward to see that the interpretation of the relation name 'SAME' in this model has four equivalence classes: $\{0, 4, 8\}, \{1, 5, 9\}, \{2, 6, 10\}, \{3, 7\}$. So, taking one representative from each equivalence class, say, 8 for the first, 1 for the second, 6 for the third, and 3 for the fourth, we obtain the following model, where the interpretation of all relation names (with respect to the chosen representatives of the various equivalence classes) are preserved, but equality behaves like 'SAME' does in the original model:

- Universe $\Omega = \{8, 1, 6, 3\}$.
- The interpretation of the constant name '0', and the interpretation of the constant name '4' are both $8 \in \Omega$ (since 8 is the representative of the equivalence class that contains both original interpretations 0 and 4).
- The interpretation of the ternary relation name 'Plus' is such that for every $\alpha, \beta, \gamma \in \Omega$, we have that (γ, α, β) is in the interpretation of 'Plus' if and only if $\gamma = \alpha + \beta$ modulo 4.

- The interpretation of the ternary relation name 'Times' is such that for every $\alpha, \beta, \gamma \in \Omega$, we have that (γ, α, β) is in the interpretation of 'Times' if and only if $\gamma = \alpha \cdot \beta$ modulo 4.

Of course, had we chosen 0 as the representative of the first equivalence class, 1 of the second, 2 of the third, and 3 of the fourth, we would have gotten what seems like a "nicer" model with $\Omega = \{0, 1, 2, 3\}$, with '0' interpreted as $0 \in \Omega$, and with 'Plus' and 'Times' interpreted, respectively, as addition and multiplication modulo 4 (and with '4' interpreted as $0 \in \Omega$, which is 4 modulo 4), but looking more closely we notice that these two models are in fact identical up to "renaming" the four elements of the model, so the latter model only seems "nicer" to us, but mathematically both are equivalent and we will be as happy with either of them.

It is worth examining what would have gone wrong had we just removed the relation name 'SAME' from the original model *without* shrinking the universe to contain only one representative from each equivalence class. First and more obviously, we would have had a problem with formulas that contain both constants: The formula 'SAME(0,4)' holds in the original model while the corresponding formula '0=4' would not have held in the new model had we not shrunk its universe. (This formula *does* hold in the new model with only one representative from each equivalence class, since the interpretations of both constants '0' and '4' in that model are the same: the universe element $8 \in \Omega$.) There is another more subtle yet more fundamental problem with not shrinking the universe, though: Consider the formula '∃v[∃w[∃x[∃y[∃z[(~SAME(v,w)&(~SAME(v,x)&· · ·(~SAME(x,z)& ~SAME(y,z))· · ·))]]]]]' where the conjunction goes over all 10 pairs of distinct variable names out of 'v'. . . 'z', checking that the interpretations of no two of these variable names are "the SAME." This formula does not hold in the original model. Nonetheless, the corresponding formula '∃v[∃w[∃x[∃y[∃z[(~v=w&(~v=x&· · ·(~x=z&~y=z)· · ·))]]]]]' would have held in the new model had we not shrunk its universe. (This formula does *not* hold in the new model with only one representative from each equivalence class, since the universe of this model does not contain five distinct elements.) Indeed, shrinking the universe to contain only one representative from each equivalence class is the only way to force equality in the new model to behave like 'SAME' does in the original model. Your final task in this chapter is to implement this conversion.

TASK 8 Implement the missing code for the function `make_equality_as_SAME_in_model(model)`, which returns an analog of the given model without the interpretation of 'SAME', and containing exactly one representative from each equivalence class of the interpretation of 'SAME' in the given model. It is required that for every formula set `formulas` and its corresponding equality-free formula set `new_formulas=replace_equality_with_SAME_in_formulas(formulas)`, for every model `model` it is the case that `model` is a model of `new_formulas` if and only if `make_equality_as_SAME_in_model(model)` is a model of `formulas`.

```
                        predicates/functions.py

def make_equality_as_SAME_in_model(model: Model[T]) -> Model[T]:
    """Converts the given model to a model where equality coincides with the
    interpretation of 'SAME' in the given model, in the sense that any set of
    formulas holds in the returned model if and only if its canonically
```

```
    corresponding set of formulas that do not contain equality holds in the
    given model.

    Parameters:
        model: model to convert, that contains no function interpretations, and
            contains an interpretation of the relation name 'SAME' that is
            reflexive, symmetric, transitive, and respected by the
            interpretations of all other relation names.

    Returns:
        A model that is a model of any set `formulas` if and only if the given
        model is a model of `replace_equality_with_SAME(formulas)`. The universe
        of the returned model corresponds to the equivalence classes of the
        interpretation of 'SAME' in the given model.
    """
    assert 'SAME' in model.relation_interpretations and \
        model.relation_arities['SAME'] == 2
    assert len(model.function_interpretations) == 0
    # Task 8.8
```

The guarantees of your solutions to Tasks 7 and 8 prove the following theorem.

THEOREM 8.2 (Redundancy of Equality)   *For every set F of formulas (which may contain equality), there exists a set F′ of equality-free formulas obtainable from F via an efficient syntactic procedure, such that F has a model if and only if F′ has a model. Moreover, given a model of F′ there is a simple natural way to convert it into a model of F and vice versa.*

Once again, we resort to an admittedly informal statement of the theorem (8.2) on the redundancy of equality. Recall that we have remarked that in the theorem (8.1) on redundancy of functions, "simple natural way" in particular meant that the correspondence between models of F and models of $F′$ was one-to-one. To make our informality in the theorem (8.2) on the redundancy of equality even worse, by now you know that when removing equality, the correspondence between models of F and models of $F′$ is not one-to-one (indeed, several models of $F′$ will be mapped to the same model of F since we are collapsing every equivalence class into a single representative, and for example it is impossible to unambiguously recover the size of each equivalence class after it had been collapsed). Nonetheless, it turns out that this correspondence maintains many of the natural properties of one-to-one correspondences – and in particular still, in a precise strong sense, the models that F and $F′$ can represent are "as rich" – as well as many additional desirable properties such as the *locality* property discussed at the end of Section 8.1. Once again, interested readers are advised to seek out a text on **model theory** (and specifically on **homomorphisms** between models) for a more detailed and formal discussion.

9   Deductive Proofs of Predicate Logic Formulas

In this chapter, we will develop the notion of formal deductive proofs for predicate logic. As in the case of propositional logic, we will have axioms and inference rules, but we will now need to handle all of the new constructs of predicate logic. The effort that we made in the study of propositional logic in Part I of this book will bear its fruits as it will allow us to use arbitrary tautologies in our proofs.

This chapter is rather technical, focusing on the exact syntactic details of our proof system for predicate logic. Before we dive into the details, let us give a high-level overview of the components of our proof system:

- **Assumptions and Axioms:** A line in a proof may be an assumption or a logical axiom, which as you will see, we will treat in the same way. The specific set of axioms that we will use will only be specified in Chapter 10. The main complication here is that we allow syntactic *families* of formulas, called **schemas**[1], as axioms. For example, we would like to be able to have a single axiom schema that says that for any formula ϕ, any variable name x, and any term τ, the following is an axiom: '$(\forall x[\phi(x)] \rightarrow \phi(\tau))$'.
- **Inference Rules:** We will have exactly two axiomatic inference rules. The first is our old acquaintance **modus ponens (MP)** that deduces the formula 'ψ' from previous lines 'ϕ' and '$(\phi \rightarrow \psi)$'. The second is called **universal generalization** and allows arbitrary universal quantifications of previous lines: deducing a formula '$\forall x[\phi]$' from a previous line 'ϕ'.
- **Tautologies:** We will allow using any tautology of propositional logic as a line in our proof (we will see in Section 9.3.4 precisely how a tautology of propositional logic can be used in a predicate-logic proof). We allow ourselves this power as we already know from our study of propositional logic that any such tautology has a proof from some short list of propositional-logic axioms (we will give the precise justification in Section 9.4, via a predicate-logic version of the tautology theorem (9.2)).

The structure of this chapter is as follows: We start with an example of a proof. We then formally define the somewhat involved notion of schemas that we will allow using. We continue by fully specifying our proof system and making sure that it is **sound**: Anything that is syntactically proven from some assumptions indeed semantically follows from them. Finally, we revisit our choice of allowing arbitrary tautologies in our proof system and show that by your solutions to the tasks of Chapter 6, this really is only a matter of convenience.

---

[1] Another frequently used plural form of "schemas," which you may encounter in many books, is "schemata." For simplicity, in this book we will stick with "schemas."

9.1   Example of a Proof

As our example we will look at a proof of the following **syllogism**: All Greeks are human, all humans are mortal; thus, all Greeks are mortal. This syllogism may be formulated and proved in predicate logic as follows.

Assumptions:

1. '∀x[(Greek(x)→Human(x))]'
2. '∀x[(Human(x)→Mortal(x))]'

Conclusion: '∀x[(Greek(x)→Mortal(x))]'

Proof:

1. '∀x[(Greek(x)→Human(x))]'. Justification: First assumption.
2. '(∀x[(Greek(x)→Human(x))]→(Greek(x)→Human(x)))'. Justification: This is an instance of an axiom schema that says that for any formula ϕ, any variable name x, and any term τ, the following is an axiom: '(∀x[$\phi(x)$]→$\phi(\tau)$))'. In this case, $\phi(x)$ is taken to be '(Greek(x)→Human(x))', and both x and τ are taken to be 'x'.
3. '(Greek(x)→Human(x))'. Justification: Modus ponens (MP) from Lines 1 and 2.
4. '∀x[(Human(x)→Mortal(x))]'. Justification: Second assumption.
5. '(∀x[(Human(x)→Mortal(x))]→(Human(x)→Mortal(x)))'. Justification: This, again, is another instance of the same axiom schema '(∀x[$\phi(x)$]→$\phi(\tau)$))', this time with $\phi(x)$ taken to be '(Human(x)→Mortal(x))', and again with x and τ both taken to be 'x'.
6. '(Human(x)→Mortal(x))'. Justification: Modus ponens (MP) from Lines 4 and 5.
7. '((Greek(x)→Human(x))→((Human(x)→Mortal(x))→(Greek(x)→Mortal(x))))'. Justification: The structure of this line has the form '((p→q)→((q→r)→(p→r)))', which is a tautology of propositional logic.
8. '((Human(x)→Mortal(x))→(Greek(x)→Mortal(x)))'. Justification: Modus ponens (MP) from Lines 3 and 7.
9. '(Greek(x)→Mortal(x))'. Justification: Modus ponens (MP) from Lines 6 and 8.
10. '∀x[(Greek(x)→Mortal(x))]'. Justification: Universal generalization of Line 9.

While this proof may look unintuitive, here is a way to think about it. Technically, our proof system allows using lines that are not **sentences**, i.e., allows using lines that have free variable names. Intuitively, a formula with free variable names should be thought of as though all of its free variable names are universally quantified. Lines 1–6 of the proof take us from the quantified assumptions to essentially equivalent formulas without the explicit quantification. The technical advantage of having omitted the universal quantifiers is that we now have formulas that "look like" propositional logic formulas, which we already know how to handle. Indeed, Lines 7–9 rely only on propositional-logic-like arguments to obtain the required conclusion. Finally, Line 10 moves back to the required explicitly quantified form of the conclusion.

9.2 Schemas

Recall that in propositional logic, we could have a formula like '(x|~x)' as an axiom, with the understanding that we can "plug in" any formula for 'x'. Thus, for example, substituting '(p→q)' for 'x' gives that the formula '((p→q)|~(p→q))' is a specialization of this axiom, which we are also allowed to use. We will need a similar mechanism for predicate logic, but here we will make the rules of what exactly can be substituted, and where, explicit. There are various possible levels of generality for defining schemas, and, as usual, we choose some sufficient intermediate level of generality, trading off elegance, ease of implementation, and ease of use.

While in propositional logic we had either assumptions that have to be taken completely literally without any substitutions on one extreme or axioms where essentially any symbol could be consistently replaced with any formula when using the axiom on the other extreme, in predicate logic we will have the full range in between these two extremes. For example we may wish to write an assumption such as 'plus(c,d)=plus(d,c)', where 'c' and 'd' are **templates** that could be (consistently) replaced by any terms but 'plus' cannot be replaced by any other function name. In contrast, we may wish to write an assumption such as 'plus(0,c)=c' where 'c' is a template that could be replaced by any term but neither 'plus' nor '0' can be replaced.

As a different example, as already mentioned in the beginning of this chapter, we will also wish to be able to represent some **axiom schemas**, each of which standing for a *collection* of axioms of a certain type. That is, in traditional mathematical textual proofs we can say things like "for any formula ϕ, any term τ, and any variable name x, the following is an axiom: '$(\forall x[\phi(x)] \to \phi(\tau))$'," and we will wish to capture such statements as axioms as well. (Attentive readers may have noticed that we had in fact already encountered this axiom schema in the proof example in Section 9.1.) In our computerized representation, we will use relation names as templates for formulas, constant names as templates for terms, and variable names as templates for variable names, so we will represent this axiom schema as '$(\forall x[R(x)] \to R(c))$' while explicitly stating that 'R', 'x', and 'c' are all templates. In this case, roughly speaking, 'R' is a template for any "formula into which a term can be substituted," 'c' is a template for any term, and 'x' is a template for any variable name. Any choice of such formula, term, and variable name to substitute for the templates creates a different **instance** of this axiom schema. All constant, variable, and relation names (if any) that we do not specify to be templates should always be taken literally in any instance of the axiom schema.

The file `predicates/proofs.py` defines (among other classes) a Python class `Schema` that represents a schema as a regular predicate-logic formula together with the set of constructs of this formula – constant names, variable names, and/or relation names – that serve as templates (placeholders).

```
                              ┌─────────────────────┐
                              │ predicates/proofs.py │
─────────────────────────────┴─────────────────────┴──────────────────────
@frozen
class Schema:
    """An immutable schema of predicate-logic formulas, comprised of a formula
    along with the constant names, variable names, and nullary or unary relation
    names in that formula that serve as templates. A template constant name is a
```

```
      placeholder for any term. A template variable name is a placeholder for any
      variable name. A template nullary or unary relation name is a placeholder
      for any (parametrized for a unary template relation name) predicate-logic
      formula that does not refer to any variable name in the schema (except
      possibly through its instantiated argument for a unary relation name).

      Attributes:
          formula: the formula of the schema.
          templates: the constant, variable, and relation names from the formula
              that serve as templates.
      """
      formula: Formula
      templates: FrozenSet[str]

      def __init__(self, formula: Formula,
                   templates: AbstractSet[str] = frozenset()):
          """Initializes a `Schema` from its formula and template names.

          Parameters:
              formula: the formula for the schema.
              templates: the constant, variable, and relation names from the
                  formula to serve as templates.
          """
          for template in templates:
              assert is_constant(template) or is_variable(template) or \
                  is_relation(template)
              if is_relation(template):
                  arities = {arity for relation,arity in formula.relations() if
                             relation == template}
                  assert arities == {0} or arities == {1}
          self.formula = formula
          self.templates = frozenset(templates)
```

The default value (for the constructor of this class) of the set of templates is the empty set, which corresponds to a schema with only one possible instance (because there are no templates that can be replaced): the original schema formula. We will now review each of the three types of syntactic constructs that can potentially serve as templates: constant names, variable names, and relation names.

9.2.1   Templates Constants Names

A constant name that is specified as a template can serve as a placeholder for any term. Thus, for example, the schema

$$\texttt{Schema(Formula.parse('c=c'), \{'c'\})}$$

has as instances all of the following formulas (among others): '0=0', 'x=x', 'plus(x,y)=plus(x,y)'.

9.2.2   Templates Variable Names

A variable name that is specified as a template can serve as a placeholder for any variable name. For example, the schema

```
Schema(Formula.parse('(times(x,0)=0&Ax[Ey[plus(x,y)=0]])'), {'x'})
```

has the following as an instance: '(times(z,0)=0&∀z[∃y[plus(z,y)=0]])'. As this example shows, all occurrences of the template variable name should be replaced, including free *and* bound occurrences, as well as occurrences that immediately follow a quantifier.

9.2.3 Templates Relation Names

A relation name that is specified as a template can serve as a placeholder for an arbitrary formula that may possibly be "parametrized" by a single "parameter." Let us first consider the simpler case of a **parameter-less** template relation name – a template whose invocations in the schema formula are nullary, such as is the case in the schema

```
Schema(Formula.parse('(Q()|~Q())'), {'Q'})
```

for the template 'Q'. A parameter-less template relation name such as 'Q' in this schema can serve as a placeholder for any formula. Thus, for example, this schema has the following as an instance: '(c=y|~c=y)'.

Let us now consider the more intricate case of a **parametrized** template relation name – a template whose invocations in the schema formula are unary, such as is the case in the schema

```
Schema(Formula.parse('(Ax[(R(x)->Q(x))]->(Az[R(z)]->Aw[Q(w)]))'),
                     {'R', 'Q'})
```

for each of the templates 'Q' and 'R'.[2] A parametrized template relation name such as 'Q' or 'R' in this schema can serve as a placeholder for any **parametrized formula**, that is, a formula that optionally contains a placeholder for the argument of the unary invocation. Thus, for example, this schema can be **instantiated** with 'R(□)' defined as '□=7' (parametrized by the placeholder □), and with 'Q(□)' defined as 'T(y,□)' to obtain the following instance of this schema: '(∀x[(x=7→T(y,x))]→(∀z[z=7]→∀w[T(y,w)]))'.

Note that when defining the parametrized template 'Q(□)' as 'T(y,□)' in the last example, and when defining the parameter-less template 'Q()' as 'c=y' in the preceding example, we allowed the formula that replaces the template relation name to contain free variable names ('y' in both examples). In order to avoid unintended (and not logically sound) quantifications, we however restrict this to only be allowed for free variable names that *do not get bound by a quantifier in the resulting instance of the schema*. Thus, for example, if we look at the schema

```
Schema(Formula.parse('(Ax[R(x)]->R(c))'), {'R', 'c', 'x'})
```

that appeared in the proof example in Section 9.1, then we allow to instantiate this schema with 'R(□)' defined as '□=0' to get '(∀x[x=0]→c=0)', but we do not allow to instantiate it with 'R(□)' defined as '□=x', so '(∀x[x=x]→c=x)' is *not* an instance of this schema (nor is it a logically sound statement), since the free variable name 'x' in '□=x' would get bound

---

[2] Note in the implementation of the constructor of class Schema that it verifies for each template relation name that its invocations in the schema formula are either all nullary – corresponding to a parameter-less template – or all unary – corresponding to a parametrized template.

by the universal quantifier in the resulting schema instance if such a substitution were to be made.[3]

Let us look more closely at the process of, e.g., taking the schema

```
Schema(Formula.parse('(Ax[R(x)]->R(c))'), {'R', 'c', 'x'})
```

just discussed and instantiating it with 's(1)' for 'c', with '($\exists$z[s(z)=$\square$]$\rightarrow$Q($\square$))' for 'R($\square$)', and with 'y' for 'x':

1. The variable name 'x' that immediately follows the universal quantification gets substituted for 'y'.
2. For the first occurrence of 'R' in the schema (i.e., for 'R(x)') we first substitute 'y' for 'x' to get the **instantiated argument** 'y' of that invocation of this template relation name. This instantiated argument then gets substituted for all occurrences of the parameter '$\square$' in the parametrized formula '($\exists$z[s(z)=$\square$]$\rightarrow$Q($\square$))' to get '($\exists$z[s(z)=y]$\rightarrow$Q(y))' as the final replacement for 'R(x)'.
3. For the second occurrence (i.e., for 'R(c)') we substitute 's(1)' for 'c' to get the instantiated argument 's(1)' of that invocation of this template relation name. This instantiated argument then gets substituted for all occurrences of the parameter '$\square$' in the parametrized formula '($\exists$z[s(z)=$\square$]$\rightarrow$Q($\square$))' to get '($\exists$z[s(z)=s(1)]$\rightarrow$Q(s(1)))' as the final replacement for 'R(c)'.
4. Altogether, we get '($\forall$y[($\exists$z[s(z)=y]$\rightarrow$Q(y))]$\rightarrow$($\exists$z[s(z)=s(1)]$\rightarrow$Q(s(1))))' as the resulting instance of this axiom schema (which is indeed a logically sound statement).

One final restriction we must verify regards quantification *within* parametrized formulas that are substituted for parametrized template relation names. Consider again the schema

```
Schema(Formula.parse('(Ax[R(x)]->R(c))'), {'R', 'c', 'x'})
```

already discussed. If we were to allow to instantiate this schema with 'R($\square$)' as '$\exists$x[$\square$=7]', then we would get '($\forall$x[$\exists$x[x=7]]$\rightarrow$$\exists$x[c=7])', which is not logically sound. Therefore, in parametrized formulas that replace (parametrized) template relation names, we do not allow quantifications that *bound any variable name in any instantiated argument of that parametrized template relation name.*[4]

---

[3] Programming language aficionados may notice that this is a classic issue of **variable scope**. We resolved it this way since our formulas do not have a syntax to allow specifying that unlike the first 'x' in 'x=x', which has "local scope," the second 'x' in 'x=x' should have "global scope" like the 'x' in 'c=x'.

[4] This is again an issue of variable scope. Some readers may at this point wonder why we do not disallow some other "scope-confusing instantiations." Consider, e.g., the "intuitively correct" schema `Schema(Formula.parse('Ex[R(c)]->R(c))'), {'c'})`. Replacing 'c' with 'x' in this schema would yield the not logically sound "instance" '$\exists$x[R(x)]$\rightarrow$R(x)', so to avoid that we could have restricted *terms* that replace template *constant* names to contain only free variable names that *do not get bound by a quantifier in the resulting instance of the schema*, analogously to the first restriction detailed in this section regarding variable names in *formulas* that replace template *relation* names. As another example, consider the "intuitively correct" schema `Schema(Formula.parse('Ey[~y=x]'), {'y'})`. Replacing 'y' with 'x' in this schema would yield the not logically sound "instance" '$\exists$x[~x=x]', so to avoid that we could have restricted substitutions of template *variable* names to only those substitutions that *do not make other existing variable names bound by quantifications over the substituted variable names*. While restrictions such as these could have been useful, and would certainly have prevented some instances of some schemas from not being logically sound, this is in fact not the case for any of the schemas that we will use in this book. More generally, there is no "right" or "wrong" set of restrictions to impose here: All that we need, as we will see in the

9.2.4   Handling Parametrized Formulas

We will represent parametrized formulas in Python as regular `Formula` objects that use the constant name '_' (underscore) as the placeholder. So, for example, the first parametrized formula given as an example in Section 9.2.3, '□=7', would be represented in Python by the formula that is returned by `Formula.parse('_=7')`. To avoid confusion, from this point onward, throughout the book and throughout all tests, we will use the constant name '_' only for this purpose.

To handle the substitution of arguments into parametrized formulas, we will implement a notion of *substitution* in a predicate-logic expression – a term or a formula – where all occurrences of a constant name (specifically, '_') are "replaced" by some term. Looking at the tree representation of the expression in which we wish to make the substitution, we simply replace every leaf labeled with the constant name '_' with a subtree that is the tree of the substituting term. Recall that by the second restriction on instantiating parametrized formulas given in Section 9.2.3, we altogether disallow any such substitution in which any variable name that appears in the substituting term gets bound by any quantifier of the formula, so we will have the code that implements the substitution raise an exception in such cases.

While for handling parametrized formulas it is enough to handle substitutions of the constant name '_', we will later want to be able to apply the same mechanics of substitution (including the "scope checking" of variable names in the term to be substituted) also to substitute a term for a variable name rather than for a constant name. In this specific use case, though, and this will become clearer in Chapter 10, we will want to be somewhat careful to only replace *free* occurrences of the variable name. Consider, for example, the formula '(R(x)&∀x[Q(x)])'. If we are asked to replace the variable name 'x' in this formula with the term 'c', we will see that it will be useful that only the 'x' in 'R(x)' be replaced, since the 'x' in 'Q(x)' refers to the variable name universally quantified over ('∀x') in the second part of the formula.

In the following two tasks, you will implement the mechanics of the substitution just described. You will be asked to implement these not only for a single constant or variable name, but in fact also for substituting several constant and/or variable names at the same time. As this functionality will be useful for us in a variety of contexts beyond handling parametrized formulas, you are asked to implement it as part of the classes `Term` and `Formula` in the file `predicates/syntax.py`.

TASK 1   Implement the missing code for the method `substitute(substitution_map, forbidden_variables)` of class `Term`, which returns the term obtained from the current term by replacing each occurrence of each variable or constant name that is a key of the given substitution map with the term to which it is mapped. This method raises a `ForbiddenVariableError` (an exception defined in the file `predicates/syntax.py`)

following chapters, is to have enough restrictions in place on the possible instances of schemas to make sure that the specific schemas that we define and use throughout this book have only logically sound instances (but do still have as legal instances all of the intended logically sound instances that we will need in our proofs). As we will see in Chapter 10, for the schemas that we chose for this book, the two restrictions detailed in the text of this section suffice.

if a term that is used in the requested substitution contains one of the given forbidden variable names.

```
                    ┌─────────────────────┐
                    │ predicates/syntax.py │
                    └─────────────────────┘
class ForbiddenVariableError(Exception):
    """Raised by `Term.substitute` and `Formula.substitute` when a substituted
    term contains a variable name that is forbidden in that context.

    Attributes:
        variable_name: the variable name that was forbidden in the context in
            which a term containing it was to be substituted.
    """
    variable_name: str

    def __init__(self, variable_name: str):
        """Initializes a `ForbiddenVariableError` from the offending variable
        name.

        Parameters:
            variable_name: variable name that is forbidden in the context in
                which a term containing it is to be substituted.
        """
        assert is_variable(variable_name)
        self.variable_name = variable_name
        ⋮

class Term:
        ⋮

    def substitute(self, substitution_map: Mapping[str, Term],
                   forbidden_variables: AbstractSet[str] = frozenset()) -> Term:
        """Substitutes in the current term, each constant name `construct` or
        variable name `construct` that is a key in `substitution_map` with the
        term `substitution_map[construct]`.

        Parameters:
            substitution_map: mapping defining the substitutions to be
                performed.
            forbidden_variables: variable names not allowed in substitution
                terms.

        Returns:
            The term resulting from performing all substitutions. Only
            constant name and variable name occurrences originating in the
            current term are substituted (i.e., those originating in one of the
            specified substitutions are not subjected to additional
            substitutions).

        Raises:
            ForbiddenVariableError: If a term that is used in the requested
                substitution contains a variable name from
                `forbidden_variables`.

        Examples:
            >>> Term.parse('f(x,c)').substitute(
            ...     {'c': Term.parse('plus(d,x)'), 'x': Term.parse('c')}, {'y'})
            f(c,plus(d,x))
```

```
        >>> Term.parse('f(x,c)').substitute(
        ...     {'c': Term.parse('plus(d,y)')}, {'y'})
        Traceback (most recent call last):
          ...
        predicates.syntax.ForbiddenVariableError: y
        """
    for construct in substitution_map:
        assert is_constant(construct) or is_variable(construct)
    for variable in forbidden_variables:
        assert is_variable(variable)
    # Task 9.1
```

Hint: Use recursion.

TASK 2   Implement the missing code for the method substitute(substitution_map, forbidden_variables) of class Formula, which returns the formula obtained from the current formula by replacing each occurrence of each constant name that is a key of the given substitution map with the term to which it is mapped, and replacing each *free* occurrence of each variable name that is a key of the given substitution map with the term to which it is mapped. This method raises a ForbiddenVariableError if a term that is used in the requested substitution contains a variable name that either is one of the given forbidden variable names or becomes bound when the term is substituted into the formula.

```
                          ┌─────────────────────┐
                          │ predicates/syntax.py │
                          └─────────────────────┘
class Formula:
    ⋮
    ⋮

    def substitute(self, substitution_map: Mapping[str, Term],
                   forbidden_variables: AbstractSet[str] = frozenset()) -> \
            Formula:
        """Substitutes in the current formula, each constant name `construct` or
        free occurrence of variable name `construct` that is a key in
        `substitution_map` with the term `substitution_map[construct]`.

        Parameters:
            substitution_map: mapping defining the substitutions to be
                performed.
            forbidden_variables: variable names not allowed in substitution
                terms.

        Returns:
            The formula resulting from performing all substitutions. Only
            constant name and variable name occurrences originating in the
            current formula are substituted (i.e., those originating in one of
            the specified substitutions are not subjected to additional
            substitutions).

        Raises:
            ForbiddenVariableError: If a term that is used in the requested
                substitution contains a variable name from `forbidden_variables`
                or a variable name occurrence that becomes bound when that term
                is substituted into the current formula.

        Examples:
            >>> Formula.parse('Ay[x=c]').substitute(
            ...     {'c': Term.parse('plus(d,x)'), 'x': Term.parse('c')}, {'z'})
```

```
        Ay[c=plus(d,x)]

        >>> Formula.parse('Ay[x=c]').substitute(
        ...     {'c': Term.parse('plus(d,z)')}, {'z'})
        Traceback (most recent call last):
          ...
        predicates.syntax.ForbiddenVariableError: z

        >>> Formula.parse('Ay[x=c]').substitute(
        ...     {'c': Term.parse('plus(d,y)')})
        Traceback (most recent call last):
          ...
        predicates.syntax.ForbiddenVariableError: y
    """
    for construct in substitution_map:
        assert is_constant(construct) or is_variable(construct)
    for variable in forbidden_variables:
        assert is_variable(variable)
    # Task 9.2
```

Hint: Use recursion, augmenting the set `forbidden_variables` in the recursive call with quantified variable names as needed. In the recursion base use your solution to Task 1.

9.2.5   Instantiating Schemas

We can now implement the most important functionality of the `Schema` class, which is to *instantiate* the schema according to a given **instantiation map**.

Recall that our plan is to use the `substitute()` method that you have implemented in Task 2 to handle the burden of substituting instantiated arguments into parametrized formulas that replace parametrized template relation names – and that this method will raise an exception if and only if the second restriction from Section 9.2.3 is violated. In addition, you will be able to use the `substitute()` method of class `Term` that you have implemented in Task 1, due to its ability to handle both constant and variable name placeholders, and furthermore to handle several such placeholders at once, to handle some of the burden of instantiating template constant and variable names by sparing you from writing any more recursions over terms. Most of the work that remains is to write a recursion over formulas that handles the overall instantiation of all types of templates – parameter-less template relation names, parametrized template relation names, template constant names, and template variable names – while verifying that we adhere also to the first restriction from Section 9.2.3. The recursive helper method that you will implement in the following task does precisely this.

TASK 3   Implement the missing code for the static method `_instantiate_helper` of class `Schema`. This recursive method takes four arguments:

1. A `formula`.
2. A map `constants_and_variables_instantiation_map` that maps each template constant name and template variable name to a term that is to be substituted for that template in `formula`. A constant name may be mapped to any term, while a variable name may only be mapped to (a term whose root is) a variable name.

3. A map `relations_instantiation_map` that maps each template relation name to a formula that is to be substituted for it. For parametrized templates relation names, the mapped formula is parametrized by the constant name `'_'`.

4. A set `bound_variables` of variable names that are to be treated as being "quantified by outer layers of the recursion." The implication is (see, in the subsequent instructions, the first case in which an exception should be raised) that a template relation name in `formula` may not be mapped by `relation_instantiation_map` to a formula that has free variable names that are in this set, just like (see, in the subsequent instructions, the second case in which an exception should be raised) it may not be mapped to a formula that has free variable names that get quantified when plugged into `formula`.

The method returns a formula resulting from performing all of the substitutions described in Sections 9.2.1 through 9.2.3 on `formula`.

This method raises a `Schema.BoundVariableError` (an exception defined for you in the class `Schema`) if any free variable name in any formula from `relations_instantiation_map` that is substituted for a (parameter-less or parametrized) template relation name gets bound in the returned formula or is in the set `bound_variables`.

The method also raises a `Schema.BoundVariableError` (this is our recommendation, but for the convenience of readers who are unfamiliar with the details of exception handling, the tests that we provide also accept raising any other exception) if for an invocation of a parametrized template relation name, the substitution of the instantiated argument into the parametrized formula to which the template relation name is mapped causes a variable name in the instantiated argument to get bound by a quantification in that parametrized formula (i.e., if the corresponding call to the method `substitute()` of that formula raises an exception).

```
                              ┌─ predicates/proofs.py ─┐
class Schema:

    ⋮

    class BoundVariableError(Exception):
        """Raised by `_instantiate_helper` when a variable name becomes bound
        during a schema instantiation in a way that is disallowed in that
        context.

        Attributes:
            variable_name: the variable name that became bound in a way that was
                disallowed during a schema instantiation.
            relation_name: the relation name during whose substitution the
                relevant occurrence of the variable name became bound.
        """
        variable_name: str
        relation_name: str

        def __init__(self, variable_name: str, relation_name: str):
            """Initializes a `~Schema.BoundVariableError` from the offending
            variable name and the relation name during whose substitution the
            error occurred.

            Parameters:
```

```
            variable_name: variable name that is to become bound in a way
                that is disallowed during a schema instantiation.
            relation_name: the relation name during whose substitution the
                relevant occurrence of the variable name is to become bound.
        """
        assert is_variable(variable_name)
        assert is_relation(relation_name)
        self.variable_name = variable_name
        self.relation_name = relation_name

    @staticmethod
    def _instantiate_helper(formula: Formula,
                            constants_and_variables_instantiation_map:
                                Mapping[str, Term],
                            relations_instantiation_map: Mapping[str, Formula],
                            bound_variables: AbstractSet[str] = frozenset()) \
            -> Formula:
        """Performs the following substitutions in the given formula:
```

1. Substitute each occurrence of each constant name or variable name
   that is a key of the given constants and variables instantiation map
   with the term mapped to this name by this map.
2. Substitute each nullary invocation of each relation name that is a
   key of the given relations instantiation map with the formula mapped
   to it by this map.
3. For each unary invocation of each relation name that is a key of the
   given relations instantiation map, first perform all substitutions
   to the argument of this invocation (according to the given constants
   and variables instantiation map), then substitute the result for
   each occurrence of the constant name '_' in the formula mapped to the
   relation name by this map, and then substitute the result for this
   unary invocation of the relation name.

Only name occurrences originating in the given formula are substituted
(i.e., name occurrences originating in one of the above substitutions
are not subjected to additional substitutions).

Parameters:
    formula: formula in which to perform the substitutions.
    constants_and_variables_instantiation_map: mapping from constant
        names and variable names in the given formula to terms to be
        substituted for them, where the roots of terms mapped to
        variable names are variable names.
    relations_instantiation_map: mapping from nullary and unary relation
        names in the given formula to formulas to be substituted for
        them, where formulas to be substituted for unary relation names
        are parametrized by the constant name '_'.
    bound_variables: variable names to be treated as bound (see below).

Returns:
    The result of all substitutions.

Raises:
    BoundVariableError: if one of the following occurs when substituting
        an invocation of a relation name:

        1. A free occurrence of a variable name in the formula

mapped to the relation name by the given relations
instantiation map is in `bound_variables` or becomes bound
by a quantification in the given formula after all variable
names in the given formula have been substituted.
2. For a unary invocation: a variable name that is in the
argument to that invocation after all substitutions have been
applied to this argument, becomes bound by a quantification
in the formula mapped to the relation name by the given
relations instantiation map.

Examples:
    The following succeeds:

```
>>> Schema._instantiate_helper(
...     Formula.parse('Ax[(Q(c)->R(x))]'), {'x': Term('w')},
...     {'Q': Formula.parse('y=_')}, {'x', 'z'})
Aw[(y=c->R(w))]
```

however the following fails since 'Q(c)' is to be substituted with
'y=c' while 'y' is specified to be treated as bound:

```
>>> Schema._instantiate_helper(
...     Formula.parse('Ax[(Q(c)->R(x))]'), {},
...     {'Q': Formula.parse('y=_')}, {'x', 'y', 'z'})
Traceback (most recent call last):
    ...
predicates.proofs.Schema.BoundVariableError: ('y', 'Q')
```

and the following fails since as 'Q(c)' is to be substituted with
'y=c', 'y' is to become bound by the quantification 'Ay':

```
>>> Schema._instantiate_helper(
...     Formula.parse('Ax[(Q(c)->R(x))]'), {'x': Term('y')},
...     {'Q': Formula.parse('y=_')})
Traceback (most recent call last):
    ...
predicates.proofs.Schema.BoundVariableError: ('y', 'Q')
```

The following succeeds:

```
>>> Schema._instantiate_helper(
...     Formula.parse('Ax[(Q(c)->R(x))]'),
...     {'c': Term.parse('plus(d,x)')},
...     {'Q': Formula.parse('Ey[y=_]')})
Ax[(Ey[y=plus(d,x)]->R(x))]
```

however the following fails since as '_' is to be substituted with
'plus(d,y)' in 'Ey[y=_]', the 'y' in 'plus(d,y)' is to become bound
by the quantification 'Ey':

```
>>> Schema._instantiate_helper(
...     Formula.parse('Ax[(Q(c)->R(x))]'),
...     {'c': Term.parse('plus(d,y)')},
...     {'Q': Formula.parse('Ey[y=_]')})
Traceback (most recent call last):
    ...
predicates.proofs.Schema.BoundVariableError: ('y', 'Q')
"""
```

```
    for construct in constants_and_variables_instantiation_map:
        assert is_constant(construct) or is_variable(construct)
        if is_variable(construct):
            assert is_variable(
                constants_and_variables_instantiation_map[construct].root)
    for relation in relations_instantiation_map:
        assert is_relation(relation)
    for variable in bound_variables:
        assert is_variable(variable)
    # Task 9.3
```

Guidelines: This method should naturally be implemented recursively. Two simple base cases are when `formula` is an invocation of a relation name that is not a template, or an equality. The required substitution here is simply given by the `substitute()` method of class `Formula` (and you should completely disregard the set `bound_variables` in these two simple base cases). Another simple base case is when `formula` is a nullary invocation of a (parameter-less) template relation name. In this case, the formula to which this relation name is mapped should simply be returned (but only after checking that the free variable names of this formula are disjoint from the set `bound_variables` – otherwise an exception should be raised). The interesting base case is when `formula` is a unary invocation of a (parametrized) template relation name, that is, of the form '$R(t)$' where R is a template relation name and t is a term. In this case, you should first use the `substitute()` method of class `Term` to make the substitutions in t to obtain the instantiated argument t' of this invocation, and then you should "plug" the instantiated argument t' into the formula ϕ to which this template relation name is mapped by using the `substitute()` method of class `Formula` with the substitution map `{'_': `t'`}`. (Of course, in this case you should also check before that the free variable names of ϕ are disjoint from the set `bound_variables` – otherwise an exception should be raised.) The recursion over the formula structure is simple, where the only nontrivial step is the case where `formula` is a quantification of the form '$\forall x[\phi]$' or '$\exists x[\phi]$'. In this case, if the quantification variable name is a template then it should be replaced as specified, and (regardless of whether or not the quantification variable name is a template) deeper recursion levels should take the quantification into account, i.e., the quantification variable name (after any replacement) should be included in the `bound_variables` set that is passed to deeper recursion levels. **Hint:** Make sure that you understand why in each of the calls that were just detailed in the guidelines to any of the `substitute()` methods, an empty set should always be specified as the set of forbidden variable names.

We are now finally ready to implement the main method of the `Schema` class.

TASK 4   Implement the missing code for the method `instantiate(instantiation_map)` of class `Schema`, which takes an instantiation map – a map that maps each template of the current schema to what it should be instantiated to – and returns the instantiated schema instance, as explained in Section 9.2.1 through 9.2.3. Templates that are not mapped by the given instantiation map remain as is in the returned instance. If the instantiation map specifies a constant, variable, or relation name that is not a template, or if an illegal instantiation (violating one of the two restrictions from Section 9.2.3) is requested, then `None` is returned instead.

```
                          ┌─────────────────────┐
                          │ predicates/proofs.py │
                          └─────────────────────┘
#: A mapping from constant names, variable names, and relation names to
#: terms, variable names, and formulas respectively.
InstantiationMap = Mapping[str, Union[Term, str, Formula]]
  ⋮
  ⋮
class Schema:
      ⋮
      ⋮
    def instantiate(self, instantiation_map: InstantiationMap) -> \
            Union[Formula, None]:
        """Instantiates the current schema according to the given map from
        templates of the current schema to expressions.

        Parameters:
            instantiation_map: mapping from templates of the current schema to
                expressions of the type for which they serve as placeholders.
                That is, constant names are mapped to terms, variable names are
                mapped to variable names (strings), and relation names are
                mapped to formulas where unary relation names are mapped to
                formulas parametrized by the constant name ``'_'``.

        Returns:
            The predicate-logic formula obtained by applying the substitutions
            specified by the given map to the formula of the current schema:

            1. Each occurrence in the formula of the current schema of each
               template constant name specified in the given map is substituted
               with the term to which that template constant name is mapped.
            2. Each occurrence in the formula of the current schema of each
               template variable name specified in the given map is substituted
               with the variable name to which that template variable name is
               mapped.
            3. Each nullary invocation in the formula of the current schema of
               each template relation name specified in the given map is
               substituted with the formula to which that template relation name
               is mapped.
            4. Each unary invocation in the formula of the current schema of
               each template relation name specified in the given map is
               substituted with the formula to which that template relation name
               is mapped, in which each occurrence of the constant name '_' is
               substituted with  the instantiated argument of that invocation of
               the template relation name (that is, the term that results from
               instantiating the argument of that invocation by performing all
               the specified substitutions on it).

            ``None`` is returned if one of the keys of the given map is not a
            template of the current schema or if one of the following occurs
            when substituting an invocation of a template relation name:

            1. A free occurrence of a variable name in the formula substituted
               for the template relation name becomes bound by a quantification
               in the instantiated schema formula, except if the template
               relation name is unary and this free occurrence originates in the
               instantiated argument of the invocation of the template relation
               name.
            2. For a unary invocation: a variable name in the instantiated
               argument of that invocation becomes bound by a quantification in
               the formula that is substituted for the invocation of the
```

```
                template relation name.

        Examples:
            >>> s = Schema(Formula.parse('(Q(c1,c2)->(R(c1)->R(c2)))'),
            ...             {'c1', 'c2', 'R'})
            >>> s.instantiate({'c1': Term.parse('plus(x,1)'),
            ...                'R': Formula.parse('Q(_,y)')})
            (Q(plus(x,1),c2)->(Q(plus(x,1),y)->Q(c2,y)))
            >>> s.instantiate({'c1': Term.parse('plus(x,1)'),
            ...                'c2': Term.parse('c1'),
            ...                'R': Formula.parse('Q(_,y)')})
            (Q(plus(x,1),c1)->(Q(plus(x,1),y)->Q(c1,y)))

            >>> s = Schema(Formula.parse('(P()->P())'), {'P'})
            >>> s.instantiate({'P': Formula.parse('plus(a,b)=c')})
            (plus(a,b)=c->plus(a,b)=c)

        For the following schema:

            >>> s = Schema(Formula.parse('(Q(d)->Ax[(R(x)->Q(f(c)))])'),
            ...             {'R', 'Q', 'x', 'c'})

        the following succeeds:

            >>> s.instantiate({'R': Formula.parse('_=0'),
            ...                'Q': Formula.parse('x=_'),
            ...                'x': 'w'})
            (x=d->Aw[(w=0->x=f(c))])

        however, the following returns ``None`` because 'd' is not a
        template of the schema:

            >>> s.instantiate({'R': Formula.parse('_=0'),
            ...                'Q': Formula.parse('x=_'),
            ...                'x': 'w',
            ...                'd': Term('z')})

        and the following returns ``None`` because 'z' that is free in the
        assignment to 'Q' is to become bound by a quantification in the
        instantiated schema formula:

            >>> s.instantiate({'R': Formula.parse('_=0'),
            ...                'Q': Formula.parse('s(z)=_'),
            ...                'x': 'z'})

        and the following returns ``None`` because 'y' in the instantiated
        argument 'f(plus(a,y))' of the second invocation of 'Q' is to become
        bound by the quantification in the formula substituted for 'Q':

            >>> s.instantiate({'R': Formula.parse('_=0'),
            ...                'Q': Formula.parse('Ay[s(y)=_]'),
            ...                'c': Term.parse('plus(a,y)')})
        """
        for construct in instantiation_map:
            if is_variable(construct):
                assert is_variable(instantiation_map[construct])
            elif is_constant(construct):
```

```
                    assert isinstance(instantiation_map[construct], Term)
           else:
                    assert is_relation(construct)
                    assert isinstance(instantiation_map[construct], Formula)
       # Task 9.4
```

Guidelines: Call your solution to Task 3 with the appropriate arguments that you will derive from `instantiation_map`. Do not forget to check for illegal arguments and to handle exceptions raised by `_instantiate_helper()`.

We conclude this section by recalling the specialization soundness lemma (4.1) of propositional logic, which states that every specialization of a sound inference rule is itself sound as well. While it would have been nice to have an analogous lemma for predicate logic, it is not clear exactly what such a lemma would mean: that every instance of a sound schema is sound? But what does it mean for a schema to be sound? In propositional logic since both an inference rule and its specializations are inference rules, this lemma has nontrivial meaning since there is a definition, that does not involve specialization, for what it means for an inference rule to be sound. In predicate logic, however, formulas are instances of schemas rather than specializations of formulas, and while it is clear what it means for a formula to be sound – to hold in every model – it is not clear what it means for a schema to be sound (without mentioning instantiation). Indeed, what would it mean for a schema to hold in every model? Therefore, in predicate logic, we do not have an analogous lemma, but rather we define the soundness[5] property of schemas so that this statement holds by definition.

DEFINITION 9.1 (Sound Formula; Sound Schema) We say that a predicate-logic formula is **sound** if it holds in every model that has interpretations for all its constant, function, and relation names, under any assignment to its free variable names. We say that a schema is **sound** if every instance of it (an instance is a predicate-logic formula) is sound.

In fact, as we will see in Chapter 10, the two restrictions on instantiations that we imposed in Section 9.2.3 are in place to make sure that the axiom schemas in our axiomatic system for predicate logic – see Chapter 10 – are sound: to disallow "instances" of these schemas that would not hold in all models, and would thus render these schemas not sound.

Before moving on to defining proofs in predicate logic, we note an important difference in the definition of soundness between propositional logic and predicate logic. Unlike in propositional logic, where the soundness of any inference rule (or formula) could be checked using a finite semantic procedure (checking all of the finitely many possible models by calling `is_sound_inference()`), in predicate logic there may be infinitely many models for a given formula, and so just semantically checking soundness by going over all possible models is infeasible.[6] We will discuss this point in Chapter 10. For Section 9.3, we

---

[5] What we call **sound** schemas are often called **valid** schemas. In this book, however, we use the term *valid* for syntactic "correctness" (e.g., valid proof) and the term *sound* for semantic "correctness," both for simplicity and to emphasize the contrast between the syntactic and semantic worlds.

[6] A certain set of formulas for which there is a finite semantic procedure for verifying their soundness – **tautologies** (in predicate logic this is no longer a synonym for a sound formula, but rather a special case of a sound formula) – will be mentioned in Section 9.3 and discussed in Section 9.4.

will assume that we are somehow assured that some basic schemas or formulas are sound, and we will wish to use them to prove that other formulas are sound as well.

9.3   Proofs

We can now move to defining formal deductive proofs in predicate logic. Just like in propositional logic, a proof gives a formal derivation of a conclusion from a list of **assumptions/axioms**, via a set of **inference rules**, where the derivation itself is a list of **lines**, each of which contains a formula that is justified as being (an instance of) an assumption/axiom, or by previous lines via an inference rule. Of course, here the formulas in the lines will be predicate-logic (rather than propositional) formulas, and we will have different axioms and inference rules (and allow different assumptions) than in propositional logic. There are many possible variants for the allowed inference rules and logical axioms for predicate logic. We will use a system that has two inference rules (that have assumptions) rather than one in propositional logic,[7] and a handful of axiom schemas that we will get to know in Chapter 10. More specifically, we will allow the following types of justifications for the lines in our proofs:

- **Assumption/Axiom**: We may, of course, use any of our assumptions/axioms of the proof in it, and note that as our assumptions/axioms are given as schemas, any instance of an assumed/axiomatic schema may be used. For simplicity, we do not make any formal or programmatic distinction between assumptions and axioms, and may refer to these both as assumptions and as axioms of the proof; however, one may pragmatically think of assumptions/axioms that are schemas with templates as playing a part somewhat similar to that of the axioms from our propositional-logic proofs, while assumptions/axioms that do not have any templates can be thought of as analogous to regular assumptions in our propositional-logic proofs.
- **Modus Ponens**: We will keep allowing modus ponens, or MP, as an inference rule. That is, from ϕ and '$(\phi \rightarrow \psi)$' (that are justified in previous proof lines) we may deduce ψ.
- **Universal Generalization**: We introduce one new allowed inference rule, named universal generalization, or UG. That is, from any formula ϕ (that is justified in a previous proof line), for any variable name x we may deduce '$\forall x[\phi]$'. For example, from the formula '$(R(x) \rightarrow Q(x))$' we may deduce '$\forall x[(R(x) \rightarrow Q(x))]$' as well as '$\forall z[(R(x) \rightarrow Q(x))]$'. As we will see in Section 9.3.5, the UG rule syntactically encompasses our *semantic* treatment of free variable names as being universally quantified.
- **Tautology**: Finally, we will also allow the use of any **predicate-logic tautology** without proof, where a predicate-logic tautology is a formula that is a propositional-logic tautology when viewed as a propositional formula (see Section 9.3.4 for the precise definition). For example, '$(R(x) \rightarrow R(x))$' is a (predicate-logic) tautology, and so is '$(\forall x[R(x)] \rightarrow \forall x[R(x)])$', but '$\forall x[(R(x) \rightarrow R(x))]$' is not a tautology (once again, see

---

[7] For simplicity, in our predicate-logic proofs we force what we only used as a convention in our propositional-logic proofs: that whenever we can "encode" a needed inference rule as an axiom, we do so. We therefore only allow two inference rules (that have assumptions) that we will need, which it turns out we cannot encode as axioms without introducing other inference rules: our tried-and-true MP and a newly introduced inference rule called UG (see the third type of justification that we will soon define).

Section 9.3.4 for the precise definition). While attentive readers would at this point protest the blatant usage within proofs of something that has to be semantically (albeit finitely) checked (i.e., whether a given formula is a tautology), we note that allowing any tautology is purely for simplicity, as we could have alternatively added a small set of schemas, each representing one of our axioms from Chapter 6, as assumptions/axioms and "inlined" the proof of any needed tautology using these axioms. We show how to do this in Section 9.4.

For example, here is a simple proof that uses each of the four justification types just defined:

Assumption: 'R(c)', where c is a template
Conclusion: '$\forall$x[~~R(x)]'

Proof:

1. 'R(x)'. Justification: Instance of the assumption, instantiated with c defined as 'x'.
2. '(R(x)→~~R(x))'. Justification: A tautology.
3. '~~R(x)'. Justification: MP from from Lines 1 and 2.
4. '$\forall$x[~~R(x)]'. Justification: UG of Line 3.

The file `predicates/proofs.py` defines the Python class `Proof` that represents such a proof and which contains a set of assumptions/axioms that are `Schema` objects, a conclusion that is a `Formula` object, and the body of the proof that consists of its lines (see the next paragraph).

```
                        ┌─────────────────────┐
                        │ predicates/proofs.py │
                        └─────────────────────┘
@frozen
class Proof:
    """An immutable deductive proof in Predicate Logic, comprised of a list of
    assumptions/axioms, a conclusion, and a list of lines that prove the
    conclusion from (instances of) these assumptions/axioms and from
    tautologies, via the Modus Ponens (MP) and Universal Generalization (UG)
    inference rules.

    Attributes:
        assumptions: the assumption/axioms of the proof.
        conclusion: the conclusion of the proof.
        lines: the lines of the proof.
    """
    assumptions: FrozenSet[Schema]
    conclusion: Formula
    lines: Tuple[Proof.Line, ...]

    def __init__(self, assumptions: AbstractSet[Schema], conclusion: Formula,
                 lines: Sequence[Proof.Line]):
        """Initializes a `Proof` from its assumptions/axioms, conclusion,
        and lines.

        Parameters:
            assumptions: the assumption/axioms for the proof.
            conclusion: the conclusion for the proof.
            lines: the lines for the proof.
        """
```

```
self.assumptions = frozenset(assumptions)
self.conclusion = conclusion
self.lines = tuple(lines)
```

Unlike in propositional logic where we had one inner class that represented any line with any of the two allowed types of line justifications (being an assumption or being the conclusion of an allowed inference rule), here we will have a different inner class for each of the four allowed types of line justifications. Each of these four line classes will adhere to the following "interface."

1. It is immutable.
2. It has a field called `formula` that contains the formula justified by the line.
3. It has a method `is_valid(assumptions, lines, line_number)` that checks if the line validly justifies its formula given the assumptions/axioms of the proof and given the other lines of the proof (the method is also given the line number of the current line within the lines of the proof).[8]

This unified "interface" allows code that operates on the lines of a proof to handle all lines similarly and transparently. For example, this allows the following simple implementation of the method `is_valid()` of class `Proof` that we have already implemented for you, which checks the validity of the current proof.

```
                          predicates/proofs.py
class Proof:
        ⋮
        ⋮
    #: An immutable proof line.
    Line = Union[AssumptionLine, MPLine, UGLine, TautologyLine]
        ⋮
        ⋮
    def is_valid(self) -> bool:
        """Checks if the current proof is a valid proof of its claimed
        conclusion from (instances of) its assumptions/axioms.

        Returns:
            ``True`` if the current proof is a valid proof of its claimed
            conclusion from (instances of) its assumptions/axioms, ``False``
            otherwise.
        """
        if len(self.lines) == 0 or self.lines[-1].formula != self.conclusion:
            return False
        for line_number in range(len(self.lines)):
            if not self.lines[line_number].is_valid(self.assumptions,
                                                    self.lines, line_number):
                return False
        return True
```

As in Chapter 4, the main functional aspect of the `Proof` class is in checking the validity of a proof. While we have already implemented the method `is_valid()` of this class for

---

[8] The motivation for the design decision of having this method take the assumptions of the proof and the lines of the proof as two separate arguments rather than just take the entire `Proof` object as one argument will become clear in Chapter 10.

you, it is missing its core components that deal with verification of the four allowed justification types – the implementations for the `is_valid()` methods of the various classes of proof lines. In the tasks of this section, you will implement these components.

9.3.1 Assumption/Axiom Lines

The inner class `Proof.AssumptionLine` is used for proof lines justified as instances of assumptions/axioms. This class holds, in addition to the formula that it justifies, also the assumption/axiom (a schema) whose instance this formula is, as well as the instantiation map according to which this assumption/axiom can be instantiated to obtain this formula (the map may be empty if the assumption/axiom has no templates).

```
                          predicates/proofs.py
class Proof:
    .
    .
    .
    @frozen
    class AssumptionLine:
        """An immutable proof line justified as an instance of an
        assumption/axiom.

        Attributes:
            formula: the formula justified by the line.
            assumption: the assumption/axiom that instantiates the formula.
            instantiation_map: the mapping instantiating the formula from the
                assumption/axiom.
        """
        formula: Formula
        assumption: Schema
        instantiation_map: InstantiationMap

        def __init__(self, formula: Formula, assumption: Schema,
                     instantiation_map: InstantiationMap):
            """Initializes an `Proof.AssumptionLine` from its formula, its
            justifying assumption/axiom, and its instantiation map from the
            justifying assumption/axiom.

            Parameters:
                formula: the formula to be justified by the line.
                assumption: the assumption/axiom that instantiates the formula.
                instantiation_map: the mapping instantiating the formula from
                    the assumption/axiom.
            """
            for construct in instantiation_map:
                if is_variable(construct):
                    assert is_variable(instantiation_map[construct])
                elif is_constant(construct):
                    assert isinstance(instantiation_map[construct], Term)
                else:
                    assert is_relation(construct)
                    assert isinstance(instantiation_map[construct], Formula)
            self.formula = formula
            self.assumption = assumption
            self.instantiation_map = frozendict(instantiation_map)
```

TASK 5   Implement the missing code for the method `is_valid(assumptions, lines, line_number)` of class `Proof.AssumptionLine`, which returns whether the formula of the current line is validly justified within the context of the specified proof (i.e., whether it really is an instantiation, as specified, of one of the assumption/axiom of this proof).

```
                           ┌─ predicates/proofs.py ─┐
class Proof:
    ⋮

    class AssumptionLine:
        ⋮

        def is_valid(self, assumptions: AbstractSet[Schema],
                     lines: Sequence[Proof.Line], line_number: int) -> bool:
            """Checks if the current line is validly justified in the context of
            the specified proof.

            Parameters:
                assumptions: assumptions/axioms of the proof.
                lines: lines of the proof.
                line_number: line number of the current line in the given lines.

            Returns:
                ``True`` if the assumption/axiom of the current line is an
                assumption/axiom of the specified proof and if the formula
                justified by the current line is a valid instance of this
                assumption/axiom via the instantiation map of the current line,
                ``False`` otherwise.
            """
            assert line_number < len(lines) and lines[line_number] is self
            # Task 9.5
```

Hint: Recall that this method takes the three arguments `assumptions`, `lines`, and `line_number` in order to take the same arguments as the `is_valid()` methods of other proof line classes. You need not use all of these in your solution to this task.

9.3.2   Modus Ponens (MP) Lines

The inner class `Proof.MPLine` is used for proof lines justified by the MP inference rule. This class holds, in addition to the formula that it justifies, also the line numbers of the previous lines from which this formula is deduced via MP.

```
                           ┌─ predicates/proofs.py ─┐
class Proof:
    ⋮

    @frozen
    class MPLine:
        """An immutable proof line justified by the Modus Ponens (MP) inference
        rule.

        Attributes:
            formula: the formula justified by the line.
            antecedent_line_number: the line number of the antecedent of the MP
```

```
                      inference justifying the line.
              conditional_line_number: the line number of the conditional of the
                  MP inference justifying the line.
      """
      formula: Formula
      antecedent_line_number: int
      conditional_line_number: int

      def __init__(self, formula: Formula, antecedent_line_number: int,
                   conditional_line_number: int):
          """Initializes a `Proof.MPLine` from its formula and line numbers of
          the antecedent and conditional of the MP inference justifying it.

          Parameters:
              formula: the formula to be justified by the line.
              antecedent_line_number: the line number of the antecedent of the
                  MP inference to justify the line.
              conditional_line_number: the line number of the conditional of
                  the MP inference to justify the line.
          """
          self.formula = formula
          self.antecedent_line_number = antecedent_line_number
          self.conditional_line_number = conditional_line_number
```

TASK 6   Implement the missing code for the method is_valid(assumptions, lines, line_number) of class Proof.MPLine, which returns whether the formula of the current line is validly justified via an application of MP to the specified previous lines.

predicates/proofs.py

```
class Proof:
      ⋮

    class MPLine:
          ⋮

        def is_valid(self, assumptions: AbstractSet[Schema],
                     lines: Sequence[Proof.Line], line_number: int) -> bool:
            """Checks if the current line is validly justified in the context of
            the specified proof.

            Parameters:
                assumptions: assumptions/axioms of the proof.
                lines: lines of the proof.
                line_number: line number of the current line in the given lines.

            Returns:
                ``True`` if the formula of the line from the given lines whose
                number is the conditional line number justifying the current
                line is '(`antecedent`->`consequent`)', where `antecedent` is
                the formula of the line from the given lines whose number is the
                antecedent line number justifying the current line and
                `consequent` is the formula justified by the current line;
                ``False`` otherwise.
            """
            assert line_number < len(lines) and lines[line_number] is self
            # Task 9.6
```

Hint: Recall again that this method takes the three arguments `assumptions`, `lines`, and `line_number` in order to take the same arguments as the `is_valid()` methods of other proof line classes. You need not use all of these in your solution to this task.

9.3.3   Universal Generalization (UG) Lines

The inner class `Proof.UGLine` is used for proof lines justified by the UG inference rule. This class holds, in addition to the formula that it justifies, also the line number of the previous line from which this formula is deduced via UG.

```
                          predicates/proofs.py
class Proof:
    ⋮

    @frozen
    class UGLine:
        """An immutable proof line justified by the Universal Generalization
        (UG) inference rule.

        Attributes:
            formula: the formula justified by the line.
            nonquantified_line_number: the line number of the statement
                quantified by the formula.
        """
        formula: Formula
        nonquantified_line_number: int

        def __init__(self, formula: Formula, nonquantified_line_number: int):
            """Initializes a `Proof.UGLine` from its formula and line number of
            the statement quantified by the formula.

            Parameters:
                formula: the formula to be justified by the line.
                nonquantified_line_number: the line number of the statement
                    quantified by the formula.
            """
            self.formula = formula
            self.nonquantified_line_number = nonquantified_line_number
```

TASK 7   Implement the missing code for the method `is_valid(assumptions, lines, line_number)` of class `Proof.UGLine`, which returns whether the formula of the current line is validly justified via an application of UG to the specified previous line.

```
                          predicates/proofs.py
class Proof:
    ⋮

    class UGLine:
        ⋮

        def is_valid(self, assumptions: AbstractSet[Schema],
                     lines: Sequence[Proof.Line], line_number: int) -> bool:
            """Checks if the current line is validly justified in the context of
            the specified proof.
```

```
            Parameters:
                assumptions: assumptions/axioms of the proof.
                lines: lines of the proof.
                line_number: line number of the current line in the given lines.

            Returns:
                ``True`` if the formula of the current line is of the form
                'A`x`[`nonquantified`]', where `nonquantified` is the formula of
                the line from the given lines whose number is the nonquantified
                line number justifying the current line and `x` is any variable
                name; ``False`` otherwise.
            """
            assert line_number < len(lines) and lines[line_number] is self
            # Task 9.7
```

Hint: Recall once more that this method takes the three arguments `assumptions`, `lines`, and `line_number` in order to take the same arguments as the `is_valid()` methods of other proof line classes. You need not use all of these in your solution to this task.

9.3.4 Tautology Lines

We now finally give a precise definition for what a predicate-logic tautology is. Predicate-logic formulas generalize propositional formulas by replacing the propositional variable names with structured subformulas whose root is a relation name, an equality, or a quantifier. We define the **propositional skeleton** of a predicate-logic formula as the propositional formula that is obtained by consistently replacing each of these subformulas with a new propositional variable name. For example, the propositional skeleton of '$(R(x)|Q(y))\rightarrow R(x))$' is '$((z1|z2)\rightarrow z1)$', the propositional skeleton of '$(\sim x=s(0)\rightarrow GT(x,1))$' is '$(\sim z1\rightarrow z2)$', and the propositional skeleton of '$\forall x[(R(x)\rightarrow R(x))]$' is '$z1$'. We call a predicate-logic formula a **(predicate-logic) tautology** if its propositional skeleton (a propositional formula) is a propositional-logic tautology.[9] The inner class `Proof.TautologyLine` is used for proof lines justified as predicate-logic tautologies.

```
                              predicates/proofs.py
    class Proof:
            ⋮
            ⋮
        @frozen
        class TautologyLine:
            """An immutable proof line justified as a tautology.

            Attributes:
                formula: the formula justified by the line.
            """
            formula: Formula
```

[9] We use the terminology *the* propositional skeleton somewhat misleadingly, as there are many propositional skeletons for any given predicate-logic formula. For example, '$((z3|z4)\rightarrow z3)$' is also a propositional skeleton of the formula '$(R(x)|Q(y))\rightarrow R(x))$'. There is no problem here, though, since either all propositional skeletons of a given formula are propositional-logic tautologies or none are.

```
        def __init__(self, formula: Formula):
            """Initializes a `Proof.TautologyLine` from its formula.

            Parameters:
                formula: the formula to be justified by the line.
            """
            self.formula = formula
```

TASK 8   Implement the missing code for the method `propositional_skeleton()` of class Formula (in the file `predicates/syntax.py`), which returns a propositional skeleton of the current (predicate-logic) formula – an object of class `propositions.syntax.Formula`[10] – along with the map from propositional variable names of the returned propositional skeleton (e.g., 'z8') to the predicate-logic subformulas of the current formula that they have replaced.

```
                            ┌─ predicates/syntax.py ─┐
class Formula:
    ⋮

    def propositional_skeleton(self) -> Tuple[PropositionalFormula,
                                              Mapping[str, Formula]]:
        """Computes a propositional skeleton of the current formula.

        Returns:
            A pair. The first element of the pair is a propositional formula
            obtained from the current formula by substituting every (outermost)
            subformula that has a relation name, equality, or quantifier at its
            root with a propositional variable name, consistently such that
            multiple identical such (outermost) subformulas are substituted with
            the same propositional variable name. The propositional variable
            names used for substitution are obtained, from left to right
            (considering their first occurrence), by calling
            `next(fresh_variable_name_generator)`. The second element of the
            pair is a mapping from each propositional variable name to the
            subformula for which it was substituted.

        Examples:
            >>> formula = Formula.parse('((Ax[x=7]&x=7)|(~Q(y)->x=7))')
            >>> formula.propositional_skeleton()
            (((z1&z2)|(~z3->z2)), {'z1': Ax[x=7], 'z2': x=7, 'z3': Q(y)})
            >>> formula.propositional_skeleton()
            (((z4&z5)|(~z6->z5)), {'z4': Ax[x=7], 'z5': x=7, 'z6': Q(y)})
        """
        # Task 9.8
```

Guidelines: The propositional variable names in the returned propositional formula should be named 'z1', 'z2', ..., ordered according to their first (left-most) occurrence in the original predicate-logic formula, with the numbering increasing between successive calls to `propositional_skeleton`. Call `next(fresh_variable_name_generator)` (this generator is imported for you from `predicates/util.py`) to generate these variable names.

---

[10] To avoid naming conflicts, this class is imported for you into `predicates/syntax.py` under the name `PropositionalFormula`.

TASK 9   Implement the missing code for the method is_valid(assumptions, lines, line_number) of class Proof.TautologyLine, which returns whether the formula of the current line really is a (predicate-logic) tautology.

```
                         ⟨ predicates/proofs.py ⟩
class Proof:
       ⋮

    class TautologyLine:
           ⋮

        def is_valid(self, assumptions: AbstractSet[Schema],
                     lines: Sequence[Proof.Line], line_number: int) -> bool:
            """Checks if the current line is validly justified in the context of
            the specified proof.

            Parameters:
                assumptions: assumptions/axioms of the proof.
                lines: lines of the proof.
                line_number: line number of the current line in the given lines.

            Returns:
                ``True`` if the formula justified by the current line is a
                (predicate-logic) tautology, ``False`` otherwise.
            """
            assert line_number < len(lines) and lines[line_number] is self
            # Task 9.9
```

Hints: Use your solution to Task 8. The function propositions.semantics .is_tautology() is imported for you into predicates/proofs.py under the name is_propositional_tautology(). Recall yet again that this method takes the three arguments assumptions, lines, and line_number in order to take the same arguments as the is_valid() methods of other proof line classes. You need not use these in your solution to this task.

As already noted, we allow for the use of tautologies without proof purely for simplicity. Indeed, by proving all needed tautologies and "inlining" the proofs we could have done away with tautology justifications, as well as with their *semantic* validation, resulting in purely syntactic validation of proofs, as one may desire. We will discuss (and implement) this in Section 9.4.

9.3.5   The Soundness of Proofs

Similarly to propositional logic, we will say that a formula ϕ is **provable** from a set of schemas A, and write $A \vdash \phi$, if there is a (valid) proof of ϕ from the assumptions/axioms A (using assumption lines, MP lines, UG lines, and tautology lines). Very similarly to propositional logic, it is not hard to prove that the proof system just defined is sound.

DEFINITION 9.2 (Entailment; Sound Inference)   We say that a set of assumptions A **entails** a conclusion ϕ if every model that satisfies each of the assumptions in A (under any assignment to its free variable names) also satisfies ϕ (under any assignment to its free variable names). We denote this by $A \models \phi$.[11] We say that the inference of ϕ from A is **sound** if $A \models \phi$. If A is the empty set then we simply write $\models \phi$, which is equivalent to saying that ϕ is sound (as defined on in Definition 9.1).

THEOREM 9.1 (The Soundness Theorem for Predicate Logic)   *Any inference that is provable via (only) sound assumptions/axioms is sound. That is, if X contains only sound schemas, and if $A \cup X \vdash \phi$, then $A \models \phi$.*

As programmatically proving the soundness theorem (9.1) for predicate logic would not add any new insights beyond your corresponding programmatic proof of the soundness theorem (4.1) for propositional logic, we will skip the involved programming, and instead prove the soundness of predicate logic in the traditional mathematical way, using induction over the lines of a proof.

Proof   Fix a model of (all of the instances of) A. All that we need to verify is that if the formulas of all previous lines hold in the model, then each type of justification that we allow results in a formula (for the line that follows) that holds in the model as well:

- Assumption/axiom line: Any instance of any schema in A holds in the model by definition of the model. Any schema in X is sound, and so by definition any of its instances is sound and so holds in any model.
- MP line: The reasoning is similar yet a bit more detailed. Fix an assignment to the free variable names of the formula justified by the line. Arbitrarily augment the assignment with values for any additional free variable names that occur in the two justifying formulas (from previous lines) – this does not change the truth value of the justified formula in the model under that assignment. By definition, each of the justifying formulas holds in the model under the augmented assignment, so by the semantic definition of the evaluation of the implication operator, so does the justified formula. So, the justified formula holds in the model under the original assignment.
- UG line: The justifying formula (from a previous line) holds in the model under any assignment to its free variable names, and in particular under any assignment to free occurrences of the variable name over which UG is taken, and that is precisely also the semantic meaning of the universal quantification in the formula justified by the UG line.[12]
- Tautology line: Any assignment to the free variable names of the formula justified by the line defines, together with the model, a truth value for each subformula whose root is a relation name, equality, or quantifier. This corresponds to an assignment of a truth value to each of the propositional variable names of the propositional skeleton of the justified formula – in other words, this corresponds to a propositional model in which this propositional skeleton can be evaluated. Since this propositional skeleton evaluates to *True* under the latter model (as it is a propositional-logic tautology), so does the justified formula itself in the original (predicate-logic) model under the original assignment.   □

---

[11] As we have remarked also in Part I of this book, the symbol $\models$ is sometimes used also in a slightly different way: For a model M and a formula ϕ one may write $M \models \phi$ (i.e., M is a model of ϕ) to mean that ϕ evaluates to *True* in the model M.

[12] This argument clarifies our cryptic comment above, that UG syntactically encompasses our *semantic* treatment of free variable names as being universally quantified.

We conclude this section with a brief discussion of why we have chosen (as is customary) to treat free variable names as universally quantified in formulas – a semantic decision that we made already at the end of Chapter 7 when we defined what it means for a model to be a model of a given formula, and which is syntactically captured in our proof system by the UG axiomatic inference rule. First, why allow free variable names at all? Well, to avoid clutter. Indeed, we could have done just as well without allowing free variable names in formulas if we would have, e.g., allowed every universal closure of a tautology, that is, every formula of the form '$\forall p_1[\forall p_1[\cdots \forall p_n[\phi]\cdots]]$' where ϕ is a tautology and the quantifications are over all of the free variable names of ϕ, but then, to avoid losing expressive power, we would have had to define MP in a much more bulky way: to allow not only to deduce, e.g., '$\sim(R(x,y)\rightarrow Q(x,y))$' from '$R(x,y)$' and from '$\sim Q(x,y)$', but also to deduce, e.g., '$\forall x[\forall y[\sim(R(x,y)\rightarrow Q(x,y))]]$' from '$\forall x[\forall y[R(x,y)]]$' and from '$\forall x[\forall y[\sim Q(x,y)]]$'. Given this example, it is easy to see that choosing to allow free occurrences of variable names and to treat them as universally quantified, in combination with allowing UG, gives a far simpler definition of proof justifications. Second, why do we treat free variable names as universally quantified and not, say, existentially quantified? Well, since in that case, while tautologies would still be valid (well, at least as long as there is at least one element in the universe), the above usage of MP would for example not be valid. Indeed, deducing '$\exists x[\exists y[\sim(R(x,y)\rightarrow Q(x,y))]]$' from '$\exists x[\exists y[R(x,y)]]$' and from '$\exists x[\exists y[\sim Q(x,y)]]$' is fundamentally flawed (make sure that you understand why). Very similarly, in Section 9.4 we will see that treating free variable names as universally quantified allows us to easily translate a propositional-logic proof of the (propositional-logic tautology) propositional skeleton of a predicate-logic tautology into a predicate-logic proof for that predicate-logic tautology, which in fact allows us to translate any predicate-logic proof into a proof without tautology line justifications.

9.4   Getting Rid of Tautology Lines

We conclude this chapter by showing that the ability to use tautologies as building blocks in our proof does not really give our proofs more proving power (and so is for convenience only). That is, in this section you will show that any (predicate-logic) tautology is provable using only assumption/axiom and MP line justifications via a set of schemas that correspond to our axiomatic system for propositional logic. For convenience, we will focus in this section only on tautologies whose propositional skeletons contain only the implication and negation operators, and will therefore only require schemas that correspond to our axiomatic system for implication and negation.[13] These schemas are defined in `predicates/proofs.py`.

predicates/proofs.py

```
# Schema equivalents of the propositional-logic axioms for implication and
# negation
```

---

[13] Readers who have worked through Section 6.A will notice that their solution to that section can be easily used to generalize everything in the current section to tautologies with arbitrary operators in their propositional skeletons.

```
#: Schema equivalent of the propositional-logic self implication axiom `I0`.
I0_SCHEMA = Schema(Formula.parse('(P()->P())'), {'P'})
#: Schema equivalent of the propositional-logic implication introduction (right)
#: axiom `I1`.
I1_SCHEMA = Schema(Formula.parse('(Q()->(P()->Q()))'), {'P', 'Q'})
#: Schema equivalent of the propositional-logic self-distribution of implication
#: axiom `D`.
D_SCHEMA = Schema(Formula.parse(
    '((P()->(Q()->R()))->((P()->Q())->(P()->R())))'), {'P', 'Q', 'R'})
#: Schema equivalent of the propositional-logic implication introduction (left)
#: axiom `I2`.
I2_SCHEMA = Schema(Formula.parse('(~P()->(P()->Q()))'), {'P', 'Q'})
#: Schema equivalent of the propositional-logic converse contraposition axiom
#: `N`.
N_SCHEMA  = Schema(Formula.parse('((~Q()->~P())->(P()->Q()))'), {'P', 'Q'})
#: Schema equivalent of the propositional-logic negative-implication
#: introduction axiom `NI`.
NI_SCHEMA = Schema(Formula.parse('(P()->(~Q()->~(P()->Q())))'), {'P', 'Q'})
#: Schema equivalent of the propositional-logic double-negation introduction
#: axiom `NN`.
NN_SCHEMA = Schema(Formula.parse('(P()->~~P())'), {'P'})
#: Schema equivalent of the propositional-logic resolution axiom `R`.
R_SCHEMA  = Schema(Formula.parse(
    '((Q()->P())->((~Q()->P())->P()))'), {'P', 'Q'})

#: Schema system equivalent of the axioms of the propositional-logic large
#: axiomatic system for implication and negation `AXIOMATIC_SYSTEM`.
PROPOSITIONAL_AXIOMATIC_SYSTEM_SCHEMAS = {I0_SCHEMA, I1_SCHEMA, D_SCHEMA,
                                         I2_SCHEMA, N_SCHEMA, NI_SCHEMA,
                                         NN_SCHEMA, R_SCHEMA}

#: Mapping from propositional-logic axioms for implication and negation to their
#: schema equivalents.
PROPOSITIONAL_AXIOM_TO_SCHEMA = {
    I0: I0_SCHEMA, I1: I1_SCHEMA, D: D_SCHEMA, I2: I2_SCHEMA, N: N_SCHEMA,
    NI: NI_SCHEMA, NN: NN_SCHEMA, R: R_SCHEMA}
```

LEMMA 9.1 *All of the above schemas are sound.*

Proof It is straightforward to see that each instance of these schemas is a (predicate-logic) tautology, so the same reasoning as in the proof of the soundness theorem (9.1) applies. □

Our strategy for proving any predicate-logic tautology (without tautology line justifications of course) from these schemas is quite straightforward at a high level: Since the propositional skeleton of the given predicate-logic tautology is a propositional-logic tautology, by the tautology theorem (6.1), this propositional skeleton is provable via our axiomatic system for propositional logic. We will syntactically "translate" this propositional-logic proof, line by line, into a predicate-logic proof of the given predicate-logic tautology. The resulting proof will have the exact same structure and arguments of the propositional-logic proof. However, instead of operating on propositional formulas constructed out of the propositional variable names of that propositional skeleton as building blocks, it will operate in exactly the same way on predicate-logic formulas constructed in exactly the same way out of the predicate-logic subformulas that replace (in the given predicate-logic tautology) these propositional variable names. Hence, of course, instead of culminating in proving the propositional skeleton of the given predicate-logic tautology, it will culminate in proving the given predicate-logic tautology itself.

Concretely, we will "translate" the formula justified by each line of the proof by simply replacing every occurrence of any of these propositional variable names with the appropriate predicate-logic subformula. What about justifying these translated formulas? First, we will notice that MP justifications from the propositional-logic proof remain valid following this translation. Second, any specialization of one of our axioms that is used in the propositional-logic proof gets translated into an instance of the schema equivalent (as just defined) of this axiom. By both of these, we will indeed be able to validly justify all of the arguments of the "translated" proof. Our first step is to "translate" a propositional skeleton of a predicate-logic formula into that predicate-logic formula using a given substitution map.

TASK 10 Implement the missing code for the static method `from_propositional_skeleton(skeleton, substitution_map)` of class Formula, which returns a predicate-logic formula `formula` such that the pair `(skeleton, substitution_map)` is a legal return value (not imposing any restrictions on variable names or their orders, though) of `formula.propositional_skeleton()`.

```
predicates/syntax.py

class Formula:
    .
    .
    .
    @staticmethod
    def from_propositional_skeleton(skeleton: PropositionalFormula,
                                    substitution_map: Mapping[str, Formula]) \
            -> Formula:
        """Computes a predicate-logic formula from a propositional skeleton and
        a substitution map.

        Arguments:
            skeleton: propositional skeleton for the formula to compute,
                containing no constants or operators beyond '~', '->', '|', and
                '&'.
            substitution_map: mapping from each propositional variable name of
                the given propositional skeleton to a predicate-logic formula.

        Returns:
            A predicate-logic formula obtained from the given propositional
            skeleton by substituting each propositional variable name with the
            formula mapped to it by the given map.

        Examples:
            >>> Formula.from_propositional_skeleton(
            ...     PropositionalFormula.parse('((z1&z2)|(~z3->z2))'),
            ...     {'z1': Formula.parse('Ax[x=7]'), 'z2': Formula.parse('x=7'),
            ...      'z3': Formula.parse('Q(y)')})
            ((Ax[x=7]&x=7)|(~Q(y)->x=7))

            >>> Formula.from_propositional_skeleton(
            ...     PropositionalFormula.parse('((z9&z2)|(~z3->z2))'),
            ...     {'z2': Formula.parse('x=7'), 'z3': Formula.parse('Q(y)'),
            ...      'z9': Formula.parse('Ax[x=7]')})
```

```
        ((Ax[x=7]&x=7)|(~Q(y)->x=7))
    """
    for operator in skeleton.operators():
        assert is_unary(operator) or is_binary(operator)
    for variable in skeleton.variables():
        assert variable in substitution_map
    # Task 9.10
```

Our next and main steps are to handle the translation of axiom justifications, and using that to translate an entire proof of a propositional skeleton of a predicate-logic formula into a proof of that formula.

TASK 11

a. Implement the missing code for the function `_axiom_specialization_map_to_schema_instantiation_map(propositional_specialization_map, substitution_map)`. This function takes as input a specialization map that specifies how a propositional-logic axiom axiom from AXIOMATIC_SYSTEM specializes into some specialization specialization, and a substitution map that specifies how to transform specialization into a predicate-logic formula formula (i.e., formula is the formula returned by calling Formula.from_propositional_skeleton(specialization, substitution_map), a call which raises no assertion errors). The function returns an instantiation map for instantiating the schema equivalent of axiom (e.g., if axiom is I0, then its schema equivalent is I0_SCHEMA) into formula.

predicates/proofs.py

```
def _axiom_specialization_map_to_schema_instantiation_map(
        propositional_specialization_map: PropositionalSpecializationMap,
        substitution_map: Mapping[str, Formula]) -> Mapping[str, Formula]:
    """Composes the given propositional-logic specialization map, specifying the
    transformation from a propositional-logic axiom to a specialization of it,
    and the given substitution map, specifying the transformation from that
    specialization (as a propositional skeleton) to a predicate-logic formula,
    into an instantiation map specifying how to instantiate the schema
    equivalent of that axiom into the same predicate-logic formula.

    Parameters:
        propositional_specialization_map: mapping specifying how some
            propositional-logic axiom `axiom` (which is not specified) from
            `AXIOMATIC_SYSTEM` specializes into some specialization
            `specialization` (which is also not specified), and containing no
            constants or operators beyond '~', '->', '|', and '&'.
        substitution_map: mapping from each propositional variable name of
            `specialization` to a predicate-logic formula.

    Returns:
        An instantiation map for instantiating the schema equivalent of `axiom`
        into the predicate-logic formula obtained from its propositional
        skeleton `specialization` by the given substitution map.

    Examples:
        >>> _axiom_specialization_map_to_schema_instantiation_map(
        ...     {'p': PropositionalFormula.parse('(z1->z2)'),
```

```
        ...        'q': PropositionalFormula.parse('~z1')},
        ...       {'z1': Formula.parse('Ax[(x=5&M())]'),
        ...        'z2': Formula.parse('R(f(8,9))')})
        {'P': (Ax[(x=5&M())]->R(f(8,9))), 'Q': ~Ax[(x=5&M())]}
    """
    for variable in propositional_specialization_map:
        assert is_propositional_variable(variable)
        for operator in propositional_specialization_map[variable].operators():
            assert is_unary(operator) or is_binary(operator)
    for variable in substitution_map:
        assert is_propositional_variable(variable)
    # Task 9.11a
```

Hint: You may assume that the keys of `propositional_specialization_map` are a subset of `{'p', 'q', 'r'}`.

b. Implement the missing code for the function `_prove_from_skeleton_proof(formula, skeleton_proof, substitution_map)`. This function takes as input a predicate-logic formula `formula`, a propositional-logic proof[14] of a propositional skeleton `skeleton` of `formula` via `AXIOMATIC_SYSTEM`, and a substitution map such that the pair `(skeleton, substitution_map)` is a legal return value of a call to `formula.propositional_skeleton()`. The function returns a predicate-logic proof of `formula` via `PROPOSITIONAL_AXIOMATIC_SYSTEM_SCHEMAS` that contains only assumption/axiom and MP lines.

```
                            ┌─ predicates/proofs.py ─┐

def _prove_from_skeleton_proof(formula: Formula,
                               skeleton_proof: PropositionalProof,
                               substitution_map: Mapping[str, Formula]) -> \
        Proof:
    """Translates the given proof of a propositional skeleton of the given
    predicate-logic formula into a proof of that predicate-logic formula.

    Parameters:
        formula: predicate-logic formula to prove.
        skeleton_proof: valid propositional-logic proof of a propositional
            skeleton of the given formula, from no assumptions and via
            `AXIOMATIC_SYSTEM`, and containing no constants or operators beyond
            '~', '->', '|', and '&'.
        substitution_map: mapping from each propositional variable name of the
            propositional skeleton of the given formula that is proven in the
            given proof to the respective predicate-logic subformula of the
            given formula.

    Returns:
        A valid predicate-logic proof of the given formula from the axioms
        `PROPOSITIONAL_AXIOMATIC_SYSTEM_SCHEMAS` via only assumption lines and
        MP lines.
    """
    assert len(skeleton_proof.statement.assumptions) == 0 and \
           skeleton_proof.rules.issubset(PROPOSITIONAL_AXIOMATIC_SYSTEM) and \
           skeleton_proof.is_valid()
```

---

[14] To avoid naming conflicts, the class `propositions.proofs.Proof` is imported for you into `predicates/proofs.py` under the name `PropositionalProof`.

```
    assert Formula.from_propositional_skeleton(
        skeleton_proof.statement.conclusion, substitution_map) == formula
    for line in skeleton_proof.lines:
        for operator in line.formula.operators():
            assert is_unary(operator) or is_binary(operator)
    # Task 9.11b
```

Guidelines: Since there are no assumptions in the given proof, each line is either the result of an application of MP to previous lines or a specialization of an axiom. In either case, "translate" the formula justified by the line using your solution to Task 10; in the latter case use also your solution to the first part of this task to "translate" the specialization map.

Hint: To allow you to use the method `formula_specialization_map()` of class `propositions.proofs.InferenceRule` (which also takes an object of this class as an argument) while maintaining readability, that class is imported for you into `predicates/proofs.py` under the name `PropositionalInferenceRule`.

You are now in good shape to use your solution of Task 11 to show that every predicate-logic tautology is provable via the schemas defined in the beginning of this section.

TASK 12 (Programmatic Proof of the Predicate-Logic Version of the Tautology Theorem (9.2)) Implement the missing code for the function `prove_tautology(tautology)`, which proves the given predicate-logic tautology from the axioms `PROPOSITIONAL_AXIOMATIC_SYSTEM_SCHEMAS` with only assumption/axiom and MP lines.

```
                          predicates/proofs.py
def prove_tautology(tautology: Formula) -> Proof:
    """Proves the given predicate-logic tautology.

    Parameters:
        tautology: predicate-logic tautology, whose propositional skeleton
            contains no constants or operators beyond '->' and '~', to prove.

    Returns:
        A valid proof of the given predicate-logic tautology from the axioms
        `PROPOSITIONAL_AXIOMATIC_SYSTEM_SCHEMAS` via only assumption lines
        and MP lines.
    """
    skeleton = tautology.propositional_skeleton()[0]
    assert is_propositional_tautology(skeleton)
    assert skeleton.operators().issubset({'->', '~'})
    # Task 9.12
```

Hint: To avoid naming conflicts, the function `propositions.tautology.prove_tautology()` is imported for you into `predicates/proofs.py` under the name `prove_propositional_tautology()`.

Section 6.A, which you may or may not have worked through, discusses how a solution to that section can be used to implement the function `propositions.tautology.prove_tautology()` in a way that can handle propositional-logic tautologies with arbitrary constant and operators, using an extended axiomatic system that we denoted by $\hat{\mathcal{H}}$ (rather than our axiomatic system for implication and negation from Chapter 6, which we denoted by $\mathcal{H}$). Even if you have not worked through

Section 6.A, it should be clear to you that plugging in such an enhanced implementation of `propositions.tautology.prove_tautology()` into your solution to Task 12 (and removing the assertion limiting operators to implication and negation in the beginning of the function you have implemented in that task) will immediately allow your solution to work with tautologies with arbitrary operators in their propositional skeletons. Your solution to Task 12 proves the following theorem.

THEOREM 9.2 (The Tautology Theorem: Predicate-Logic Version)   *For every predicate-logic tautology ϕ, there exists a valid proof of ϕ that uses only assumption/axiom and MP line justifications (and not tautology or UG line justifications), from the schema equivalents of $\mathcal{H}$ (or from the schema equivalents of $\hat{\mathcal{H}}$ if the propositional skeleton of ϕ contains any operators beyond implication and negation).*

We therefore obtain that indeed tautology line justifications can be dropped from our proofs without losing any proving power (as long as we add a few schemas).

COROLLARY 9.1   *If a predicate-logic formula ϕ is provable from a set of assumptions/axioms A, then it is provable without tautology line justifications from A as well as the schema equivalents of $\hat{\mathcal{H}}$.*

10 Working with Predicate Logic Proofs

In this chapter we will introduce a specific axiomatic system for predicate logic and prove some theorems using this system. You will be asked to both prove things "manually" to and implement some helper functions/methods that will make writing proofs easier (but no worries – you will not be asked to re-implement `inline_proof()` for predicate logic).

10.1 Our Axiomatic System

Our axiomatic system will of course have the following components that you have already dealt with in the `Proof` class in Chapter 9:

- Inference Rules. As specified in Chapter 9, we have only two inference rules:
  - **Modus Ponens (MP):** From ϕ and '$(\phi \rightarrow \psi)$', deduce ψ. (Just like in propositional logic.)
  - **Universal Generalization (UG):** From ϕ deduce '$\forall x[\phi]$'. Note that ϕ may have x as a free variable name (and may of course have any other free variable name).
- Tautologies ("imported" from propositional logic). As discussed in Chapter 9, we directly allow all (predicate-logic) tautologies as axioms purely for convenience, as it is also possible instead to leverage our analysis from Part I of this book to prove them from the schema equivalents of the axioms of propositional logic.
  - **Tautology:** Any formula ϕ that is a tautology. Note that we allow tautologies to have free variable names, such as in the tautology '$((R(x)\&Q(x))\rightarrow R(x))$'.

In addition to these components, our axiomatic system will also have the following six additional axiom schemas that deal with quantification and equality, which will be part of the assumptions/axioms of every proof that you will write from this point onward. These schemas are defined as constants in the file `predicates/prover.py` inside the class `Prover`, which we will discuss below.

- Quantification Axioms. These ensure that the universal and existential quantifiers have the meanings that we want:
  - **Universal Instantiation (UI):** The schema '$(\forall x[\phi(x)]\rightarrow\phi(\tau))$', where $\phi(\Box)$, x, and τ are (placeholders for) a parametrized formula, a variable name, and a term, respectively.

178

```
                          ┌─────────────────────┐
                          │ predicates/prover.py │
                          └─────────────────────┘
class Prover:
        ⋮

    #: Axiom schema of universal instantiation
    UI = Schema(Formula.parse('(Ax[R(x)]->R(c))'), {'R', 'x', 'c'})
```

- **Existential Introduction (EI):** The schema '($\phi(\tau) \to \exists x[\phi(x)]$)', where $\phi(\square)$, x, and τ are a parametrized formula, a variable name, and a term, respectively.

```
                          ┌─────────────────────┐
                          │ predicates/prover.py │
                          └─────────────────────┘
class Prover:
        ⋮

    #: Axiom schema of existential introduction
    EI = Schema(Formula.parse('(R(c)->Ex[R(x)])'), {'R', 'x', 'c'})
```

- **Universal Simplification (US):** The schema '($\forall x[(\psi \to \phi(x))] \to (\psi \to \forall x[\phi(x)])$)', where ψ is a (parameter-less) formula, $\phi(\square)$ is a parametrized formula, and x is a variable name. Note that the rules from Chapter 9 that define the legal instances of schemas require in particular that (the formula that is substituted for) ψ does not have (the variable that name is substituted for) x as a free variable name.

```
                          ┌─────────────────────┐
                          │ predicates/prover.py │
                          └─────────────────────┘
class Prover:
        ⋮

    #: Axiom schema of universal simplification
    US = Schema(Formula.parse('(Ax[(Q()->R(x))]->(Q()->Ax[R(x)]))'),
                {'Q', 'R', 'x'})
```

- **Existential Simplification (ES):** The schema '($(\forall x[(\phi(x) \to \psi)] \& \exists x[\phi(x)]) \to \psi$)', where ψ is a formula, $\phi(\square)$ is a parametrized formula, and x is a variable name. Note once more that the rules from Chapter 9 that define the legal instances of schemas require in particular that ψ does not have x as a free variable name.

```
                          ┌─────────────────────┐
                          │ predicates/prover.py │
                          └─────────────────────┘
class Prover:
        ⋮

    #: Axiom schema of existential simplification
    ES = Schema(Formula.parse('((Ax[(R(x)->Q())]&Ex[R(x)])->Q())'),
                {'Q', 'R', 'x'})
```

- Equality Axioms. These ensure that the equality relation has the meaning that we want:[1]
  - **Reflexivity (RX):** The schema '$\tau = \tau$', where τ is a term.

---

[1] It is instructive to compare these two equality axioms with the formulas that you created in Chapter 8 to capture the properties of the interpretation of the 'SAME' relation name that replaced equality there. RX of course corresponds to the reflexivity property, and ME in particular also implies being respected by all relation interpretations. What about symmetry and transitivity, though? As it turns out – you will show this in Tasks 6 and 9 – these can be deduced from RX and ME due to the fact that ME allows substitution in arbitrary formulas and not only in relation invocations.

```
                              ┌─────────────────────┐
                              │ predicates/prover.py │
                              └─────────────────────┘
  class Prover:
              ⋮

      #: Axiom schema of reflexivity
      RX = Schema(Formula.parse('c=c'), {'c'})
```

– **Meaning of Equality (ME):** The schema '$(\tau{=}\sigma{\rightarrow}(\phi(\tau){\rightarrow}\phi(\sigma)))$', where $\phi(\square)$ is a parametrized formula, and τ and σ are terms.

```
                              ┌─────────────────────┐
                              │ predicates/prover.py │
                              └─────────────────────┘
  class Prover:
              ⋮

      #: Axiom schema of meaning of equality
      ME = Schema(Formula.parse('(c=d->(R(c)->R(d)))'), {'R', 'c', 'd'})
```

```
                              ┌─────────────────────┐
                              │ predicates/prover.py │
                              └─────────────────────┘
  class Prover:
            ⋮

      #: Axiomatic system for Predicate Logic, consisting of `UI`, `EI`, `US`,
      #: `ES`, `RX`, and `ME`.
      AXIOMS = frozenset({UI, EI, US, ES, RX, ME})
```

We once again emphasize that we explicitly allow our proofs to use formulas that are not **sentences**, i.e., to use formulas that have free variable names. As discussed in Chapter 9, this gives a convenient way to manipulate formulas using tautologies and MP.[2] However, notice that a formula $\phi(x_1,\ldots,x_n)$ whose free variable names are $x_1,\ldots,x_n$ is essentially equivalent to the sentence '$\forall x_1[\forall x_2[\cdots \forall x_n[\phi(x_1,\ldots,x_n)]\cdots]]$', not only semantically (which it is by definition of how we evaluate universal quantifications and formulas with free variable names) but also, using our axiomatic system, syntactically within a proof. Indeed, the inference rule of universal generalization (UG) allows us to deduce from the former formula the latter one (by applying UG with the variable name x_n, then with the variable name x_{n-1}, etc.), while the axiom schema of Universal Instantiation (UI) allows us to deduce from the latter formula the former one (by instantiating UI with the placeholder τ substituted by the term 'x_1', then with the placeholder τ substituted by the term 'x_2', etc.).

Our first order of business is to verify that the six axiom schemas just defined are sound. While for our axioms of propositional logic (and for their schema equivalents for predicate logic) this was an easy finite check, for the six axiom schemas just defined this is no longer the case, as even for a single instance of any of these schemas there are infinitely many possible models, and no clear "shortcut" for showing that only finitely many values in

---

[2] Recall that the **propositional skeleton** of any predicate-logic formula with a quantification at its root, such as '$\forall x[(Q(x){\rightarrow}(P(x){\rightarrow}Q(x)))]$', is simply a propositional variable name, and therefore not a tautology, and so such formulas are not considered axiomatic in our system. On the other hand, the propositional skeleton of '$(Q(x){\rightarrow}(P(x){\rightarrow}Q(x)))$' is a tautology, and so it is an axiom of our system.

these models affect its value. We will thus have to resort to "standard" mathematical proofs for proving the soundness of these axiom schemas:[3]

LEMMA 10.1   *The six axiom schemas UI, EI, US, ES, RX, and ME are sound.*

Proof   We will prove this for the axiom schema UI. The proof for each of the other five axiom schemas is either similar or easier.

We have to prove that every instance of the schema UI is sound. This may seem intuitively trivial: If '$\phi(x)$' holds for every possible value of x, then '$\phi(\tau)$' should hold regardless of the value of τ. However, as we have already seen in Chapter 9, due to the possibility of certain variable names appearing in the parametrized formula that is substituted for the placeholder $\phi(\square)$ or in the term that is substituted for the placeholder τ in this schema, there in fact would have been non-sound instances of UI were it not for the two rules that we defined in Chapter 9 that restrict the legal instances of schemas. The entirety of this proof will in fact be dedicated to carefully verifying that these two rules suffice to "rule out" every possible issue of this sort, or in other words, that indeed subject to these two rules, every conceivable instance of UI really is sound.[4]

Our proof will therefore intimately depend on the two rules from Chapter 9 that define the legal instances of schemas. Let '$(\forall \tilde{x}[\psi] \to \xi)$' be an instance of UI obtained by instantiating UI by substituting some variable name $\tilde{x}$ for the placeholder x in UI, some parametrized formula $\tilde{\phi}(\square)$ for the placeholder $\phi(\square)$ in UI (so 'ψ' is the result of substituting the instantiated argument $\tilde{x}$ into the parametrized formula $\tilde{\phi}(\square)$), and some term $\tilde{\tau}$ for the placeholder τ in UI (so 'ξ' is the result of substituting the instantiated argument $\tilde{\tau}$ into the parametrized formula $\tilde{\phi}(\square)$) without violating any of these two rules from Chapter 9.

We will first claim that if we take ψ and replace every free occurrence of $\tilde{x}$ in it by $\tilde{\tau}$, then we obtain ξ.[5] To see this, we notice that by the definition of instantiating parametrized template relation names, the only difference between ψ and ξ is that some occurrences of $\tilde{x}$ in ψ (those that are the result of substituting $\tilde{x}$ for the parameter $\square$ of $\tilde{\phi}(\square)$) have in their stead a $\tilde{\tau}$ in ξ. We have to show that these occurrences of $\tilde{x}$ in ψ are precisely all the free occurrences of $\tilde{x}$ in ψ – no more and no less. By the first rule from Chapter 9 that defines the legal instances of schemas, the formula $\tilde{\phi}(\square)$ does not have any free occurrences of $\tilde{x}$. Therefore, *every* free occurrence of $\tilde{x}$ in ψ is the result of substituting $\tilde{x}$ for the parameter $\square$ of $\tilde{\phi}(\square)$ and therefore has in its stead a $\tilde{\tau}$ in ξ. By the second rule from Chapter 9 that defines the legal instances of schemas, when $\tilde{x}$ is substituted into $\tilde{\phi}(\square)$ it does not get bound by a quantifier in $\tilde{\phi}(\square)$. Therefore, *only* free occurrences of $\tilde{x}$ in ψ

---

[3] While these "standard" mathematical proofs will *convince you* that these axiom schemas are sound, we note that we do have a problem of circularity here: if we ever wanted to formalize these mathematical proofs (that prove the soundness of these axiom schemas) as Proof objects, we would in fact need these axiom schemas – whose soundness these proofs prove – for formalizing these proofs. This is precisely why axioms are needed in mathematics: To avoid such circularity, we must assume *something* without a proof. We nonetheless write a "standard" mathematical proof for the soundness of these axiom schemas (even though this proof will implicitly assume things about quantifications, equality, etc.), to convince ourselves that they are reasonable axiom schemas to assume.

[4] As noted, we defined these two rules precisely to make sure that all legal instances of each of our six axiom schemas are sound (and that these schemas have rich enough legal instances for our proofs).

[5] In fact, the traditional way to define UI is via such replacements rather than via parametrized formulas. We chose the latter so that our schema syntax may be more intuitive for programmers.

are the result of substituting $\tilde{x}$ for the parameter $\square$ of $\tilde{\phi}(\square)$ and therefore only these occurrences of $\tilde{x}$ have in their stead a $\tilde{\tau}$ in ξ. So, the occurrences of $\tilde{x}$ in ψ that have in their stead a $\tilde{\tau}$ in ξ are all the free occurrences of $\tilde{x}$ in ψ and only these occurrences. So, ξ is the result of replacing every free occurrence of $\tilde{x}$ in ψ by $\tilde{\tau}$.

We will now claim that whenever the instance '$(\forall \tilde{x}[\psi] \rightarrow \xi)$' is evaluated in any model M (that has interpretations for all its constant, function, and relation names), under any assignment A (to its free variable names), the value of every variable name occurrence in ξ that originates in $\tilde{\tau}$ (when substituted for the parameter $\square$ of $\tilde{\phi}(\square)$) gets its values from A. Indeed, by the second rule from Chapter 9 that defines the legal instances of schemas, no such variable name occurrence gets bound by a quantifier in $\tilde{\phi}(\square)$, and therefore every such variable name occurrence is free in '$(\forall \tilde{x}[\psi] \rightarrow \xi)$', and so gets its value from A.

We are now ready to show that '$(\forall \tilde{x}[\psi] \rightarrow \xi)$' sound, i.e., evaluates to *True* in any model M, under any assignment A. By definition of how the *implies* operator is evaluated, it is enough to show that for any such model M and assignment A for which '$\forall \tilde{x}[\psi]$' evaluates to *True*, ξ also evaluates to *True*. So let M and A be such so that '$\forall \tilde{x}[\psi]$' evaluates to *True*. Let α be the element in the universe of M to which $\tilde{\tau}$ evaluates in M under A. As we have argued, each of the variable name occurrences in ξ that originates in $\tilde{\tau}$ gets its value from A when ξ is evaluated. Therefore, and since ξ is the result of replacing every free occurrence of $\tilde{x}$ in ψ by $\tilde{\tau}$, we have that the value of ξ in M under A is the value of ψ in M under the assignment created from A by assigning the element α to the variable name $\tilde{x}$. But this value is *True* (which is what we want to prove!) since by the definition of '$\forall \tilde{x}[\psi]$' evaluating to *True* in M under A, we have that ψ evaluates to *True* in M under any assignment created from A by assigning *any* element in the universe of M to the variable name $\tilde{x}$. $\square$

Combining Lemma 10.1 with the soundness theorem (9.1) for predicate logic, we therefore obtain that any inference proven from these six axiom schemas is sound.

In this chapter, you will write proofs using the axiomatic system just defined, by using the `Proof` class that you built in Chapter 9, with UI, EI, US, ES, RX, and ME as axioms (in addition to any assumptions) in every proof that you will write. In some of the tasks in this chapter, you are asked to write some proof; the corresponding programming task is to return an object of class `Proof` that has as assumptions/axioms the axiom schemas UI, EI, US, ES, RX, and ME, as well as the assumptions/axioms specified in that task, and has the specified conclusion (and is a valid proof, of course). Manually writing these proofs may turn out to be a bit (OK, very) cumbersome, so you will not work directly with the `Proof` class, but rather with a new class called `Prover` that "wraps around" the `Proof` class and provides a more convenient way to write proofs.

predicates/prover.py

```
class Prover:
    """A class for gradually creating a predicate-logic proof from given
    assumptions as well as from the six axioms (`AXIOMS`) Universal
    Instantiation (`UI`), Existential Introduction (`EI`), Universal
    Simplification (`US`), Existential Simplification (`ES`), Reflexivity
    (`RX`), and Meaning of Equality (`ME`).
```

```
    Attributes:
        _assumptions: the assumptions/axioms of the proof being created, which
            include `AXIOMS`.
        _lines: the lines so far of the proof being created.
        _print_as_proof_forms: flag specifying whether the proof being created
            is being printed in real time as it forms.
    """
    _assumptions: FrozenSet[Schema]
    _lines: List[Proof.Line]
    _print_as_proof_forms: bool

    ⋮
    ⋮

    def __init__(self, assumptions: Collection[Union[Schema, Formula, str]],
                 print_as_proof_forms: bool=False):
        """Initializes a `Prover` from its assumptions/additional axioms. The
        proof created by the prover initially has no lines.

        Parameters:
            assumptions: the assumptions/axioms beyond `AXIOMS` for the proof
                to be created, each specified as either a schema, a formula that
                constitutes the unique instance of the assumption, or the string
                representation of the unique instance of the assumption.
            print_as_proof_forms: flag specifying whether the proof to be
                created is to be printed in real time as it forms.
        """
        self._assumptions = \
            Prover.AXIOMS.union(
                {assumption if isinstance(assumption, Schema)
                 else Schema(assumption) if isinstance(assumption, Formula)
                 else Schema(Formula.parse(assumption))
                 for assumption in assumptions})
        self._lines = []
        self._print_as_proof_forms = print_as_proof_forms
        if self._print_as_proof_forms:
            print('Proving from assumptions/axioms:\n'
                  '  AXIOMS')
            for assumption in self._assumptions - Prover.AXIOMS:
                print('   ' + str(assumption))
            print('Lines:')
```

A single instance of class Prover is used to "write" a single proof that initially has no lines when the prover is constructed, and which the methods of the prover can be used to gradually extend. As can be seen, for your convenience the constructor of class Prover is very flexible with respect to the types of the arguments that it can take: While Proof assumptions are schemas, they can be passed to the Prover constructor not only as objects of type Schema, but also as objects of type Formula and even as their string representations, and the Prover constructor will convert them to type Schema. This flexibility is also a feature of the other methods of class Prover. For example, the method add_instantiated_assumption(), which adds an assumption line to the proof being created by the prover, can take the added instance not only as a Formula object but also as its string representation, and can even have string representations instead of Formula and Term objects in the instantiation map that it takes. The basic methods of class Prover, which we have already implemented for you, are add_assumption(), add_instantiated_assumption(), add_tautology(), add_mp(), and add_ug().

Each of these methods adds to the proof being created by the prover a single line justified by one of the four allowed justification types, and we will get to know them momentarily.[6]

In addition to these five basic methods that add a single line to the proof being created by the prover, some of the tasks in this chapter will ask you to implement more advanced methods of the `Prover` class, each of which will add to the proof being created several lines with a single call. **Important:** In all of these methods that you will implement, you will of course access the `_lines` instance variable of the current `Prover` object that holds the lines already added to the proof being created, however you should *never* modify this instance variable directly via `self._lines`, but *only* via the methods `add_assumption()`, `add_instantiated_assumption()`, `add_tautology()`, `add_mp()`, and `add_ug()` (or via other methods that you will have already implemented). By convention, each of these `Prover` methods (the basic ones already mentioned and the additional ones that you will implement) returns the line number, in the proof being created by the prover, of the last (or the only) line that was added – the line that holds the conclusion that the method was asked to deduce.

Once you are done adding all desired lines to a prover, you can obtain the final proof, as an object of class `Proof`, by calling the `qed()` method of the prover.

```
predicates/prover.py

class Prover:
      ⋮

    def qed(self) -> Proof:
        """Concludes the proof created by the current prover.

        Returns:
            A valid proof, from the assumptions of the current prover as well as
            `AXIOMS`', of the formula justified by the last line appended to the
            current prover.
        """
        conclusion = self._lines[-1].formula
        if self._print_as_proof_forms:
            print('Conclusion:', str(conclusion) + '. QED\n')
        return Proof(self._assumptions, conclusion, self._lines)
```

10.2   Syllogisms

From Wikipedia ("Syllogism," 2021, para. 1):[7]

> *A syllogism (Greek: syllogismos, 'conclusion, inference') is a kind of logical argument that applies deductive reasoning to arrive at a conclusion based on two propositions that are asserted or assumed to be true.*
> *In its earliest form, defined by Aristotle, from the combination of a general statement (the major premise) and a specific statement (the minor premise), a conclusion is deduced. For*

---

[6] You can ignore the additional already-implemented method `add_proof()` for the duration this chapter – you will use this method, which is a predicate-logic equivalent of sorts of the `inline_proof()` function that you implemented for propositional logic, in Chapters 11 and 12.

[7] Wikipedia, *The Free Encyclopedia*, s.v. "Syllogism," (accessed June 22, 2021), `https://en.wikipedia.org/w/index.php?title=Syllogism&oldid=1028905379`.

example, knowing that all men are mortal (major premise) and that Socrates is a man (minor premise), we may validly conclude that Socrates is mortal.

Let us try to formalize and prove this syllogism in our system.

Assumptions: (In addition to the six axiom schemas UI, EI, US, ES, RX, ME)

1. '∀x[(Man(x)→Mortal(x))]'
2. 'Man(aristotle)'

Conclusion:[8] 'Mortal(aristotle)'

Proof:

1. '∀x[(Man(x)→Mortal(x))]'. Justification: First assumption.
2. '(∀x[(Man(x)→Mortal(x))]→(Man(aristotle)→Mortal(aristotle)))'. Justification: UI with $\phi(\square)$ defined as '(Man($\square$)→Mortal($\square$))', with x defined as 'x', and with τ defined as 'aristotle'.
3. '(Man(aristotle)→Mortal(aristotle))'. Justification: MP from Steps 1 and 2.
4. 'Man(aristotle)'. Justification: Second assumption.
5. 'Mortal(aristotle)'. Justification: MP from Steps 4 and 3.

A programmatic implementation of this proof (and of all other proofs from this chapter) using the Prover class can be found in a corresponding function in the file predicates/some_proofs.py.

```
                        predicates/some_proofs.py

def prove_syllogism(print_as_proof_forms: bool = False) -> Proof:
    """Proves from the assumptions:

    1. All men are mortal ('Ax[(Man(x)->Mortal(x))]'), and
    2. Aristotle is a man ('Man(aristotle)')

    the conclusion: Aristotle is mortal ('Mortal(aristotle)').

    Parameters:
        print_as_proof_forms: flag specifying whether the proof is to be printed
            in real time as it is being created.

    Returns:
        A valid proof of the above inference via `Prover.AXIOMS`.
    """
    prover = Prover({'Ax[(Man(x)->Mortal(x))]', 'Man(aristotle)'},
                    print_as_proof_forms)
    step1 = prover.add_assumption('Ax[(Man(x)->Mortal(x))]')
    step2 = prover.add_instantiated_assumption(
        '(Ax[(Man(x)->Mortal(x))]->(Man(aristotle)->Mortal(aristotle)))',
        Prover.UI, {'R': '(Man(_)->Mortal(_))', 'c': 'aristotle'})
    step3 = prover.add_mp('(Man(aristotle)->Mortal(aristotle))', step1, step2)
```

---

[8] We have replaced Socrates with Aristotle in our conclusion not as a philosophical statement of any sort, but rather to make the conclusion (and the formulas in the proof) look more intuitive in our predicate-logic language, in which 'aristotle' is a valid constant name but 'socrates' is not.

```
step4 = prover.add_assumption('Man(aristotle)')
step5 = prover.add_mp('Mortal(aristotle)', step4, step3)
return prover.qed()
```

This is a good opportunity to start to get to know the Prover class by going over this Python implementation and comparing it to the preceding proof. In both programming and text, it is a tad annoying to go through Step 2 to obtain Step 3, so in the next task you will write a helper method called add_universal_instantiation() that can do this automatically for you and allows for the following shorter implementation.

predicates/some_proofs.py

```
def prove_syllogism_with_universal_instantiation(print_as_proof_forms: bool =
                                                 False) -> Proof:
    """Using the method `Prover.add_universal_instantiation`, proves from the
    assumptions:

    1. All men are mortal ('Ax[(Man(x)->Mortal(x))]'), and
    2. Aristotle is a man ('Man(aristotle)')

    the conclusion: Aristotle is mortal ('Mortal(aristotle)').

    Parameters:
        print_as_proof_forms: flag specifying whether the proof is to be printed
            in real time as it is being created.

    Returns:
        A valid proof, created with the help of the method
        `Prover.add_universal_instantiation`, of the above inference via
        `AXIOMS`.
    """
    prover = Prover({'Ax[(Man(x)->Mortal(x))]', 'Man(aristotle)'},
                    print_as_proof_forms)
    step1 = prover.add_assumption('Ax[(Man(x)->Mortal(x))]')
    step2 = prover.add_universal_instantiation(
        '(Man(aristotle)->Mortal(aristotle))', step1, 'aristotle')
    step3 = prover.add_assumption('Man(aristotle)')
    step4 = prover.add_mp('Mortal(aristotle)', step3, step2)
    return prover.qed()
```

TASK 1   Implement the missing code for the method add_universal_instantiation(instantiation, line_number, term) of class Prover, which adds to the prover a sequence of validly justified lines, the last of which has the formula instantiation.[9] The line with the given line number must hold a universally quantified formula '$\forall x[\phi(x)]$' for some variable name x and formula $\phi(x)$, and the derived formula instantiation should have the given term substituted into the free occurrences of x in $\phi(x)$.

---

[9] The instantiation parameter can also be passed as a string representation of a formula. The code of the method that we have already implemented for you converts it to a Formula if needed. The same holds for all Formula and Term objects passed, whether directly as arguments or even indirectly within maps, to any of the other Prover methods that you will be asked to implement in this chapter.

```
                        ┌─ predicates/prover.py ─┐
class Prover:
    :
    :

    def add_universal_instantiation(self, instantiation: Union[Formula, str],
                                    line_number: int, term: Union[Term, str]) \
            -> int:
        """Appends to the proof being created by the current prover a sequence
        of validly justified lines, the last of which validly justifies the
        given formula, which is the result of substituting a term for the
        outermost universally quantified variable name in the formula in the
        specified already existing line of the proof.

        Parameters:
            instantiation: conclusion of the sequence of lines to be appended,
                specified as either a formula or its string representation.
            line_number: line number in the proof of a universally quantified
                formula of the form 'A`x`[`statement`]'.
            term: term, specified as either a term or its string representation,
                that when substituted into the free occurrences of `x` in
                `statement` yields the given formula.

        Returns:
            The line number of the newly appended line that justifies the given
            formula in the proof being created by the current prover.

        Examples:
            If Line `line_number` contains the formula
            'Ay[Az[f(x,y)=g(z,y)]]' and `term` is 'h(w)', then `instantiation`
            should be 'Az[f(x,h(w))=g(z,h(w))]'.
        """
        if isinstance(instantiation, str):
            instantiation = Formula.parse(instantiation)
        assert line_number < len(self._lines)
        quantified = self._lines[line_number].formula
        assert quantified.root == 'A'
        if isinstance(term, str):
            term = Term.parse(term)
        assert instantiation == \
            quantified.statement.substitute({quantified.variable: term})
        # Task 10.1
```

Example: If we have in Line 17 of the proof being created by a prover prover the formula '$\forall y[(Q(y,z) \rightarrow R(w,y))]$', then the call

```
prover.add_universal_instantiation('(Q(f(1,w),z)->R(w,f(1,w)))',
                                   17, 'f(1,w)')
```

will add to the proof a few lines, the last of which has the formula '$(Q(f(1,w),z) \rightarrow R(w,f(1,w)))$'.

Let us try to formalize and prove another syllogism: All Greeks are human, all humans are mortal; thus, all Greeks are mortal.

Assumptions:

1. '$\forall x[(Greek(x) \rightarrow Human(x))]$'
2. '$\forall x[(Human(x) \rightarrow Mortal(x))]$'

Conclusion: '∀x[(Greek(x)→Mortal(x))]'

Proof:

1. '∀x[(Greek(x)→Human(x))]'. Justification: First assumption.
2. '(Greek(x)→Human(x))'. Justification: Universal instantiation of Step 1 (substituting the term 'x' for the quantification variable name 'x').
3. '∀x[(Human(x)→Mortal(x))]'. Justification: Second assumption.
4. '(Human(x)→Mortal(x))'. Justification: Universal instantiation of Step 3.
5. '((Greek(x)→Human(x))→((Human(x)→Mortal(x))→(Greek(x)→Mortal(x))))'. Justification: A tautology.
6. '((Human(x)→Mortal(x))→(Greek(x)→Mortal(x)))'. Justification: MP from Steps 2 and 5.
7. '(Greek(x)→Mortal(x))'. Justification: MP from Steps 4 and 6.
8. '∀x[(Greek(x)→Mortal(x))]'. Justification: UG of Step 7.

```
predicates/some_proofs.py

def prove_syllogism_all_all(print_as_proof_forms: bool = False) -> Proof:
    """Proves from the assumptions:

    1. All Greeks are human ('Ax[(Greek(x)->Human(x))]'), and
    2. All humans are mortal ('Ax[(Human(x)->Mortal(x))]')

    the conclusion: All Greeks are mortal ('Ax[(Greek(x)->Mortal(x))]').

    Parameters:
        print_as_proof_forms: flag specifying whether the proof is to be printed
            in real time as it is being created.

    Returns:
        A valid proof of the above inference via `Prover.AXIOMS`.
    """
    prover = Prover({'Ax[(Greek(x)->Human(x))]', 'Ax[(Human(x)->Mortal(x))]'},
                    print_as_proof_forms)
    step1 = prover.add_assumption('Ax[(Greek(x)->Human(x))]')
    step2 = prover.add_universal_instantiation(
        '(Greek(x)->Human(x))', step1, 'x')
    step3 = prover.add_assumption('Ax[(Human(x)->Mortal(x))]')
    step4 = prover.add_universal_instantiation(
        '(Human(x)->Mortal(x))', step3, 'x')
    step5 = prover.add_tautology(
        '((Greek(x)->Human(x))->((Human(x)->Mortal(x))->(Greek(x)->Mortal(x))))')
    step6 = prover.add_mp(
        '((Human(x)->Mortal(x))->(Greek(x)->Mortal(x)))', step2, step5)
    step7 = prover.add_mp('(Greek(x)->Mortal(x))', step4, step6)
    step8 = prover.add_ug('Ax[(Greek(x)->Mortal(x))]', step7)
    return prover.qed()
```

Steps 5–7 of this proof seem a bit cumbersome, so in the next task you will write a helper method called add_tautological_implication() that provides an easier way to derive a tautological implication of previous lines and allows for the following shorter implementation:[10]

```python
def prove_syllogism_all_all_with_tautological_implication(print_as_proof_forms:
                                                          bool = False) -> \
        Proof:
    """Using the method `Prover.add_tautological_implication`, proves from the
    assumptions:

    1. All Greeks are human ('Ax[(Greek(x)->Human(x))]'), and
    2. All humans are mortal ('Ax[(Human(x)->Mortal(x))]')

    the conclusion: All Greeks are mortal ('Ax[(Greek(x)->Mortal(x))]').

    Parameters:
        print_as_proof_forms: flag specifying whether the proof is to be printed
            in real time as it is being created.

    Returns:
        A valid proof, created with the help of the method
        `Prover.add_tautological_implication`, of the above inference via
        `AXIOMS`.
    """
    prover = Prover({'Ax[(Greek(x)->Human(x))]', 'Ax[(Human(x)->Mortal(x))]'},
                    print_as_proof_forms)
    step1 = prover.add_assumption('Ax[(Greek(x)->Human(x))]')
    step2 = prover.add_universal_instantiation(
        '(Greek(x)->Human(x))', step1, 'x')
    step3 = prover.add_assumption('Ax[(Human(x)->Mortal(x))]')
    step4 = prover.add_universal_instantiation(
        '(Human(x)->Mortal(x))', step3, 'x')
    step5 = prover.add_tautological_implication(
        '(Greek(x)->Mortal(x))', {step2, step4})
    step6 = prover.add_ug('Ax[(Greek(x)->Mortal(x))]', step5)
    return prover.qed()
```

Similar to the propositional skeleton of a single predicate-logic formula, we define the **propositional skeleton** of a predicate-logic inference as the propositional-logic inference rule obtained from the predicate-logic inference by consistently (across all of the assumptions and the conclusion) replacing each (outermost) subformula whose root is a relation name, an equality, or a quantifier, with a new propositional variable name. For example, the propositional skeleton of the predicate-logic inference with assumptions '(R(x)|Q(y))' and '~R(x)' and conclusion 'Q(y)' is the propositional-logic inference rule with assumptions

---

[10] It is instructive to compare the six-step proof that follows not only with its eight-step version that we have just given, which already makes some shortcuts by using universal instantiation steps, but also with its full ten-step version that we gave as an example of a proof in the beginning of Chapter 9. Together, the ability to use both universal instantiation steps and tautological implication steps allows us to cut the number of explicitly specified proof steps almost in half. The number of actual lines in the resulting proof does not change, of course, but what we are interested in is making our life when coding proofs easier, which being able to explicitly specify considerably fewer steps (and this will of course be even more significant in more elaborate proofs) certainly does. Indeed, the shortcuts that you are accumulating under your belt in this chapter will together save you from explicitly specifying more than just a few proof steps in subsequent tasks and in the following chapters.

'(z1|z2)' and '~z1' and conclusion 'z2'. We say that a (predicate-logic) formula ϕ is a **(predicate-logic) tautological implication** of some set of (predicate-logic) formulas A if the propositional skeleton (a propositional-logic inference rule) of the predicate-logic inference with assumptions A and conclusion ϕ is sound.[11]

TASK 2   Implement the missing code for the method `add_tautological_implication(` `implication`, `line_numbers`) of class `Prover`, which adds to the prover a sequence of validly justified lines, the last of which has the formula `implication`. The derived formula `implication` should be a tautological implication of the formulas from the lines with the given line numbers.

```
                          ┌─────────────────────┐
                          │  predicates/prover.py │
                          └─────────────────────┘
class Prover:
    ⋮

    def add_tautological_implication(self, implication: Union[Formula, str],
                                     line_numbers: AbstractSet[int]) -> int:
        """Appends to the proof being created by the current prover a sequence
        of validly justified lines, the last of which validly justifies the
        given formula, which is a tautological implication of the formulas in
        the specified already existing lines of the proof.

        Parameters:
            implication: conclusion of the sequence of lines to be appended,
                specified as either a formula or its string representation.
            line_numbers: line numbers in the proof of formulas of which
                `implication` is a tautological implication.

        Returns:
            The line number of the newly appended line that justifies the given
            formula in the proof being created by the current prover.
        """
        if isinstance(implication, str):
            implication = Formula.parse(implication)
        for line_number in line_numbers:
            assert line_number < len(self._lines)
        # Task 10.2
```

Hint: Think back to your solution to Task 4 in Chapter 6 (the implementation of `prove_sound_inference()`) and understand why a formula ϕ is a tautological implication of some set of formulas A if and only if the (predicate-logic) formula that "encodes" the inference with assumptions A and conclusion ϕ is a predicate-logic tautology.

One nice thing about your solution to Task 2 is that it allows you to never bother with "double MP" maneuvers again, even when the original conditional statement (the statement of the form '$(\phi\rightarrow(\psi\rightarrow\xi))$') is not a tautology. If you have somehow proven the three statements '$(\phi\rightarrow(\psi\rightarrow\xi))$', ϕ, and ψ, then instead of deriving ξ from these using a "double MP" maneuver (first deriving '$(\psi\rightarrow\xi)$' via MP, and then deriving ξ via yet another MP),

---

[11] We once again use the terminology *the* propositional skeleton somewhat misleadingly, as there are many propositional skeletons for any given predicate-logic inference. For example, the inference rule with assumptions '(z3|z4)' and '~z3' and conclusion 'z4' is also a propositional skeleton of the above predicate-logic inference. There is once again no problem here, though, since either all propositional skeletons of a given predicate-logic inference are sound, or none are.

you can instead derive ξ as a tautological implication of these three statements in one proof step (i.e., using one Python line).

Finally, let us try to formalize and prove the syllogism that we gave as our first example in the beginning of Chapter 7: All men are mortal, some men exist; thus, some mortals exist.

Assumptions:

1. '$\forall x[(Man(x) \rightarrow Mortal(x))]$'
2. '$\exists x[Man(x)]$'

Conclusion: '$\exists x[Mortal(x)]$'

Proof:

1. '$\forall x[(Man(x) \rightarrow Mortal(x))]$'. Justification: First assumption.
2. '$\exists x[Man(x)]$'. Justification: Second assumption.
3. '$(Man(x) \rightarrow Mortal(x))$'. Justification: Universal instantiation of Step 1.
4. '$(Mortal(x) \rightarrow \exists x[Mortal(x)])$'. Justification: EI with $\phi(\square)$ defined as '$Mortal(\square)$' and with x and τ both defined as 'x'.
5. '$(Man(x) \rightarrow \exists x[Mortal(x)])$'. Justification: Tautological implication of Steps 3 and 4.
6. '$\forall x[(Man(x) \rightarrow \exists x[Mortal(x)])]$'. Justification: UG of Step 5.
7. '$((\forall x[(Man(x) \rightarrow \exists x[Mortal(x)])] \& \exists x[Man(x)]) \rightarrow \exists x[Mortal(x)])$'. Justification: ES with $\phi(\square)$ defined as '$Man(\square)$', with x defined as 'x', and with ψ defined as '$\exists x[Mortal(x)]$' (which does not have 'x' free).
8. '$\exists x[Mortal(x)]$'. Justification: Tautological implication of Steps 2, 6, and 7.

```
                    predicates/some_proofs.py

def prove_syllogism_all_exists(print_as_proof_forms: bool = False) -> Proof:
    """Proves from the assumptions:

    1. All men are mortal ('Ax[(Man(x)->Mortal(x))]'), and
    2. Some men exist ('Ex[Man(x)]')

    the conclusion: Some mortals exist ('Ex[Mortal(x)]').

    Parameters:
        print_as_proof_forms: flag specifying whether the proof is to be printed
            in real time as it is being created.

    Returns:
        A valid proof of the above inference via
        `~predicates.prover.Prover.AXIOMS`.
    """
    prover = Prover({'Ax[(Man(x)->Mortal(x))]', 'Ex[Man(x)]'},
                    print_as_proof_forms)
    step1 = prover.add_assumption('Ax[(Man(x)->Mortal(x))]')
    step2 = prover.add_assumption('Ex[Man(x)]')
    step3 = prover.add_universal_instantiation(
        '(Man(x)->Mortal(x))', step1, 'x')
    step4 = prover.add_instantiated_assumption(
        '(Mortal(x)->Ex[Mortal(x)])', Prover.EI,
        {'R': 'Mortal(_)', 'c': 'x'})
```

```
step5 = prover.add_tautological_implication(
    '(Man(x)->Ex[Mortal(x)])', {step3, step4})
step6 = prover.add_ug('Ax[(Man(x)->Ex[Mortal(x)])]', step5)
step7 = prover.add_instantiated_assumption(
    '((Ax[(Man(x)->Ex[Mortal(x)])]&Ex[Man(x)])->Ex[Mortal(x)])', Prover.ES,
    {'R': 'Man(_)', 'Q': 'Ex[Mortal(x)]'})
step8 = prover.add_tautological_implication(
    'Ex[Mortal(x)]', {step2, step6, step7})
return prover.qed()
```

The maneuver in the last three steps of this proof is quite useful in general, where the idea is that once we have shown that some x with a property '$P(x)$' exists (e.g., 'Ex[Man(x)]'), and that '$(P(x){\rightarrow}Q)$' (e.g., '(Man(x)->Ex[Mortal(x)])'), then we can deduce Q (e.g., 'Ex[Mortal(x)]'). In the next task you will write a helper method called add_existential_derivation() that automates this maneuver and allows for the following shorter implementation:

```
                          predicates/some_proofs.py

def prove_syllogism_all_exists_with_existential_derivation(print_as_proof_forms:
                                                    bool = False) -> \
        Proof:
    """Using the method `~predicates.prover.Prover.add_existential_derivation`,
    proves from the assumptions:

    1. All men are mortal ('Ax[(Man(x)->Mortal(x))]'), and
    2. Some men exist ('Ex[Man(x)]')

    the conclusion: Some mortals exist ('Ex[Mortal(x)]').

    Parameters:
        print_as_proof_forms: flag specifying whether the proof is to be printed
            in real time as it is being created.

    Returns:
        A valid proof, created with the help of the method
        `~predicates.prover.Prover.add_existential_derivation`, of the above
        inference via `~predicates.prover.Prover.AXIOMS`.
    """
    prover = Prover({'Ax[(Man(x)->Mortal(x))]', 'Ex[Man(x)]'},
                    print_as_proof_forms)
    step1 = prover.add_assumption('Ax[(Man(x)->Mortal(x))]')
    step2 = prover.add_assumption('Ex[Man(x)]')
    step3 = prover.add_universal_instantiation(
        '(Man(x)->Mortal(x))', step1, 'x')
    step4 = prover.add_instantiated_assumption(
        '(Mortal(x)->Ex[Mortal(x)])', Prover.EI, {'R': 'Mortal(_)', 'c': 'x'})
    step5 = prover.add_tautological_implication(
        '(Man(x)->Ex[Mortal(x)])', {step3, step4})
    step6 = prover.add_existential_derivation('Ex[Mortal(x)]', step2, step5)
    return prover.qed()
```

TASK 3   Implement the missing code for the method add_existential_derivation(consequent, line_number1, line_number2) of class Prover, which adds to the prover a sequence of validly justified lines, the last of which has the formula consequent.

The line with number line_number1 must hold an existential formula '$\exists x[\phi(x)]$' (for some variable name x) and the line with number line_number2 must hold the implication '$(\phi(x) \to \psi)$', where ψ is the derived formula consequent.

```
                      ┌─ predicates/prover.py ─┐
class Prover:
     ⋮

    def add_existential_derivation(self, consequent: Union[Formula, str],
                                   line_number1: int, line_number2: int) -> int:
        """Appends to the proof being created by the current prover a sequence
        of validly justified lines, the last of which validly justifies the
        given formula, which is the consequent of the formula in the second
        specified already existing line of the proof, whose antecedent is
        existentially quantified by the formula in the first specified already
        existing line of the proof.

        Parameters:
            consequent: conclusion of the sequence of lines to be appended,
                specified as either a formula or its string representation.
            line_number1: line number in the proof of an existentially
                quantified formula of the form 'E`x`[`antecedent(x)`]', where
                `x` is a variable name that may have free occurrences in
                `antecedent(x)` but has no free occurrences in `consequent`.
            line_number2: line number in the proof of the formula
                '(`antecedent(x)`->`consequent`)'.

        Returns:
            The line number of the newly appended line that justifies the given
            formula in the proof being created by the current prover.
        """
        if isinstance(consequent, str):
            consequent = Formula.parse(consequent)
        assert line_number1 < len(self._lines)
        quantified = self._lines[line_number1].formula
        assert quantified.root == 'E'
        assert quantified.variable not in consequent.free_variables()
        assert line_number2 < len(self._lines)
        conditional = self._lines[line_number2].formula
        assert conditional == Formula('->', quantified.statement, consequent)
        # Task 10.3
```

It is now finally time for you to prove a few statements on your own. The functions that you are asked to implement the next two tasks are contained in the file predicates/some_proofs.py.

TASK 4 Prove the following inference:

Assumptions:

1. Everybody loves somebody: '$\forall x[\exists y[Loves(x,y)]]$'
2. Everybody loves a lover:[12] '$\forall x[\forall z[\forall y[(Loves(x,y) \to Loves(z,x))]]]$'

---

[12] An astute reader may notice that it would also have been possible to understand (and formalize) this sentence in various other ways, such as '$\forall z[\exists x[\exists y[(Loves(x,y)\&Loves(z,x))]]]$' ("each person loves some lover") or

Conclusion: Everybody loves everybody: '∀x[∀z[Loves(z,x)]]'

The proof should be returned by the function `prove_lovers()`, whose missing code you should implement.

```
                    ┌─ predicates/some_proofs.py ─┐
def prove_lovers(print_as_proof_forms: bool = False) -> Proof:
    """Proves from the assumptions:

    1. Everybody loves somebody ('Ax[Ey[Loves(x,y)]]'), and
    2. Everybody loves a lover ('Ax[Az[Ay[(Loves(x,y)->Loves(z,x))]]]')

    the conclusion: Everybody loves everybody ('Ax[Az[Loves(z,x)]]').

    Parameters:
        print_as_proof_forms: flag specifying whether the proof is to be printed
            in real time as it is being created.

    Returns:
        A valid proof of the above inference via `Prover.AXIOMS`.
    """
    prover = Prover({'Ax[Ey[Loves(x,y)]]',
                     'Ax[Az[Ay[(Loves(x,y)->Loves(z,x))]]]'},
                    print_as_proof_forms)
    # Task 10.4
    return prover.qed()
```

TASK 5   Prove the following inference:

Assumptions:

1. No homework is fun: '~∃x[(Homework(x)&Fun(x))]'
2. Some homework is reading: '∃x[(Homework(x)&Reading(x))]'

Conclusion: Some reading is not fun: '∃x[(Reading(x)&~Fun(x))]'

The proof should be returned by the function `prove_homework()`, whose missing code you should implement.

```
                    ┌─ predicates/some_proofs.py ─┐
def prove_homework(print_as_proof_forms: bool = False) -> Proof:
    """Proves from the assumptions:

    1. No homework is fun ('~Ex[(Homework(x)&Fun(x))]'), and
    2. Some reading is homework ('Ex[(Homework(x)&Reading(x))]')

    the conclusion: Some reading is not fun ('Ex[(Reading(x)&~Fun(x))]').

    Parameters:
        print_as_proof_forms: flag specifying whether the proof is to be printed
            in real time as it is being created.
```

'∃x[∃y[(Loves(x,y)&∀z[Loves(z,x)])]]' ("there is some lover that everybody loves"). Indeed, as already remarked in passing, human-language sentences are many times not easy to understand, let alone without context. We think that in the context of the famous song by this name, though, "everybody loves a lover" is meant as in our understanding of it: "everybody loves every lover."

```
    Returns:
        A valid proof of the above inference via `Prover.AXIOMS`.
    """
    prover = Prover({'~Ex[(Homework(x)&Fun(x))]',
                     'Ex[(Homework(x)&Reading(x))]'}, print_as_proof_forms)
    # Task 10.5
    return prover.qed()
```

Hint: Notice that for any formula ϕ, we have that '$\phi \rightarrow \exists x[\phi]$' is an instance of EI. Use this once for deriving '~(Homework(x)&Fun(x))', and once again for deriving '((Reading(x)&~Fun(x))$\rightarrow \exists$x[(Reading(x)&~Fun(x))])'. Note that since the left-hand side of the latter formula is not true in general, you'll need to use this latter formula in a clever way in your proof in order to derive its right-hand side – but how? Well, since you have not used your second assumption yet, it is time to use it, and since it is existentially quantified, you will have to use it via an existential derivation. Can you see how what you have proven so far can be used to prove the other formula needed for the existential derivation to give you the desired overall conclusion?

10.3 Some Mathematics

We now move on to using logic to express basic mathematical structures. In particular we will use functions and equality much more.

10.3.1 Groups

We start with one of the simplest mathematical structures, that of a **group**. While a **field** has two operators: addition and multiplication, a group only has one operator, which we will denote by addition. The **language** in which we will describe a group has, accordingly, two function names – a binary function name 'plus' and a *unary* function name 'minus' – and a constant name '0'. A group has only three axioms:

Group Axioms:

- Zero Axiom: 'plus(0,x)=x'
- Negation Axiom: 'plus(minus(x),x)=0'
- Associativity Axiom: 'plus(plus(x,y),z)=plus(x,plus(y,z))'

```
                          predicates/some_proofs.py
#: The three group axioms
GROUP_AXIOMS = frozenset({'plus(0,x)=x', 'plus(minus(x),x)=0',
                          'plus(plus(x,y),z)=plus(x,plus(y,z))'})
```

While our programs will stick to this simple functional notation, in this chapter we will use the equivalent standard, infix notation for better readability:

- Zero Axiom: $0 + x = x$
- Negation Axiom: $-x + x = 0$
- Associativity Axiom: $(x + y) + z = x + (y + z)$

We note that group addition may possibly be non-commutative, i.e., it is not necessarily the case that $x + y = y + x$. Therefore, since we only defined 0 to be neutral to addition when it is on the left, it is not clear that it is also neutral to addition when it is on the right (i.e., it is not clear that also $x + 0 = x$). However, it turns out that one can carefully prove this from the three group axioms, and we will now formulate this proof.

Assumptions: Group axioms
Conclusion: $x + 0 = x$

Proof:

We will trace and formalize the following mathematical proof, which you may have seen written on the board if you took a course on algebraic structures. The basic "trick" of this proof is to add the term $(- - x + -x)$ on the left:

$$x + 0 = 0 + (x + 0) = (0 + x) + 0 = ((- - x + -x) + x) + 0 =$$
$$= (- - x + (-x + x)) + 0 = (- - x + 0) + 0 = - - x + (0 + 0) =$$
$$= - - x + 0 = - - x + (-x + x) = (- - x + -x) + x = 0 + x = x.$$

Let us formalize this proof in our system. We start by listing the axioms as the first steps of the proof:

1. $0 + x = x$. Justification: Zero axiom.
2. $-x + x = 0$. Justification: Negation axiom.
3. $(x + y) + z = x + (y + z)$. Justification: Associativity axiom.

```
                      predicates/some_proofs.py
def prove_group_right_neutral(···, print_as_proof_forms: bool = False) -> Proof:
    """Proves from the group axioms that x+0=x ('plus(x,0)=x').

    Parameters:
        :
        :

        print_as_proof_forms: flag specifying whether the proof is to be printed
            in real time as it is being created.

    Returns:
        A valid proof of the above inference via `Prover.AXIOMS`.
    """
    prover = Prover(GROUP_AXIOMS, print_as_proof_forms)
    zero = prover.add_assumption('plus(0,x)=x')
    negation = prover.add_assumption('plus(minus(x),x)=0')
    associativity = prover.add_assumption('plus(plus(x,y),z)=plus(x,plus(y,z))')
    :
    :
```

We will also want to use the "flipped" equalities that follow from these axioms by the symmetry of equality. While we have not defined the symmetry of equality as a logical axiom, it can be derived from the logical axioms of equality (RX and ME), and the next task will provide a convenient interface to doing so and performing this kind of flipping.

TASK 6   Implement the missing code for the method `add_flipped_equality(flipped, line_number)` of class `Prover`, which adds to the prover a sequence of validly justified lines, the last of which has the formula `flipped`. The derived formula `flipped` must be of the form '$\tau=\sigma$' (for some terms τ and σ), where the line with the given `line_number` must hold the "non-flipped" equality '$\sigma=\tau$'.

```
                         ┤ predicates/prover.py ├
class Prover:
        :
        :
    def add_flipped_equality(self, flipped: Union[Formula, str],
                             line_number: int) -> int:
        """Appends to the proof being created by the current prover a sequence
        of validly justified lines, the last of which validly justifies the
        given equality, which is the result of exchanging the two sides of the
        equality in the specified already existing line of the proof.

        Parameters:
            flipped: conclusion of the sequence of lines to be appended,
                specified as either a formula or its string representation.
            line_number: line number in the proof of an equality that is the
                same as the given equality, except that the two sides of the
                equality are exchanged.

        Returns:
            The line number of the newly appended line that justifies the given
            equality in the proof being created by the current prover.
        """
        if isinstance(flipped, str):
            flipped = Formula.parse(flipped)
        assert is_equality(flipped.root)
        assert line_number < len(self._lines)
        equality = self._lines[line_number].formula
        assert equality == Formula('=', [flipped.arguments[1],
                                         flipped.arguments[0]])
        # Task 10.6
```

We can continue our proof:

4. $x = 0 + x$. Justification: Flipped zero axiom.
5. $0 = -x + x$. Justification: Flipped negation axiom.
6. $x + (y + z) = (x + y) + z$. Justification: Flipped associativity axiom.

```
                        ┤ predicates/some_proofs.py ├
def prove_group_right_neutral(···, print_as_proof_forms: bool = False) -> Proof:
        :
        :
    flipped_zero = prover.add_flipped_equality('x=plus(0,x)', zero)
    flipped_negation = prover.add_flipped_equality(
        '0=plus(minus(x),x)', negation)
    flipped_associativity = prover.add_flipped_equality(
        'plus(x,plus(y,z))=plus(plus(x,y),z)', associativity)
        :
        :
```

Notice that early in the mathematical proof that we are tracing, we used the equality $0 = --x + -x$, so we should certainly derive it somewhere in our formalized proof. This equation is an instance of the flipped negation axiom, obtained by plugging $-x$ into x. We can derive it in our proof by first applying UG to the flipped negation axiom to obtain $\forall x[0 = -x + x]$, and then using our `add_universal_instantiation()` method, substituting $-x$ into x. The next task will provide a convenient interface to performing this kind of derivation, and will also allow making several substitutions in one call.

TASK 7   Implement the missing code for the method `add_free_instantiation(instantiation, line_number, substitution_map)` of class `Prover`, which adds to the prover a sequence of validly justified lines, the last of which has the formula `instantiation`. The derived formula `instantiation` should be the result of substituting free variable names of the formula in the line with the given number with terms, according to the given map, which maps variable names to terms.

```
                        ┌─ predicates/prover.py ─┐
class Prover:
    ⋮

    def add_free_instantiation(self, instantiation: Union[Formula, str],
                               line_number: int,
                               substitution_map:
                               Mapping[str, Union[Term, str]]) -> int:
        """Appends to the proof being created by the current prover a sequence
        of validly justified lines, the last of which validly justifies the
        given formula, which is the result of substituting terms for free
        variable names in the formula in the specified already existing line of
        the proof.

        Parameters:
            instantiation: conclusion of the sequence of lines to be appended,
                specified as either a formula or its string representation.
            line_number: line number in the proof of a formula with free
                variable names, which contains no variable names that are ``z``
                followed by a number.
            substitution_map: mapping from free variable names of the formula
                with the given line number to terms that contain no variable
                names that are ``z`` followed by a number, to be substituted for
                them to obtain the given formula. Each value of this map may
                also be given as a string representation (instead of a term).
                Only variable name occurrences originating in the formula with
                the given line number are substituted (i.e., variable names
                originating in one of the specified substitutions are not
                subjected to additional substitutions).

        Returns:
            The line number of the newly appended line that justifies the given
            formula in the proof being created by the current prover.

        Examples:
            If Line `line_number` contains the formula
            '(z=5&Az[f(x,y)=g(z,y)])' and `substitution_map` is
            ``{'y': 'h(w)', 'z': 'y'}``, then `instantiation` should be
            '(y=5&Az[f(x,h(w))=g(z,h(w))])'.
        """
```

```
       if isinstance(instantiation, str):
           instantiation = Formula.parse(instantiation)
       substitution_map = dict(substitution_map)
       for variable in substitution_map:
           assert is_variable(variable)
           term = substitution_map[variable]
           if isinstance(term, str):
               substitution_map[variable] = term = Term.parse(term)
           for variable in term.variables():
               assert not is_z_and_number(variable)
       assert line_number < len(self._lines)
       original = self._lines[line_number].formula
       for variable in original.variables():
           assert not is_z_and_number(variable)
       assert original.free_variables().issuperset(substitution_map.keys())
       assert instantiation == original.substitute(substitution_map)
       # Task 10.7
```

Example: If we have in Line 17 of the proof being created by a prover `prover` the formula 'plus(x,y)=plus(y,x)', then the call

```
prover.add_free_instantiation('plus(f(y),g(x,0))=plus(g(x,0),f(y))',
                    17, {'x': 'f(y)', 'y': 'g(x,0)'})
```

will add to the proof a few lines, the last of which has the formula 'plus(f(y),g(x,0))= plus(g(x,0),f(y))'.

Guidelines: As already mentioned, substituting a term into a single variable name is easy by calling the method `add_ug()` and then calling the method `add_universal_instantiation()`. While in simple cases this could be done sequentially for all variable names in the given substitution map, a sequential substitution will not give the required results if the substituted terms themselves contain in them some of the substituted variable names. For instance, in the example just given, if we first replaced 'x' with 'f(y)' to obtain the intermediate formula 'plus(f(y),y)=plus(y,f(y))', then a second-stage replacement of 'y' with 'g(x,0)' would also *incorrectly* cause 'f(y)' to be replaced with 'f(g(x,0))', obtaining the formula 'plus(f(g(x,0)),g(x,0))=plus(g(x,0),f(g(x,0)))' instead of the requested 'plus(f(y),g(x,0)) =plus(g(x,0),f(y))'. To avoid this, first sequentially replace all variable names that need to be instantiated with new variable names, e.g., in our example obtaining an intermediate formula 'plus(z1,z2)=plus(z2,z1)' (remember that `next(fresh_variable_name_generator)` is your friend...), and then instantiate each of these temporary unique variable names with the target term.

We can now obtain arbitrary instances of the basic rules, so here is a good place in our proof to list those that we will need:

7. $0 = --x + -x$. Justification: Free instantiation of the flipped negation axiom, substituting x with $-x$.
8. $--x + -x = 0$. Justification: Flipped equality of Step 7.
9. $(--x+-x)+x = --x+(-x+x)$. Justification: Free instantiation of the associativity axiom, substituting x with $--x$, substituting y with $-x$, and substituting z with x.
10. $0 + 0 = 0$. Justification: Free instantiation of the zero axiom, substituting x with 0.

```
                        ┤ predicates/some_proofs.py ├
def prove_group_right_neutral(···, print_as_proof_forms: bool = False) -> Proof:
    ⋮
    step7 = prover.add_free_instantiation(
        '0=plus(minus(minus(x)),minus(x))', flipped_negation, {'x': 'minus(x)'})
    step8 = prover.add_flipped_equality(
        'plus(minus(minus(x)),minus(x))=0', step7)
    step9 = prover.add_free_instantiation(
        'plus(plus(minus(minus(x)),minus(x)),x)='
        'plus(minus(minus(x)),plus(minus(x),x))',
        associativity, {'x': 'minus(minus(x))', 'y': 'minus(x)', 'z': 'x'})
    step10 = prover.add_free_instantiation('plus(0,0)=0', zero, {'x': '0'})
    ⋮
```

We can now "really start" tracing the mathematical proof given earlier, step by step:

11. $x + 0 = 0 + (x + 0)$. Justification: Free instantiation of the flipped zero axiom, substituting x with $(x + 0)$.
12. $0 + (x + 0) = (0 + x) + 0$. Justification: Free instantiation of the flipped associativity axiom, substituting x and z with 0, and substituting y with x.

```
                        ┤ predicates/some_proofs.py ├
def prove_group_right_neutral(···, print_as_proof_forms: bool = False) -> Proof:
    ⋮
    step11 = prover.add_free_instantiation(
        'plus(x,0)=plus(0,plus(x,0))', flipped_zero, {'x': 'plus(x,0)'})
    step12 = prover.add_free_instantiation(
        'plus(0,plus(x,0))=plus(plus(0,x),0)', flipped_associativity,
        {'x': '0', 'y': 'x', 'z': '0'})
    ⋮
```

The next thing that we would like to deduce is $(0 + x) + 0 = ((- - x + -x) + x) + 0$, by "substituting" both sides of the equality $0 = - - x + -x$ from Step 7 into the expression $(\Box + x) + 0$. This type of substitution can be performed using the logical axioms of equality (RX and ME), and your solution to the following task will provide a convenient interface to performing it.

TASK 8   Implement the missing code for the method `add_substituted_equality(substituted, line_number, parametrized_term)` of class `Prover`, which adds to the prover a sequence of validly justified lines, the last of which has the formula `substituted`. The line with number `line_number` must hold an equality '$\tau=\sigma$' (for some terms τ and σ) and the derived formula `substituted` should be '$\phi(\tau)=\phi(\sigma)$', where $\phi(\Box)$ is the given parametrized term.

```
                        ┤ predicates/prover.py ├
class Prover:
    ⋮
    def add_substituted_equality(self, substituted: Union[Formula, str],
```

```
                                     line_number: int,
                         parametrized_term: Union[Term, str]) -> int:
    """Appends to the proof being created by the current prover a sequence
    of validly justified lines, the last of which validly justifies the
    given equality, whose two sides are the results of substituting the two
    respective sides of the equality in the specified already existing line
    of the proof into the given parametrized term.

    Parameters:
        substituted: conclusion of the sequence of lines to be appended,
            specified as either a formula or its string representation.
        line_number: line number in the proof of an equality.
        parametrized_term: term parametrized by the constant name '_',
            specified as either a term or its string representation, such
            that substituting each of the two sides of the equality with the
            given line number into this parametrized term respectively
            yields each of the two sides of the given equality.

    Returns:
        The line number of the newly appended line that justifies the given
        equality in the proof being created by the current prover.

    Examples:
        If Line `line_number` contains the formula 'g(x)=h(y)' and
        `parametrized_term` is '_+7', then `substituted` should be
        'g(x)+7=h(y)+7'.
    """
    if isinstance(substituted, str):
        substituted = Formula.parse(substituted)
    assert is_equality(substituted.root)
    assert line_number < len(self._lines)
    equality = self._lines[line_number].formula
    assert is_equality(equality.root)
    if isinstance(parametrized_term, str):
        parametrized_term = Term.parse(parametrized_term)
    assert substituted == \
        Formula('=', [parametrized_term.substitute(
                          {'_': equality.arguments[0]}),
                      parametrized_term.substitute(
                          {'_': equality.arguments[1]})])
    # Task 10.8
```

We can now continue with our proof:

13. $(0 + x) + 0 = ((- - x + -x) + x) + 0$. Justification: Substituting both sides of the equality $0 = - - x + -x$ from Step 7 into the expression $(\Box + x) + 0$.

14. $((- - x + -x) + x) + 0 = (- - x + (-x + x)) + 0$. Justification: Substituting both sides of the equality $(- - x + -x) + x = - - x + (-x + x)$ from Step 9 into the expression $\Box + 0$.

15. $(- - x + (-x + x)) + 0 = (- - x + 0) + 0$. Justification: Substituting both sides of the equality $-x + x = 0$ from Step 2 into the expression $(- - x + \Box) + 0$.

16. $(- - x + 0) + 0 = - - x + (0 + 0)$. Justification: Free instantiation of the associativity axiom, substituting x with $- - x$ and substituting y and z with 0.

17. $--x + (0+0) = --x+0$. Justification: Substituting both sides of the equality $0+0=0$ from Step 10 into the expression $--x+\square$.

18. $--x + 0 = --x + (-x+x)$. Justification: Substituting both sides of the equality $0 = -x+x$ from Step 5 into the expression $--x+\square$.

19. $--x + (-x+x) = (--x+-x) + x$. Justification: Free instantiation of the flipped associativity axiom, substituting x with $--x$, substituting y with $-x$, and substituting z with x.

20. $(--x+-x) + x = 0+x$. Justification: Substituting in both sides of the equality $--x+-x = 0$ from Step 8 into the expression $\square + x$.

```
                      ┌─ predicates/some_proofs.py ─┐
def prove_group_right_neutral(···, print_as_proof_forms: bool = False) -> Proof:
    ⋮

    step13 = prover.add_substituted_equality(
        'plus(plus(0,x),0)=plus(plus(plus(minus(minus(x)),minus(x)),x),0)',
        step7, 'plus(plus(_,x),0)')
    step14 = prover.add_substituted_equality(
        'plus(plus(plus(minus(minus(x)),minus(x)),x),0)='
        'plus(plus(minus(minus(x)),plus(minus(x),x)),0)',
        step9, 'plus(_,0)')
    step15 = prover.add_substituted_equality(
        'plus(plus(minus(minus(x)),plus(minus(x),x)),0)='
        'plus(plus(minus(minus(x)),0),0)',
        negation, 'plus(plus(minus(minus(x)),_),0)')
    step16 = prover.add_free_instantiation(
        'plus(plus(minus(minus(x)),0),0)=plus(minus(minus(x)),plus(0,0))',
        associativity, {'x': 'minus(minus(x))', 'y': '0', 'z': '0'})
    step17 = prover.add_substituted_equality(
        'plus(minus(minus(x)),plus(0,0))=plus(minus(minus(x)),0)',
        step10, 'plus(minus(minus(x)),_)')
    step18 = prover.add_substituted_equality(
        'plus(minus(minus(x)),0)=plus(minus(minus(x)),plus(minus(x),x))',
        flipped_negation, 'plus(minus(minus(x)),_)')
    step19 = prover.add_free_instantiation(
        'plus(minus(minus(x)),plus(minus(x),x))='
        'plus(plus(minus(minus(x)),minus(x)),x)', flipped_associativity,
        {'x': 'minus(minus(x))','y': 'minus(x)','z': 'x'})
    step20 = prover.add_substituted_equality(
        'plus(plus(minus(minus(x)),minus(x)),x)=plus(0,x)', step8, 'plus(_,x)')
    ⋮
```

Recalling that the zero axiom gives $0+x = x$, we now have a sequence of equalities (Steps 11–20 in order, followed by Step 1) that we would like to "chain" together using the transitivity of equality to get the final conclusion that we are after. While we have not defined the transitivity of equality as a logical axiom, it can be derived from ME, and your solution to the next task will provide a convenient interface to doing so and performing this kind of chaining.

TASK 9   Implement the missing code for the method `add_chained_equality(chained, line_numbers)` of class `Prover`, which adds to the prover a sequence of validly justified lines, the last of which has the formula `chained`. The derived formula `chained` must be of the form '$\tau=\sigma$', where the lines with the given `line_numbers` hold (in the given order) a sequence of equalities '$\tau_1=\tau_2$', '$\tau_2=\tau_3$', ..., '$\tau_{n-1}=\tau_n$', with τ_1 being τ and τ_n being σ.

```
                              ┌─ predicates/prover.py ─┐
class Prover:
    ⋮

    def _add_chaining_of_two_equalities(self, line_number1: int,
                                        line_number2: int) -> int:
        """Appends to the proof being created by the current prover a sequence
        of validly justified lines, the last of which validly justifies an
        equality that is the result of chaining together the two equalities in
        the specified already existing lines of the proof.

        Parameters:
            line_number1: line number in the proof of an equality of the form
                '`first`=`second`'.
            line_number2: line number in the proof of an equality of the form
                '`second`=`third`'.

        Returns:
            The line number of the newly appended line that justifies the
            equality '`first`=`third`' in the proof being created by the current
            prover.

        Examples:
            If Line `line_number1` contains the formula 'a=b' and Line
            `line_number2` contains the formula 'b=f(b)', then the last appended
            line will contain the formula 'a=f(b)'.
        """
        assert line_number1 < len(self._lines)
        equality1 = self._lines[line_number1].formula
        assert is_equality(equality1.root)
        assert line_number2 < len(self._lines)
        equality2 = self._lines[line_number2].formula
        assert is_equality(equality2.root)
        assert equality1.arguments[1] == equality2.arguments[0]
        # Task 10.9a

    def add_chained_equality(self, chained: Union[Formula, str],
                             line_numbers: Sequence[int]) -> int:
        """Appends to the proof being created by the current prover a sequence
        of validly justified lines, the last of which validly justifies the
        given equality, which is the result of chaining together the equalities
        in the specified already existing lines of the proof.

        Parameters:
            chained: conclusion of the sequence of lines to be appended,
                specified as either a formula or its string representation,
                of the form '`first`=`last`'.
            line_numbers: line numbers in the proof of equalities of the form
                '`first`=`second`', '`first`=`third`', ...,
                '`before_last`=`last`', i.e., the left-hand side of the first
                equality is the left-hand side of the given equality, the
                right-hand of each equality (except for the last) is the
```

```
                left-hand side of the next equality, and the right-hand side of
                the last equality is the right-hand side of the given equality.

        Returns:
            The line number of the newly appended line that justifies the given
            equality in the proof being created by the current prover.

        Examples:
            If `line_numbers` is ``[7,3,9]``, Line 7 contains the formula
            'a=b', Line 3 contains the formula 'b=f(b)', and Line 9 contains the
            formula 'f(b)=0', then `chained` should be 'a=0'.
    """
    if isinstance(chained, str):
        chained = Formula.parse(chained)
    assert is_equality(chained.root)
    assert len(line_numbers) >= 2
    current_term = chained.arguments[0]
    for line_number in line_numbers:
        assert line_number < len(self._lines)
        equality = self._lines[line_number].formula
        assert is_equality(equality.root)
        assert equality.arguments[0] == current_term
        current_term = equality.arguments[1]
    assert chained.arguments[1] == current_term
    # Task 10.9b
```

Guidelines: First implement the missing code for the private method _add_chaining_
of_two_equalities(line_number1, line_number2) that has similar functionality
but with only two equalities to chain (see the method *docstring* for details), and then use
that method to solve this task in full generality.

We can now finally conclude our proof:

21. $x + 0 = x$. Justification: Chaining Steps 11–20 in order, followed by Step 1.

```
                          ┤ predicates/some_proofs.py ├
def prove_group_right_neutral(···, print_as_proof_forms: bool = False) -> Proof:
    ⋮

    step21 = prover.add_chained_equality(
        'plus(x,0)=x',
        [step11, step12, step13, step14, step15, step16, step17, step18, step19,
         step20, zero])
    return prover.qed()
```

During this proof you have developed enough helper functions to prepare yourself for
the remainder of this chapter, in which you will prove additional important mathematical
theorems. The functions that you are asked to implement the remainder of this chapter are
contained in the file predicates/some_proofs.py. We start by showing that not only is
zero neutral to addition on both the left and the right, but this property is also unique to zero.

TASK 10   Prove the following inference:

Assumptions: Group axioms and $a + c = a$

Conclusion: $c = 0$

The proof should be returned by the function `prove_group_unique_zero()`, whose missing code you should implement.

```
predicates/some_proofs.py
```
```python
def prove_group_unique_zero(print_as_proof_forms: bool = False) -> Proof:
    """Proves from the group axioms and from the assumption a+c=a
    ('plus(a,c)=a') that c=0 ('c=0').

    Parameters:
        print_as_proof_forms: flag specifying whether the proof is to be printed
            in real time as it is being created.

    Returns:
        A valid proof of the above inference via `Prover.AXIOMS`.
    """
    prover = Prover(GROUP_AXIOMS.union({'plus(a,c)=a'}), print_as_proof_forms)
    # Task 10.10
    return prover.qed()
```

10.3.2 Fields

We move on from groups to **fields**. We will represent addition in a field using the function name 'plus', multiplication in a field using the function name 'times', zero (the neutral to additivity) using the constant name '0', and one (the neutral to multiplication) using the constant name '1'.

Field Axioms:

- $0 + x = x$
- $-x + x = 0$
- $(x + y) + z = x + (y + z)$
- $x + y = y + x$
- $x \cdot 1 = x$
- $x \cdot y = y \cdot x$
- $(x \cdot y) \cdot z = x \cdot (y \cdot z)$
- $(x \neq 0 \rightarrow \exists y[y \cdot x = 1])$ (where $x \neq 0$ should be read as '~x=0', of course)
- $x \cdot (y + z) = (x \cdot y) + (x \cdot z)$

```
predicates/some_proofs.py
```
```python
#: The six field axioms
FIELD_AXIOMS = frozenset(GROUP_AXIOMS.union(
    {'plus(x,y)=plus(y,x)', 'times(x,1)=x', 'times(x,y)=times(y,x)',
     'times(times(x,y),z)=times(x,times(y,z))', '(~x=0->Ey[times(y,x)=1])',
     'times(x,plus(y,z))=plus(times(x,y),times(x,z))'}))
```

TASK 11   Prove the following inference:

Assumptions: Field axioms
Conclusion: $0 \cdot x = 0$

The proof should be returned by the function `prove_field_zero_multiplication()`, whose missing code you should implement.

```
                                   ┌─────────────────────────┐
                                   │ predicates/some_proofs.py │
                                   └─────────────────────────┘
def prove_field_zero_multiplication(print_as_proof_forms: bool = False) -> \
        Proof:
    """Proves from the field axioms that 0*x=0 ('times(0,x)=0').

    Parameters:
        print_as_proof_forms: flag specifying whether the proof is to be printed
            in real time as it is being created.

    Returns:
        A valid proof of the above inference via `Prover.AXIOMS`.
    """
    prover = Prover(FIELD_AXIOMS, print_as_proof_forms)
    # Task 10.11
    return prover.qed()
```

Hint: If you have seen a proof of this in a linear algebra course, you can try to formalize that proof. Alternatively, one possible proof strategy is to first prove that $0 \cdot x + 0 \cdot x = 0 \cdot x$, and to then continue similarly to Task 10. (Note that the field axioms for addition contain all of the group axioms. However, we do not have a convenient interface for inlining the solution to Task 10 in another proof as is, because of its assumption, so feel free to duplicate code rather than build an inlining interface just for the sake of this task.)

10.3.3 Peano Arithmetic

Peano arithmetic, named after the nineteenth-century Italian mathematician Giuseppe Peano, attempts to capture the natural numbers. (In logic courses and set theory courses, the natural numbers customarily start from zero rather than from one.) In Peano arithmetic, apart from multiplication and addition, we have the unary "successor" function, named 's', which should be thought of as returning one when applied to zero, two when applied to one, etc.

Axioms of Peano Arithmetic:

- $(s(x) = s(y) \rightarrow x = y)$
- $s(x) \neq 0$
- $x + 0 = x$
- $x + s(y) = s(x + y)$
- $x \cdot 0 = 0$
- $x \cdot s(y) = x \cdot y + x$
- Axiom Schema of Induction: The schema $((\phi(0) \& \forall x[(\phi(x) \rightarrow \phi(s(x)))]) \rightarrow \forall x[\phi(x)])$, where $\phi(\square)$ is a placeholder for a parametrized formula.

```
                         ( predicates/some_proofs.py )
#: Axiom schema of induction
INDUCTION_AXIOM = Schema(
    Formula.parse('((R(0)&Ax[(R(x)->R(s(x)))])->Ax[R(x)])'), {'R'})
#: The seven axioms of Peano arithmetic
PEANO_AXIOMS = frozenset({'(s(x)=s(y)->x=y)', '~s(x)=0', 'plus(x,0)=x',
                          'plus(x,s(y))=s(plus(x,y))', 'times(x,0)=0',
                          'times(x,s(y))=plus(times(x,y),x)', INDUCTION_AXIOM})
```

Note that we do not have commutativity of addition or multiplication as axioms of Peano arithmetic, and these need to be proven from the given axioms. Let us see an example of a first step toward this. The axioms of Peano arithmetic state that $x \cdot 0 = 0$; let us try to prove that also $0 \cdot x = 0$, which is the first step toward proving the commutativity of multiplication in set theory courses.

Assumptions: Axioms of Peano arithmetic
Conclusion: $0 \cdot x = 0$

Proof:
   The idea is to prove the conclusion by induction (i.e., use the axiom schema of induction with $0 \cdot \square = 0$ as $\phi(\square)$). We already know that the base case $0 \cdot 0 = 0$ holds. The induction step would need to show that $0 \cdot x = 0 \rightarrow 0 \cdot s(x) = 0$, and then, by induction, these should imply that $0 \cdot x = 0$ for all x. So how do we show the induction step, $0 \cdot x = 0 \rightarrow 0 \cdot s(x) = 0$? Well, the mathematical reasoning is simple: $0 \cdot s(x) = 0 \cdot x + 0 = 0 \cdot x = 0$, where the first equality is an instance of the sixth axiom, the second equality is an instance of the third axiom, and the third equality is the assumption of the induction step. Let us formalize this mathematical reasoning. We start by proving the basis of the induction:

1. $x \cdot 0 = 0$. Justification: Axiom.
2. $0 \cdot 0 = 0$. Justification: Free instantiation of Step 1.

We proceed by proving the induction step:

3. $x \cdot s(y) = x \cdot y + x$. Justification: Axiom.
4. $0 \cdot s(x) = 0 \cdot x + 0$. Justification: Free instantiation of Step 3.
5. $0 \cdot x + 0 = 0 \cdot x$. Justification: Free instantiation of Step 1.
6. $0 \cdot s(x) = 0 \cdot x$. Justification: Chaining Steps 4 and 5.
7. $0 \cdot x = 0 \cdot s(x)$. Justification: Flipped equality of Step 6.
8. $(0 \cdot x = 0 \cdot s(x) \rightarrow (0 \cdot x = 0 \rightarrow 0 \cdot s(x) = 0))$. Justification: An instance of ME.
9. $(0 \cdot x = 0 \rightarrow 0 \cdot s(x) = 0)$. Justification: MP from Steps 7 and 8.
10. $\forall x[(0 \cdot x = 0 \rightarrow 0 \cdot s(x) = 0)]$. Justification: UG of Step 9.

Finally we apply the axiom schema of induction:

11. $(0 \cdot 0 = 0 \mathbin{\&} \forall x[(0 \cdot x = 0 \rightarrow 0 \cdot s(x) = 0)])$. Justification: Tautological implication of Steps 2 and 10.
12. $((0 \cdot 0 = 0 \mathbin{\&} \forall x[(0 \cdot x = 0 \rightarrow 0 \cdot s(x) = 0)]) \rightarrow \forall x[0 \cdot x = 0])$. Justification: An instance of the axiom schema of induction.
13. $\forall x[0 \cdot x = 0]$. Justification: MP from Steps 11 and 12.
14. $0 \cdot x = 0$. Justification: Universal instantiation of Step 13.

In a similar way one can prove that not only $x + 0 = x$ as was given as an axiom, but also $0 + x = x$, which is the first step toward proving the commutativity of addition in set theory courses, and what we ask you to do in the next task.

TASK 12   Prove the following inference:

Assumptions: Axioms of Peano arithmetic
Conclusion: $0 + x = x$

The proof should be returned by the function `prove_peano_left_neutral()`, whose missing code you should implement.

```
                          ┌─────────────────────────────┐
                          │ predicates/some_proofs.py   │
def prove_peano_left_neutral(print_as_proof_forms: bool = False) -> Proof:
    """Proves from the axioms of Peano arithmetic that 0+x=x ('plus(0,x)=x').

    Parameters:
        print_as_proof_forms: flag specifying whether the proof is to be printed
            in real time as it is being created.

    Returns:
        A valid proof of the above inference via
        `~predicates.prover.Prover.AXIOMS`.
    """
    prover = Prover(PEANO_AXIOMS, print_as_proof_forms)
    # Task 10.12
    return prover.qed()
```

Hint: Use induction on x (i.e., use the axiom schema of induction with $0 + \square = \square$ as $\phi(\square)$). The challenge is again in proving the "induction step," which in this case is '(plus(0,x)=x→plus(0,s(x))=s(x))'. To prove the induction step, start by proving that '(plus(0,x)=x→s(plus(0,x))=s(x))', and whenever you get stuck in the proof of the induction step, try to use ME.

In the same somewhat tedious way one may continue proving the commutativity of addition and multiplication, as well as, it turns out, (essentially) all other properties of the natural numbers, from the fact that $\sqrt{2}$ is not a rational number (i.e. $(x \neq 0 \rightarrow x \cdot x \neq 2 \cdot y \cdot y)$) to Fermat's last theorem. Significant parts of mathematics, such as the theory of computation, may be expressed in the language of Peano arithmetic, and these too can be proven formally using the axioms of Peano arithmetic. What Peano arithmetic cannot do, it turns out, is handle infinite objects. Doing that requires a somewhat stronger and trickier axiomatic system, that we present next and with which we conclude this chapter.

10.3.4 Zermelo–Fraenkel Set Theory

Predicate logic turns out to suffice for capturing all of mathematics from a handful of axioms. The standard formalization is to have **sets** as the basic building blocks (elements) of our universe, and to define everything from there. That is, in terms of predicate logic, there is a single binary relation name that denotes membership of an item in a set, 'In(x,y)', meaning $x \in y$.

The axioms for sets are stated so that they imply that an empty set exists (we may or may not have a constant name $\emptyset$ that denotes it), and once we have the empty set we can continue to define the natural numbers as: $0 = \emptyset$, $1 = \{\emptyset\}$, $2 = \{\emptyset, \{\emptyset\}\}$, $3 = \{\emptyset, \{\emptyset\}, \{\emptyset, \{\emptyset\}\}\}$, etc.,[13] and the set theory axioms will suffice for proving all the required properties of natural numbers (in particular all the axioms of Peano arithmetic). Notice however that this construction also provides *sets* of natural numbers, and sets of sets of natural numbers, etc., which Peano arithmetic does not provide. Once we have natural numbers, we can continue defining integers, rationals, real numbers, complex numbers, real-valued functions, vector fields, and the rest of mathematics.

Some of the set theory axioms give basic intended properties for sets. For example, the **extensionality axiom** states that two sets are equal (are the same set) if they have the same elements. Formally, '$\forall x[\forall y[(\forall z[((\text{In}(z,x) \rightarrow \text{In}(z,y))\&(\text{In}(z,y) \rightarrow \text{In}(z,x)))] \rightarrow x=y)]]$'. Most of the axioms, however, are devoted to ensuring that certain types of sets exist.

To understand the need for this, let us look at our naïve notion of how we get a set: We usually specify a condition and then look at the set of all elements that satisfy it. Formally, for every parametrized formula (condition) $\phi(\square)$ we imagine an **axiom schema of (unrestricted) comprehension** stating that the set of all elements satisfying this condition exists: $\exists y[\forall x[x \in y \leftrightarrow \phi(x)]]$.

```
                    predicates/some_proofs.py
#: Axiom schema of (unrestricted) comprehension
COMPREHENSION_AXIOM = Schema(
    Formula.parse('Ey[Ax[((In(x,y)->R(x))&(R(x)->In(x,y)))]]'), {'R'})
```

However, in 1901, the British philosopher, logician, mathematician, writer, and Nobel laureate (in Literature!) Bertrand Russell, noticed what has come to be known as "Russell's paradox": that by looking at the set $\{x|x \notin x\}$, the axiom schema of comprehension turns out to lead to a contradiction. You will now formalize his argument.

TASK 13   Prove the following inference:

Assumption: Axiom schema of comprehension
Conclusion: The contradiction '$(z=z \,\&\, z \neq z)$'

The proof should be returned by the function `prove_russell_paradox()`, whose missing code you should implement.

```
                    predicates/some_proofs.py
def prove_russell_paradox(print_as_proof_forms: bool = False) -> Proof:
    """Proves from the axioms schema of unrestricted comprehension the
    contradiction '(z=z&~z=z)'.

    Parameters:
        print_as_proof_forms: flag specifying whether the proof is to be printed
            in real time as it is being created.
```

---

[13] This encoding of the natural numbers is due to the Jewish-Hungarian-born American mathematician, physicist, computer scientist, and game theorist John von Neumann. For more details, including why such a seemingly cumbersome encoding of the natural numbers is needed, you are highly encouraged to take a course on set theory.

```
Returns:
    A valid proof of the above inference via
    `~predicates.prover.Prover.AXIOMS`.
    """
    prover = Prover({COMPREHENSION_AXIOM}, print_as_proof_forms)
    # Task 10.13
    return prover.qed()
```

Hint: Following Russell's paradox, instantiate the axiom schema of unrestricted comprehension by defining '$\phi(\Box)$' as '$\sim$In($\Box$,$\Box$)'.

We conclude that we cannot just assume that there is a set for any condition that we wish to use (like we would have wanted the axiom schema of comprehension to guarantee), but rather need axioms to tell us which sets exist. In particular, instead of the general axiom schema of comprehension, it is customary to have a weaker axiom schema of specification that only allows imposing conditions on elements of a given set: For every parametrized formula (condition) $\phi(\Box)$ the following is an axiom: $\forall z[\exists y[\forall x[x \in y \leftrightarrow (x \in z \,\&\, \phi(x))]]]$. This allows one to take arbitrary subsets of a given, preexisting set. A number of other set theory axioms specify the ways in which one may go "up," that is, build larger sets from those that one already has: by taking unions, by taking a power set, by pairing two items, by taking a functional image of a set, and there is also an axiom that guarantees the existence of an infinite set. Beyond these, there is an axiom of foundation that essentially states that there cannot be "cycles" of inclusion such as $x \in y \in z \in x$. All of these axioms together are the axiomatic basis for the celebrated Zermelo–Fraenkel (**ZF**) set theory, named after German mathematician Ernst Zermelo and Jewish-German (and later Israeli) mathematician Abraham Fraenkel.

Finally, mathematicians also assume, when needed, the axiom of choice, which states that for every set Z of non-empty sets there exists a function f that chooses, for each set $Y \in Z$, some element in Y. The resulting axiomatic system, called **ZFC** (Zermelo–Fraenkel with choice) forms the canonical basis of modern mathematics.

11 The Deduction Theorem and Prenex Normal Form

In this chapter, we will prove two important and general tools, which beyond being useful each on its own, will also be of utmost importance in our proof of the completeness theorem for predicate logic in Chapter 12, in which our analysis of this entire book will culminate.

- The **deduction theorem** (11.1) for predicate logic, which shows (much like the deduction theorem (5.2) for propositional logic, which you proved in Chapter 5) that if some statement ξ is provable (in predicate logic) from some assumptions that include an assumption ψ, then under certain mild conditions, the statement '$(\psi \to \xi)$' is provable from the same set of assumptions, without ψ. From the deduction theorem (11.1), much like in propositional logic, we will derive a theorem (11.2) on **soundness of proofs by way of contradiction** in predicate logic.
- The **prenex normal form theorem** (11.3), which shows that every formula can be transformed into an equivalent formula in **prenex normal form**, that is, a formula where all quantifiers appear at the beginning (top levels) of the formula.

11.1 The Deduction Theorem

Recall that in Chapter 5, you have proved the deduction theorem (5.2) for propositional logic, and in particular its "hard direction" (which is often referred to by itself as the deduction theorem for propositional logic).

THEOREM 5.2' ("Hard Direction" of the Deduction Theorem for Propositional Logic) *Let $\mathcal{R}$ be a set of inference rules that includes MP, I1, and D, and may additionally include only inference rules with no assumptions. Let A be an arbitrary set of formulas, and let ϕ and ψ be two additional formulas. If $A \cup \{\phi\} \vdash_{\mathcal{R}} \psi$, then $A \vdash_{\mathcal{R}} '(\phi \to \psi)'$.*

This establishes that under certain conditions, the converse of MP holds as well: not only can we prove ψ from some assumptions that include ϕ if we can prove '$(\phi \to \psi)$' from the same assumptions without ϕ, but also conversely, if we can prove ψ from some assumptions that include ϕ, then (under mild conditions on the inference rules that may be used), we can prove '$(\phi \to \psi)$' from the same assumptions without ϕ.

Since this theorem turned out to be an extremely useful tool in writing proofs in propositional logic, and in particular in proving the tautology theorem (6.1) and therefore the completeness theorem (6.5/6.6) for propositional logic, we will now prove an analogue of this theorem for predicate logic. Since our proof system in predicate logic does not allow for any inference rules that have assumptions except MP and UG, we will not need any analogue of the condition from the deduction theorem (5.2/5.2') for propositional logic regarding which inference rules may have assumptions. The condition from that theorem on the set of inference rules containing MP, I1, and D will be replaced, strictly speaking, by being able to use MP, UG, and all tautologies (which all of our proofs can), and the axiom schema US, which was introduced in Chapter 10 (but which we have in fact so far not used at all!).

We will also have an additional new condition that has no analogue in propositional logic: that the proof of ψ from the set of assumptions that includes ϕ does not involve UG over any variable name that is free in ϕ. Unlike the former conditions, which are technical, this new condition is crucial. To see this, notice for example that from only the assumption 'y=0' (which remember that we semantically interpret as "for any assignment to 'y' of an element from the universe of the model, it holds that that element is the interpretation of '0'") one can use UG over the variable name 'y' to deduce '∀y[y=0]' (which has the exact same semantic interpretation). Nonetheless, it is not the case that without any assumptions whatsoever, one can prove '(y=0→∀y[y=0])' (which remember that semantically we interpret as "if any element is the interpretation of zero, then this implies that all elements are the interpretation of zero"), but this would have been implied by the deduction theorem (11.1) that we will state soon if it were not for the constraint on UG. Indeed, in all but very specific models (those with only one element) the formula '(y=0→∀y[y=0])' is simply not satisfied. More generally, if one can prove from 'R(x)' that 'Q(x)', then due to our convention on interpreting assumptions/conclusions with free variable names, this proof in fact shows that '(∀x[R(x)]→∀x[Q(x)])' rather than that (for every 'x' separately) '(R(x)→Q(x))', which has a very different semantic interpretation. Our main uses of the deduction theorem (11.1) for predicate logic will however be when ϕ is a **sentence** – a formula with no free variable names at all – in which case this constraint is always trivially satisfied regardless of the structure of the proof of ψ from (among other assumptions) ϕ, so we will not have to worry about this constraint in that case. We will now formally state this theorem (or rather, only its "hard part," since its "easy part" follows from the ability to use MP precisely as in propositional logic).

THEOREM 11.1 (The Deduction Theorem for Predicate Logic)   *Let A be a set of schemas that includes US, and let ϕ and ψ be two formulas. If $A \cup \{\phi\} \vdash \psi$ via a proof that does not use UG over any variable name that is free in ϕ, then $A \vdash$ '($\phi \rightarrow \psi$)'.*

You will now prove the deduction theorem (11.1) for predicate logic. All of the functions that you are asked to implement in this section are contained in the file `predicates/deduction.py`.

TASK 1 (Programmatic Proof of the Deduction Theorem (11.1))   Implement the missing code for the function `remove_assumption(proof, assumption)`. This function takes as input a (predicate-logic) proof of some conclusion ψ that:

- has our six logical axiom schemas[1] among its assumptions/axioms,

---

[1] While we strictly only need US, we assume all six logical axiom schemas so that you may easily use the `Prover` class in your solution.

- has the given assumption ϕ as a simple assumption/axiom (with no templates), and
- does not use UG over any variable name that is free in ϕ.

The function returns a proof of '$(\phi \rightarrow \psi)$' from the same assumptions/axioms except ϕ.

```
                        predicates/deduction.py
def remove_assumption(proof: Proof, assumption: Formula,
                      print_as_proof_forms: bool = False) -> Proof:
    """Converts the given proof of some `conclusion` formula, an assumption of
    which is `assumption`, to a proof of '(`assumption`->`conclusion`)' from the
    same assumptions except `assumption`.

    Parameters:
        proof: valid proof to convert, from assumptions/axioms that include
            `Prover.AXIOMS`.
        assumption: formula that is a simple assumption (i.e., without any
            templates) of the given proof, such that no line of the given proof
            is a UG line over a variable name that is free in this assumption.
        print_as_proof_forms: flag specifying whether the proof of
            '(`assumption`->`conclusion`)' is to be printed in real time as it
            is being created.

    Returns:
        A valid proof of '(`assumption`->`conclusion`)' from the same
        assumptions/axioms as the given proof except `assumption`.
    """
    assert proof.is_valid()
    assert Schema(assumption) in proof.assumptions
    assert proof.assumptions.issuperset(Prover.AXIOMS)
    for line in proof.lines:
        if isinstance(line, Proof.UGLine):
            assert line.formula.variable not in assumption.free_variables()
    # Task 11.1
```

Hints: As in Chapter 5, for each formula ξ that is deduced by some line of the original proof, the new proof should deduce '$(\phi \rightarrow \xi)$'; that is, the suggested strategy is to create your proof by going over the lines of the given proof, in order, and whenever a line of the given proof deduces some ξ, to add one or more lines to the new proof that together deduce '$(\phi \rightarrow \xi)$'. Use tautological implications generously; when the original proof line uses UG, you will need to work a bit harder—try to understand how to use US in this case.

As we have seen in Chapter 5, one important implication of (any version of) the deduction theorem is that we can use it to formally explain why a **proof by way of contradiction** works. Recall that in a proof by way of contradiction, we make an assumption, use it to prove the negation of an axiom (recall that we encourage you to think of a proof by way of contradiction as a **proof by way of contradicting an axiom**) and deduce from this that the assumption that we made is in fact false. Since in predicate logic (thanks to your proof of the tautology theorem (6.1) in propositional logic) we can use all tautologies as axioms of our proofs, we will allow the "proof of the negation of an axiom" that we are given to be a proof of any **contradiction**,[2] i.e., of the negation of any tautology.[3]

THEOREM 11.2 (Soundness of Proofs by Way of Contradiction in Predicate Logic)   *Let A be a set of schemas that includes US, and let ϕ be a formula. If a contradiction (i.e., negation of a tautology) is provable from $A \cup \{\phi\}$ without using UG over any variable name that is free in ϕ, then $A \vdash$ '$\sim\phi$'.*

You will now prove the theorem (11.2) on soundness of proofs by way of contradiction in predicate logic. The proof will once again be considerably simpler than the proof for propositional logic due to the ability to use all tautologies freely at this point.

TASK 2 (Programmatic Proof of the theorem (11.2) on Soundness of Proofs by Way of Contradiction)   Implement the missing code for the function `prove_by_way_of_contradiction(proof, assumption)`. This function takes as input a (predicate-logic) proof of some contradiction that:

- has our six logical axiom schemas[4] among its assumptions/axioms,
- has the given assumption ϕ as a simple assumption/axiom (with no templates), and
- does not use UG over any variable name that is free in ϕ.

The function returns a proof of '$\sim\phi$' from the same assumptions/axioms except ϕ.

```
                    ⌐ predicates/deduction.py ⌐

def prove_by_way_of_contradiction(proof: Proof, assumption: Formula) -> Proof:
    """Converts the given proof of a contradiction, an assumption of which is
    `assumption`, to a proof of '~`assumption`' from the same assumptions except
    `assumption`.

    Parameters:
        proof: valid proof of a contradiction (i.e., a formula whose negation is
            a tautology) to convert, from assumptions/axioms that include
            `Prover.AXIOMS`.
        assumption: formula that is a simple assumption (i.e., without any
            templates) of the given proof, such that no line of the given proof
            is a UG line over a variable name that is free in this assumption.

    Returns:
        A valid proof of '~`assumption`' from the same assumptions/axioms as the
        given proof except `assumption`.
    """
    assert proof.is_valid()
    assert Schema(assumption) in proof.assumptions
    assert proof.assumptions.issuperset(Prover.AXIOMS)
    for line in proof.lines:
```

---

[2] In some sense, this may be thought of as further justifying the common name "proof by (way of) contradiction."

[3] Similarly to Chapter 5, it is possible also in predicate logic to have other equivalent definitions for this notion of inconsistency, and in particular ones that do not involve tautologies. For example, since every formula is a tautological implication of a contradiction, the ability to prove a contradiction from certain assumptions/axioms is equivalent to the ability to prove every formula from the same assumptions/axioms, so this notion of inconsistency can be phrased in a purely syntactic way and is precisely the same as in propositional logic.

[4] Once again, we strictly only need US.

```
            if isinstance(line, Proof.UGLine):
                assert line.formula.variable not in assumption.free_variables()
        # Task 11.2
```

Guidelines: Recall that `Proof` objects are immutable. Therefore, you cannot simply add lines to any `Proof` object. Instead, construct a new `Prover` object, use the `add_proof()` method of that object (which we have already implemented for you) to insert all the lines of any `Proof` object into the proof of this prover, and then add more lines to that proof using the `Prover` API, including the methods that you implemented in Chapter 10 (and in particular, `add_tautological_implication()`).

11.2 Prenex Normal Form

According to Wiktionary ("prenex," 2021),[5] the term "prenex" comes from the Late Latin *praenexus*, meaning "bound up in front." A formula is said to be in **prenex normal form** if all of its quantifications are at the beginning/at the top-most levels. More precisely:

DEFINITION 11.1 (Prenex Normal Form)   A formula is said to be in **prenex normal form** if there is an initial sequence of nodes of the formula that all contain quantifications, and all other nodes in the formula do not contain quantifications.

For example, the formula '$\forall x[\exists y[(R(x,y) \rightarrow Q(y))]]$' is in prenex normal form, while the formula '$\forall x[(R(x) \rightarrow \exists y[Q(x,y)])]$' is *not* in prenex normal form since the existential quantification is only on the second part of the implication (or more precisely, the *implies* node, which is not a quantification node, precedes the node of that quantification). The formula '$\forall x[(\exists y[R(x,y)] \rightarrow Q(x))]$' is similarly *not* in prenex normal form since the existential quantification is only on the first part of the implication (and again the *implies* node precedes it). In this section, we will explore this form. The functions that you are asked to implement in this section are contained in the file `predicates/prenex.py` unless otherwise noted.

TASK 3   Implement the missing code for the function `is_in_prenex_normal_form(formula)`, which checks whether a given formula is in prenex normal form.

```
                        ┌─────────────────────┐
                        │ predicates/prenex.py │
                        └─────────────────────┘
def is_quantifier_free(formula: Formula) -> bool:
    """Checks if the given formula contains any quantifiers.

    Parameters:
        formula: formula to check.

    Returns:
        ``False`` if the given formula contains any quantifiers, ``True``
        otherwise.
    """
    # Task 11.3a
```

[5] Wiktionary, *The Free Dictionary*, s.v. "prenex," (accessed June 22, 2021), https://en.wiktionary.org/w/index.php?title=prenex&oldid=60445646.

```
def is_in_prenex_normal_form(formula: Formula) -> bool:
    """Checks if the given formula is in prenex normal form.

    Parameters:
        formula: formula to check.

    Returns:
        ``True`` if the given formula in prenex normal form, ``False``
        otherwise.
    """
    # Task 11.3b
```

Guidelines: First implement the missing code for the recursive function `is_quantifier_free(formula)`, which checks whether a given formula contains no quantifiers, and then use that function to solve this task.

As you will show in this section, and this will be incredibly useful in Chapter 12, every formula can be converted into prenex normal form, and moreover, the equivalence of the original formula and the one in prenex normal form is provable by a predicate-logic proof via just our four logical axiom schemas of quantification from Chapter 10:

THEOREM 11.3 (The Prenex Normal Form Theorem) *For every formula ϕ there exists an equivalent formula ψ in prenex normal form, such that the equivalence between ϕ and ψ (i.e., '$((\phi \rightarrow \psi) \& (\psi \rightarrow \phi))$') is provable from UI, EI, US, and ES.*

The idea of this conversion is to use various logical equivalences to "pull out" the quantifications. This becomes doable if we make sure that quantified variable names in different parts of the formula do not "clash" with one another, nor with the free variable names of the formula, so that each variable name occurrence *remains* bound by the same quantifier, or *remains* free, before and after "pulling out" the quantifications, despite the scopes of the various quantifications having changed. Specifically, let x be a variable name, let $\phi(x)$ be an arbitrary formula, and let ψ be a formula that *does not have x as a free variable name*. Then the following logical equivalences can be used to "pull out" the quantifications:

1. '$\sim\forall x[\phi(x)]$' is equivalent to '$\exists x[\sim\phi(x)]$'.
2. '$\sim\exists x[\phi(x)]$' is equivalent to '$\forall x[\sim\phi(x)]$'.
3. '$(\forall x[\phi(x)] \& \psi)$' is equivalent to '$\forall x[(\phi(x) \& \psi)]$'.
4. '$(\exists x[\phi(x)] \& \psi)$' is equivalent to '$\exists x[(\phi(x) \& \psi)]$'.
5. '$(\psi \& \forall x[\phi(x)])$' is equivalent to '$\forall x[(\psi \& \phi(x))]$'.
6. '$(\psi \& \exists x[\phi(x)])$' is equivalent to '$\exists x[(\psi \& \phi(x))]$'.
7. '$(\forall x[\phi(x)] | \psi)$' is equivalent to '$\forall x[(\phi(x) | \psi)]$'.
8. '$(\exists x[\phi(x)] | \psi)$' is equivalent to '$\exists x[(\phi(x) | \psi)]$'.
9. '$(\psi | \forall x[\phi(x)])$' is equivalent to '$\forall x[(\psi | \phi(x))]$'.
10. '$(\psi | \exists x[\phi(x)])$' is equivalent to '$\exists x[(\psi | \phi(x))]$'.
11. '$(\forall x[\phi(x)] \rightarrow \psi)$' is equivalent to '$\exists x[(\phi(x) \rightarrow \psi)]$'.
12. '$(\exists x[\phi(x)] \rightarrow \psi)$' is equivalent to '$\forall x[(\phi(x) \rightarrow \psi)]$'.
13. '$(\psi \rightarrow \forall x[\phi(x)])$' is equivalent to '$\forall x[(\psi \rightarrow \phi(x))]$'.
14. '$(\psi \rightarrow \exists x[\phi(x)])$' is equivalent to '$\exists x[(\psi \rightarrow \phi(x))]$'.

Each of these equivalences "pulls" a quantification "out" of a logical operator, so multiple applications of these equivalences will pull all of the quantifications outside. When we say above that a formula L "is equivalent to" a formula R, it is more than just saying that they have the same value in all models. Indeed, we are actually stating that the formula '$((L \rightarrow R)\&(R \rightarrow L))$' is provable from our four logical axiom schemas of quantification. As noted, all the equivalences just defined require that ψ does not have x as a free variable name. If ψ does happen to have x as a free variable name, then we can easily change the quantification to be over some other variable name, since '$\forall x[\phi(x)]$' is equivalent to '$\forall z[\phi(z)]$' (and similarly, '$\exists x[\phi(x)]$' is equivalent to '$\exists z[\phi(z)]$') for every variable name z that does not appear in ϕ. We will thus need two additional maneuvers, that handle not only replacing a variable name in a single formula (i.e., that '$Qx[\phi(x)]$' is equivalent to '$Qz[\phi(z)]$'), but also quantifying (with and without replacing variable names) over equivalent formulas. Specifically, let x and y be variable names, and let $\phi(\square)$ and $\psi(\square)$ be arbitrary parametrized formulas that have neither x nor y as free variable names. Then we will need the following:

15. If $\phi(x)$ and $\psi(x)$ are equivalent, then '$\forall x[\phi(x)]$' and '$\forall y[\psi(y)]$' are equivalent.
16. If $\phi(x)$ and $\psi(x)$ are equivalent, then '$\exists x[\phi(x)]$' and '$\exists y[\psi(y)]$' are equivalent.

In this section, you will prove the prenex normal form theorem (11.3). Our main strategy will be, as outlined above, to first make sure that no two variable names "clash," and then "pull out" all quantifications using the above equivalences. Let us consider an example: say that we wish to convert the following formula into prenex normal form:

$$\text{'}{\sim}(z{=}x|\forall z[(\exists x[(x{=}z\&\forall z[z{=}x])]\rightarrow\forall x[x{=}y])])\text{'}$$

Let us carefully try and make sense of all of the occurrences of the same variables names (variable name occurrences left without a numbered label are free):

$$\boxed{1}\ \boxed{2}\,\boxed{2}\,\boxed{1}\ \ \boxed{3}\,\boxed{3}\,\boxed{2}\ \ \ \boxed{4}\,\boxed{4}$$
$$\text{'}{\sim}(z{=}x|\forall z[(\exists x[(x{=}z\&\forall z[z{=}x])]\rightarrow\forall x[x{=}y])])\text{'}$$

We first replace each quantified variable name with a new unique variable name:

$$\boxed{1}\ \ \boxed{2}\,\boxed{2}\ \boxed{1}\ \ \ \boxed{3}\,\boxed{3}\ \boxed{2}\ \ \ \ \boxed{4}\ \boxed{4}$$
$$\text{'}{\sim}(z{=}x|\forall z1[(\exists z2[(z2{=}z1\&\forall z3[z3{=}z2])]\rightarrow\forall z4[z4{=}y])])\text{'}$$

We now start by pulling out the quantification '$\forall z3$' from the conjunction:

$$\text{'}{\sim}(z{=}x|\forall z1[(\exists z2[(z2{=}z1\&\forall \mathbf{z3}[z3{=}z2])]\rightarrow\forall z4[z4{=}y])])\text{'}$$
$$\Downarrow$$
$$\text{'}{\sim}(z{=}x|\forall z1[(\exists z2[\forall \mathbf{z3}[(z2{=}z1\&z3{=}z2)]]\rightarrow\forall z4[z4{=}y])])\text{'}$$

We now pull out both of the quantifications '$\exists z2$' and '$\forall z3$' from the implication (note that the universal quantification becomes an existential quantification and *vice versa*, due to the rules of pulling out quantifications from the left side of an implication):

$$\text{'}{\sim}(z{=}x|\forall z1[(\exists \mathbf{z2}[\forall \mathbf{z3}[(z2{=}z1\&z3{=}z2)]]\rightarrow\forall z4[z4{=}y])])\text{'}$$
$$\Downarrow$$
$$\text{'}{\sim}(z{=}x|\forall z1[\forall \mathbf{z2}[\exists \mathbf{z3}[((z2{=}z1\&z3{=}z2)\rightarrow\forall z4[z4{=}y])]]])\text{'}$$

We now pull out the quantification '$\forall z4$' from the implication (note that this remains a universal quantification due to the rules of pulling out quantifications from the right side of an implication):

$$\text{`}{\sim}(z{=}x|\forall z1[\forall z2[\exists z3[((z2{=}z1\&z3{=}z2)\to\forall z4[z4{=}y])]]])\text{'}$$
$$\Downarrow$$
$$\text{`}{\sim}(z{=}x|\forall z1[\forall z2[\exists z3[\forall z4[((z2{=}z1\&z3{=}z2)\to z4{=}y)]]]])\text{'}$$

We now pull out all of the quantifications from the disjunction:

$$\text{`}{\sim}(z{=}x|\forall z1[\forall z2[\exists z3[\forall z4[((z2{=}z1\&z3{=}z2)\to z4{=}y)]]]])\text{'}$$
$$\Downarrow$$
$$\text{`}{\sim}\forall z1[\forall z2[\exists z3[\forall z4[(z{=}x|((z2{=}z1\&z3{=}z2)\to z4{=}y))]]]]\text{'}$$

Finally, we pull out all of the quantifications from the negation, noting that each universal quantifier is replaced with an existential quantifier and *vice versa*:

$$\text{`}{\sim}\forall z1[\forall z2[\exists z3[\forall z4[(z{=}x|((z2{=}z1\&z3{=}z2)\to z4{=}y))]]]]\text{'}$$
$$\Downarrow$$
$$\text{`}\exists z1[\exists z2[\forall z3[\exists z4[{\sim}(z{=}x|((z2{=}z1\&z3{=}z2)\to z4{=}y))]]]]\text{'}$$

That's it: We have reached an equivalent formula that is in prenex normal form. In the remainder of this section, you will write code that not only performs the above conversion for any formula, but also produces a proof of the equivalence of the original formula and the resulting formula, thus proving the prenex normal form theorem (11.3).

To make things easier, we will allow the proofs that you will program in the remainder of this section to use all of the sixteen above-stated equivalences and implications as additional axiom schemas, even though each of these is provable from our four basic axiom schemas of quantification. All of these additional axiom schemas are already defined for you in the file `predicates/prenex.py`.

```
                        predicates/prenex.py
#: Additional axioms of quantification for Predicate Logic.
ADDITIONAL_QUANTIFICATION_AXIOMS = (
    Schema(Formula.parse('((~Ax[R(x)]->Ex[~R(x)])&(Ex[~R(x)]->~Ax[R(x)]))'),
           {'x', 'R'}),
    Schema(Formula.parse('((~Ex[R(x)]->Ax[~R(x)])&(Ax[~R(x)]->~Ex[R(x)]))'),
           {'x', 'R'}),
    Schema(Formula.parse('(((Ax[R(x)]&Q())->Ax[(R(x)&Q())])&'
                         '(Ax[(R(x)&Q())]->(Ax[R(x)]&Q())))'), {'x', 'R', 'Q'}),
    Schema(Formula.parse('(((Ex[R(x)]&Q())->Ex[(R(x)&Q())])&'
                         '(Ex[(R(x)&Q())]->(Ex[R(x)]&Q())))'), {'x', 'R', 'Q'}),
    Schema(Formula.parse('(((Q()&Ax[R(x)])->Ax[(Q()&R(x))])&'
                         '(Ax[(Q()&R(x))]->(Q()&Ax[R(x)])))'), {'x', 'R', 'Q'}),
    Schema(Formula.parse('(((Q()&Ex[R(x)])->Ex[(Q()&R(x))])&'
                         '(Ex[(Q()&R(x))]->(Q()&Ex[R(x)])))'), {'x', 'R', 'Q'}),
    Schema(Formula.parse('(((Ax[R(x)]|Q())->Ax[(R(x)|Q())])&'
                         '(Ax[(R(x)|Q())]->(Ax[R(x)]|Q())))'), {'x', 'R', 'Q'}),
    Schema(Formula.parse('(((Ex[R(x)]|Q())->Ex[(R(x)|Q())])&'
                         '(Ex[(R(x)|Q())]->(Ex[R(x)]|Q())))'), {'x', 'R', 'Q'}),
    Schema(Formula.parse('(((Q()|Ax[R(x)])->Ax[(Q()|R(x))])&'
                         '(Ax[(Q()|R(x))]->(Q()|Ax[R(x)])))'), {'x', 'R', 'Q'}),
    Schema(Formula.parse('(((Q()|Ex[R(x)])->Ex[(Q()|R(x))])&'
```

```
                            '(Ex[(Q()|R(x))]->(Q()|Ex[R(x)]))'), {'x', 'R', 'Q'}),
         Schema(Formula.parse('(((Ax[R(x)]->Q())->Ex[(R(x)->Q())])&'
                            '(Ex[(R(x)->Q())]->(Ax[R(x)]->Q())))'), {'x', 'R', 'Q'}),
         Schema(Formula.parse('(((Ex[R(x)]->Q())->Ax[(R(x)->Q())])&'
                            '(Ax[(R(x)->Q())]->(Ex[R(x)]->Q())))'), {'x', 'R', 'Q'}),
         Schema(Formula.parse('(((Q()->Ax[R(x)])->Ax[(Q()->R(x))])&'
                            '(Ax[(Q()->R(x))]->(Q()->Ax[R(x)])))'), {'x', 'R', 'Q'}),
         Schema(Formula.parse('(((Q()->Ex[R(x)])->Ex[(Q()->R(x))])&'
                            '(Ex[(Q()->R(x))]->(Q()->Ex[R(x)])))'), {'x', 'R', 'Q'}),
         Schema(Formula.parse('(((R(x)->Q(x))&(Q(x)->R(x)))->'
                            '((Ax[R(x)]->Ay[Q(y)])&(Ay[Q(y)]->Ax[R(x)])))'),
             {'x', 'y', 'R', 'Q'}),
         Schema(Formula.parse('(((R(x)->Q(x))&(Q(x)->R(x)))->'
                            '((Ex[R(x)]->Ey[Q(y)])&(Ey[Q(y)]->Ex[R(x)])))'),
             {'x', 'y', 'R', 'Q'}))
```

Notice that in the example just given, we have in fact used these equivalences to replace a *sub*formula with an equivalent subformula. While our sixteen new additional axiom schemas do not allow us to do precisely that (they formally handle full rather than partial formulas), as we will see the additional ability of Additional Axioms 15 and 16 to quantify over equivalent formulas will allow us to proceed in essentially the same way nonetheless.

As we will handle a lot of equivalence-between-formulas proofs on our way to proving the prenex normal form theorem (11.3), it will be convenient to use the following function, which we have already implemented for you and which takes two formulas and returns the formula that asserts their equivalence.

predicates/prenex.py

```
def equivalence_of(formula1: Formula, formula2: Formula) -> Formula:
    """States the equivalence of the two given formulas as a formula.

    Parameters:
        formula1: first of the formulas the equivalence of which is to be
            stated.
        formula2: second of the formulas the equivalence of which is to be
            stated.

    Returns:
        The formula '((`formula1`->`formula2`)&(`formula2`->`formula1`))'.
    """
    return Formula('&', Formula('->', formula1, formula2),
                   Formula('->', formula2, formula1))
```

Before we start proving the prenex normal form theorem (11.3) using our sixteen new additional axiom schemas, however, we invite you to prove (all instances of) the first of these schemas, Additional Axiom 1, yourself from the four basic axiom schemas of quantification (and to save yourself the work of proving the remaining fifteen schemas). Your proof will also demonstrate the incredible usefulness of the deduction theorem (11.1).

OPTIONAL TASK 4   In this task, you will prove, for every variable name x and for every arbitrary formula $\phi(x)$, that '$\sim\forall x[\phi(x)]$' is equivalent to '$\exists x[\sim\phi(x)]$'. In the first two parts below you will show both directions of the equivalence, and in the third you will tautologically infer the equivalence. The functions that you are asked to implement in this task are contained in the file `predicates/some_proofs.py`.

a. Prove, for every variable name x and for every arbitrary formula $\phi(x)$, that '$(\sim\exists x[\sim\phi(x)]\rightarrow\forall x[\phi(x)])$' holds. That is, implement the missing code for the function `_prove_not_exists_not_implies_all(variable, formula)`, which takes x and $\phi(x)$, and returns a proof of '$(\sim\exists x[\sim\phi(x)]\rightarrow\forall x[\phi(x)])$'.[6]

```
predicates/some_proofs.py

def _prove_not_exists_not_implies_all(variable: str, formula: Formula,
                              print_as_proof_forms: bool = False) -> \
        Proof:
    """Proves that '(~E`variable`[~`formula`]->A`variable`[`formula`])'.

    Parameters:
        variable: variable name for the quantifications in the formula to be
            proven.
        formula: statement to be universally quantified, and whose negation is
            to be existentially quantified, in the formula to be proven.
        print_as_proof_forms: flag specifying whether the proof is to be printed
            in real time as it is being created.

    Returns:
        A valid proof of the above formula via `Prover.AXIOMS`.
    """
    assert is_variable(variable)
    # Optional Task 11.4a
```

Guidelines: Use the deduction theorem (11.1), that is, assume '$\sim\exists x[\sim\phi(x)]$' and prove '$\forall x[\phi(x)]$'. As your first step, use '$\sim\phi(x)\rightarrow\exists x[\sim\phi(x)]$'.

b. Prove, for every variable name x and for every arbitrary formula $\phi(x)$, that '$(\exists x[\sim\phi(x)]\rightarrow\sim\forall x[\phi(x)])$' holds. That is, implement the missing code for the function `_prove_exists_not_implies_not_all(variable, formula)`, which takes x and $\phi(x)$, and returns a proof of '$(\exists x[\sim\phi(x)]\rightarrow\sim\forall x[\phi(x)])$'.

```
predicates/some_proofs.py

def _prove_exists_not_implies_not_all(variable: str, formula: Formula,
                              print_as_proof_forms: bool = False) -> \
        Proof:
    """Proves that '(E`variable`[~`formula`]->~A`variable`[`formula`])'.

    Parameters:
        variable: variable name for the quantifications in the formula to be
            proven.
        formula: statement to be universally quantified, and whose negation is
            to be existentially quantified, in the formula to be proven.
        print_as_proof_forms: flag specifying whether the proof is to be printed
            in real time as it is being created.

    Returns:
        A valid proof of the above formula via `Prover.AXIOMS`.
```

---

[6] Once again, here and below, we allow the usage of all six basic logical axiom schemas so that you may easily use the Prover class in your solution.

```
"""
assert is_variable(variable)
# Optional Task 11.4b
```

Guidelines: Use the deduction theorem (11.1), that is, assume '$\exists x[\sim\phi(x)]$' and prove '$\sim\forall x[\phi(x)]$'. Your last step should be calling `add_existential_derivation()` with the consequent argument to this method being '$\sim\forall x[\phi(x)]$' and with the `line_number1` argument to this method pointing to a line with the assumption '$\exists x[\sim\phi(x)]$'.

c. Prove, for every variable name x and for every arbitrary formula $\phi(x)$, that '$\sim\forall x[\phi(x)]$' is equivalent to '$\exists x[\sim\phi(x)]$'. That is, implement the missing code for the function `prove_not_all_iff_exists_not(variable, formula)`, which takes x and $\phi(x)$, and returns a proof of this equivalence.

```
─────────────────( predicates/some_proofs.py )─────────────────
def prove_not_all_iff_exists_not(variable: str, formula: Formula,
                                 print_as_proof_forms: bool = False) -> Proof:
    """Proves that
    `equivalence_of('(~A`variable`[`formula`]', 'E`variable`[~`formula`]')`.

    Parameters:
        variable: variable name for the quantifications in the formula to be
            proven.
        formula: statement to be universally quantified, and whose negation is
            to be existentially quantified, in the formula to be proven.
        print_as_proof_forms: flag specifying whether the proof is to be printed
            in real time as it is being created.

    Returns:
        A valid proof of the above formula via `Prover.AXIOMS`.
    """
    assert is_variable(variable)
    # Optional Task 11.4c
```

Guidelines: Tautologically infer this from the previous two parts. Use the method `add_proof()` of class `Prover` to insert these two proofs into a new prover (the `add_proof()` method takes care of properly shifting all line numbers that justify MP and UG lines, to retain the validity of proof lines that are added when the prover already has some proof lines), and continue the proof from there using the `Prover` API.

Examining the proof of equivalence that Optional Task 4 outputs, you will note that it uses all four basic logical axioms of quantifications (UI, EI, US, and ES). We note that your solution to Optional Task 4 indeed completely proves (all instances of) the first of our sixteen new additional axiom schemas. Therefore, in any proof that has this schema as an assumption/axiom (recall that in Python, this schema is referenced as `ADDITIONAL_QUANTIFICATION_AXIOMS[0]`), any step that instantiates this assumption/axiom, i.e., any proof step of the following form:

```
stepN = prover.add_instantiated_assumption(
            instance, ADDITIONAL_QUANTIFICATION_AXIOMS[0],
            {'R': formula, 'x': variable})
```

can be replaced with the following equivalent proof step, which does not require `ADDITIONAL_QUANTIFICATION_AXIOMS[0]` as an assumption/axiom:

```
stepN = prover.add_proof(
            not_all_iff_exists_not_proof(
                variable, formula.substitute({'_': Term(variable)})))
```

Now that we have had a small taste of what proving our sixteen new additional axiom schemas entails, we will very happily move on to proving the prenex normal form theorem (11.3), using *all* sixteen schemas as additional assumptions/axioms. (The fact that all of these sixteen schemas are provable from our four basic axiom schemas of quantification implies, by the soundness theorem (9.1) for predicate logic, that they are all sound. Since you have not seen a proof of Additional Axioms 2 through 16, we invite you to try and prove their soundness directly to be convinced that they are all indeed sound.) We start by making sure that the quantified variable names in different parts of a given formula do not "clash" with one another, nor with the free variable names of the formula.

DEFINITION 11.2 (Uniquely Named Variables)   A formula is said to have **uniquely named variables** if no two quantifications in the formula quantify over the same variable name, and no variable name has both bound and free occurrences in the formula.

The function `has_uniquely_named_variables(formula)`, which we have already implemented for you, checks whether a given formula has uniquely named variables.

predicates/prenex.py

```
def has_uniquely_named_variables(formula: Formula) -> bool:
    """Checks if the given formula has uniquely named variables.

    Parameters:
        formula: formula to check.

    Returns:
        ``False`` if in the given formula some variable name has both bound and
        free occurrences or is quantified by more than one quantifier, ``True``
        otherwise.

    Examples:
        >>> has_uniquely_named_variables(
        ...     Formula.parse('(x=0&(Ax[R(x)]|Ex[R(x)]))'))
        False
        >>> has_uniquely_named_variables(
        ...     Formula.parse('(x=0&(Ax[R(x)]|Ey[R(y)]))'))
        False
        >>> has_uniquely_named_variables(
        ...     Formula.parse('(y=0&(Ax[R(x)]|Ex[R(x)]))'))
        False
        >>> has_uniquely_named_variables(
        ...     Formula.parse('(x=0&(Ay[R(y)]|Ez[R(z)]))'))
        True
    """
    forbidden_variables = set(formula.free_variables())
    def has_uniquely_named_variables_helper(formula: Formula) -> bool:
        if is_unary(formula.root):
            return has_uniquely_named_variables_helper(formula.first)
```

```
        elif is_binary(formula.root):
            return has_uniquely_named_variables_helper(formula.first) and \
                has_uniquely_named_variables_helper(formula.second)
        elif is_quantifier(formula.root):
            if formula.variable in forbidden_variables:
                return False
            forbidden_variables.add(formula.variable)
            return has_uniquely_named_variables_helper(formula.statement)
        else:
            assert is_equality(formula.root) or is_relation(formula.root)
            return True

    return has_uniquely_named_variables_helper(formula)
```

TASK 5   Implement the missing code for the function `_uniquely_rename_quantified_variables(formula)`, which takes a formula and returns an equivalent formula with uniquely named variables, along with a proof of the equivalence of the given and returned formulas.

predicates/prenex.py

```
def _uniquely_rename_quantified_variables(formula: Formula) -> \
        Tuple[Formula, Proof]:
    """Converts the given formula to an equivalent formula with uniquely named
    variables, and proves the equivalence of these two formulas.

    Parameters:
        formula: formula to convert, which contains no variable names that are
            ``z`` followed by a number.

    Returns:
        A pair. The first element of the pair is a formula equivalent to the
        given formula, with the exact same structure but with the additional
        property of having uniquely named variables, obtained by consistently
        replacing each variable name that is bound in the given formula with a
        new variable name obtained by calling
        `next(fresh_variable_name_generator)`. The second element of the pair is
        a proof of the equivalence of the given formula and the returned
        formula (i.e., a proof of `equivalence_of(formula, returned_formula)`)
        via `Prover.AXIOMS` and `ADDITIONAL_QUANTIFICATION_AXIOMS`.

    Examples:
        >>> formula = Formula.parse('~(w=x|Aw[(Ex[(x=w&Aw[w=x])]->Ax[x=y])])')
        >>> returned_formula, proof = _uniquely_rename_quantified_variables(
        ...     formula)
        >>> returned_formula
        ~(w=x|Az58[(Ez17[(z17=z58&Az4[z4=z17])]->Az32[z32=y])])
        >>> proof.is_valid()
        True
        >>> proof.conclusion == equivalence_of(formula, returned_formula)
        True
        >>> proof.assumptions == Prover.AXIOMS.union(
        ...     ADDITIONAL_QUANTIFICATION_AXIOMS)
        True
    """
    for variable in formula.variables():
        assert not is_z_and_number(variable)
    # Task 11.5
```

Guidelines: Use recursion. To modify, combine, and extend the proofs returned by recursive calls, construct a new `Prover` object, use the `add_proof()` method of that object with each proof returned by a recursive call to insert it into the proof of this prover (the `add_proof()` method takes care of properly shifting all line numbers that justify MP and UG lines, to retain the validity of proof lines that are added when the prover already has some proof lines), and then complete the proof using the `Prover` API, including the methods that you implemented in Chapter 10 (in particular, with the last two of our sixteen new additional axiom schemas – Additional Axioms 15 and 16).

Recall that Additional Axioms 1 and 2 allow you to "pull out" a single quantification across a negation. The next building block toward proving the prenex normal form theorem (11.3) is to show how to use that (in conjunction with Additional Axioms 15 and 16) to "pull out" any number of quantifications across a negation.

TASK 6   Implement the missing code for the function `_pull_out_quantifications_across_negation(formula)`, which takes a formula whose root is a negation, i.e., a formula of the form '$\sim Q_1 x_1[Q_2 x_2[\cdots Q_n x_n[\phi]\cdots]]$' where $n \geq 0$, each Q_i is a quantifier, each x_i is a variable name, and ϕ does not start with a quantifier, and returns an equivalent formula of the form '$Q'_1 x_1[Q'_2 x_2[\cdots Q'_n x_n[\sim\phi]\cdots]]$' where each Q'_i is a quantifier (and where each x_i and ϕ are the same as in `formula`), along with a proof of the equivalence of the given and returned formulas.

predicates/prenex.py

```
def _pull_out_quantifications_across_negation(formula: Formula) -> \
        Tuple[Formula, Proof]:
    """Converts the given formula with uniquely named variables of the form
    '`~`Q1``x1`[`Q2``x2`[...`Qn``xn`[`inner_formula`]...]]' to an equivalent
    formula of the form
    '`Q'1``x1`[`Q'2``x2`[...`Q'n``xn`[`~`inner_formula`]...]]', and proves the
    equivalence of these two formulas.

    Parameters:
        formula: formula to convert, whose root is a negation, i.e., which is of
            the form '`~`Q1``x1`[`Q2``x2`[...`Qn``xn`[`inner_formula`]...]]'
            where `n`>=0, each `Qi` is a quantifier, each `xi` is a variable
            name, and `inner_formula` does not start with a quantifier.

    Returns:
        A pair. The first element of the pair is a formula equivalent to the
        given formula, but of the form
        '`Q'1``x1`[`Q'2``x2`[...`Q'n``xn`[`~`inner_formula`]...]]' where each
        `Q'i` is a quantifier, and where the `xi` variable names and
        `inner_formula` are the same as in the given formula. The second element
        of the pair is a proof of the equivalence of the given formula and the
        returned formula (i.e., a proof of
        `equivalence_of(formula, returned_formula)`) via `Prover.AXIOMS` and
        `ADDITIONAL_QUANTIFICATION_AXIOMS`.

    Examples:
        >>> formula = Formula.parse('~Ax[Ey[R(x,y)]]')
        >>> returned_formula, proof = _pull_out_quantifications_across_negation(
        ...         formula)
        >>> returned_formula
```

```
        Ex[Ay[~R(x,y)]]
        >>> proof.is_valid()
        True
        >>> proof.conclusion == equivalence_of(formula, returned_formula)
        True
        >>> proof.assumptions == Prover.AXIOMS.union(
        ...        ADDITIONAL_QUANTIFICATION_AXIOMS)
        True
    """
    assert is_unary(formula.root)
    # Task 11.6
```

Guidelines: Call the function recursively with '$\sim Q_2 x_2[\cdots Q_n x_n[\phi]\cdots]$' to obtain '$Q'_2 x_2[\cdots Q'_n x_n[\sim\phi]\cdots]$' (and the proof of equivalence). From this show that '$Q'_1 x_1[\sim Q_2 x_2[\cdots Q_n x_n[\phi]\cdots]]$' and '$Q'_1 x_1[Q'_2 x_2[\cdots Q'_n x_n[\sim\phi]\cdots]]$' are equivalent (don't forget that add_proof() is your friend); now apply Additional Axiom 1 or Additional Axiom 2. As a base case for the recursion, use the case $n = 0$ (no quantifications after the negation at the root of formula) rather than the case $n = 1$.

Our next building block, which you will develop throughout Tasks 7 and 8, is to "pull out" any number of quantifications from both operands of a binary operator. We start with "pulling out" any number of quantifications from one of the operands of a binary operator.

TASK 7

a. Implement the missing code for the function _pull_out_quantifications_ from_left_across_binary_operator(formula), which takes a formula with uniquely named variables whose root is a binary operator, i.e., a formula with uniquely named variables that is of the form '$(Q_1 x_1[Q_2 x_2[\cdots Q_n x_n[\phi]\cdots]]*\psi)$' where $*$ is a binary operator, $n \geq 0$, each Q_i is a quantifier, each x_i is a variable name, and ϕ does not start with a quantifier, and returns an equivalent formula of the form '$Q'_1 x_1[Q'_2 x_2[\cdots Q'_n x_n[(\phi*\psi)]\cdots]]$' where each Q'_i is a quantifier (and where $*$, each x_i, ϕ, and ψ are the same as in formula), along with a proof of the equivalence of the given and returned formulas.

```
predicates/prenex.py
```

```python
def _pull_out_quantifications_from_left_across_binary_operator(formula:
                                                    Formula) -> \
        Tuple[Formula, Proof]:
    """Converts the given formula with uniquely named variables of the form
    '(`Q1``x1`[`Q2``x2`[...`Qn``xn`[`inner_first`]...]]`*``second`)' to an
    equivalent formula of the form
    '`Q'1``x1`[`Q'2``x2`[...`Q'n``xn`[(`inner_first``*``second`)]...]]' and
    proves the equivalence of these two formulas.

    Parameters:
        formula: formula with uniquely named variables to convert, whose root
            is a binary operator, i.e., which is of the form
            '(`Q1``x1`[`Q2``x2`[...`Qn``xn`[`inner_first`]...]]`*``second`)'
            where `*` is a binary operator, `n`>=0, each `Qi` is a quantifier,
            each `xi` is a variable name, and `inner_first` does not start with
            a quantifier.
```

```
    Returns:
        A pair. The first element of the pair is a formula equivalent to the
        given formula, but of the form
        '`Q'1``x1`[`Q'2``x2`[...`Q'n``xn`[(`inner_first``*``second`)]...]]'
        where each `Q'i` is a quantifier, and where the operator `*`, the `xi`
        variable names, `inner_first`, and `second` are the same as in the given
        formula. The second element of the pair is a proof of the equivalence of
        the given formula and the returned formula (i.e., a proof of
        `equivalence_of(formula, returned_formula)`) via `Prover.AXIOMS` and
        `ADDITIONAL_QUANTIFICATION_AXIOMS`.

    Examples:
        >>> formula = Formula.parse('(Ax[Ey[R(x,y)]]&Ez[P(1,z)])')
        >>> returned_formula, proof = \
        ...     _pull_out_quantifications_from_left_across_binary_operator(
        ...             formula)
        >>> returned_formula
        Ax[Ey[(R(x,y)&Ez[P(1,z)])]]
        >>> proof.is_valid()
        True
        >>> proof.conclusion == equivalence_of(formula, returned_formula)
        True
        >>> proof.assumptions == Prover.AXIOMS.union(
        ...         ADDITIONAL_QUANTIFICATION_AXIOMS)
        True
    """
    assert has_uniquely_named_variables(formula)
    assert is_binary(formula.root)
    # Task 11.7a
```

Guidelines: The logic is almost identical to that of Task 6: call the function recursively with '$(Q_2 x_2[\cdots Q_n x_n[\phi]\cdots]*\psi)$' to obtain '$Q'_2 x_2[\cdots Q'_n x_n[(\phi*\psi)]\cdots]$' (and the proof of equivalence). From this show that '$Q'_1 x_1[(Q_2 x_2[\cdots Q_n x_n[\phi]\cdots]*\psi)]$' and '$Q'_1 x_1[Q'_2 x_2[\cdots Q'_n x_n[(\phi*\psi)]\cdots]]$' are equivalent (don't forget that add_proof() is your friend); now apply one of the additional quantification axioms. As a base case for the recursion, use the case $n = 0$ rather than the case $n = 1$.

Hint: Q'_i depends not only on Q_i, but also on the operator $*$.

b. Implement the missing code for the function _pull_out_quantifications_from_right_across_binary_operator(formula), which takes a formula with uniquely named variables whose root is a binary operator, i.e., a formula with uniquely named variables that is of the form '$(\phi*Q_1 x_1[Q_2 x_2[\cdots Q_n x_n[\psi]\cdots]])$' where $*$ is a binary operator, $n \geq 0$, each Q_i is a quantifier, each x_i is a variable name, and ψ does not start with a quantifier, and returns an equivalent formula of the form '$Q'_1 x_1[Q'_2 x_2[\cdots Q'_n x_n[(\phi*\psi)]\cdots]]$' where each Q'_i is a quantifier (and where $*$, each x_i, ϕ, and ψ are the same as in formula), along with a proof of the equivalence of the given and returned formulas.

```
                                                    predicates/prenex.py
def _pull_out_quantifications_from_right_across_binary_operator(formula:
                                                    Formula) -> \
        Tuple[Formula, Proof]:
    """Converts the given formula with uniquely named variables of the form
    '(`first``*``Q1``x1`[`Q2``x2`[...`Qn``xn`[`inner_second`]...]])' to an
```

```
    equivalent formula of the form
    '`Q'1``x1`[`Q'2``x2`[...`Q'n``xn`[(`first``*``inner_second`)]...]]' and
    proves the equivalence of these two formulas.

    Parameters:
        formula: formula with uniquely named variables to convert, whose root
            is a binary operator, i.e., which is of the form
            '(`first``*``Q1``x1`[`Q2``x2`[...`Qn``xn`[`inner_second`]...]])'
            where `*` is a binary operator, `n`>=0, each `Qi` is a quantifier,
            each `xi` is a variable name, and `inner_second` does not start with
            a quantifier.

    Returns:
        A pair. The first element of the pair is a formula equivalent to the
        given formula, but of the form
        '`Q'1``x1`[`Q'2``x2`[...`Q'n``xn`[(`first``*``inner_second`)]...]]'
        where each `Q'i` is a quantifier, and where the operator `*`, the `xi`
        variable names, `first`, and `inner_second` are the same as in the given
        formula. The second element of the pair is a proof of the equivalence of
        the given formula and the returned formula (i.e., a proof of
        `equivalence_of(formula, returned_formula)`) via `Prover.AXIOMS` and
        `ADDITIONAL_QUANTIFICATION_AXIOMS`.

    Examples:
        >>> formula = Formula.parse('(Ax[Ey[R(x,y)]]|Ez[P(1,z)])')
        >>> returned_formula, proof = \
        ...     _pull_out_quantifications_from_right_across_binary_operator(
        ...         formula)
        >>> returned_formula
        Ez[(Ax[Ey[R(x,y)]]|P(1,z))]
        >>> proof.is_valid()
        True
        >>> proof.conclusion == equivalence_of(formula, returned_formula)
        True
        >>> proof.assumptions == Prover.AXIOMS.union(
        ...         ADDITIONAL_QUANTIFICATION_AXIOMS)
        True
    """
    assert has_uniquely_named_variables(formula)
    assert is_binary(formula.root)
    # Task 11.7b
```

Guidelines: Almost identical to the first part: call the function recursively with '$(\phi * Q_2 x_2 [\cdots Q_n x_n [\psi] \cdots])$' to obtain '$Q'_2 x_2 [\cdots Q'_n x_n [(\phi * \psi)] \cdots]$' (and the proof of equivalence). From this show that '$Q'_1 x_1 [(\phi * Q_2 x_2 [\cdots Q_n x_n [\psi] \cdots])]$' and '$Q'_1 x_1 [Q'_2 x_2 [\cdots Q'_n x_n [(\phi * \psi)] \cdots]]$' are equivalent (don't forget that add_proof() is your friend); now apply one of the additional quantification axioms. As a base case for the recursion, use the case $n = 0$ rather than the case $n = 1$.

You are now ready to complete the building block that "pulls out" all quantifications from *both* operands of a binary operator – this turns out to be slightly trickier than simply applying both parts of Task 7.

TASK 8 Implement the missing code for the function _pull_out_quantifications_ across_binary_operator(formula), which takes a formula with uniquely named variables whose root is a binary operator, i.e., a formula with uniquely named variables that is of the form

$$\text{`}(Q_1x_1[Q_2x_2[\cdots Q_nx_n[\phi]\cdots]]*P_1y_1[P_2y_2[\cdots P_my_m[\psi]\cdots]])\text{'}$$

where $*$ is a binary operator, $n \geq 0$, $m \geq 0$, each Q_i and each P_i is a quantifier, each x_i and each y_i is a variable name, and neither ϕ nor ψ starts with a quantifier, and returns an equivalent formula of the form

$$\text{`}Q'_1x_1[Q'_2x_2[\cdots Q'_nx_n[P'_1y_1[P'_2x_2[\cdots P'_my_m[(\phi*\psi)]\cdots]]]\cdots]]\text{'}$$

where each Q'_i and each P'_i is a quantifier (and where $*$, each x_i, each y_i, ϕ, and ψ are the same as in `formula`), along with a proof of the equivalence of the given and returned formulas.

```
                          predicates/prenex.py
def _pull_out_quantifications_across_binary_operator(formula: Formula) -> \
        Tuple[Formula, Proof]:
    """Converts the given formula with uniquely named variables of the form
    '(`Q1``x1`[`Q2``x2`[...`Qn``xn`[`inner_first`]...]]`*`
      `P1``y1`[`P2``y2`[...`Pm``ym`[`inner_second`]...]]])'
    to an equivalent formula of the form
    '`Q'1``x1`[`Q'2``x2`[...`Q'n``xn`[
        `P'1``y1`[`P'2``y2`[...`P'm``ym`[(`inner_first``*``inner_second`)]...]]
    ]...]]'
    and proves the equivalence of these two formulas.

    Parameters:
        formula: formula with uniquely named variables to convert, whose root
            is a binary operator, i.e., which is of the form
            '(`Q1``x1`[`Q2``x2`[...`Qn``xn`[`inner_first`]...]]`*`
              `P1``y1`[`P2``y2`[...`Pm``ym`[`inner_second`]...]]])'
            where `*` is a binary operator, `n`>=0, `m`>=0, each `Qi` and `Pi`
            is a quantifier, each `xi` and `yi` is a variable name, and neither
            `inner_first` nor `inner_second` starts with a quantifier.

    Returns:
        A pair. The first element of the pair is a formula equivalent to the
        given formula, but of the form
        '`Q'1``x1`[`Q'2``x2`[...`Q'n``xn`[
            `P'1``y1`[`P'2``y2`[...`P'm``ym`[
                (`inner_first``*``inner_second`)
            ]...]]
        ]...]]'
        where each `Q'i` and `P'i` is a quantifier, and where the operator `*`,
        the `xi` and `yi` variable names, `inner_first`, and `inner_second` are
        the same as in the given formula. The second element of the pair is a
        proof of the equivalence of the given formula and the returned formula
        (i.e., a proof of `equivalence_of(formula, returned_formula)`) via
        `Prover.AXIOMS` and `ADDITIONAL_QUANTIFICATION_AXIOMS`.

    Examples:
        >>> formula = Formula.parse('(Ax[Ey[R(x,y)]]->Ez[P(1,z)])')
        >>> returned_formula, proof = \
        ...     _pull_out_quantifications_across_binary_operator(
        ...         formula)
        >>> returned_formula
```

```
          Ex[Ay[Ez[(R(x,y)->P(1,z))]]]
          >>> proof.is_valid()
          True
          >>> proof.conclusion == equivalence_of(formula, returned_formula)
          True
          >>> proof.assumptions == Prover.AXIOMS.union(
          ...       ADDITIONAL_QUANTIFICATION_AXIOMS)
          True
      """
      assert has_uniquely_named_variables(formula)
      assert is_binary(formula.root)
      # Task 11.8
```

Guidelines: First use the first part of Task 7 on `formula` to obtain '$Q'_1 x_1 [Q'_2 x_2 [\cdots Q'_n x_n [$ $(\phi * P_1 y_1 [P_2 y_2 [\cdots P_m y_m [\psi] \cdots]])] \cdots]]$' (and the proof of equivalence). Then use the second part on '$(\phi * P_1 y_1 [P_2 y_2 [\cdots P_m y_m [\psi] \cdots]])$' to obtain '$P'_1 y_1 [P'_2 y_2 [\cdots P'_m y_m [$ $(\phi * \psi)] \cdots]]$' (and the proof of equivalence). Use the latter to show that '$Q'_1 x_1 [Q'_2 x_2 [\cdots$ $Q'_n x_n [(\phi * P_1 y_1 [P_2 y_2 [\cdots P_m y_m [\psi] \cdots]])] \cdots]]$' is equivalent to $Q'_1 x_1 [Q'_2 x_2 [\cdots Q'_n x_n [P'_1 y_1 [$ $P'_2 x_2 [\cdots P'_m y_m [(\phi * \psi)] \cdots]]] \cdots]]$. (And don't forget that `add_proof()` is your friend.)

You are now ready to combine Tasks 6 and 8 to convert a formula with no "clashing" variable names (as output by Task 5) into a formula in prenex normal form.

TASK 9   Implement the missing code for the function `_to_prenex_normal_form_` `from_uniquely_named_variables(formula)`, which takes a formula with uniquely named variables and returns an equivalent formula in prenex normal form, along with a proof of the equivalence of the given and returned formulas.

```
                    ┌─────────────────────┐
                    │ predicates/prenex.py │
                    └─────────────────────┘
def _to_prenex_normal_form_from_uniquely_named_variables(formula: Formula) -> \
        Tuple[Formula, Proof]:
    """Converts the given formula with uniquely named variables to an equivalent
    formula in prenex normal form, and proves the equivalence of these two
    formulas.

    Parameters:
        formula: formula with uniquely named variables to convert.

    Returns:
        A pair. The first element of the pair is a formula equivalent to the
        given formula, but in prenex normal form. The second element of the pair
        is a proof of the equivalence of the given formula and the returned
        formula (i.e., a proof of `equivalence_of(formula, returned_formula)`)
        via `Prover.AXIOMS` and `ADDITIONAL_QUANTIFICATION_AXIOMS`.

    Examples:
        >>> formula = Formula.parse('(~(Ax[Ey[R(x,y)]]->Ez[P(1,z)])|S(w))')
        >>> returned_formula, proof = \
        ...     _to_prenex_normal_form_from_uniquely_named_variables(
        ...         formula)
        >>> returned_formula
        Ax[Ey[Az[(~(R(x,y)->P(1,z))|S(w))]]]
        >>> proof.is_valid()
        True
        >>> proof.conclusion == equivalence_of(formula, returned_formula)
```

```
      True
      >>> proof.assumptions == Prover.AXIOMS.union(
      ...         ADDITIONAL_QUANTIFICATION_AXIOMS)
      True
      """
      assert has_uniquely_named_variables(formula)
      # Task 11.9
```

Guidelines: In the cases in which the root of `formula` is an operator, use recursion to convert each operand into prenex normal form (and to obtain the proof of equivalence); complete the proof of each of these cases using Task 6 or Task 8. (Don't forget that `add_proof()` is your friend.)

Now that all of the recursions are behind you, you are finally ready to prove the prenex normal form theorem (11.3).

TASK 10 (Programmatic Proof of the Prenex Normal Form Theorem (11.3))   Implement the missing code for the function `to_prenex_normal_form(formula)`, which takes a formula and returns an equivalent formula in prenex normal form, along with a proof of the equivalence of the given and returned formulas.

```
                    ┤ predicates/prenex.py ├
def to_prenex_normal_form(formula: Formula) -> Tuple[Formula, Proof]:
    """Converts the given formula to an equivalent formula in prenex normal
    form, and proves the equivalence of these two formulas.

    Parameters:
        formula: formula to convert, which contains no variable names that are
            ``z`` followed by a number.

    Returns:
        A pair. The first element of the pair is a formula equivalent to the
        given formula, but in prenex normal form. The second element of the pair
        is a proof of the equivalence of the given formula and the returned
        formula (i.e., a proof of `equivalence_of(formula, returned_formula)`)
        via `Prover.AXIOMS` and `ADDITIONAL_QUANTIFICATION_AXIOMS`.

    Examples:
        >>> formula = Formula.parse('~(w=x|Aw[(Ex[(x=w&Aw[w=x])]->Ax[x=y])])')
        >>> returned_formula, proof = to_prenex_normal_form(formula)
        >>> returned_formula
        Ez58[Ez17[Az4[Ez32[~(w=x|((z17=z58&z4=z17)->z32=y))]]]]
        >>> proof.is_valid()
        True
        >>> proof.conclusion == equivalence_of(formula, returned_formula)
        True
        >>> proof.assumptions == Prover.AXIOMS.union(
        ...         ADDITIONAL_QUANTIFICATION_AXIOMS)
        True
    """
    for variable in formula.variables():
        assert not is_z_and_number(variable)
    # Task 11.10
```

Guidelines: Use Tasks 5 and 9 (and don't forget that `add_proof()` is your friend).

12   The Completeness Theorem

In this chapter, in which the analysis of this entire book culminates, we will take the final steps toward proving the **completeness theorem** (12.1/12.4) for predicate logic – the main theorem of predicate logic, which states that a set of formulas is **consistent** if and only if it has a model. Similarly to propositional logic, we call a set of formulas in predicate logic **consistent** if a contradiction (i.e., the negation of a tautology, such as '(R(x)&~R(x))') cannot be proven from it and from our six axiom schemas (equivalently, from it and from these six schemas plus the sixteen additional schemas from Chapter 11).[1] So, consistency is a syntactic concept, while having a model is a semantic one, and the completeness theorem relates these two seemingly very different concepts. While we will not be able to create a fully programmatic proof for the completeness theorem (12.1/12.4) (we will have to complete the very last step mathematically, as it involves infinite models), we will be able to programmatically prove almost all of the required lemmas and to describe the general flow of the mathematical proof.

As in propositional logic, there is an "easy direction" to the completeness theorem that follows from (or rather, is a restatement of) the soundness theorem. Recall that the soundness theorem (9.1) for predicate logic from Chapter 9 states that if a set of formulas A can be used, alongside our (basic and additional) twenty-two (sound) axiom schemas, to prove a formula ϕ, then ϕ holds in any model where all of A hold. In particular, if A has a model, then ϕ must hold in that model, so ϕ cannot be a contradiction, and so A is consistent. This chapter is therefore dedicated to proving the "hard direction" of the ("consistency" version of the) completeness theorem (12.1): that every consistent set of formulas has a model.

In this chapter, we will assume that we are in a setting without any function names and without the equality symbol – as you have shown in Chapter 8, this does not make predicate logic lose any expressive power. Furthermore, it will suffice to carry out the core of our proof with formulas that are given in prenex normal form, since you have shown in Chapter 11 that this does not lose any generality. Finally, it will also be convenient to work with formulas that are actually **sentences**, i.e., have no free variable names. Again, this is without loss of generality since as we have seen, we can go back and forth between

---

[1] Recall from propositional logic that we call a set inconsistent if the negation of an axiom is provable from it via our axiomatic system. In propositional logic we defined this with respect to the axiom I0 (but saw that defining this with respect to any other axiom would have been equivalent), and in predicate logic we define this with respect to any tautology, since we allow all tautologies as axioms in our proof thanks to your proof of the tautology theorem (6.1) in propositional logic (and once again, defining this with respect to any other axiom would have been an equivalent completely syntactic definition). This is completely analogous to our reinterpretation of proofs by way of contradiction for predicate logic in Chapter 11 as compared to Chapter 5.

sentences and formulas by universally quantifying over any free variable name using UG on the one hand and by removing universal quantifications using UI (replacing any quantified variable name "with itself") on the other hand. So, we wish to show that every consistent set of sentences in prenex normal form (that, as will always be the case in this chapter, are without function names or equalities) has a model. All of the functions that you are asked to implement in this chapter are contained in the file `predicates/completeness.py`.

Since we have "assumed away" function names, to construct a model of a given consistent set of sentences we will need to figure out three things:

1. which universe to use for the model,
2. which interpretation to give for each constant name, i.e., how to map each constant name to an element from the universe, and
3. which interpretation to give for each relation name, i.e., for every relation name R and every tuple of elements from the universe $(\alpha_1, \ldots, \alpha_n)$ where n is the arity of R, whether the tuple $(\alpha_1, \ldots, \alpha_n)$ is in the interpretation of R.

Since we have "assumed away" the equality symbol, we will handle the first two of these questions (which universe to use, and which interpretation to give for each constant name) in a very simple (yet quite ingenious) manner: Our universe will be the set of the constant names that we use, and the interpretation of each constant name (when viewed as a constant name) will be the constant name itself (when viewed as an element of the universe).[2]

To handle the third of these questions (regarding which interpretation to give for each relation name), it would be quite convenient if for each relation name R, for every tuple of constant names $(c_1, \ldots, c_n)$ where n is the arity of R, the given consistent set of sentences already had in it either the **primitive** sentence '$R(c_1, \ldots, c_n)$' or its negation '$\sim R(c_1, \ldots, c_n)$' (the set of sentences cannot contain both since then it would not be consistent), since then we could simply "read off" the interpretation of R from such sentences: If the set of sentences had this primitive sentence (without any negation), then the tuple $(c_1, \ldots, c_n)$ should be in the interpretation of R, while if the set of sentences had the negation of this primitive sentence, then this tuple should *not* be in the interpretation of R. The basic strategy of our proof of the ("hard direction" of the) completeness theorem (12.1) will therefore be to add enough sentences (and in particular, enough sentences that are either primitive sentences or the negation of primitive sentences) to the given set of sentences – *while leaving it consistent* – so that we will indeed be able to "read off" the interpretations of all relation names from such primitive sentences, or from their negations, in the set. In particular, we will consider ourselves to have added "enough" sentences to the given set if after having added them, the set satisfies the following condition.

DEFINITION 12.1 (Closed Set of Sentences; Primitively Closed Set of Sentences; Universally Closed Set of Sentences; Existentially Closed Set of Sentences)   Let S be a (possibly infinite) set of sentences in prenex normal form. We say that S is **closed** if all of the following hold:

---

[2] Had we not assumed away the equality symbol, we would have had to be far more careful here and take the elements of the universe to be equivalence classes of constant names, similarly to our construction from Chapter 8. The approach that we have adopted therefore allows for that argument to be handled in a separate proof (that we have already given in Chapter 8), instead of being intertwined into our proof of the completeness theorem (12.1).

- S is **primitively closed**: For every relation name R that appears somewhere in S and for every tuple of (not necessarily distinct) constant names $(c_1, \ldots, c_n)$ where n is the arity of R and each c_i appears somewhere in S, either the **primitive** sentence '$R(c_1, \ldots, c_n)$' or its negation '$\sim R(c_1, \ldots, c_n)$' (or both) is in S.
- S is **universally closed**: For every universally quantified sentence '$\forall x[\phi(x)]$' in S and every constant name c that appears somewhere in S, the **universal instantiation** '$\phi(c)$' is also in S.[3]
- S is **existentially closed**: For every existentially quantified sentence '$\exists x[\phi(x)]$' in S, there exists a constant name c such that the **existential witness**[4] '$\phi(c)$' is also in S.

The function `is_closed(sentences)` takes a (finite) set of sentences in prenex normal form and returns whether this set is closed. While we have already implemented this function for you, it is missing a few core components, which you will implement in the next task.

```
                    ┌─────────────────────────────┐
                    │ predicates/completeness.py  │
────────────────────┴─────────────────────────────┴──────────────
def is_closed(sentences: AbstractSet[Formula]) -> bool:
    """Checks whether the given set of prenex-normal-form sentences is closed.

    Parameters:
        sentences: set of prenex-normal-form sentences to check.

    Returns:
        ``True`` if the given set of sentences is primitively, universally, and
        existentially closed; ``False`` otherwise.
    """
    for sentence in sentences:
        assert is_in_prenex_normal_form(sentence) and \
                len(sentence.free_variables()) == 0
    return is_primitively_closed(sentences) and \
            is_universally_closed(sentences) and \
            is_existentially_closed(sentences)
```

The function `get_constants(formulas)`, which takes a (finite) set of formulas and returns the set of constant names that appear in these formulas, will be useful in implementing the three missing core components of the function `is_closed()` in the next task. We have already implemented this function for you using the method `constants()` of class `Formula` that you have implemented in Chapter 7.

```
                    ┌─────────────────────────────┐
                    │ predicates/completeness.py  │
────────────────────┴─────────────────────────────┴──────────────
def get_constants(formulas: AbstractSet[Formula]) -> Set[str]:
    """Finds all constant names in the given formulas.
```

---

[3] Here and henceforth in this chapter, similarly to the notation used in previous chapters, by $\phi(x)$ we mean any formula that may have x as a free variable name (but may have no other free variable names, as otherwise '$\forall x[\phi(x)]$' would not be a sentence), and by '$\phi(c)$' we mean the sentence obtained from $\phi(x)$ by replacing every free occurrence of x with c.

[4] The sentence '$\phi(c)$' is called an **existential witness** to '$\exists x[\phi(x)]$' since if the former holds in a model, then it "witnesses" that there really *exists* an element of the universe (the interpretation of c) such that if it is assigned to x then '$\phi(x)$' holds in that model.

```
Parameters:
    formulas: formulas to find all constant names in.

Returns:
    A set of all constant names used in one or more of the given formulas.
"""
constants = set()
for formula in formulas:
    constants.update(formula.constants())
return constants
```

TASK 1   Implement the missing components of the function is_closed(), that is:

a. Implement the missing code for the function is_primitively_closed(
sentences), which returns whether the given (finite) set of sentences in prenex
normal form is primitively closed.

predicates/completeness.py

```
def is_primitively_closed(sentences: AbstractSet[Formula]) -> bool:
    """Checks whether the given set of prenex-normal-form sentences is
    primitively closed.

    Parameters:
        sentences: set of prenex-normal-form sentences to check.

    Returns:
        ``True`` if for every n-ary relation name from the given sentences, and
        for every n (not necessarily distinct) constant names from the given
        sentences, either the invocation of this relation name over these
        constant names (in order), or the negation of this invocation (or both),
        is one of the given sentences; ``False`` otherwise.
    """
    for sentence in sentences:
        assert is_in_prenex_normal_form(sentence) and \
                len(sentence.free_variables()) == 0
    # Task 12.1a
```

Hint: The relations() method of class Formula may be useful here, and so may the
product() method (with its repeat argument) from the standard Python itertools
module.

b. Implement the missing code for the function is_universally_closed(
sentences), which returns whether the given (finite) set of sentences in prenex
normal form is universally closed.

predicates/completeness.py

```
def is_universally_closed(sentences: AbstractSet[Formula]) -> bool:
    """Checks whether the given set of prenex-normal-form sentences is
    universally closed.

    Parameters:
        sentences: set of prenex-normal-form sentences to check.
```

```
    Returns:
        ``True`` if for every universally quantified sentence from the given set
        of sentences, and for every constant name from these sentences, the
        statement quantified by this sentence, with every free occurrence of the
        universal quantification variable name replaced with this constant name,
        is also in the given set; ``False`` otherwise.
    """
    for sentence in sentences:
        assert is_in_prenex_normal_form(sentence) and \
               len(sentence.free_variables()) == 0
    # Task 12.1b
```

Hint: The substitute() method of class Formula may be useful here.

c. Implement the missing code for the function is_existentially_closed(sentences), which returns whether the given (finite) set of sentences in prenex normal form is existentially closed.

predicates/completeness.py

```
def is_existentially_closed(sentences: AbstractSet[Formula]) -> bool:
    """Checks whether the given set of prenex-normal-form sentences is
    existentially closed.

    Parameters:
        sentences: set of prenex-normal-form sentences to check.

    Returns:
        ``True`` if for every existentially quantified sentence from the given
        set of sentences there exists a constant name such that the statement
        quantified by this sentence, with every free occurrence of the
        existential quantification variable name replaced with this constant
        name, is also in the given set; ``False`` otherwise.
    """
    for sentence in sentences:
        assert is_in_prenex_normal_form(sentence) and \
               len(sentence.free_variables()) == 0
    # Task 12.1c
```

Hint: The substitute() method of class Formula may be useful here as well.

Our strategy for the remainder of this chapter will be as follows. In Section 12.1, we will show that once we have a closed set of sentences S then we will be able to either create a model of it that has the set of constant names that appear in S as the universe of the model (by "reading off" the interpretations of all relation names from S, as outlined in the discussion preceding Definition 12.1) or otherwise explicitly prove a contradiction from S (showing S to be inconsistent). In Section 12.2, we will show that any set of sentences S can have sentences added to it in a way that makes it closed, yet leaves it consistent if it originally were consistent. In Sections 12.3 and 12.4 we will state and discuss the completeness theorem (12.1) and alternate versions thereof, as well as other conclusions and consequences of this important theorem.

12.1   Deriving a Model or a Contradiction for a Closed Set

In this section, we will show that once we have a closed set of sentences S, then we will be able to either create a model of it with the set of constant names that appear in S as its universe or, if in creating such a model, then show how to explicitly prove a contradiction from S (showing that it is in fact inconsistent). That is, in this section we will prove the following lemma.

LEMMA 12.1 (Completeness for Closed Sets)   *Let S be a (possibly infinite) closed set of sentences in prenex normal form. If S is consistent, then S has a model.*

We will start by attempting to construct a model of S with the set of constant names that appear in S as its universe. Specifically, if the primitive sentence '$R(c_1,\ldots,c_n)$' is contained in S then any such model of S must have the tuple $(c_1,\ldots,c_n)$ in the interpretation of R, and so we will add this tuple to this interpretation in the model that we are creating. Conversely, if '$\sim R(c_1,\ldots,c_n)$' is in S, then this tuple must *not* be in the interpretation of R in any such model of S, so we will *not* add this tuple to this interpretation in the model that we are creating. (If both of these sentences are in S, then S is inconsistent since the contradiction '$(R(c_1,\ldots,c_n)\&\sim R(c_1,\ldots,c_n))$' is provable from it, and we are done.) Due to the primitive closure condition, S is assured to contain one of these primitive sentences for every relation name R and every tuple of constant names that each appear somewhere in S, so the model that we are creating is uniquely determined, and is in fact the only possible candidate (among those whose universe is the set of constant names that appear somewhere in S) for being a model of S. If this model satisfies all of the sentences in S, then we are done. Otherwise, some sentence in S is unsatisfied by the model, and we will want to show that S is in fact inconsistent. Our first order of business is to show that due to the universal and existential closure conditions, one can remove all of the quantifiers from this unsatisfied sentence, to find a quantifier-free sentence that is unsatisfied by the model.

TASK 2   Implement the missing code for the function find_unsatisfied_quantifier_free_sentence(sentences, model, unsatisfied), which takes a universally and existentially closed (finite) "set" (this will be clarified momentarily) of sentences in prenex normal form sentences, takes a model model whose universe is the set of constant names that appear somewhere in sentences, and takes a sentence (which possibly contains quantifiers) from sentences that model does not satisfy, and returns a quantifier-free sentence from sentences that model does not satisfy. To verify that you indeed use the universal and existential closure conditions in your solution (and not simply iterate over sentences until you find a suitable sentence to return), the tests for this task are implemented such that the "set" sentences that this function is given in fact may not be iterated over. Instead, it may only be accessed using containment queries, i.e., using the Python in operator as in: if sentence in sentences. (In Python terminology, the parameter sentences is a Container but not an AbstractSet.)

predicates/completeness.py

```
def find_unsatisfied_quantifier_free_sentence(sentences: Container[Formula],
                                              model: Model[str],
                                              unsatisfied: Formula) -> Formula:
```

```
"""
Given a universally and existentially closed set of prenex-normal-form
sentences, given a model whose universe is the set of all constant names
from the given sentences, and given a sentence from the given set that the
given model does not satisfy, finds a quantifier-free sentence from the
given set that the given model does not satisfy.

Parameters:
    sentences: universally and existentially closed set of
        prenex-normal-form sentences, which is only to be accessed using
        containment queries, i.e., using the ``in`` operator as in:

        >>> if sentence in sentences:
        ...     print('contained!')

    model: model for all element names from the given sentences, whose
        universe is `get_constants(sentences)`.
    unsatisfied: sentence (which possibly contains quantifiers) from the
        given sentences that is not satisfied by the given model.

Returns:
    A quantifier-free sentence from the given set of sentences that is not
    satisfied by the given model.
"""
# We assume that every formula in sentences is in prenex normal form and has
# no free variable names, that sentences is universally and existentially
# closed, and that the set of constant names that appear somewhere in
# sentences is model.universe; but we cannot assert these since we cannot
# iterate over sentences.
for constant in model.universe:
    assert is_constant(constant)
assert is_in_prenex_normal_form(unsatisfied)
assert len(unsatisfied.free_variables()) == 0
assert unsatisfied in sentences
assert not model.evaluate_formula(unsatisfied)
# Task 12.2
```

Hint: Use recursion to "peel off" one quantifier at a time (replacing the quantified variable name with some constant name) while maintaining that the resulting sentence is in the given set of sentences and is unsatisfied by the given model. Use the fact that the given set of sentences is universally and existentially closed to guide your implementation and ensure its correctness.

Your solution to Task 2 and the reasoning behind it essentially prove the following lemma (in particular, the reasoning behind your code does not hinge in any way on the finiteness of the set of sentences or constant names[5]).

LEMMA 12.2   *Let S be a (possibly infinite) universally and existentially closed set of sentences in prenex normal form. If S is not satisfied by some model M, then there exists a quantifier-free sentence in S that is not satisfied by M.*

---

[5] While you do iterate over the set of constant names in your solution, you do so only to find a constant name that when substituted into a given sentence yields a sentence that does not hold in the model. The existence of such a constant name is guaranteed by the closure conditions, and this would continue to hold even if the set of constant names were infinite.

So, returning to our proof outline from before Task 2, we now have a quantifier-free sentence that is not satisfied by the model that we created using the primitive closure condition of S. We will notice that this quantifier-free sentences is composed, using logical operators, of only primitive sentences. Generally speaking, the formulas in our language are of course composed of relation invocations and equalities, with operators and quantifications applied to them to create compound formulas. However, having assumed away equalities for the analysis of this chapter, we have that all formulas are composed, using operators and quantifications, solely of relation invocations; and specifically that all quantifier-free sentences are composed, using only operators, of relation invocations applied solely to constant names (since we have assumed away function names, and since any variable name would be free, making the quantifier-free "sentence" in fact not a sentence). In other words, all quantifier-free sentences are composed, using only logical operators, of what we called, exactly for this reason, **primitive** sentences.

To complete our proof we will prove momentarily, as you will demonstrate in the next task, that the quantifier-free sentence from S that is not satisfied by the model that we created (using the primitive closure condition of S) must tautologically contradict the sentences in S that correspond to the primitive sentences from which this quantifier-free sentence is composed, and therefore S is inconsistent.

TASK 3   Implement the missing code for the function `model_or_inconsistency(sentences)`, which either returns a model of the given closed (finite) set of sentences in prenex normal form (if such a model exists), or returns a proof of a contradiction from these sentences (as well as our axioms) as assumptions.

```
                          ┌─ predicates/completeness.py ─┐
def get_primitives(quantifier_free: Formula) -> Set[Formula]:
    """Finds all primitive subformulas of the given quantifier-free formula.

    Parameters:
        quantifier_free: quantifier-free formula that contains no function names
            and no equalities, whose subformulas are to be searched.

    Returns:
        The primitive subformulas (i.e., relation invocations) of which the
        given quantifier-free formula is composed using logical operators.

    Examples:
        The primitive subformulas of '(R(c1,d)|~(Q(c1)->~R(c2,a)))' are
        'R(c1,d)', 'Q(c1)', and 'R(c2,a)'.
    """
    assert is_quantifier_free(quantifier_free)
    assert len(quantifier_free.functions()) == 0
    assert '=' not in str(quantifier_free)
    # Task 12.3a

def model_or_inconsistency(sentences: AbstractSet[Formula]) -> \
        Union[Model[str], Proof]:
    """Either finds a model in which the given closed set of prenex-normal-form
    sentences holds, or proves a contradiction from these sentences.
```

```
    Parameters:
        sentences: closed set of prenex-normal-form sentences that contain no
            function names and no equalities, to either find a model of, or
            prove a contradiction from.

    Returns:
        A model in which all of the given sentences hold if such exists,
        otherwise a valid proof of  a contradiction from the given formulas via
        `Prover.AXIOMS`.
    """
    assert is_closed(sentences)
    for sentence in sentences:
        assert len(formula.functions()) == 0
        assert '=' not in str(sentence)
    # Task 12.3b
```

Guidelines: First construct the model with `get_constants(sentences)` as its universe and with relation interpretations according to the primitive (and negation-of-primitive) sentences in `sentences` (ignoring any sentence in `sentences` that is not a primitive sentence or its negation while constructing this model). If this model satisfies `sentences`, then you are done. Otherwise, find some sentence from `sentences` that this model does not satisfy, and use Task 2 to consequently find a quantifier-free sentence from `sentences` that this model does not satisfy. Then, tautologically prove a contradiction from (1) this quantifier-free sentence, (2) the primitive sentences in `sentences` that appear in this quantifier-free sentence, and (3) the negation-of-primitive sentences in `sentences` whose primitive negation appears in this quantifier-free sentence. For the last part (proving a contradiction), first implement the missing code for the recursive function `get_primitives(quantifier_free)` (see the function *docstring* for details), and then use that function to complete your solution of this task.

Your solution to Task 3 demonstrates the lemma (12.1) on completeness for closed sets stated in the beginning of this section. We do not consider your solution to programmatically prove this lemma, though, as the implementation of your solution most probably does not explain *why* a key step of this solution works. Specifically, the last key remaining step in the proof of the lemma (12.1) on completeness for closed sets, that of deriving a contradiction from the quantifier-free sentence that you found in Task 2, is not necessarily *explained* by your implementation. If you followed our guidelines above, then your implementation states that a contradiction is a tautological implication of this quantifier-free sentence, as well as its primitive components – or their negations – that are in S. Otherwise, you may have done something slightly different but essentially the same such as stating that the negation of the conjunction of this quantifier-free sentence and its primitive components – or their negations – that are in S, is a tautology, and as such simply listed that as a line in the proof of the contradiction. Either way, we will now explicitly, mathematically, prove that a contradiction can in fact be derived as needed.

LEMMA 12.3 *Let ϕ be a quantifier-free sentence, let $p_1, \ldots, p_n$ be its primitive subformulas, and let S be a set of formulas that for every $i = 1, \ldots, n$ contains either the primitive sentence p_i or its negation '$\sim p_i$'. Denote by S' the set of these primitive or negated-primitive sentences that are in S. If ϕ evaluates to False in some model of S', then $S' \cup \{\phi\}$ is inconsistent.*

Proof   Fix a model M of S' in which ϕ does not hold. By definition, M must give the value *True* to every primitive sentence $p_i \in S'$ and must give the value *False* to every primitive sentence $p_i \notin S'$, since in the latter case we have that '$\sim p_i$' $\in S'$. Let ψ be the conjunction (i.e., concatenation using '&' operators) of all sentences in S', i.e., the conjunction of all the p_i sentences/their negations, as each appears in S'. By the semantic definition of evaluating conjunctions, there is a single possible truth-value assignment to all the p_i sentences that makes ψ evaluate to *True*, and this naturally is precisely the above-described truth-value assignment to the p_i sentences by our model M.

We claim that '$(\psi \to \sim \phi)$' is a tautology. To see this, we will view ϕ as a propositional formula over the p_i sentences (to be completely formally, we would have had to phrase the discussion that follows in terms of the propositional skeleton of ϕ). Since ϕ is quantifier-free and $p_1, ..., p_n$ are *all* of its primitive subformulas, ϕ indeed is a propositional formula over the p_i sentences, that is, it is composed of the p_i sentences using only logical operators. Therefore, the truth value of ϕ in any model is completely determined by the truth values of the p_i sentences in that model, and therefore the truth value of '$(\psi \to \sim \phi)$' in any model is also completely determined by the truth values of the p_i sentences in that model. In order to show that '$(\psi \to \sim \phi)$' is a tautology it therefore suffices to show that any truth-value assignment to the p_i sentences satisfies '$(\psi \to \sim \phi)$'. Since, as already noted, there is a single truth-value assignment to the p_i sentences that satisfies ψ, we only need to show that this assignment also satisfies '$\sim \phi$', but this exactly is the meaning of our assumption that ϕ gets value *False* in the model M (which we have argued to correspond to the unique assignment that makes ψ evaluate to *True*).

We can now obtain a proof of a contradiction from $S' \cup \{\phi\}$ by first proving ψ from all of its primitive subformulas/their negations (that are all in S'), and then applying MP to the tautology '$(\psi \to \sim \phi)$' to deduce '$\sim \phi$'. Together with ϕ we thus prove the contradiction '$(\phi \& \sim \phi)$'. (Or, concisely as you have probably done in your code, since ψ is a tautological implication of its primitive subformulas/their negations that are in S', and since MP is also tautological, simply derive '$(\phi \& \sim \phi)$', or any other contradiction, as a tautological implication of ϕ as well as all of its primitive subformulas/their negations that are in S'.)

$\square$

Note that the proof of Lemma 12.3 uses the fact that we have *every* tautology at our disposal when writing a proof. This is in unlike our "usual" usage of tautologies in proofs so far, which was limited to *specific* "nice" or "simple" tautologies that do save some clutter in our proofs but each of which we could have manually proved separately had we wanted to. The fact that we have *every* tautology at our disposal, as really is required in the proof of the above Lemma 12.3, even if we are not allowed to use tautology lines (as long as we can use the schema equivalents of our propositional axiomatic system instead), is due to the tautology theorem (6.1/9.2) that your work in Part I of this book proved. This is a key place on the way to proving the completeness theorem (12.1) for predicate logic, where the tautology theorem (6.1/9.2) is used.

12.2   Closing a Set

With the lemma (12.1) on completeness for closed sets in hand, to deduce the completeness theorem (12.1) it is enough to show that every set of sentences in prenex normal form can be "closed" (i.e., can have sentences added to it to obtain a closed set of sentences in prenex normal form) without losing consistency (i.e., so that if the original set is consistent, then so is the closed set), since then we will be able to first "close" this set and then "read off" a model (or generate a contradiction, if the "original" set of sentences was not consistent to begin with) as in Task 3. It is therefore enough to prove the following lemma.

LEMMA 12.4 (Consistency-Preserving Closure)   *For every (possibly infinite) consistent set of sentences in prenex normal form S, there exists a closed consistent superset of sentences in prenex normal form $\bar{S} \supseteq S$.*

The high-level idea of "closing" S is to iteratively add more and more sentences that help satisfy one of the three closure conditions, in a way that does not lose consistency. In the following sequence of tasks you will indeed show that given any nonclosed set of sentences, it is always possible to add to this set an additional sentence that satisfies an additional closure condition, and, crucially, to do this without losing consistency. In the end of this section, we will discuss how to combine your solutions to these various tasks to "close" a set S. This last step will be somewhat involved, and in fact as we will see, for more than one reason we will have no choice but to carry out parts of the proof of this last step mathematically rather than programmatically.

12.2.1 Primitive Closure

We start addressing the three closure conditions by showing how to satisfy a primitive closure condition. We would like to show that for any primitive sentence ϕ, we can add either ϕ or its negation '$\sim\phi$' to our consistent set of sentences S without losing consistency. We will actually show more generally that if S is consistent, then for every arbitrary (not necessarily primitive) sentence ϕ, we can add either ϕ or its negation '$\sim\phi$' to S without losing consistency. It is not programmatically easy to figure out which of these can be added without losing consistency, but in the next task you will nonetheless programmatically prove that one of these is possible, by showing that if both $S \cup \{\phi\}$ is inconsistent and $S \cup \{'\sim\phi'\}$ is inconsistent, then S was already inconsistent to begin with.

TASK 4   Implement the missing code for the function combine_contradictions(proof_from_affirmation, proof_from_negation). This function takes as input two proofs of contradictions, both from *almost* the same set of assumption/axiom sentences, with the only difference between the assumptions of the two proofs being that each has an extra simple assumption (with no templates), with the extra assumption of proof_from_negation being the negation of the extra assumption of proof_from_affirmation. The function returns a proof of a contradiction from the assumptions/axioms that are common to both proofs.

```
                        predicates/completeness.py
def combine_contradictions(proof_from_affirmation: Proof,
                           proof_from_negation: Proof) -> Proof:
    """Combines the given two proofs of contradictions, both from the same
    assumptions/axioms except that the latter has an extra assumption that is
    the negation of an extra assumption that the former has, into a single proof
    of a contradiction from only the common assumptions/axioms.
```

```
    Parameters:
        proof_from_affirmation: valid proof of a contradiction from one or more
            assumptions/axioms that are all sentences and that include
            `Prover.AXIOMS`.
        proof_from_negation: valid proof of a contradiction from the same
            assumptions/axioms of `proof_from_affirmation`, but with one
            simple assumption (i.e., without any templates) `assumption`
            replaced with its negation '~`assumption`'.

    Returns:
        A valid proof of a contradiction from only the assumptions/axioms common
        to the given proofs (i.e., without `assumption` or its negation).
    """
    assert proof_from_affirmation.is_valid()
    assert proof_from_negation.is_valid()
    common_assumptions = proof_from_affirmation.assumptions.intersection(
        proof_from_negation.assumptions)
    assert len(common_assumptions) == \
            len(proof_from_affirmation.assumptions) - 1
    assert len(common_assumptions) == len(proof_from_negation.assumptions) - 1
    affirmed_assumption = list(proof_from_affirmation.assumptions -
                                common_assumptions)[0]
    negated_assumption = list(proof_from_negation.assumptions -
                                common_assumptions)[0]
    assert len(affirmed_assumption.templates) == 0
    assert len(negated_assumption.templates) == 0
    assert negated_assumption.formula == \
            Formula('~', affirmed_assumption.formula)
    assert proof_from_affirmation.assumptions.issuperset(Prover.AXIOMS)
    assert proof_from_negation.assumptions.issuperset(Prover.AXIOMS)
    for assumption in common_assumptions.union({affirmed_assumption,
                                                negated_assumption}):
        assert len(assumption.formula.free_variables()) == 0
    # Task 12.4
```

Hint: One possible approach is to start by applying the function `proof_by_way_of_contradiction()` to each of the given proofs.[6]

Your solution to Task 4 proves the following lemma.

LEMMA 12.5   *Let S be a (possibly infinite) consistent set of sentences. For every sentence ϕ, either $S \cup \{\phi\}$ is consistent or $S \cup \{`\sim \phi`\}$ is consistent (or both).*

Notice that while Task 4 applies to any sentence ϕ, to get the primitive closure condition we only need to apply it to primitive sentences of the form '$R(c_1, \ldots, c_n)$' where R is one of the relation names that appear in S and n is the arity of R, and each c_i is a constant name that appears somewhere in S. So, to "primitively close" a finite S, since there are only finitely many such primitive sentences that contain relation names and constant names from S, we could simply go over all of them one by one, adding each of them or its negation (whichever does not violate consistency at that point) until we reach a state in which for each sentence

---

[6] While this approach results in an implementation that is conceptually not dissimilar from your implementation of `reduce_assumption()` from Chapter 6, and while the functionalities of these two functions are not dissimilar and each of them crucially relies on a respective deduction theorem, we note that each of these two functions plays a decidedly different role in the proof of the completeness theorem that corresponds to it.

of this form, either it or its negation is in S, i.e., a state in which S is primitively closed. As already noted, it is not programmatically easy to figure out which of these two sentences (the primitive or its negation) can be added without losing consistency,[7] so we will not program this step of the construction, but will rather make do for the mathematical proof ahead with the knowledge that one of these can indeed be done, as you have proved in Task 4.

12.2.2 Universal Closure

The next two tasks deal with satisfying a universal closure condition. We would like to show that for any universal sentence '$\forall x[\phi(x)]$' that our consistent set of sentences S contains, we can add to S any universal instantiation '$\phi(c)$' of it, for any constant name c, without losing consistency. To prove this, we will show that if the enlarged set is inconsistent, then S was already inconsistent to begin with.

TASK 5   Implement the missing code for the function `eliminate_universal_instantiation_assumption(proof, universal, constant)`. This function takes as input a proof of a contradiction from a set of assumption/axiom sentences, a sentence `universal` that is an assumption of the given proof of the form '$\forall x[\phi(x)]$' for some variable name x, and a constant name `constant` such that another assumption of the given proof is the universal instantiation '$\phi(\text{constant})$' of `universal` with this constant name. The function returns a proof of a contradiction from the same assumptions/axioms except the universal instantiation '$\phi(\text{constant})$'.

```
predicates/completeness.py

def eliminate_universal_instantiation_assumption(proof: Proof,
                                                 universal: Formula,
                                                 constant: str) -> Proof:
    """Converts the given proof of a contradiction, whose assumptions/axioms
    include `universal` and `instantiation`, where the latter is the universal
    instantiation of the former with the constant name `constant`, to a proof
    of a contradiction from the same assumptions without `instantiation`.

    Parameters:
        proof: valid proof of a contradiction from one or more
            assumptions/axioms that are all sentences and that include
            `Prover.AXIOMS`.
        universal: assumption of the given proof that is universally quantified.
        constant: constant name such that the formula `instantiation` obtained
            from the statement quantified by `universal` by replacing all free
            occurrences of the universal quantification variable name by the
            given constant name, is an assumption of the given proof.

    Returns:
        A valid proof of a contradiction from the assumptions/axioms of the
        given proof except `instantiation`.
    """
    assert proof.is_valid()
    assert Schema(universal) in proof.assumptions
```

---

[7] If it were easy, then we would not have any conjectures since we would immediately know for each sentence whether or not it contradicts our axioms, and so all mathematicians would be out of a job...

```
    assert universal.root == 'A'
    assert is_constant(constant)
    assert Schema(universal.statement.substitute({universal.variable:
                                                  Term(constant)})) in \
            proof.assumptions
    for assumption in proof.assumptions:
        assert len(assumption.formula.free_variables()) == 0
    # Task 12.5
```

Hint: Once again, one possible approach is to start by applying the function `proof_by_way_of_contradiction()` to the given proof.

Your solution to Task 5 proves the following lemma.

LEMMA 12.6   *Let S be a (possibly infinite) consistent set of sentences. For every universally quantified sentence '$\forall x[\phi(x)]$' $\in$ S and every constant name c, we have that $S \cup \{'\phi(c)'\}$ is consistent.*

So, to "universally close" a finite S, for each universal sentence in S we could go ahead and start by adding to S, without losing consistency, all of the universal instantiations of this sentence with respect to all constant names that appear somewhere in S. This, however, would not guarantee that the enlarged S is universally closed, since some of the added instantiations may themselves be universally quantified. For example, if we start with '$\forall x[\forall y[R(x,y,a,b)]]$', then the set after adding all of the universal instantiations of '$\forall x[\forall y[R(x,y,a,b)]]$' will be $\{'\forall x[\forall y[R(x,y,a,b)]]', '\forall y[R(a,y,a,b)]', '\forall y[R(b,y,a,b)]'\}$, which is not universally closed since it is missing universal instantiations of the two added sentences '$\forall y[R(a,y,a,b)]$' and '$\forall y[R(b,y,a,b)]$'. So, we would have to repeat this process to add all of their universal instantiations and so on, until we would reach a state in which S is universally closed. Fortunately, this would only take a finite number of repetitions, which equals the maximum number of universal quantifications at the top level of a single formula in the original S (since in each repetition, a newly added universal instantiation has one fewer quantifier than the universal sentence from the previous repetition that it instantiates). In the next task you will perform one round of this process.

TASK 6   Implement the missing code for the function `universal_closure_step(sentences)`, which returns a superset of the given (finite) set of sentences in prenex normal form, that additionally contains, for every universally quantified sentence '$\forall x[\phi(x)]$' in the given set, all of the universal instantiations of this sentence with respect to every constant name that appears somewhere in the given sentences.

predicates/completeness.py

```
def universal_closure_step(sentences: AbstractSet[Formula]) -> Set[Formula]:
    """Augments the given sentences with all universal instantiations of each
    universally quantified sentence from these sentences, with respect to all
    constant names from these sentences.

    Parameters:
        sentences: prenex-normal-form sentences to augment with their universal
            instantiations.
```

```
    Returns:
        A set of all of the given sentences, and in addition any formula that
        can be obtained from the statement quantified by any universally
        quantified sentence from the given sentences by replacing all
        occurrences of the quantification variable name with some constant name
        from the given sentences.
    """
    for sentence in sentences:
        assert is_in_prenex_normal_form(sentence) and \
            len(sentence.free_variables()) == 0
    # Task 12.6
```

Example: If we call this function with a set containing only the sentence '∀x[∀y[R(x,y,a,b)]]', then the returned set will contain, in addition to the original sentence, also the two sentences '∀y[R(a,y,a,b)]' and '∀y[R(b,y,a,b)]', and if we call this function again on this returned set, then the new returned set will contain, in addition to these three sentences, also the four sentences 'R(a,a,a,b)', 'R(a,b,a,b)', 'R(b,a,a,b)', and 'R(b,b,a,b)' (and if we call this function again on this returned set, then the same set would again be returned).

12.2.3 Existential Closure

Finally, we get to satisfying an existential closure condition. We would like to show that for any existential sentence '∃x[φ(x)]' that our consistent set of sentences S contains, we can add to S an existential witness of the form 'φ(c)', where c is a new (not previously in S) "witnessing" constant name,[8] without losing consistency. Similarly to Task 5, to prove this we will show that if the enlarged set is inconsistent, then S (which does not use this new witnessing constant name at all) was already inconsistent to begin with. To do so, given the proof of a contradiction from all of the sentences including the added existential witness 'φ(c)', you will start with an intermediate step that replaces all of the occurrences of this new witnessing constant name c, in this proof and in all of its assumptions, with a new variable name. So, for example, if this new variable name is 'zz', then the assumption 'φ(c)' becomes 'φ(zz)' after the replacement (both as an assumption and as the formula of any lines in which this assumption is instantiated). As it turns out, the validity of the proof is actually maintained following this replacement: The propositional skeletons of line formulas do not change, so tautologies remain tautologies (and for the same reason, the conclusion of the proof remains a contradiction); any MP application remains valid since the same replacements are made in all three formulas involved; any UG application remains valid since variable names remain variable names and the same replacements are made in both formulas involved; and finally, any formula justified by an assumption/axiom remains a legal instance since we perform the replacement also in the assumption/axiom and in any instantiation map, and since there are no quantifications anywhere over the new variable name, so no instance of it can become illegally bound during any instantiation. Given the

---

[8] Such a witnessing constant name is often called a "Henkin" constant name, after the Jewish-American logician Leon Henkin. While the completeness theorem (12.1) was first proven by the Austrian (and later American) logician Kurt Gödel, after whom it is customarily named **Gödel's completeness theorem**, the simpler strategy for proving this theorem that has become standard in mathematical logic courses, and which we also follow, is due to Henkin.

proof that results from this replacement, you will then show that a contradiction can be proven from the assumptions of this proof even without the assumption '$\phi(zz)$' (which in this proof replaced the existential witness assumption '$\phi(c)$' of the original proof). In other words (since the witnessing constant name is a new constant name that does not appear in any assumption of the original proof other than '$\phi(c)$'), a contradiction can be proven from the assumptions of the original proof even without the existential witness '$\phi(c)$', which is what we set out to show.

TASK 7

a. Implement the missing code for the function `replace_constant(proof, constant, variable)`, which takes a proof, a constant name that (potentially) appears in the assumptions of the proof and/or in the proof itself, and a variable name that does not appear anywhere in the proof or in the assumptions, and returns a "similar" (and still valid) proof where every occurrence of the given constant name in the assumptions and in the proof is replaced with the given variable name.

```
                         predicates/completeness.py
def replace_constant(proof: Proof, constant: str, variable: str = 'zz') -> \
        Proof:
    """Replaces all occurrences of the given constant name in the given proof
    with the given variable name.

    Parameters:
        proof: valid proof in which to replace.
        constant: constant name that does not appear as a template constant name
            in any of the assumptions of the given proof.
        variable: variable name that does not appear anywhere in the given proof
            or in its assumptions.

    Returns:
        A valid proof where every occurrence of the given constant name in the
        given proof and in its assumptions is replaced with the given variable
        name.
    """
    assert proof.is_valid()
    assert is_constant(constant)
    assert is_variable(variable)
    for assumption in proof.assumptions:
        assert constant not in assumption.templates
        assert variable not in assumption.formula.variables()
    for line in proof.lines:
        assert variable not in line.formula.variables()
    # Task 12.7a
```

Hint: The `substitute()` methods of the classes `Formula` and `Term` may be useful here.

b. Implement the missing code for the function `eliminate_existential_witness_assumption(proof, existential, constant)`. This function takes as input a proof of a contradiction from a set of assumption/axiom sentences, a sentence `existential` that is an assumption of the given proof of the form '$\exists x[\phi(x)]$' for some variable name x, and a constant name `constant` such that another assumption of the given proof is the existential witness '$\phi(\texttt{constant})$' of `existential` with this (witnessing) constant name and such that this constant name does not appear anywhere else in the assumptions/axioms. The function returns a proof of a contradiction from the same assumptions/axioms except the existential witness '$\phi(\texttt{constant})$'.

predicates/completeness.py

```
def eliminate_existential_witness_assumption(proof: Proof,
                                             existential: Formula,
                                             constant: str) -> Proof:
    """Converts the given proof of a contradiction, whose assumptions/axioms
    include `existential` and `witness`, where the latter is the existential
    witness of the former with the witnessing constant name `constant`, to a
    proof of a contradiction from the same assumptions without `witness`.

    Parameters:
        proof: valid proof, which does not contain the variable name 'zz' in its
            lines or assumptions, of a contradiction from one or more
            assumptions/axioms that are all sentences and that include
            `Prover.AXIOMS`.
        existential: assumption of the given proof that is existentially
            quantified.
        constant: constant name such that the formula `witness` obtained from
            from the statement quantified by `existential` by replacing all free
            occurrences of the existential quantification variable name by the
            given constant name, is an assumption of the given proof, and such
            that this constant name does not appear in any assumption of the
            given proof except `witness`.

    Returns:
        A valid proof of a contradiction from the assumptions/axioms of the
        given proof except `witness`.
    """
    assert proof.is_valid()
    assert Schema(existential) in proof.assumptions
    assert existential.root == 'E'
    assert is_constant(constant)
    witness = existential.statement.substitute({existential.variable:
                                                Term(constant)})
    assert Schema(witness) in proof.assumptions
    for assumption in proof.assumptions:
        assert len(assumption.formula.free_variables()) == 0
        assert 'zz' not in assumption.formula.variables()
    for assumption in proof.assumptions - {Schema(witness)}:
        assert constant not in assumption.formula.constants()
    for line in proof.lines:
        assert 'zz' not in line.formula.variables()
    # Task 12.7b
```

Guidelines: In the given proof, replace the given constant name with the new variable name 'zz' that you may assume does not appear anywhere in the original proof, use `proof_by_way_of_contradiction()` to prove '$\sim\phi(zz)$' from the assumptions without `witness`, and finally prove a contradiction from this and from '$\exists x[\phi(x)]$'.

Your solution to Task 7 (along with the preceding reasoning of why the replacement in the first part of that task maintains the validity of the proof) proves the following lemma.

LEMMA 12.7 *Let S be a (possibly infinite) consistent set of sentences. For every existentially quantified sentence '$\exists x[\phi(x)]$' $\in$ S and new constant name c that does not appear anywhere in S, we have that $S \cup \{`\phi(c)'\}$ is consistent.*

So, to "existentially close" a finite S, for each existential sentence in S we could go ahead and start by adding to S, without losing consistency, an existential witness for this sentence using a new witnessing constant name that does not appear anywhere in S. Once again, since some of the added existential witnesses may themselves be existentially quantified (and so each of these would itself require an existential witness for the set to be existentially closed), we may need to repeat this process a finite number of times (which equals the maximum number of existential quantifications at the top level of a single formula in the original S) until we reach a state in which S is existentially closed. Analogously to Task 6, in the next task you will perform one round of this process.

TASK 8 Implement the missing code for the function `existential_closure_step(sentences)`, which returns a superset of the given (finite) set of sentences in prenex normal form, that additionally contains, for every existentially quantified sentence '$\exists x[\phi(x)]$' in the given set, an existential witness for this sentence with a new witnessing constant name that does not appear anywhere in S, if a witness for this sentence is not already contained in the given sentences.

```
                        ┌─────────────────────────────┐
                        │ predicates/completeness.py  │
┌───────────────────────┴─────────────────────────────┴───────────────────────┐
def existential_closure_step(sentences: AbstractSet[Formula]) -> Set[Formula]:
    """Augments the given sentences with an existential witness that uses a new
    constant name, for each existentially quantified sentence from these
    sentences for which an existential witness is missing.

    Parameters:
        sentences: prenex-normal-form sentences to augment with any missing
            existential witnesses.

    Returns:
        A set of all of the given sentences, and in addition for every
        existentially quantified sentence from the given sentences, a formula
        obtained from the statement quantified by that sentence by replacing all
        occurrences of the quantification variable name with a new constant name
        obtained by calling `next(fresh_constant_name_generator)`.
    """
    for sentence in sentences:
        assert is_in_prenex_normal_form(sentence) and \
               len(sentence.free_variables()) == 0
    # Task 12.8
```

Guidelines: Use `next(fresh_constant_name_generator)` (imported for you from `logic_utils.py`) to generate new constant names. You may assume that the given set of sentences does not contain constant names that you have generated this way.

Hint: The `substitute()` method of class `Formula` may be useful both for checking if an existential witness for a given sentence already exists, and for creating such a witness if one does not already exist.

Example: If we call this function with a set containing only the sentence '$\exists x[\exists y[R(x,y)]]$', then the returned set will contain, in addition to the original sentence, also the sentence

'∃y[R(e1,y)]', where 'e1' stands here for a constant name returned by calling `next(`
`fresh_constant_name_generator)`, and if we call this function again on this returned
set, then the new returned set will contain, in addition to these two sentences, also the
sentence 'R(e1,e2)', where 'e2' stands here for an additional constant name returned by
calling `next(fresh_constant_name_generator)` (and if we call this function again on
this returned set, then the same set would again be returned).

12.2.4 "Combined" Closure

Let us recap our proposed strategy for proving the completeness theorem (12.1) for predicate logic: Given a finite set of formulas F, we can convert each formula in F into a sentence
in prenex normal form to obtain an equivalent set S. Now, given this finite S, we can first add
each primitive sentence (composed of a relation name that is used in S and constant names
that appear somewhere in S) or its negation to S so that S becomes primitively closed. While
for a given primitive sentence it is hard to determine whether it or its negation should be
added to S without losing consistency (i.e,. so that if S were consistent before the addition,
it would remain consistent), which is why we have not programmed this step, you have
shown in Task 4 that one of the two can be added without losing consistency. Once S is
primitively closed, we can then add to S all universal instantiations with respect to constant
names that appear anywhere in S of all universal sentences from S, as in Task 6, and repeat
this process finitely many times until S becomes universally closed. (You have shown in
Task 5 that consistency is not lost while doing so.) Once S is primitively and universally
closed, we can then add to S existential witnesses for all existential sentences in S as in
Task 8, and repeat this process finitely many times until S is existentially closed. (You have
shown in Task 7 that consistency is not lost while doing so.) So – have we arrived at a
set S that is closed with respect to C? Unfortunately, while the resulting set S is indeed
existentially closed, it may no longer necessarily still be primitively or universally closed,
for two reasons. The first reason, which is easy to fix, is that existentially closing S may
have added universal sentences to it that are missing instantiations in S – this can be easily
fixed by repeatedly alternating between running your solutions of Tasks 6 and 8, so that
sentences that start with sequences of alternating quantifications are properly dealt with.
The second, more major reason, is that since in the last step (existentially closing S) we
have added more constant names to S, we have thus changed the primitive- and universal-
closure conditions, as these require that S contain primitive sentences or their negations,
and universal instantiations, that are constructed using any constant names that appear
somewhere in S. The natural tendency is to keep iterating and alternate between primitively,
universally, and existentially closing S, hoping that a closed S will eventually be reached.
If a closed S is indeed reached, then as you have shown in Task 3, we can either:

- "read off" a model of S, which is therefore also a model of the "original" S (since the
  latter is a subset of the "new" S), and is therefore also a model of F since you have
  shown in Chapter 11 that the prenex normal form of any formula implies that formula
  (and since the sentence corresponding to a formula implies that formula via UI), and so
  by the soundness theorem (9.1), any model of the prenex-normal-form sentence is also
  a model of the original formula.
  —or—

- prove a contradiction from S and from our six logical axiom schemas, in which case due to Tasks 4, 5, and 7, we can prove a contradiction from the "original" S, in which case we can prove a contradiction from F and from our six logical axiom schemas since you have shown in Chapter 11 that the prenex normal form of any formula is provable from that formula and from our six (or equivalently twenty-two) logical axiom schemas (and since the sentence corresponding to a formula is provable from that formula via UG),[9] so F is inconsistent.

Recall that all of this can be done if we indeed eventually reach a closed S. However, as it turns out, reaching a closed S may fail to happen within any finite number of steps. Consider, for example, the consistent set S containing only the sentences '$\forall y[\exists x[GT(x,y)]]$' and 'SAME(0,0)'. Since the constant name '0' appears in this set of sentences, in order to universally close S our construction adds an existential sentence '$\exists x[GT(x,0)]$'. Now, to existentially close S we need to add an existential witness for this sentence, say, 'GT(e1,0)'. Once we have added this existential witness, 'e1' appears in S, so in order to universally close S again, we need to "go back" and add the sentence '$\exists x[GT(x,e1)]$' to S, which in turn requires adding a new existential witness 'GT(e2,e1)' to S, which in turn requires adding the sentence '$\exists x[GT(x,e2)]$' to S, which in turn requires adding a new existential witness 'GT(e3,e2)' to S, and so on. (And of course, for any pair of two constant names 'ei' and 'ej' added this way, we would also need to add either 'GT(ei,ej)' or its negation – whichever does not make S lose consistency, or whichever we want if neither does – to get primitive closure, etc.) In fact, if we happened to start with a few more sentences that force 'GT' to be a **strict total order** (and in particular, transitive: '$\forall x[\forall y[\forall z[((GT(x,y)\&GT(y,z))\rightarrow GT(x,z))]]]$' and antisymmetric: '$\forall x[\forall y[(GT(x,y)\rightarrow \sim GT(y,x))]]$'), then no finite model can satisfy these as well as '$\forall y[\exists x[GT(x,y)]]$' and 'SAME(0,0)'.[10] So, indeed it is not possible to stop after any finite number of steps of any kind, regardless of their order, as otherwise we would reach a closed S with a finite number of constant names, which would imply the existence of a finite model for the consistent set of sentences (including transitivity and antisymmetry) with which we started, while as we explained such a model cannot exist. Programmatically, we will thus not be able to close our set of sentences. Luckily, as we will now see, mathematically we may continue alternating between our three different step types "to infinity" and obtain a closed set. Then we will be able to complete the proof of the completeness theorem (12.1) exactly as you have done in Task 3 and as just detailed: by either "reading off" a model of S from this closed set, which is also a model of F, or proving a contradiction from S, which can be transformed via Tasks 4, 5, and 7, and via your solution of Chapter 11, to a proof of a contradiction from F.

---

[9] And as you have shown in Chapter 9, by Part I of this book this may even be proven without tautology lines, with the schema equivalents of our propositional axiomatic system instead.

[10] Intuitively, if we interpret 'GT(x,y)' as $x > y$, then '$\forall y[\exists x[GT(x,y)]]$' implies that for every element there exists an even-greater element, and 'GT' being a strict total order means, loosely speaking, that no "cycles" of any length (such as $0 > e2 > e1 > 0$ or even $0 > 0$) are allowed. So, to satisfy all of these, an infinite chain $0 < e1 < e2 < \cdots$ is required.

Proof of the Lemma (12.4) on Consistency-Preserving Closure We start with a consistent set S of sentences in prenex normal form that we enumerate[11] as $S = \{s_1, s_2, s_3, \ldots\}$. We will assume that we have access to an infinite reservoir of constant names (say, those generated by `next(fresh_constant_name_generator)`) that do not appear in S. We will build a sequence of finite sets $S_0 \subseteq S_1 \subseteq S_2 \subseteq \cdots$ (therefore only finitely many constant names and relation names appear in each) such that $S \cup S_i$ is consistent for every i, and such that each S_i (1) contains $s_1, \ldots, s_i$, (2) contains either '$R(c_1, \ldots, c_n)$' or '$\sim R(c_1, \ldots, c_n)$' for every relation name R that appears somewhere in S_{i-1} and every tuple of constant names $(c_1, \ldots, c_n)$ where n is the arity of R and each c_j appears somewhere in S_{i-1}, (3) contains all universal instantiations via constant names that appear somewhere in S_{i-1} of every universal formula in S_{i-1}, and (4) contains an existential witness for every existential formula in S_{i-1}.

As the basis of our construction, we set $S_0 = \emptyset$. At step i, we start with $S_i = S_{i-1}$, and augment it as follows:

1. Add s_i to S_i. (This does not change $S \cup S_i$, so its consistency is maintained.)
2. Sequentially iterating over all (finitely many) relation names R that appear somewhere in S_{i-1} and (finitely many) tuples of constant names $(c_1, \ldots, c_n)$ where n is the arity of R and each c_j appears somewhere in S_{i-1}, we in turn add either '$R(c_1, \ldots, c_n)$' or its negation '$\sim R(c_1, \ldots, c_n)$' to S_i, so that $S \cup S_i$ remains consistent at each point (one of these must maintain consistency by the lemma (12.5) that corresponds to Task 4).
3. As you have implemented in Task 6, for every universally quantified sentence '$\forall x[\phi(x)]$' $\in S_{i-1}$ and every constant name c that appears somewhere in S_{i-1}, we add the universal instantiation '$\phi(c)$' to S_i (which keeps $S \cup S_i$ consistent by the lemma (12.6) that corresponds to Task 5).
4. As you have implemented in Task 8, for every existentially quantified sentence '$\exists x[\phi(x)]$' $\in S_{i-1}$ for which an existential witness is not yet present in S_{i-1}, we take a fresh constant name c from our reservoir (so c does not appear anywhere in S and was not used previously), and add the existential witness '$\phi(c)$' to S_i (which keeps $S \cup S_i$ consistent by the lemma (12.7) that corresponds to Task 7).

Notice that in each step we only add a finite number of sentences and constant names, and therefore at no step is our reservoir of fresh constant names depleted. Now, let us define $\bar{S} = \bigcup_{i=1}^{\infty} S_i$. First note that $S \subseteq \bar{S}$ since for every i, we have that s_i was added to S_i and so $s_i \in S_i \subseteq \bar{S}$. Second, $\bar{S}$ is consistent: otherwise there would have been a proof of a contradiction from $\bar{S}$, and since this proof would have involved only a finite set of sentences, which would all have thus already been in the same S_i for some (finite) i (since for each k, sentence number k of these finitely many sentences would have been in S_{i_k} for some i_k, and so all of these finitely many sentences would have been in S_i for $i = \max_k S_{i_k}$), this proof would have shown S_i to be inconsistent, contradicting that by

---

[11] By Theorem 7.3, as in propositional logic, by the way in which we defined predicate-logic formulas, there are only countably many of them since they are represented by finite-length strings over a finite alphabet, so we can enumerate them. If we allowed using constant names or relation names from a set of greater infinite cardinality (e.g., constant names like c_α where α is a real number), then the set of all possible formulas would no longer be countable, and therefore we would not be able to enumerate it. A closed consistent superset of S would still exist, though, and could be constructed via analogous core arguments but with some additional supporting arguments that would require some background in set theory.

construction it is consistent. Third, $\bar{S}$ is closed: For primitive closure, take some relation name R that appears in $\bar{S}$ and tuple of constant names $(c_1, \ldots, c_n)$ where n is the arity of R and each c_j appears somewhere in $\bar{S}$, then for some i we already have that the relation name R and all $c_1, \ldots, c_n$ appear in S_i, so either '$R(c_1, \ldots, c_n)$' or its negation is in $S_{i+1} \subseteq \bar{S}$. Similarly for universal closure, take some universally quantified formula '$\forall x[\phi(x)]$' $\in \bar{S}$ and constant name c that appears somewhere in $\bar{S}$, then for some i we already have that '$\forall x[\phi(x)]$' $\in S_i$ and that c appears somewhere in S_i, so the formula '$\phi(c)$' is in $S_{i+1} \subseteq \bar{S}$. Finally, for existential closure take some existentially quantified formula '$\exists x[\phi(x)]$' $\in \bar{S}$, then for some i we already have that '$\exists x[\phi(x)]$' $\in S_i$, so an existential witness $\phi(c)$ for some constant name c exists in $S_{i+1} \subseteq \bar{S}$.   □

12.3   The Completeness Theorem

The lemma (12.4) on consistency-preserving closure and the lemma (12.1) on completeness for closed sets (along with the prenex normal form theorem (11.3), which allows us to restrict our analysis in these lemmas to sentences in prenex normal form) together prove the "hard direction" of the completeness theorem (12.1) for predicate logic. Since, as explained in the beginning of this chapter, the "easy direction" of this theorem follows from the soundness theorem (9.1) for predicate logic, we have thus completed our proof of the completeness theorem for predicate logic:

THEOREM 12.1 (The Completeness Theorem for Predicate Logic: "Consistency" Version) *A (possibly infinite) set of predicate-logic formulas has a model if and only if it is consistent.*

Looking at our proof of the completeness theorem (12.1), and in particular at our proof of the lemma (12.4) on consistency-preserving closure, focusing on the case of (at most) countably infinite sets of sentences, we notice that we have actually proved a somewhat stronger result: that every finite or countably infinite consistent set of formulas has a (at most) countable model. Since by the soundness theorem (9.1) if a set of formulas has a (even uncountable) model then it is consistent, we get the following quite remarkable semantic theorem named after German mathematician Leopold Löwenheim and Norwegian mathematician Thoralf Skolem.

THEOREM 12.2 (The Löwenheim–Skolem Theorem)   *Every finite or countably infinite set of formulas that has a model, also has a (at most) countable model.*

Thus, in predicate logic we cannot express, using countably many formulas/schemas, conditions that require uncountability. This may sound strange since, as mentioned in Chapter 10, all of mathematics can be expressed in predicate logic using the (finitely many) ZFC axiom schemas, and in particular these schemas can be used to prove **Cantor's theorem**, which states that the real numbers (a subset of the universe of any model of ZFC) are uncountable! How is this possible? This riddle is known as "Skolem's paradox." The solution (which was also given by Skolem, and which explains why this is in fact not a paradox) is that while indeed the Löwenheim–Skolem theorem (12.2) ensures a countable model of ZFC, that countability is from the point of view of looking from "our model of ZFC" in which this model was constructed. From the constructed model's point of view, however, this set of "reals of the constructed countable model" is *not* countable! This may happen since countability of a set is defined as the existence of a 1:1 map from that set to the integers. Such a map will not exist as a set in the constructed model, even though it does exist in "our math." (And to make things even more confusing, if from the point of view of that model, you were to create within it an "inner" model of ZFC, then its universe would be countable both from our point of view and from the point of view of the original model, but not from the point of view of the "inner" model, and so forth.)

12.4 The Compactness Theorem and the "Provability" Version of the Completeness Theorem

We will now wish to derive an analogue for predicate logic of the compactness theorem (6.4) for propositional logic.

THEOREM 12.3 (The Compactness Theorem for Predicate Logic) *A set of predicate-logic formulas has a model if and only if every finite subset of it has a model.*

Recall that in Chapter 6, we used the compactness theorem (6.4), together with the completeness theorem (6.3) for finite sets and with the fact that the syntactic notions of proofs and consistency are inherently finite concepts, to prove the general (for possibly infinite sets) completeness theorem (6.5). Since we have already proven the completeness theorem (12.1) for predicate logic for any—even infinite—sets, we can use the reverse order of implication to prove the compactness theorem (12.3) for predicate logic. First we will note that it is still the case that since proofs are by definition finite, any proof uses finitely many assumptions, and so if an infinite set of formulas is inconsistent, then a contradiction can already be proven from finitely many of these assumptions:

LEMMA 12.8 *A set of predicate-logic formulas is consistent if and only if every finite subset of it is consistent.*

We will use the completeness theorem (12.1) for predicate logic together with Lemma 12.8 to prove the compactness theorem (12.3) for predicate logic: A set of predicate-logic formulas has a model if and only if it is consistent (by the completeness theorem (12.1)), which is true if and only if every finite subset of it is consistent (by Lemma 12.8), which is true of and only if every finite subset of it has a model (by the completeness theorem (12.1) once again). That's it! An illustration of this argument, as well as, for comparison, the argument that we used in Chapter 6 to prove the completeness theorem (6.5) from the compactness theorem (6.4), is given in Figure 12.1. As in propositional logic, the compactness theorem (12.3) for predicate logic is also very useful even on its own.

Finally, as in propositional logic, we will want to rephrase the completeness theorem (12.1) also in a way that talks about provability rather than consistency—a way that is analogous to the tautology theorem (6.1) in giving a converse to our original statement of the soundness theorem (9.1) for predicate logic.

THEOREM 12.4 (The Completeness Theorem for Predicate Logic: "Provability" Version) *Let X be the set of our basic six logical axiom schemas. For any set A of predicate-logic*

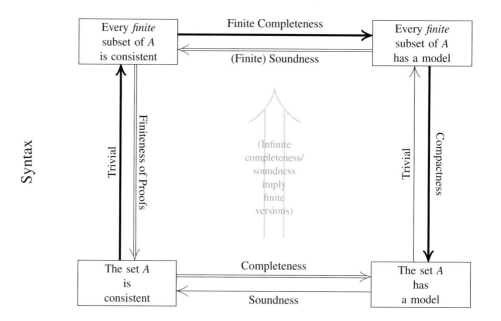

Finite

Figure 12.1 Diagram relating the completeness and compactness theorems in either propositional logic or predicate logic. The **thick** arrows trace our proof of (the "hard direction" of) the completeness theorem (6.5) for propositional logic in Chapter 6 using finite completeness (Theorem 6.3) and compactness (Theorem 6.4). The double arrows trace our proof of (the "hard direction" of) the compactness theorem (12.3) for predicate logic in this chapter using the finiteness of proofs (Lemma 12.8) and completeness (Theorem 12.1).

formulas and any predicate-logic formula ϕ, it is the case that $A \models \phi$ if and only if $A \cup X \vdash \phi$.

Proof   We will first show that the theorem holds when ϕ is a sentence. Since ϕ holds in every model that satisfies A, there is no model of A where '$\sim\phi$' holds, so the set $A \cup \{`\sim\phi'\}$ has no model, and so by the "consistency" version of the completeness theorem (12.1) it is inconsistent, so a contradiction is provable from it and from X. By the theorem (11.2) on soundness of proofs by way of contradiction, which is applicable since ϕ has no free variable names, this means that '$\sim\sim\phi$' is provable from $A \cup X$. Since ϕ is a tautological implication of '$\sim\sim\phi$', we therefore have that ϕ is also provable from $A \cup X$.

  For general ϕ, we first universally quantify over all free variable names in ϕ to obtain a sentence ϕ'. Since ϕ holds in every model that satisfies A, so does ϕ', and so, by the previous argument, ϕ' is provable from $A \cup X$. Since ϕ is provable from ϕ' using UI, we therefore have that ϕ is also provable from $A \cup X$.   □

This version of the completeness theorem (12.4), the crowning achievement of your work throughout this entire book, is, in a sense, justification for the mathematical use of proofs to try and understand what is true in every mathematical structure. Taking A to be the field axioms as in Chapter 10, for instance, this theorem tells us that whatever is true in *every* field can *always* be proven using the field axioms and our six (or equivalently twenty-two) logical axiom schemas. This is quite remarkable: to be fully convinced that a formula holds in every field, instead of (semantically) checking all the infinitely many possible fields, it is always enough to (syntactically) verify the validity of some finite proof! Furthermore, this is true for not only fields, but any possible axiomatically defined mathematical structure, be it a group, a vector space, the set of natural numbers, or even, as already briefly mentioned in Chapter 10, the entirety of modern mathematics using the axiomatization of ZFC (Zermelo–Fraenkel with choice) set theory. Knowing that a proof always exists for any true statement motivates our search for it. Finding the proof (and figuring out what to prove), of course, is an entirely different matter.

13 Sneak Peek at Mathematical Logic II: Gödel's Incompleteness Theorem

The journey toward the formalization of all of mathematics has two legs: (1) understanding the logic by which we formulate proofs and (2) understanding the basic axioms from which said proofs can derive all of the truths of mathematics. In this book we completely figured out the first leg: We have a small number of simple logical axiomatic schemas and inference rules that allow us to syntactically prove anything that follows semantically from any set of axioms!

But what about the other leg, that of choosing the "correct" set of axioms for the whole of mathematics? As we have briefly mentioned in Chapter 10, the "usual" set of axioms accepted by mathematicians is called **ZFC**: Zermelo–Fraenkel set theory with the axiom of choice. All of the "usual" mathematics that you have learned is ultimately proved from these axioms: analysis, algebra, combinatorics, everything in this book, the theory of computation, and so on.

But, do these axioms suffice for proving *all of mathematics*? What does that even mean? If not, maybe we need to add a single extra axiom or axiom schema? A few extra axioms or axiom schemas? The attempt to find a set of axioms that would suffice for settling any mathematical question was a central challenge during the beginning of the twentieth century. Let us make this question more concrete.

13.1 Complete and Incomplete Theories

Consider the group axioms that we have seen in Chapter 10:

Group Axioms:

- Zero Axiom: $0 + x = x$
- Negation Axiom: $-x + x = 0$
- Associativity Axiom: $(x + y) + z = x + (y + z)$

```
                    predicates/some_proofs.py
#: The three group axioms
GROUP_AXIOMS = frozenset({'plus(0,x)=x', 'plus(minus(x),x)=0',
                          'plus(plus(x,y),z)=plus(x,plus(y,z))'})
```

Beyond the basic symbols of predicate logic, the "language" used in these axioms contains the binary function symbol $+$ (or alternatively in our programs, the binary function name 'plus'), the unary function symbol − (or alternatively in our programs, the unary function name 'minus'), and the constant name '0'. Now we can ask a question: Do these axioms suffice for answering *any question* in this language? That is, suppose that we have some sentence, e.g. '∀x∀y[x+y=y+x]'. Is it necessarily true that one can either prove or disprove it from our given axioms?

DEFINITION 13.1 (Complete Set of Axioms)   A set of axioms A is **complete** if for any predicate-logic sentence in its language (i.e., that only uses the function names, relation names, and constant names that appear somewhere in A) we have either $A \vdash \phi$ or $A \vdash$ '∼ϕ'.

Note that we have used the term "complete" here in a totally different sense than in the "completeness" theorem that was the main focus of this book. The completeness theorem, whether for predicate logic (Theorem 12.4) or for propositional logic (Theorem 6.6), talks about completeness of a *proof system*, which asks whether a proof system can syntactically prove everything that is semantically correct. Completeness of *a set of axioms* in the sense just defined in Definition 13.1 talks about whether an axiomatic system can answer (positively or negatively) every mathematical question in its language. It is worthwhile to note that using the completeness theorem (12.4) for predicate logic, we can equivalently replace the condition of "either $A \vdash \phi$ or $A \vdash$ '∼ϕ' " in Definition 13.1 by "either $A \models \phi$ or $A \models$ '∼ϕ'."

Back to the group axioms, it is not difficult to see that neither '∀x∀y[x+y=y+x]' nor its negation is provable from the group axioms. Why? because some groups are commutative (e.g., the real numbers) and some groups are not commutative (e.g., permutation groups[1]). That is, we have two models, one in which '∀x∀y[x+y=y+x]' holds and the other in which its negation holds. So since the answer is not fully determined semantically by the group axioms, then by the soundness theorem (9.1) for predicate logic it follows that these axioms can neither syntactically prove it nor its negation.

On the other hand, suppose that we *add* to the group axioms another axiom that states that there are exactly two elements: '(∃y[∼y=0]&∀x∀y∀z[((x=y|y=z)|x=z)])', and get the axiomatic system for groups with two elements. It turns out that now we can answer not only the question of commutativity but also *every* question. How do we know this? Again we can go through the semantics and observe (using just a little bit of thought) that there is only a single possible model of a group with two elements (i.e., in a course on algebraic structures we would say that up to trivial degrees of freedom such as renaming the elements, there is only one group with two elements), and thus by the completeness theorem (12.4) for predicate logic everything that is true in that group is provable from the axioms for a group with two elements. Thus, since for any statement, either it or its negation is true in that group, one of these is provable from the four axioms for a group with two elements (i.e., the three group axioms and the additional two-element axiom just stated), and so this set of axioms is complete – the theory of groups with two elements is complete (but also quite boring).

So some sets of axioms are complete and others are not complete. While we are perfectly happy with certain theories not being complete – indeed, field theory would be quite boring if each statement held in either all fields or no field – we would very much like

---

[1] For more details, you are highly encouraged to take a course on algebraic structures.

other theories to be complete. For example, since "in our minds" it is clear what the natural numbers are, we would want to axiomatize the natural numbers in a way that completely determines every truth about them – to find a set of axioms for the theory of the natural numbers so that given any sentence about the natural numbers, either this sentence or its negation follows from these axioms. One of the foundational challenges faced by early twentieth-century mathematicians and logicians was indeed to find a complete set of axioms for the language of natural numbers that has the constant name '0', the unary successor function name 's', and the binary function symbols $+$ and $\cdot$ (multiplication), and more generally, to find a complete set of axioms for "all of mathematics," say for the language of set theory that only has the binary relation symbol '$\in$'. More concretely: Is Peano arithmetic complete? Is ZFC itself complete?

Gödel's **incompleteness theorem** (13.2), to which this chapter is dedicated, gives a resounding *negative* answer: not only is Peano arithmetic *not* complete for the language of natural numbers and ZFC is *not* complete for the language of set theory, but these deficiencies *cannot* be fixed: For any additional axioms (or axiom schemas) that we add to any of these axiomatic systems, provided that it is possible to tell whether a formula is a valid axiom, the enlarged set of axioms remains incomplete! In fact, any sound axiomatic system that is sufficiently powerful is necessarily incomplete. Thus, the quest to find the "ultimate" set of axioms for mathematics is inherently doomed to failure.

So for the rest of this chapter let us fix some sound **"ultimate" axiomatic system (UAS)** that is at least as powerful as Peano arithmetic in the sense that it can prove the axioms of Peano arithmetic.

```
#: An ultimate axiomatic system; can you find such a set of schemas?
UAS = frozenset({···})
```

We will prove that this "ultimate" axiomatic system still cannot be complete.

13.2   Gödel Numbering

Gödel's main ingenious "trick" was to let the axiomatic system "talk about itself." But since Peano arithmetic talks about natural numbers, Gödel's first order of business was to encode formulas, proofs, etc., as natural numbers. In this chapter we will want our formulas to talk about **programs**, which are technically not really that far from logical formulas, so we will encode these instead. Here the program can be given in any general purpose ("Turing complete") language, e.g., a Python program given as a string.[2] Thus we can formalize this as the following programming "tasks:"[3]

---

[2] One language for programs, which may seem less intuitive for programmers at first sight, but which is designed to capture any program in a theoretically simple way that allows for easy analysis, is to describe each program as a **Turing machine**, named after the English mathematician, computer scientist, cryptanalyst, philosopher, and theoretical biologist Alan Turing, who is widely considered to be the father of theoretical computer science and artificial intelligence and who played a pivotal role in cracking Nazi cyphers during World War II, but who was persecuted during his lifetime due to his homosexuality, eventually leading to his tragic early death.

[3] Note that in Python, integers are not restricted in size.

```
def encode_program(program: Program) -> int:
    """Encodes the given program as a natural number.

    Parameters:
        program: program to encode.

    Returns:
        A natural number encoding the given program.
    """
    # Task 13.1
```

```
def is_validly_encoded_program(encoded_program: int) -> bool:
    """Checks whether the given natural number validly encodes a program.

    Parameters:
        encoded_program: natural number to check.

    Returns:
        ``True`` if the given natural number validly encodes a program, ``False``
        otherwise.
    """
    # Task 13.2
```

We could naturally encode programs in, say, ASCII (or unicode), but Gödel was careful to choose a simple encoding, called **Gödel numbering**, that is "compatible" with Peano arithmetic. Specifically, Gödel's encoding allows the implementation of the following task for Peano arithmetic.

```
def sentence_saying_program_halts_on_input(encoded_program: int, input: int) \
        -> Formula:
    """Computes a predicate-logic sentence in the language of Peano arithmetic
    that states that the given encoded program halts when run on the given input.

    Parameters:
        encoded_program: natural number encoding a program.
        input: input to the given encoded program.

    Returns:
        A predicate-logic sentence in the language of Peano arithmetic that
        holds in any model for (the axioms of) Peano arithmetic if the program
        encoded by `encoded_program` halts (i.e., eventually terminates rather
        than gets stuck in an infinite loop) when run on the given input, and
        does not hold in any such model otherwise.
    """
    assert is_validly_encoded_program(encoded_program)
    # Task 13.3
```

To implement `sentence_saying_program_halts_on_input()`, we desire to be able to express, using a logical formula in the language of Peano arithmetic, the behavior of a computer program on a certain input. In general we would like to be able to express any question about what the program is doing at any given point in time (e.g., is it still running?, what is the content of its memory?, etc.), but for simplicity we will focus on the simple question of whether it **halts** or keeps running forever (e.g., gets stuck in an infinite loop).

Technically, there is some quite nontrivial work in allowing logical formulas to capture the behavior of programs, and that is beyond the scope of this chapter. (Presumably, that is what a second book on mathematical logic that is written in the same vein as this book would do.) To get some insight, though, let us give a high-level overview of what the "sentence saying x halts on y" would look like. The basic idea is simple: It would claim the existence of a natural number T and a sequence $\bar{s} = s_1, \ldots, s_T$ (encoded as a natural number) that describes the state of the program (i.e., content of all memory) at all time steps, and then say that the sequence of steps encodes a correct computation. That is, the sentence saying that the program encoded by x halts when run on input y may be expressed as '$\exists \bar{s}[(Start_x(s_1,y)\&(\forall i[Follows_x(s_{i+1},s_i)]\&HaltingState_x(s_T)))]$', where '$Start_x(s_1,y)$' is a (sub)formula stating that the initial state s_1 corresponds to the the initial state of the program x when run with input y, '$Follows_x(s_{i+1},s_i)$' is a formula stating that state s_{i+1} is the result of a single computation step of the program x applied to state s_i, and '$HaltingState_x(s_T)$' is a formula stating that state s_T is a halting state of the program x. Each of these three statements requires significant work for us to be able to express it via a predicate-logic formula. For example, the logic of "reading" from the code of a program the information saying what one step of it does to the state of the whole memory is a complex task. Even the basic building blocks of encoding a whole sequence $\bar{s} = s_1, \ldots, s_T$ as a single number (since Peano arithmetic only has numbers) is a nontrivial task.

Despite the many details that are needed for the implementation of this task (and which could easily fill an entire separate "Mathematical Logic II through Programming" follow-up book), the overall picture should be clear: Programming (including, say, the Python programming language) is part of mathematics, and thus it should not surprise us that a language that should handle "usual" mathematics can also logically express whatever we want about the behavior of a computer program.

To conclude this section, we make the crucial observation that since we assumed that our "ultimate" axiomatic system UAS is at least as powerful as Peano arithmetic, any model of UAS is a model of Peano arithmetic, and therefore the guarantee of `sentence_saying_program_halts_on_input()` with respect to Peano arithmetic in fact *also holds with respect to the language and axioms of UAS*: The returned sentence is in the language of UAS, holds in any model of UAS if the program encoded by `encoded_program` halts when run on `input`, and does not hold in any such model if that program does not halt when run on `input`.

13.3   Undecidability of the Halting Problem

So, say that we sorted out the technical details of how to express the notion that "the program encoded by x halts when run on input y" as a predicate-logic sentence. (Once again, this is nontrivial to pull off technically, and the bulk of a second course on mathematical logic is usually dedicated to this.) Since it is natural to have programs (such as compilers) that handle programs, it is tempting to implement a *program* (rather than a logical formula) to answer the question of whether "the program encoded by x halts when run on input y," i.e., to implement the following function.

```
def does_halt(encoded_program: int, input: int) -> bool:
    """Checks if the given encoded program halts when run on the given input.

    Parameters:
        encoded_program: natural number encoding a program.
        input: input to the given encoded program.

    Returns:
        ``True`` if the program encoded by `encoded_program` halts (i.e.,
        eventually terminates rather than gets stuck in an infinite loop) when
        run on the given input, ``False`` otherwise.
    """
    assert is_validly_encoded_program(encoded_program)
    # Can you implement this function?
```

Turing's famous result is that the **halting problem** is **undecidable**, i.e., it is impossible to correctly implement the function does_halt()! Historically, Turing's **undecidability theorem** (13.1) came after Gödel's incompleteness theorem (13.2), but we will still use it (after proving it without using Gödel's incompleteness theorem (13.2), of course) as an intermediate step in the proof of the the incompleteness theorem (13.2).

THEOREM 13.1 (Undecidability of the Halting Problem) *There does not exist any way to implement* does_halt() *correctly.*

Proof We assume by way contradiction that does_halt() is implemented correctly and provide a contradiction. For this consider the following function:

```
def diagonalize(encoded_program: int) -> None:
    """Halts if the given encoded program does not halt when run on its given
    encoding as input, and enters an infinite loop otherwise.

    Parameters:
        encoded_program: natural number encoding a program.
    """
    assert is_validly_encoded_program(encoded_program)

    if does_halt(encoded_program, encoded_program):
        while True: pass # Infinite loop.
    else:
        return
```

Looking at the code of diagonalize(), we see that if it gets (an encoding of) a program x that halts when run on x itself, then diagonalize enters an infinite loop, while if x does *not* halt when run on x, then diagonalize halts immediately. All this, assuming of course, that the function does_halt() was indeed implemented correctly (an assumption that, recall, we are really trying to disprove by way of contradiction).

Let us look at the encoding of this function diagonalize() (an encoding that contains also all the sub-functions used in its implementation, including in particular the assumed does_halt() function), and let us call it $n_{diagonalize}$. Question: what happens when we run diagonalize($n_{diagonalize}$)? Well, looking at the code of diagonalize(), there are two possibilities, either the function call does_halt($n_{diagonalize}$, $n_{diagonalize}$) returns True or it returns `False` (notice that by assumption `does_halt()` was implemented correctly so it never gets stuck in an infinite loop and it always halts, returning either `False` or `True`).

Case I: `does_halt(`$n_{diagonalize}$`, `$n_{diagonalize}$`)` **returns** `True`

By the specification of `does_halt()` this means that the program encoded by $n_{diagonalize}$ when run on input $n_{diagonalize}$ halts. That is, when we run `diagonalize(`$n_{diagonalize}$`)`, it halts. But now look at the implementation of `diagonalize()`: Since `does_halt(`$n_{diagonalize}$`,`$n_{diagonalize}$`)` returns `True`, we have that `diagonalize(`$n_{diagonalize}$`)` immediately enters an infinite loop. That is, the program encoded by $n_{diagonalize}$ when run on input $n_{diagonalize}$ does *not* halt. A contradiction.

Case II: `does_halt(`$n_{diagonalize}$`, `$n_{diagonalize}$`)` **returns** `False`

By the specification of `does_halt()` this means that the program encoded by $n_{diagonalize}$ when run on input $n_{diagonalize}$ does *not* halt. That is, when we run `diagonalize(`$n_{diagonalize}$`)`, it does *not* halt. But look again at the implementation of `diagonalize()`: Since `does_halt(`$n_{diagonalize}$`,`$n_{diagonalize}$`)` returns `False`, we have that `diagonalize(`$n_{diagonalize}$`)` immediately halts. That is, the program encoded by $n_{diagonalize}$ when run on input $n_{diagonalize}$ halts. A contradiction. □

13.4   The Incompleteness Theorem

So, we have seen that the halting problem is undecidable. But now comes the final blow: If our axiomatic system UAS is complete then we *can* implement the `does_halt()` function after all. To do so, in a nutshell, we will simply search for a proof of either the sentence saying that the given program halts or a the negation of this sentence. More technically, we will need to be able to iterate over all possible proofs. For this it would first be convenient to implement parsing for proofs, similar to the parsing that you implemented for formulas.

```
                          ┌─ predicates/proofs.py ─┐
class Proof:
        ⋮

    @staticmethod
    def parse(string: str) -> Union[Proof, None]:
        """Parses the given valid string representation into a proof.

        Parameters:
            string: string to parse.

        Returns:
            A proof `p` such that `str(p)` returns the given string, or ``None``
            if the given string is not a valid representation of any proof.
        """
        # Task 13.4
```

Finally, it will also be convenient to have access to a generator (very similar to the generator `fresh_variable_name_generator` that you have used throughout this book) that simply generates all one-character Python strings, then all two-character Python strings, and so forth. (So for each Python string, if we invoke the generator enough times we will eventually get that string.) Writing such a generator is quite an easy exercise for anyone familiar with writing Python generators (and specifically, since you used our implementation of `fresh_variable_name_generator`, it should be clear to you that there is no problem in implementing such a generator), so we will assume that we have it implemented as `string_generator` (possibly imported from, say, `logic_utils`).

Now, assuming that our "ultimate" axiomatic system UAS is complete, we can finally show how to implement `does_halt()` after all.

```python
def does_halt(encoded_program: int, input: int) -> bool:
    """Checks if the given encoded program halts when run on the given input.

    Parameters:
        encoded_program: natural number encoding a program.
        input: input to the given encoded program.

    Returns:
        ``True`` if the program encoded by `encoded_program` halts (i.e.,
        eventually terminates rather than gets stuck in an infinite loop) when
        run on the given input, ``False`` otherwise.
    """
    assert is_validly_encoded_program(encoded_program)

    program_halts_sentence = \
        sentence_saying_program_halts_on_input(encoded_program, input)
    program_loops_sentence = Formula('~', program_halts_sentence)

    while True:
        proof_string = next(string_generator)
        proof = Proof.parse(proof_string)
        if proof is not None and proof.assumptions == UAS and proof.is_valid():
            if proof.conclusion == program_halts_sentence:
                return True
            if proof.conclusion == program_loops_sentence:
                return False
```

Our implementation just looks at all possible proofs, trying to find a proof that the given encoded program either halts on the given input or does not halt on the given input. Had UAS been complete, then it would have been assured that one of these would have been found. Since this would have contradicted the undecidability theorem (13.1), we have that UAS cannot be complete.

THEOREM 13.2 (The Incompleteness Theorem) *Any such axiomatic system UAS is not complete.*

Proof   We will show that if UAS had been a complete axiomatic system then our implementation of `does_halt()` would have been correct, which would have contradicted the undecidability of the halting problem (Theorem 13.1). So, assume by way of contradiction that UAS is complete.

Let `encoded_program` be an encoded program and let `input` be an input to the program encoded by `encoded_program`. Let ϕ be the formula called `program_halts_sentence` in our alleged implementation of `does_halt()` when run on `encoded_program` and on `input`. That is, let ϕ be the formula returned by `sentence_saying_program_halts_on_input(encoded_program, input)`. Due to our assumption that UAS is a complete axiomatic system (an assumption that, recall, we are really trying to disprove by way of contradiction), we have that either ϕ or '$\sim\phi$' has a valid proof from UAS. Recall that by definition, this proof is finite and so is its string representation. Call the string representation of that proof (i.e., the string returned by calling `str()` on that proof) s^*. Now, at some point (i.e., after finitely many steps) during the execution of `does_halt(encoded_program, input)`, the call to `next(string_generator)` will return s^*. If the proof represented by s^* is a valid proof from UAS of ϕ, then our implementation of `does_halt()` will return `True`. In this case, due to the soundness theorem (9.1) for predicate logic,[4] the given program indeed halts when run on `input`. Thus the answer returned by our implementation of `does_halt()` is the correct one! Similarly, if the proof represented by s^* is a valid proof from UAS of '$\sim\phi$', then our implementation of `does_halt()` will return `False`. In this case, again due to the soundness theorem (9.1) for predicate logic, the given program indeed does *not* halt when run on `input`. Thus the answer returned by our implementation of `does_halt()` is again the correct one!

Since we are assured that for any possible `encoded_program` and `input`, one of these two possibilities (a proof of ϕ or a proof of its negation) will be found after finitely many steps, our implementation of `does_halt()` always returns the correct answer, hence solving the halting problem. A contradiction.   □

Re-examining the chain of arguments in the proof just given, we note that indeed all that it requires is that the function `sentence_saying_program_halts_on_input()` can be implemented, or in other words, that the axioms of Peano arithmetic are sufficiently strong to deal with programs. Implied here is that if such a sentence is provable from Peano arithmetic then indeed it soundly describes the behavior of the given encoded program when run on the given input. As already noted in Section 13.2, there is no problem in implementing this function, but it is technically challenging, and the bulk of a second book on mathematical logic following this book would be dedicated to developing the techniques to do this.

Have we made any other assumptions regarding our hypothetical "ultimate" axiomatic system UAS? As you may have noticed, for convenience we have implicitly assumed (in the Python code, at least) that it consists of finitely many schemas. We nonetheless note that in fact nothing in our proof depends on such finiteness or on our specific definition of how schemas may be instantiated. Indeed, we could have replaced the test for whether `proof.assumptions == UAS` in our implementation of `does_halt()` with any arbitrary code that tests that all of the assumptions of `proof` are in UAS (or are instantiations of schemas in UAS, however we may wish to define schemas and instantiation).[5] This code could even be very inefficient, but all that would be required of it for our proof to still follow through would be that such code (that never gets stuck in an infinite loop) would exist, i.e., that given a formula, it would be possible to unambiguously decide on whether or not it is a valid axiom of UAS.

---

[4] That is, since UAS is sound, whatever is provable from UAS is sound.

[5] Similarly, we could have changed the test for whether `proof.is_valid()` to allow for more inference rules in our proofs, etc.

Let us conclude by briefly discussing this decidability condition. We first note that this is a reasonable condition since an axiomatic system is useless if we cannot verify whether an assumption used in a proof is part of that system or not. Second, we note that this condition really is a necessary and meaningful condition of our analysis. Indeed, consider the following strategy for constructing UAS: We could have "closed" (as in Chapter 12) the set of axioms of Peano arithmetic without losing consistency, to obtain a closed superset of them, and could have chosen this (infinite) closed set as our axiomatic set. As shown in Chapter 12, a consistent closed set essentially has a single model, so for any sentence, either the sentence or its negation is true in this model (and hence in any model of this closed set of axioms), so this closed set of axioms is complete! Nonetheless, our proof shows that the fatal flaw with this approach is that while such a closed set that contains the axioms of Peano arithmetic does exist (we have proved this in Chapter 12), and while any such closed set indeed is a complete set of axioms, for any such closed set it is undecidable whether a formula belongs to it or not – i.e., it is impossible to implement code that correctly answers the question "is the following axiom/schema in this set?". This of course means that it is hopeless to verify proofs that use any such set as their axiomatic system, and so such a closed (and hence complete) axiomatic system, while theoretically existing, is useless to us.

Indeed, the condition of decidability of the axiomatic system really is rather weak, and the fact that our proof hinges on only this condition shows that the dream of finding a complete axiomatic system for mathematics is indeed just that: a dream.

Cheatsheet: Axioms and Axiomatic Inference Rules Used in This Book

A.1 Propositional Logic

MP: Assumptions: 'p', '(p→q)'; Conclusion: 'q'

I0: '(p→p)'   **(I0_SCHEMA:** '(P()→P())')

I1: '(q→(p→q))'   **(I1_SCHEMA:** '(Q()→(P()→Q()))')

D: '((p→(q→r))→((p→q)→(p→r)))'   ⋮

I2: '(~p→(p→q))'

N: '((~q→~p)→(p→q))'

NI: '(p→(~q→~(p→q)))'

NN: '(p→~~p)'

R: '((q→p)→((~q→p)→p))'

A: '(p→(q→(p&q)))'   **NA1:** '(~q→~(p&q))'   **NA2:** '(~p→~(p&q))'

O1: '(q→(p|q))'   **O2:** '(p→(p|q))'   **NO:** '(~p→(~q→~(p|q)))'

T: 'T'   **NF:** '~F'

A.2 Predicate Logic

- **Modus Ponens (MP):** From ϕ and '($\phi\to\psi$)', deduce ψ.
- **Universal Generalization (UG):** From ϕ deduce '$\forall x[\phi]$'.
- **Tautology:** Any formula ϕ that is a tautology.
- **Universal Instantiation (UI):** The schema '$(\forall x[\phi(x)]\to\phi(\tau))$', where $\phi(\square)$, x, and τ are (placeholders for) a parametrized formula, a variable name, and a term, respectively.
- **Existential Introduction (EI):** The schema '$(\phi(\tau)\to\exists x[\phi(x)])$', where $\phi(\square)$, x, and τ are a parametrized formula, a variable name, and a term, respectively.
- **Universal Simplification (US):** The schema '$(\forall x[(\psi\to\phi(x))]\to(\psi\to\forall x[\phi(x)]))$', where ψ is a (parameter-less) formula, $\phi(\square)$ is a parametrized formula, and x is a variable name. Note that the rules that define the legal instances of schemas require in particular that (the formula that is substituted for) ψ does not have (the variable name that is substituted for) x as a free variable name.
- **Existential Simplification (ES):** The schema '$((\forall x[(\phi(x)\to\psi)]\&\exists x[\phi(x)])\to\psi)$', where ψ is a formula, $\phi(\square)$ is a parametrized formula, and x is a variable name. Note

once more that the rules that define the legal instances of schemas require in particular that ψ does not have x as a free variable name.

- **Reflexivity (RX):** The schema '$\tau = \tau$', where τ is a term.
- **Meaning of Equality (ME):** The schema '$(\tau = \sigma \rightarrow (\phi(\tau) \rightarrow \phi(\sigma)))$', where $\phi(\square)$ is a parametrized formula, and τ and σ are terms.

A.2.1 Additional Axioms

In the following schemas, $\phi(\square)$ is a parametrized formula, ψ is a formula, and x is a variable name. Note yet again that the rules that define the legal instances of schemas require in particular that ψ does not have x as a free variable name.

1. '$\sim\forall x[\phi(x)]$' is equivalent to '$\exists x[\sim\phi(x)]$'.
2. '$\sim\exists x[\phi(x)]$' is equivalent to '$\forall x[\sim\phi(x)]$'.
3. '$(\forall x[\phi(x)]\&\psi)$' is equivalent to '$\forall x[(\phi(x)\&\psi)]$'.
4. '$(\exists x[\phi(x)]\&\psi)$' is equivalent to '$\exists x[(\phi(x)\&\psi)]$'.
5. '$(\psi\&\forall x[\phi(x)])$' is equivalent to '$\forall x[(\psi\&\phi(x))]$'.
6. '$(\psi\&\exists x[\phi(x)])$' is equivalent to '$\exists x[(\psi\&\phi(x))]$'.
7. '$(\forall x[\phi(x)]|\psi)$' is equivalent to '$\forall x[(\phi(x)|\psi)]$'.
8. '$(\exists x[\phi(x)]|\psi)$' is equivalent to '$\exists x[(\phi(x)|\psi)]$'.
9. '$(\psi|\forall x[\phi(x)])$' is equivalent to '$\forall x[(\psi|\phi(x))]$'.
10. '$(\psi|\exists x[\phi(x)])$' is equivalent to '$\exists x[(\psi|\phi(x))]$'.
11. '$(\forall x[\phi(x)]\rightarrow\psi)$' is equivalent to '$\exists x[(\phi(x)\rightarrow\psi)]$'.
12. '$(\exists x[\phi(x)]\rightarrow\psi)$' is equivalent to '$\forall x[(\phi(x)\rightarrow\psi)]$'.
13. '$(\psi\rightarrow\forall x[\phi(x)])$' is equivalent to '$\forall x[(\psi\rightarrow\phi(x))]$'.
14. '$(\psi\rightarrow\exists x[\phi(x)])$' is equivalent to '$\exists x[(\psi\rightarrow\phi(x))]$'.

In the following schemas, $\phi(\square)$ and $\psi(\square)$ are parametrized formulas, and x and y are variable names.

15. If $\phi(x)$ and $\psi(x)$ are equivalent, then '$\forall x[\phi(x)]$' and '$\forall y[\psi(y)]$' are equivalent.
16. If $\phi(x)$ and $\psi(x)$ are equivalent, then '$\exists x[\phi(x)]$' and '$\exists y[\psi(y)]$' are equivalent.

Index

∃, *see* existential quantifier
∀, *see* universal quantifier
⊕, *see* xor operator
→, *see* implies operator
&̄, *see* nand operator
|̄, *see* nor operator
↔, *see* iff operator
&, *see* and operator
|, *see* or operator
⊢, *see* provability
⊨, *see* entailment
~, *see* not operator
3-CNF, 40

affineness of a Boolean function, 51
and operator
    semantics, 26, 34, 35, 49, 50, 52
    syntax, 14, 31, 34, 98, 104, 112
antecedent, 74
arity
    of a function, 125, 130
    of a relation, 126, 130, 136, 232, 233
    of an operator, 41, 43, 46, 49, 112
assignment (in predicate logic), 124–127, 133, 159,
    170, 182
assumption
    of a proof
        in predicate logic, 94, 144, 160, 161, 163, 169,
        170, 177, 253, 265
        in propositional logic, 60, 67, 74, 77, 89, 90
    of an inference rule, 53, 54, 60, 74, 77, 78, 80, 83,
        92
axiom, *see also* axiomatic system
    in predicate logic, 160, 163, 169, 177, 178, 181,
        182, 218, 255, 257, 258, 264
    in propositional logic, 76, 80, 84, 98, 173
axiom schema, *see* schema, *see also* axiom
axiomatic system
    for predicate logic, 178, 180, 218, 231, 250, 253,
        255, 257, 258, 263, 265, 266
    for propositional logic, 74, 76, 84, 85, 87, 98, 172,
        266, *see also* Hilbert axiomatic system, *see
        also* schema equivalents of a propositional
        axiomatic system

binary operator, 14, 41, 112, 225, *see also* arity of an
    operator
bound occurrence (of a variable name), 120, 127, 216,
    222

Cantor's theorem, 252
capturing an assignment by a formula, 86, 89, 101
clause
    conjunctive, 31, 32
    disjunctive, 33, 34, 40
closed set of sentences, 232, 236, 237, 240, 241,
    249–252, 265
closure of a set of sentences, *see* closed set of
    sentences
CNF, 34, 35, 39, 40
CNF theorem, 34, 35
coloring (of a graph), 36–40
compactness theorem
    for predicate logic, 253, 254
    for propositional logic, 95–98, 253, 254
compilation, 133
completeness
    of a proof system
        in predicate logic, 236, 252, 257
        in propositional logic, 84, 93, 94, 97, 257
    of a set of axioms, 257, 258, 263, 265
    of a set of operators, 46, 49–52, 84, 97, 112
completeness theorem
    for predicate logic, 231, 240, 249, 250, 252–255,
        257
    for propositional logic, 90, 92–94, 97, 98, 253,
        254, 257
computational search, 36, 39, 40
conclusion
    of a proof
        in predicate logic, 144, 160, 161
        in propositional logic, 60, 67, 77
    of an inference rule, 53, 54, 60, 74
conjunction operator, *see* and operator
conjunctive normal form, *see* CNF
consequent, 74
consistency, 80–83, 93–95, 97, 98, 214, 231, 236, 239,
    241–245, 248–254, 265
consistency-preserving closure lemma, 241, 251, 252

constant (in propositional logic), 14, *see also* nullary
operator
constant name (in predicate logic)
as a template (in a schema), 146, 181
semantics, 122, 125, 232
syntax, 110, 116, 233, 238, 242–245, 248, 249,
251
contradiction
semantic, 30, 79, 80, 214
syntactic, 79, 80, *see also* inconsistency, *see also*
proof by way of contradiction
countable, *see* countably infinite
countably infinite, 22, 96, 121, 251–253

D axiom, 76–78, 83, 85, 172
deduction theorem
for predicate logic, 212, 242
for propositional logic, 78, 79, 82, 90, 101, 211
derivation tree, 15, 18, 21, 118, 119
diagonalization, 261
disjunction operator, *see* or operator
disjunctive normal form, *see* DNF
DNF, 32, 33, 35, 36, 39, 40, 46
DNF theorem, 32, 33, 46
double implication operator, *see* iff operator

EI axiom schema, 179, 181, 185, 216
encoding an inference rule by an axiom, 74, 86, 92
entailment
in predicate logic, 169, 170, 254, 257
in propositional logic, 54, 55, 66, 67, 73, 92,
93, 97
equality relation
semantics, 126, 138, 139, 141, 179
syntax, 112, 116, 138, 142, 231, 232, 238
equality-free analog
of a formula, 138
of a model, 139–141
of a set of formulas, 142
ES axiom schema, 179, 181, 185, 216
evaluation
of a formula, *see* truth value
of a term (in predicate logic), *see* value
exclusive or operator, *see* xor operator
existential derivation, 192
existential introduction, *see* EI axiom schema
existential quantifier
semantics, 126, 127, 171, 178, 236
syntax, 112, 179, 215–217, 233, 237–239, 248,
249, 251, 252
existential simplification, *see* ES axiom schema
existential witness, 233, 245, 248, 249, 251
existentially closed set of sentences, 232, 236, 245,
248, 249, 252
expression (in predicate logic), 121

F constant (nullary operator)
semantics, 26, 49–52

syntax, 13, 79, 98
field, 205, 257
first-order logic, *see* predicate logic
first-order predicate logic, *see* predicate logic
formula
in predicate logic, 112, 115, 116, 119, 121,
126–128, 132–134, 137, 142, 159, 167,
170, 214, 216, 222, 231, 238, 249,
251–254, 258, 259, 260, *see also* sentence
in propositional logic, 13, 15, 16, 18, 20–22, 25,
26, 29, 30, 32–36, 39, 40, 49, 53, 54, 56,
60, 80, 83, 86, 87, 92–97, 167
Formula class
of the `predicates` package (predicate logic),
112, 115
of the `propositions` package (propositional
logic), 15, 16
free instantiation, 198
free occurrence (of a variable name), 120, 126, 127,
170, 171, 181, 216, 222
free variable name, 120, 126, 133, 159, 170, 171, 180,
212, 214, 216, 231, 238, 254
`@frozen` decorator, 16, 115
function invocation
semantics, 125, 130, 133
syntax, 110, 129, 132, 133, 137, 231, 232, 238
function name, 110, 122, 125, 130, 131, 133
function-free analog
of a formula, 132–134
of a model, 130, 131, 133
of a set of formulas, 137

Gödel numbering, 258, 259
group, 195, 256, 257

$\mathcal{H}$, *see* Hilbert axiomatic system
halting (by a program), 259–264
halting problem, 261–264
Henkin constant, *see* witnessing constant name
Hilbert axiomatic system, 86, 89, 92–94, 97, 99, 101,
103, 104, 177
hypothetical syllogism, 78, 101

I0 axiom, 65, 76–78, 80, 83, 85, 172
I1 axiom, 76–78, 83, 85, 87, 172
I2 axiom, 80, 81, 83, 85, 87, 172
iff operator
semantics, 42, 50, 51
syntax, 42
implication operator, *see* implies operator
implies operator
semantics, 26, 27, 49, 50, 73, 170
syntax, 14, 74, 77, 78, 87, 112
incompleteness, *see* completeness of a set of axioms
incompleteness theorem, 258, 261–263
inconsistency, *see* consistency
induction axiom schema, 206
inference (in predicate logic), 169, 170, 182, 189

inference rule
  in predicate logic, 160, 164, 166, 264
  in propositional logic, 53–56, 60, 66, 67, 71, 72,
    74, 76, 78, 92, 189
`InferenceRule` class, 53
instance (of a schema), 145–148, 152, 159, 161, 172,
    173, 181, 245
instantiation (of a schema), *see* instance
interpretation, 122, 130, 136, 138, 232

lemma, 69, 71, 72
lemma theorem, 71, 72, 77, 78, 83, 86, 99, 101, 103,
    104
Löwenheim–Skolem theorem, 252

ME axiom schema, 181, 185, 196, 200, 202
meaning of equality axiom schema, *see* ME axiom
    schema
model
  in predicate logic, 122, 123, 125, 126, 128, 130,
    131, 133, 137, 140–142, 159, 169–171,
    182, 231, 232, 236, 237, 239, 249,
    252–254, 260, 265
  in propositional logic, 25–30, 32, 34, 36, 37, 54,
    55, 67, 73, 86, 87, 89, 90, 94–98, 101, 170,
    254
`Model` class, 123
modus ponens, *see* MP inference rule
monotonicity of a Boolean function, 50
MP inference rule, 73, 74, 77, 78, 80, 83, 85, 86, 160,
    161, 164, 169–171, 173, 177, 190, 245
multiplexer operator, *see* mux operator
mux operator, 43, 49, 50, 52

N axiom, 82, 83, 85, 172
n-ary function, *see* arity of a function
n-ary operator, *see* arity of an operator
n-ary relation, *see* arity of a relation
nand operator
  semantics, 42, 49
  syntax, 42
negation operator, *see* not operator
NI axiom, 85, 87, 172
NN axiom, 85, 87, 172
non-implication operator, 52
nor operator
  semantics, 42, 49
  syntax, 42
not operator
  semantics, 26, 30, 35, 49, 51
  syntax, 13, 31, 33, 40, 79, 80, 86, 87, 103, 112,
    214, 224, 233, 236, 239, 241, 242, 251, 254
notation
  infix, 22, 115
  polish, 22, 115
  postfix, *see* notation, reverse polish
  prefix, *see* notation, polish
  reverse polish, 22, 115

NP-completeness, 39, 40, 79
nullary operator, 41, *see also* arity of an operator

operator, 14, 41, 43, 46, 49, 52, 97, 112, 238
or operator
  semantics, 26, 32, 35, 50, 52
  syntax, 14, 32, 33, 40, 98, 104, 112

parametrized formula, 147, 149, 178–181, 217
parsing, 15, 18, 20, 117, 262
Peano arithmetic, 206, 258–260, 264, 265
predicate logic, 109
prefix-free, 20, 116
prenex normal form, 215, 216, 236, 237, 241, 249, 251
prenex normal form theorem, 216, 217, 230, 231, 252
primitive sentence, 232, 233, 236, 238, 239, 241, 242,
    249
primitively closed set of sentences, 232, 236, 241,
    242, 249, 252
program, 258–260, 262–264
proof, *see also* provability
  in predicate logic, 144, 160, 161, 169, 171, 172,
    177, 182, 245, 251, 253, 255, 258, 262–265
  in propositional logic, 60, 61, 66, 67, 69, 70, 74,
    77, 87, 89, 90, 92, 94, 171, 172
proof by way of contradiction, 79, 80, 82, 83, 213, 214
`Proof` class
  of the `predicates` package (predicate logic),
    161, 182
  of the `propositions` package (propositional
    logic), 61, 69
propositional formula, *see* formula in propositional
    logic
propositional logic, 13
propositional skeleton
  of a predicate-logic formula, 167, 170–173, 180,
    240, 245
  of an inference (in predicate logic), 189
provability, *see also* proof
  in predicate logic, 169, 170, 177, 182, 214, 216,
    246, 250, 254, 257, 264
  in propositional logic, 60, 66, 71, 72, 74, 77, 78,
    80, 82, 83, 85, 89, 90, 92, 93, 97, 101, 172
`Prover` class, 182

quantification
  existential, *see* existential quantifier
  universal, *see* universal quantifier
Quine arrow operator, *see* nor operator

R axiom, 85, 90, 172
reduction, 39, 40
redundance of equality theorem, 142, 231, 232, 238
redundance of functions theorem, 137, 231,
    232, 238
reflexivity
  axiom schema, *see* RX axiom schema
  of equality, 138

relation invocation
  syntax, 112
relation corresponding to function, 130, 131, 133,
      135, 136
relation invocation
  semantics, 126, 130, 232
  syntax, 133, 136, 233, 238
relation name, 112, 122, 126, 130, 131, 133, 138, 251
  as a template (in a schema), 147, 181
Russell's paradox, 209
RX axiom schema, 179, 181, 185, 196, 200

satisfiability, 30, 36, 37, 39, 40
schema, 145–147, 159, 169, 177–182, 231, 250, 252,
      253, 255, 258, 264
Schema class, 145–147
schema equivalents of a propositional axiomatic
      system, 171, 172, 177, 178, 240, 250, 266
scope of quantification, 112, 127, 216
sentence, 180, 212, 231, 236–239, 241, 242, 244, 248,
      249, 251, 254, 257, 260, 262, 265
Sheffer stroke operator, *see* nand operator
Skolem's paradox, 252
soundness
  of a predicate-logic formula, 159, 170
  of a propositional formula, *see* tautology in
      propositional logic
  of a schema, 159, 170, 172, 181
  of an inference (in predicate logic), 169, 170, 182
  of an inference rule, 54, 55, 66, 67, 73, 74, 76, 80,
      82, 85, 92–94, 98, 190
soundness theorem
  for predicate logic, 170, 172, 182, 231, 249,
      252–254, 257, 264
  for propositional logic, 66, 67, 84, 92, 93, 98, 254
  of proofs by way of contradiction
    for predicate logic, 214, 254
    for propositional logic, 82, 83, 93, 97
specialization (of an inference rule), 56, 57, 60, 66,
      67, 71, 173
specialization provability lemma, 70, 71
specialization soundness lemma, 66, 67, 159
syllogism, 144, 184, 187, 191, *see also* hypothetical
      syllogism
symmetry of equality, 138, 196

T constant (nullary operator)
  semantics, 26, 50, 51
  syntax, 13, 98
T-preservation, 50
tautological implication, 188, 190, 191, 214, 240
tautology
  in predicate logic, 160, 161, 167, 169–172, 177,
      180, 214, 231, 240, 245, 250
  in propositional logic, 30, 36, 39, 55, 73, 90, 92,
      160, 167, 171, 172
tautology theorem
  predicate-logic version, 176, 177, 240
  propositional-logic version, 90, 92, 143, 172

template (in a schema), 145–147
term (in predicate logic), 110, 111, 116, 118, 121, 125
Term class, 110, 111
ternary operator, 43, *see also* arity of an operator
testing, 7, 8
transitivity of equality, 138, 202
truth table, 29, 32–35, 43, 46, 49, 84
truth value
  of a predicate-logic formula, 126, 128, 133, 170,
      180, 182, 240
  of a propositional formula, 25–30, 32–35, 54, 67,
      89, 97, 101, 170

UG inference rule, 160, 161, 166, 169–171, 180, 212,
      214, 232, 245, 250
UI axiom schema, 178, 180, 181, 185, 216, 232, 249,
      254
unary operator, 14, 41, 112, *see also* arity of an
      operator
undecidability theorem, 261–263
unique readability theorem
  of predicate-logic formulas, 119
  of propositional formulas, 21
  of terms (in predicate logic), 118
uniquely named variables, 222
universal generalization, *see* UG inference rule
universal instantiation
  axiom schema, *see* UI axiom schema
  of a predicate-logic formula, 186, 233, 243, 244,
      249, 251
universal quantifier
  semantics, 126, 127, 170, 171, 178, 180, 182, 236
  syntax, 112, 144, 178, 179, 215–217, 232, 233,
      237–239, 244, 249, 251, 252, 254
universal simplification, *see* US axiom schema
universally closed set of sentences, 232, 236, 243,
      244, 249, 252
universe (of a model), 122, 130, 141, 232
US axiom schema, 179, 181, 185, 212–214, 216

value (of a term in predicate logic), 125, 139, 182
variable name
  in predicate logic
    as a template (in a schema), 146, 181
    semantics, 125–127, 133, 182
    syntax, 110, 112, 116, 133, 217, 222, 238
  in propositional logic
    semantics, 25, 26, 28, 29, 32–37, 86, 97, 170
    syntax, 13, 20, 22, 31, 33, 40, 56, 57, 86, 96,
      167, 189

witnessing constant name, 245, 248

xor operator
  semantics, 42, 51, 52
  syntax, 42

ZF, 210
ZFC, 210, 252, 253, 255, 258